C000054942

A guide to the Pembrokeshire Coast Path

By the same author, all published by Constable

A guide to the Pennine Way
A guide to Offa's Dyke Path
A guide to the Pilgrim's Way
  and North Downs Way

Published by Cicerone Press
The Westmorland Heritage Walk

Christopher John Wright

A guide to

The Pembrokeshire Coast Path

Constable London

First published in Great Britain 1986
by Constable and Company Limited
3 The Lanchesters, 162 Fulham Palace Road
London W6 9ER
Copyright © 1986 by Christopher John Wright
Set in Times New Roman by
Inforum Ltd, Portsmouth
Printed and bound in Great Britain
at The Bath Press, Avon

Second Edition 1989
Reprinted 1993

British Library CIP Data
Wright, Christopher John, *1943-*
A guide to the Pembrokeshire coast path.
1. Trails   2. Pembrokeshire Coast Path
(Wales)-Guide-books
I. Title
914.29'6204858   DA740.P3

ISBN 0 09 469260 2

Contents

Illustrations

Maps

Plans

Pictorial guide to maps and plans
Symbols and abbreviations used in the maps and plans

- ▬ ▬ ▬ Official footpath
- · · · · · · Recommended footpath
- ───── **Boundaries: wall, fence, hedge, etc**
- ～◡►═ Stream or river (*arrow indicates direction of flow*)
- ⊣⊢ Bridge
- *FB*⊣⊢ Footbridge
- ⸎ ⸎ ⸎ Marshy ground
- ▬ ▮ ▰▄ Buildings
- ⸸ ⸸ † Church or chapel
- ⬭ Lake or pond

- ⬗ Sands at low water
- ⬯ Rocks at low water
- ⌣⌣ Earthwork
- N ┼ North is top of map (*unless otherwise indicated*)

Abbreviations

YH	Youth Hostel
PO	Post Office
TCB	Telephone call box

KEY TO SKETCH MAPS

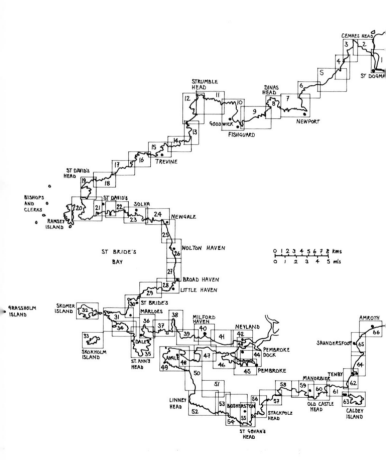

Acknowledgements

I much appreciated the total freedom extended to me by my understanding publishers during the five years of research, survey and production for this guide (1980–1985).

In the first edition I thanked Miss Lola Jarowiecki for typing my revised manuscript and the following for their help and guidance whilst preparing this book: the Institute of Oceanographic Sciences, Natural Environment Research Council; Mr S R Richards, Regional Controller, HM Coastguard, Department of Trade; The Harbourmaster, Milford Haven Conservancy Board; Nick Wheeler, National Park Officer, Pembrokeshire National Park Authority; Mr J Terroni and Mr P W Ridgway, Public Relations, Trinity House Lighthouse Service; The Dyfed Wildlife Trust; the Maritime Trust; the National Trust; the Editor, *Western Telegraph;* Mr M Walsh, Employee Relations, Esso Milford Haven; Mr A C Warlow, Gulf Oil Refining Ltd; Mr D M Lloyd, Public Relations, Texaco Ltd; Mr J S Harris, Public Relations, Milford Haven Refinery, Amoco (UK) Ltd; B P Oil Llandarcy Refinery Ltd; Mr S E Hinton, Station Manager, Pembroke Power Station, Central Electricity Generating Board; Lt Col B Couzens RTR and Major A F Gradidge, Castlemartin Royal Armoured Corps Range; WO R A Rowe, Officer Commanding, R A Range, Manorbier.

The sketch maps in this guide are based on the Ordnance Survey 1:10,000 scale, with the sanction of the Controller of HM Stationery Office. Crown Copyright Reserved.

Abbreviations used in the book are as follows: AHA – Area Health Authority; BMC – British Mountaineering Council; BTA – British Tourist Authority; CEGB – Central Electricity Generating Board; DWT – Dyfed Wildlife Trust; MHCB – Milford Haven Conservancy Board; MOD – Ministry of Defence; MSC – Manpower Services Commission; NCC – Nature Conservancy Council; NT – National Trust; PNPA – Pembrokeshire National Park Authority; RSPB – Royal Society for the Protection of Birds; YHA – Youth Hostels' Association.

CJW
1989

A general survey

The Pembrokeshire Coast was designated as Britain's fifth and smallest national park in 1952, and soon afterwards the then National Parks Commission submitted a report proposing that a long-distance footpath following the cliffs, bays and beaches of its fine coastline should be established. A survey had already been made for the Commission by the author and naturalist Ronald M Lockley, and the Commission's report was approved on 3 July 1953.

Eventually, after years of negotiation for the new rights of way needed to complete the line, and the construction of nearly 500 stiles and more than 100 footbridges, the path was officially opened. On 16 May 1970 at the Regency Hall, Saundersfoot, during National Footpath Week, Wynford Vaughan Thomas, President of the Council for the Protection of Rural Wales, and also himself a keen walker and owner of a property on the Path, declared the Coast Path open. It became Britain's third long-distance footpath, and the first in Wales.

The line of the Pembrokeshire Coast Path is as near to the cliff edge or high-water mark as is practicable, and there are few serious route-finding or navigational difficulties. The 'official' length of the Path as quoted in the Countryside Commission's publications is 167ml/269km but I have found this length to be somewhat short. Since the 'official' length was designated and approved by the Secretary of State there have been improvements and Footpath Diversion Orders (for example, as at Carregwastad, Sandy Haven and Manorbier) which have lengthened the Path, so that it is now 174.7ml/281km long. However, the total route walked can be as long as 192.9ml/310.45km, as I shall try to show.

To the amended 'official' length of 174.7ml/281km there must be added 8.75ml/14km to take into account those several short stretches through built-up areas which are not 'designated', and the total length becomes 183.45ml/295km as follows:

Hakin Point–Milford Haven link	1ml/1.6km
Hazelbeach–Pembroke Dock link	4.5ml/7.25km
Pembroke Dock missing link	1.5ml/2.5km
Pembroke–Monkton Quoit link	1ml/1.6km

| Tenby missing link | 0.5ml/0.8km |
| Saundersfoot missing link | 0.25ml/0.4km |

Strangely, why is the Coast Path 'designated' through the built-up areas of Fishguard and Goodwick but not through the built-up areas of Milford Haven, Neyland, Pembroke Dock, Pembroke, Tenby and Saundersfoot? After all, these are as urban as Fishguard and Goodwick and it is supposed to be a *coastal* footpath. One must also take into account the recommended detours around the Deer Park and Lydstep Head: the 'official' route does not carry the Path around these headlands for some strange reason, yet the true Coast Path walker is unlikely to miss them out:

| Deer Park circuit | 1ml/1.6km |
| Lydstep Head circuit | 1ml/1.6km |

The total now becomes 185.45ml/298.4km. Furthermore, high tide in the Milford Haven may require diversions at Dale and Sandy Haven, which will add 7.5ml/12km to this figure, giving a grand total of 192.95ml/310.45km.

Taking further into account the recommended detours to places of special interest near the route – for example, visits to St David's Cathedral and the Bishop's Palace, Skomer Island, Pembroke Castle, Manorbier Castle, Caldey Island and Tenby – it is likely that the total distance covered will be in the region of 200ml/322km.

The Dyfed County Council and the Pembrokeshire National Park Authority (PNPA) have carried out an energetic programme of waymarking and have erected many stiles of a uniform pattern, and the sight of one of these helps confirm the route of the Path. I have counted 479 numbered stiles along the route, and these are all shown on my sketch maps. Many of the stiles were in existence long before the coast path became continuous, and since 1980 several old stiles have been removed or blocked off, and new ones erected, yet still there are stiles which serve no useful purpose. Almost all stiles are marked with the acorn symbol.

In some places around the coast the line of the Path had to be prepared by using a small bulldozer, and a great deal of skill and courage was needed by the operator on steeply sloping cliffland. These sections were usually where new lengths of path had to be created, but they have weathered so well, growing fresh vegetation, that it is hard today to find where the hand of man has been.

In most places around the coast the agricultural or cultivated land stops short of the actual cliff-face and is defined by either the traditional Pembrokeshire hedge-bank, or a wall or a fence, and the Coast Path generally runs along the seaward side of such a boundary. The Coast Path therefore mostly runs through uncultivated land, and on little-used sections sea-buckthorn, brambles and gorse can present problems to people who walk with bare legs.

The existence of the Coast Path opens up many miles of coast to the increasing number of visitors and holiday-makers who are prepared to leave their cars for an hour or so to explore and enjoy the magnificent coastline, as only walkers on the cliffs can appreciate the distinctive character of this coastal National Park. A number of circular walks are possible, and I have indicated where public rights of way lead down to the coast from the nearest coast road or village. Car parking places are also shown where access to the coast is possible.

Parts of the Coast Path are steep, and some are very steep, and this may cause difficulties to the old, the infirm, young children and even the strong long-distance footpath walker carrying a heavy pack on his back. These steep sections are more often to be found where the underlying geology consists of shales and sandstones, and when the ground is wet the slopes can become very slippery and sometimes dangerous. In some places steps have been constructed to make the going a little easier.

In many parts the seaward side of the Coast Path is unfenced or unprotected, and you must be careful of your footing, particularly on the narrow paths and above the cliffs. Erosion is still taking place around the coastline and cliff-falls may occur at any time, causing the Coast Path to be diverted over the hedge-bank into the neighbouring field. These known hazards have been charted and marked on my maps, but one needs to keep a careful watch at all times where the Path comes close to the cliff edge.

This guide adopts a series of strip maps at a scale of 1:20,000 (approximately 3in to 1 mile). Details of contours and features of

the countryside off-route have had to be omitted from the strip
maps for clarity, and this deficiency will have to be remedied by
the use of the appropriate Ordnance Survey maps. The strip maps
are drawn, unless otherwise indicated, with grid N at the top of
the map when held to be read in the normal manner. Each map
tells you where the adjoining map can be found, and a key map
on p.10 shows you the relationship of the maps to each other.

However, you may need to know that the following Ordnance
Survey maps cover the route:

1:50,000 Landranger Series: 145 Cardigan; 157 St David's and
Haverfordwest: 158 Tenby.
1:25,000 Pathfinder Series and First Series: SM 70 Skomer Island;
SM 72 St David's; SM 80 Angle; SM 81 St Bride's Bay; SM 82
Newgale; SM 83 Mathry; SM 90 Pembroke; SM 93 Fishguard; SN
00/10 Tenby and Saundersfoot; SN 03 Newport; SN 04 Dinas Head;
SN 14 Cardigan; SR 89/99 Castlemartin; SS 09/19 Manorbier and
Tenby.

Maps are listed in numerical order, and are not necessarily in the
order in which they are used for walking the route.

One of the other principal objects of the guide is to deal with
some of those subjects which make a visit to the Pembrokeshire
coast such a delight and fascination. The author recognises that not
all of the visitors and holidaymakers to this area come solely with
the intention of walking the long-distance coastal footpath: the
PNPA estimates that about 1½ million holiday-makers visit the area
annually, and of this figure only about 600 are Coast-Path walkers
throughout its length. But the coast has attractions for all kinds of
holiday-maker, and I have included introductory chapters on those
subjects which highlight an appreciation of what this coastal
national park has to offer: chapters on ornithology, botany, and the
complex and fascinating geology and scenery of the coast. Language
and cultural history have not been forgotten either, and it is hoped
that the book will serve not only as a guide to the Pembrokeshire
Coast Path but also as a guide to many other aspects of the coast.

There is no 'best time' for walking the Coast Path: any time is a good time. In the months of April, May and June there is a better chance of settled weather, the hours of daylight are long, and the flora and fauna are at their best. However, accommodation is not so easy to find until July and August, but in high summer one has to cope with more holiday-makers and undergrowth on the paths. Autumn is the time to see the migrations of many thousands of birds travelling down the coast, and winter is the time to see spectacular seas as the storms crash the waves on the cliffs and the sands. The Pembrokeshire Coast Path is a path for all seasons.

Coastal scenery and geology

Geologically Pembrokeshire is an ancient county. The landscape is
of outstanding geological interest because it is based upon an
unbroken series of rocks ranging from the Pre-Cambrian series, as
much as 3000 million years old, through to the youngest rocks of the
Coal Measures of the Carboniferous age of 250 million years ago.
The systems pass upwards through the geological timescale from the
Pre-Cambrian through the Cambrian, Ordovician, Silurian,
Devonian and Carboniferous series. Any hard rocks deposited since
then have all been eroded off again, leaving only the soft rocks of
the last 2 million years or so.

One of the most striking features of the geology is the amazing
diversity of rock types seen from the Coast Path, where they are
magnificently exposed along the cliffs. Some examples of rock type
and rock formations are world standard stratotypes for part of the
geological timescale, and the many rock types can be recognised by
the geologist or the observant amateur.

The essential feature of Pembrokeshire is its peninsular
character. The land mass is broken up into a number of peninsulas –
jutting out northwards is the Pen Caer peninsula; westward is that
of Dewisland; SW is the Dale Peninsula, with its subsidiary Marloes
Peninsula; and in the extreme S is the Angle or Castlemartin
Peninsula. Each of these in turn is broken up into lesser peninsulas
by the erosive action of the sea, thereby intensifying the peninsular
character of the coast.

The Lower Palaeozoic Era
This era (*c*570–400 million years ago) includes the igneous and
sedimentary rocks of the Pre-Cambrian systems and the
sedimentary rocks of the Cambrian, Ordovician and Silurian
systems.

Pre-Cambrian Rocks, the oldest of rocks, are to be seen only on
the coast within a few square miles of outcrop around St David's –
in the area S of Whitesand Bay and the extreme SW peninsula
around Porthlysgi.

Cambrian Rocks dominate the cliffs between Porth Clais and

Solva, and between Porthselau and Porthstinian. At Porth Clais,
Caerfai and Caer Bwdy the lower beds rest uncomfortably on the
Pre-Cambrian rocks, a conglomerate at their base, while the highest
beds are best seen at Whitesand Bay, Porth-y-Rhaw and Solva. A
particular feature of these rocks is the great variety of fossils.
Bivalved brachiopods (genus *Linguella*) are to be found in the
bedding planes in Whitesand Bay, but the most notable fossils are
the trilobites – specimens of the genus *Paradoxides* 12in/30cm long
have been found in Solva harbour.

Ordovician Rocks include sandstones and grits and great
thicknesses of shale, but they also include volcanic ashes and lavas.
The shales dominate the N coast between Cemaes Head and
Trefin. In mid-Ordovician times volcanoes became active: those
around Ramsey Island and Llanrhian were powerful, but there was
some exceptional volcanic activity around Strumble Head, where
the eroded cliffs show layer upon layer of lava flows. The surface
flows here cooled rapidly and the rock is fine-grained 'pillow' lava.
Complementing these surface flows of volcanic lava are deep-seated
formations of intrusive igneous rocks which commonly form
headlands along the cost – Penclegyr (at Porthgain), Penllechwen
and St David's Head, and the monadnock hills inland at Carn Llidi,
Carn Penberry, Garn Fawr, Garn Foloch, Garn Ysgubor, Garn
Llundain, Carn Ffald and Garn Gilfach, as well as Ramsey Island
and the Prescelly Hills. These intrusions are extremely hard and
form the most prominent features hereabouts. The masses cooled
and solidified very slowly: large crystals developed and the rock is
coarse-grained. At St David's Head it is gabbro, and at Porth Clais
granophyre. Medium-grained intrusive rocks include dolerite, such
as that found at Porthgain.

In many of the Ordovician sediments fossils are to be found in
abundance, far exceeding the fossils of the Cambrian rocks. Many
trilobites and brachiopods have been found on Ramsey Island, as
well as graptolites: the shales in and near Abereiddy are
exceptionally rich in tuning-fork graptolites, and trilobites are not
uncommon.

Silurian Rocks outcrop on the N coast from the Teifi estuary to
Newport Bay and Dinas Head. Other sediments run in a narrow

belt from Freshwater West to Freshwater East. The only sign of volcanic activity is the Skomer Volcanic Series that stretches across the Marloes Peninsula from Watch House Point (St Ishmael's) across to Dale and the Deer Park, and continues into the islands of Skomer, Grassholm and The Smalls. This series results in the formation of an extrusive igneous rock. Under atmospheric pressure the lava solidified rapidly and consequently the rock is **fine-grained basalt in the cliffs at Marloes Sands and at the** coastguard lookout near Wooltack Point.

Caledonian Earth Movements. At the end of Silurian times much of Britain, including Pembrokeshire, was subject to intense earth pressures which radically transformed the geology and land form. About 400 million years ago the Caledonian Earth Movements mightily disrupted the Lower Palaeozoic rocks, imposing the WSW-ENE grain in the N of the county and producing St David's Peninsula. The line between the Upper and Lower Palaeozoics runs between Druidston in St Bride's Bay in the W, through Haverfordwest and Narberth to Amroth in the E.

The Upper Palaeozoic Era

This era (c400–250 million years ago) includes the sedimentary rocks of the Devonian or Old Red Sandstone and Carboniferous systems.

Devonian Rocks. After the disturbance by the Caledonian Earth Movements the Lower Palaeozoic era was radically transformed. The Upper Palaeozoic rocks accumulated under conditions wholly different from the Lower. Sands and muds were transported from a harsh desert source, sufficiently oxidised to allow a red colouration of the iron minerals, and these are consolidated in coastal lagoons. These formations are very well displayed in South Pembrokeshire, particularly in the Dale Peninsula, the Angle Peninsula, from between Stackpole Quay and Old Castle Head, at Skrinkle Haven and on Caldey Island. The N side of Milford Haven is substantially of Old Red Sandstone, which is particularly noticeable around Sandy Haven and Great Castle Head, and around St Bride's.

Carboniferous Rocks. Local subsidence of the non-marine Old Red Sandstones, complemented by a rising of the land-mass to the

N, brought about the marine accumulations of the Main Limestone
in warm, clear seas, and it was these conditions which created the
magnificent coastal sections between Linney Head and Stackpole
Head, and the cliffs at Lydstep and Giltar Point. Limestone
deposition was brought to an end by an influx of sands and muds
from the land to the N, presumably following renewed uplift of the
land and an intensification of erosion by rivers. The sandstones and
shales that overlie the Carboniferous limestone are first the
Millstone Grit, which is only exposed on the coast at Druidston
Haven in the W and between Tenby's North Sands and Waterwynch
in the E. Above the grits are the Coal Measures, which accumulated
300 million years ago as a rising sea level submerged the forests,
swamps and peat beds. The Coal Measures are well exposed along
the coast of St Bride's Bay from Newgale to Talbenny, and again
along the coast from Monkstone Point to Amroth, but they are
greatly deformed by later earth movements.

Armorican Earth Movements. After the deposition of the Coal
Measures a second major series of earth movements affected
Pembrokeshire, about 290 million years ago. They were not so
intense as the Caledonian Earth Movements of 150 million years
earlier, but their effects were similar. They folded and faulted the
Carboniferous and Old Red Sandstone series and imposed the
WNW-ESE grain upon them, and they also no doubt further
contorted the more ancient systems in the N. These folds and faults
are extremely complex, but nevertheless some of the features
observed can be simply interpreted. The layering (or bedding) of
undisturbed sedimentary rocks is more or less horizontal, but the
rocks of Pembrokeshire are everywhere folded strongly, resulting in
high angles of tilt in the strata. Pressure from the sides results in
anticlines (an upfold or arched structure) and synclines (a downfold
or trough structure). Some of these folds are small enough to be
seen in their entirety – for example, at Poppit, Sleek Stone (Broad
Haven), Fox Hole (Little Haven), West Angle Bay and Lydstep.
These earth movements marked the end of the Palaeozoic period,
and after this the area mainly remained dry land.

Erosion of the Landform. The complexities of the bedrock
contrast strongly with the near-flatness of the landscape. This

Geology

Legend:

Pattern	Description
Alluvial Deposit	Recent
Coal Measures	Carboniferous
Millstone Grit	
Limestone	
Old Red Sandstone	Devonian
Sedimentary	Silurian
Igneous	
Sedimentary	Ordovician
Igneous	
Sedimentary	Cambrian
Igneous	Pre-Cambrian

Place names: Fishguard, Strumble Head, Ramsey Is., St. David's, Broad Haven, Skomer, Skokholm, Haverfordwest, Milford Haven, Narberth, Tenby, Caldey Is.

mls 0   5
kms 0   8

plateau-like character is probably the most striking aspect of the scenery because, with the exception of the Prescelly Hills and the smaller 'island' hills on the N coast, the horizon is everywhere remarkably flat.

Much of this plateau surface was produced by wave erosion about 17 million years ago when sea level was much higher than today, during the geologically fairly recent late Tertiary and early Pleistocene periods. This broad, flat, coastal zone is frequently referred to as the '200ft platform' as the present surface is today at a height of about 200ft/61m above sea level. Irrespective of the complicated differences in rock type, rock age, folding or faulting, the general plateau form cut right across large areas of the coastal landscape.

The 200ft platform varies between 100–250ft/30–76m. S of Milford Haven it is magnificently developed – 100–150ft/30–46m above sea level between Linney Head and Stackpole Head, where it cuts quite indiscriminatingly across the Carboniferous limestone. Between Freshwater East and Lydstep Haven parts of the platform cut across the Carboniferous and Old Red Sandstone rocks, exceeding 200ft/61m; and offshore the pattern is continued on the remarkably flat-topped Caldey Island.

N of the Haven the surface varies between 150–250ft/46–76m. It is planed across the folded and faulted Old Red Sandstone and Silurian sandstones and shales, as well as the Silurian igneous rocks forming the Dale/Marloes Peninsula. The platform developed on the Pre-Cambrian igneous rocks and sedimentary Cambrian rocks of the St David's Peninsula and offshore Ramsey Island is at a similar elevation, and the monotonous continuity of the surface is broken only by the isolated hill masses such as Garn Ysgubor, Garn Llundain, Carn Llidi, Carn Ffald and Carn Penberry, as well as the smaller and less craggy outcrops of Carn Treglemais and Clegyr Boia. Garn Fawr and Garn Gilfach rise above the same surfaces developed across Pen Caer. These monadnocks or former islands stood above the sea, and as they are generally composed of hard, intrusive, resistant, igneous Ordovician rock they yielded less readily under the sweeping action of the sea. These resilient outcrops highlight the dramatic coast to the N of St David's.

As the sea level advanced across the land surface the coastal cliffs gradually retreated under the influence of wave attack and at their base was left a wave-cut rock platform. As sea level began to fall, some 2 million years ago, the wave-cut platforms and raised beaches were exposed. These features are common phenomena around the coast: extensive platforms fringe the cliffs between Little and Great Furzenip in the middle of Freshwater West, beneath the limestone cliffs between Linney Head and Stackpole Head, and between Saundersfoot and Amroth. Raised beaches are well seen at Porth Clais, West Angle Bay, Freshwater West, Swanlake Bay, Manorbier Bay and on Caldey Island.

The Last Ice Age, a further remarkable episode in the geological history of the area, occurred during the later part of the Pleistocene era, approximately 20–17,000 years ago, when a mass of ice, known as the Irish Sea Glacier, overwhelmed much of the land N of the Milford Haven. Ice-scratched surfaces on some bare-rock exposures on the slopes of Carn Llidi, at an altitude of 500ft/152m, and in Whitesand Bay can be found, but otherwise erosion features carved by the ice itself are relatively scarce. The effects of glaciation are evident in the ice-deposited till or boulder clay which is widely spread over the plateau surface, and which fills many of the valleys and bays between Cemaes Head and Strumble Head; Aber Mawr is a good example.

About 15,000 years ago, as the climate became progressively warmer, the most spectacular land-forms of glacial origin were created by the action of meltwater. Water was produced that flowed within the ice, and in tunnels beneath it, with such force and erosive energy that it carved several deep and steep-sided gorges as it roared down to the sea. The most impressive meltwater channel in the British Isles is the Gwaun valley, which has its outlet at Fishguard's Lower Town. This and its side-channel form a complex interlinked system quite unlike normal river valleys, and their scale of development is out of all proportion to the small streams that now occupy them. A few other examples of meltwater channels are: Cwm Dewi, the valley separating Dinas Island from the mainland; that linking Porthgain and Abereiddy and isolating Ynys Barry; the Merry Vale between St David's and Porth Clais; the Solfach valley at Solva, and the adjoining St Elvis valley carrying the Gribin stream.

The worldwide rise in sea level and associated eustatic fluctuations of the land following the melting of the last ice masses about 12,000 years ago drowned the lower courses of many river valleys: Milford Haven and the river valleys of the Daucleddau provide the classic example of a ria in the British Isles. Solva harbour is a fine smallscale example, and there are numerous other minor havens. The submerged river inlets allowed warm Gulf Stream waters into the heart of the country. The drowning of wooded land surfaces led to the formation of the submerged forests, which are exposed occasionally at Whitesand Bay, Freshwater West and Amroth. Later vagaries of the climate also created numerous sand dune areas behind uncliffed and gently sloping beaches, as at Freshwater West, Freshwater East, Broad Haven (Bosherston), Manorbier and Lydstep.

The walker around the Pembrokeshire coast will learn a great deal about the geological nature of the area. The diversity of the basic rock-types, the sedimentary and volcanic rocks, the contorted folding and faulting as a result of the earth movements, the plateau created by the sea and the valleys carved by the ice are all there to be seen. The coastline is constantly evolving, through the formation of the storm beaches and the accumulations of the sand dunes, and by erosion through the sequence of headland, promontory, cave, arch and stack on the cliffs. The great diversity of geological features is justification enough for a walk along this magnificent coast.

Flora and fauna

The Pembrokeshire coast is noted for its profusion and variety of
flowers and birds, as the wild and varied coastline provides an ideal
habitat. To a large extent this is influenced by the equable climate,
but it is also due to a considerable degree to the variety of the soils
and the underlying rocks.

For detailed descriptions of the birds that may be seen along the
coast; the autumn bird migration; the commonest wild flowers; and
butterflies, moths and shore plants, the reader is referred to the
several excellent leaflets prepared by the PNPA Information
Service.

Flora
Even in January more than 50 species are in flower, but the
coastline is seen at its best towards the end of May and during the
first half of June when the offshore islands and mainland cliffs are
thickly carpeted with hundreds of different flowers. There is a wide
spectrum of colours, white and pink, blue and yellow, often set
against brilliant orange lichen or green turf, against the ever-
changing sea and sky, or the curious folds of different coloured
rocks.

The range of habitats for plant species is extremely wide: beaches
and sand dunes, rocky cliffs, steep slopes, narrow valleys, marshy
streams, salt marshes, shingle banks, and the occasional wood.
Some of the major habitat types are examined below, with an
indication of the plants to be found within them.

The vegetation of the highly exposed and rocky *sea cliffs* is one of
the best examples of its type in Britain. The more exposed the cliff,
the greater the diversity of the flora. Several rare and uncommon
plants are to be found and, in terms of species rarity and community
diversity, vegetation of the greatest value can be found on the sea
cliffs of the northern coast. Some of the nationally rare sea-cliff
species that can be found along the Pembrokeshire coast are, from
N to S: the bright pink perennial centaury, only on the cliffs and
sand dunes near Newport; hairy greenweed, in several places
between Newport and Fishguard, although the major British

concentrations are on the stretch of cliffs between Strumble Head and St David's Head; on the same stretch, the deep-blue spiked speedwell; on St David's Head itself the rock sea lavender. Prostrate broom occurs sporadically between Cemaes Head and St Ann's Head, but is found most frequently on the cliffs of the Dale-Marloes Peninsula. On the limestone cliffs in the S are sea-stock, golden samphire and rock samphire. The tall, yellow wild cabbage is found only on Tenby's cliffs.

Sand dunes are found in a few places on the N coast – in the bays of the Teifi estuary, at Newport Sands and at Porth Mawr (Whitesand Bay) – but there are more in the bays on the S coast: Broad Haven (Bosherston), Barafundle, Stackpole, Freshwater East, Manorbier. Those at Freshwater West and The Burrows (between Penally and Tenby) are the most extensive.

The plant regimes of the sand dunes vary according to the age and stability of the dune, and the specialised habitats they create. At the seaward foot, nourished on the tideline of rotting vegetation, grow tall lilac or white sea rocket, sprawling sea beet, sea couchgrass and orache. Marram grass stabilises the sand and flourishes so long as fresh sand is added by the winds, storms and tides. Once this provides shelter tall, yellow ragwort, thistles and sand sedge can survive, and then creeping silverweed, sea spurge and creeping buttercup thicken up the turf. From this stage on the turf becomes an enchanting mosaic of lovely flowers: scarlet pimpernel, dog violet, deep blue/purple heath milkwort, common milkwort in shades of blue, mauve or pink, creeping lilac, common speedwell and tiny white flowers of the thyme-leaved sandwort; and winding in among them is the sea bindweed with its pale purple trumpets. Perennial centaury and dune gentian are two nationally rare plants, but other flora usually well represented include the spiny sea holly, the creeping, prickly burnet rose with its white flowers, blue fleabane, greenish-yellow Carline thistle with white flowers, yellow seaside pansy, tall yellow ploughman's spikenard, and pyramidal orchid and bee orchid, both found in limestone areas.

The extensive dunes at Freshwater West and The Burrows each have a rarity. The Marsh Helleborine grows in the slacks at Freshwater West, probably its only site in Pembrokeshire, whilst the dark-green-stemmed sharp sea rush grows only in the dunes of The Burrows. The Burrows is now largely covered in a dense growth of sea buckthorn, introduced in 1930 to stabilise the sand, and as a consequence some of the most attractive dune plants have been lost from this habitat.

All the tidal reaches of the Milford Haven have at least a narrow fringe of *salt marsh*, and other salt marshes are usually to be found behind the shingle banks where they are covered by high spring tides but not reached at all by the low neap tides, e.g. Aber Mawr and Aber Bach. Only a few species of flowering plant can survive the salinity of these areas. Perennial glasswort (a low, much-branched plant with fleshy green articulated stems which grows in large patches) and sea blite both colonise the mud, and thick mattresses of sea purslane with mealy-grey leaves and yellowish fluffy flowers border the drainage channels. The sward at the top of the salt marsh is covered by sea pink or thrift in May, where it flowers later than on the cliffs. The turf round the edges of the marsh is colonised by sea milkwort, with its tall purple spikes.

Scurvy grass is the first to flower in spring, followed by thrift in May, common salt-marsh grass in June, followed by sea aster and shrubby sea purslane in July, and then in August the lax-flowered sea lavender. This species commonly occurs throughout the Haven and does not appear anywhere else in the county, but the common sea lavender is absent.

The *shingle banks* in Pembrokeshire are generally small and in most cases the covering vegetation has been worn away, yet there are places where sea twitch, sea beet and orache invade the spring-tide level, while just above grow woody nightshade with its blue-purple flowers and scarlet berries and curled dock. A graceful but scarce flower of this habitat is the yellow-horned poppy, with glaucous crinkled leaves, surmounted by the pale watery-yellow flower which later develops the long, bent seed-pod from which the plant gets its name.

Several flowers are conspicuous in lush, marshy *stream valley* bottoms and damp places, including yellow flag, a large iris with bright yellow flowers and the large, white-flowered hemlock water dropwort, both of which flower in May and June, followed by other tall flowers – meadowsweet, hemp agrimony, purple loosestrife, ragged robin–dark purple marsh cinquefoil, and the low, creeping marsh pennywort and bog pimpernel. Banks of streams are often clothed in common sallow and alder.

There are really only three places around the coast where there are *woods* close to the sea – Goultrop Roads (near Little Haven), Dale and around Saundersfoot. The first and last are remnants of what the wooded areas once were. Originally of oak and sycamore, they are now supplemented by pine, larch and spruce. The floors of the woods are deeply covered in ferns: male, soft shield, polypody and often, too, the thick, shiny, dark-green hart's tongue fern or the yellower long lance leaves of the hairy woodrush. Other plants which also grow are the yellow/green wood sage, creeping, white wood sorrel and wood groundsel, whilst primroses, bluebells, white wood anemone and red campion provide colour.

Hillsides, steep banks and uncultivated cliff-tops are usually covered with brambles, bracken, heather, gorse, blackthorn and hawthorn, and in high summer they may dominate the flowers which seek shelter beneath them.

One special local flower which should be mentioned is the Tenby Daffodil (*Narcissus obvallaris*), which flowers by the end of February. Legends that it was brought into Pembrokeshire from the Continent have been discounted by the fact that it is not known as a native species anywhere in Europe. Originally to be found only in the Ritec valley near Tenby, it is now to be found in many places on roadside hedge-banks, near dwellings or ruins, in pastures close to farmsteads, and in woods, with every indication that it is thoroughly naturalised.

There is one man-made feature which dominates the rural landscape of Pembrokeshire and which provides an excellent habitat for a variety of plants, birds and small animals, and this is the high hedge-bank – a field and roadside boundary, essentially an earth mound with stone and turf facings, and still constructed in the traditional manner throughout most of Dyfed. On the banks grow lesser celandine, primrose, lesser stitchwort, cow parsley, ragged robin, foxglove, herb robert, rough chervil and red campion, all of which make the banks colourful from early spring onwards. The tops of the banks are crowned with hedges of hawthorn, blackthorn, gorse, honeysuckle and dog rose, adding to the colourful appearance. As a recognition of their contribution to the scenery of the area and as a haven for wildlife, some sections – particularly on minor roads inland of St Bride's Bay – have been designated as Roadside Nature Reserves and are managed in such a way as to preserve their character.

Under the Conservation of Wild Creatures and Wild Plants Act, 1975, it is now illegal to disturb 21 species of wild plants. Taking wild plants in order to try and grow them in a garden at home is a practice to be deplored. They seldom survive. Wild flowers should be left where they grow so that their seed may be allowed to ripen and propagate and other people can enjoy their beauty.

Birds

Nowhere in England and Wales is there a richer sea-bird life than along the Pembrokeshire coast. The number of birds recorded in Pembrokeshire in a year is nearly 300, but the Coast Path walker will be lucky if he sees even a half or a third of that number, as his visit to the coast will be limited to a particular season.

The offshore islands of Skomer, Skokholm and Grassholm are internationally important for the following three species of breeding sea birds:

	No. of breeding pairs	% Welsh popln	% British popln	No. of larger colonies in Britain
Manx Shearwater	130,000	99	50	Nil
Storm Petrel	7,000	99	15	2
Gannet	17,000	100	13	2

The breeding numbers of other sea birds such as guillemots and razorbills are of major importance in Wales. St Margaret's Island supports the largest colony of cormorants in England and Wales.

The walker on the Coast Path will have on his one hand the birds of the sea and on his other the birds of the land, all through the year, and the walker who is also an ornithologist will have difficulty in deciding in which season to walk the Coast Path, such is the variety of birds to be seen. Some headlands and the offshore islands are particularly important, and there are a dozen locations where birds may be seen in abundance. The high cliffs, headlands and peninsulas between Cemaes Head and St Govan's Head are frequented by guillemots, razorbills, cormorants, shags, great and lesser black-backed, herring and kittiwake gulls. They are also the favourite retreat and nesting-place for a number of land birds – raven, buzzard, kestrel, rock pipit, rock dove, chough and peregrine falcon.

Along the furze-grown tops between the cliff-face and the cultivated ground, wheatears and stonechats are common, and many pairs of meadow pipits touch upon their territory.

The rocky coasts are not suited to the habits of the majority of wading birds. The only waders which breed along the Pembrokeshire coast are the oystercatcher and the ringed plover. Wading birds, sea ducks and some diving birds find that the estuary of Milford Haven is their principal feeding ground.

The most important locations for birds around the coast are Cardigan Island, Dinas Island, Strumble Head, Ramsey Island, Skomer Island, Skokholm Island, Grassholm Island, Milford Haven, Stack Rocks, Stackpole Head, St Margaret's Island and Caldey Island. Further details about these places, and means of access to them, are given in the main text.

Coastal safety

Pembrokeshire has a delightful coastline, varying from high, sheer cliffs to broad, sandy beaches. Nevertheless, coastal path walkers and other holiday-makers should be aware that there are dangers on the coast. The coastal path is everywhere safe, but every year there are accidents through cliff-falls: be extremely careful when walking the cliff paths, especially on windy days. Some parts of the coastline are continuously being eroded, so beware of unmarked sheer drops and falling rocks. In those places where there have been landslips the Path can be followed with care by following the diversions: the maps in this guide show the condition of the Path at the time of the survey. Do not allow children to walk ahead without due supervision lest there be some new, uncharted dangers in the Path. All beaches facing W tend to have strong cross-currents. Be wary and remember that heavy surf on any beach is always dangerous. Poppit Sands, Porth Mawr/Whitesand Bay, Newgale and Freshwater West can be dangerous places: again, the guide gives local bathing dangers. The beachcomber may be cut off by rising tide, the climber may be stranded on some cliff-face, or the sailor may have his dinghy carried out to sea by tidal currents. In such circumstances one should know where and how to seek help.

Of paramount importance is an understanding of the tidal streams. In two places the Coast Path route is affected by tides – at the crossings of The Gann and Sandy Haven, both in Milford Haven. In other places the walker has access to the beach as an alternative to the cliff-top – for example, Porth Mawr/Whitesand Bay, Newgale Sands and Marloes Sands – and he may wish to plan his walk to time with low-tide conditions. The following general advice is given: local details are given in the main part of the guide.

Tides
Tides are controlled mainly by the pull or gravitation attraction of the moon and are essentially a vertical movement of water.

If you stood on a beach for 24 hours you would notice the tide gradually rise to a peak, fall to a minimum level, rise to a second peak, and then fall to a second minimum. The peaks are called 'high tide' and the minima 'low tide'. All high tides are not equally high, and if you went back to the beach at high water every day for a month you would notice another cycle in which the high tides gradually got higher, reached a peak, fell off to a minimum, rose to a second peak, and then fell again to a second minimum. These peaks are called 'spring tides' and the minima 'neap tides', there being two springs and two neaps for every lunar month. At springs there are the highest high tides and the lowest low tides, whilst at neaps there are the lowest high tides and the highest low tides. Spring tides come a few days after full and new moons, while neaps follow the first and last quarters.

In Pembrokeshire low-water spring tides (i.e. the lowest of all low tides) are always at midday or soon after, and again, of course, at midnight, whilst low-water neaps are in the morning and evening. The time of high and low water is later each successive day, half an hour later at springs, becoming up to 1¼ hours later at neaps, and averaging out at 50 minutes.

Waves are due almost entirely to the sweeping of winds over the surface of the sea and are independent of the tides. In the open sea waves move forward in the same direction as the wind. The prevailing winds affecting Pembrokeshire blow from a southwesterly or westerly quarter, and hence the waves generally approach the coast from a similar direction. Wave size depends on the strength of the wind, and the distance it has been blowing over the sea – 'the fetch'.

The rising and lowering of the sea under the influences of tides results in the formation of tidal currents which may run towards, away from, or along the shore. Very strong tidal currents run between the mainland and the offshore islands of Ramsey and Skomer, and during high spring tides the 'race' through Jack Sound, off the mainland between the Deer Park and Skomer, may reach 6 knots.

Tide tables are available from local information centres and show high water at Milford Haven. Low water is 6 hours 10 minutes after high water. All times are given on a 24-hour clock, noon being 1200. Heights of tides are usually given in metres.

Unfortunately very little information is available about the high-

water time differences for all the access points to the water around
the Pembrokeshire coast. The Tidal Computation Section of the
Institute of Oceanographic Sciences has only been able to supply
me with predictions for about a dozen places, and these are given in
the main text. The times given must be added to, or subtracted
from, the time of high water at Milford Haven. These times are the
average and may be subject to appropriate variations between
spring and neap tides and local weather conditions, as well as
barometric pressure and wind influence.

Weather Forecasts. A valuable indication of expected weather
conditions is given by the shipping forecasts transmitted mainly on
BBC Radio 4, but also on Radio 3. Radio 4 Long Wave (200kHz/
1500m) gives forecasts for deep waters daily at 0015, 0625, 1355 and
1750, and for inshore waters every day at 0020, immediately after
the main daily shipping forecast. Radio 3 (1215kHz/247m) gives
forecasts for inshore waters only at 0655 Monday-Friday and 0755
on Saturdays and Sundays. General weather forecasts can be heard
on Radio 4 VHF (92–95 MHz) at 0625, 0655, 0755, 0857, 1255, 1755
and 2400 (midnight). Radio programmes will also be interrupted to
give gale warnings.

The regular pattern of radio broadcasts is to give forecasts for the
sea areas around Britain's coast and then the station reports. Listen
for sea areas Fastnet, Lundy and Irish Sea, and for coastal stations
Scilly, Valentia and Ronaldsway.

Other weather forecasts and reports may be obtained by
contacting the Meteorological Office, Brawdy (tel. Solva 528)
during office hours, or the Meteorological Office (tel. Aberporth
810777 or Gloucester 23122, both on a 24-hour service).

The Coastguard Service is the rescue organisation for all coastal
emergencies – at sea or on the cliffs. Be alert to people who may be
in distress. You could save life. If you see a red flare, orange smoke,
or a craft or person in difficulty do the following:

Dial 999 and ask for Coastguard. When connected give your
name and telephone number and say where you are speaking
from.
Give all the information you can about the incident: what you
have seen and where it is from your position as accurately as

possible. This will help save time.

Stay by the telephone in case further information is needed. Ring again if the situation changes.

HM Coastguard will provide whatever rescue units may be required – lifeboats, helicopter, or coastguard rescue teams. The coastguard organisation for Pembrokeshire is based upon the Maritime Rescue Co-ordination Centre at the Mumbles, Swansea, and the Milford Haven Rescue Sub-Centre at St Ann's Head. They are the reception points for all '999' calls relating to coastal and marine emergencies, and have direct contact with all Maritime Search and Rescue Units in the area. Coastguard stations are not open to visitors.

Danger Areas. Unfortunately, military training still takes place in the National Park, and some of the best parts of the coast are prohibited or have restricted access. There are range areas on land, and target areas at sea, which are bombed, shelled, or harassed by torpedoes, mines and other devices, and all unauthorised persons and craft have to leave the areas in good time. On land mobile patrols and at sea fast launches are used to speed trespassers on their way.

Danger areas are in St Bride's Bay, off the W, S and E coasts of the Castlemartin Peninsula, off Manorbier, and at Penally. Details of access restrictions to these areas are given in relevant places in the guide.

The Water Sport Safety Code gives the following points of advice for anyone venturing on or near the sea:

1   Never bathe or swim alone.
2   Never allow your children to bathe or swim without supervision.
3   Ask the advice of lifeguards or local people before entering the water.
4   Look for and read notices on or near bathing areas.
5   A red flag means danger – *do not enter the water*.
6   Red and yellow flags mean that the area between them is **patrolled by lifeguards** – *use this area*.

7   Never bathe immediately after strenuous exercise, or after a meal, or if the water is very cold – cramp!

8   Never remain in the water when cold.

9   Swim parallel to the shoreline and keep within your depth.

10 Don't swim off headlands – strong currents.

11 Be wary of undertow currents, even when the water looks calm.

12 Air beds, rubber rings, tyres or rubber dinghies can easily be swept out to sea by offshore winds and tidal currents. Use them with a line to the shore, or *don't use them*.

13 Do not sit under cliffs. You may be hit by falling stones dislodged by erosion or by a bird, or by a Coast Path walker.

14 If climbing you may fall or be trapped. Don't climb unless you are properly equipped and in an organised climbing party.

15 When you are on a beach beware of being trapped by the incoming tide. Make sure there is an easy exit from the beach near at hand. You could get cut off.

16 Do not leave your litter on the beach. Please take it home. Bottles may get broken by the waves smashing them on rocks, and then they may be left partially covered by sand, ready to gash bare feet.

17 Don't touch strange objects. Hazardous items, such as flares or canisters of chemicals, may sometimes be washed ashore. Tell the Coastguard or police about them.

18 When angling from rocks be wary of incoming tides and the occasional big wave. If night-fishing, do not go alone.

19 When surfing wear ankle leashes. Return to shore when you are cold.

20 Water skiers should have two people in the boat, one to drive, and one to watch the skier.

21 Sub-aqua divers should use surface marker buoys. Cover boats can lose the location of divers.

22 If boating, only go to sea in well-equipped boats. Have an auxiliary means of propulsion in case the outboard fails. An anchor, a bailer, oars and personal buoyancy are all essential in small craft. Always inform a friend ashore before and after making a boat trip.

23   When yachting in tenders, and always at night, wear a
     lifejacket.
24   When dinghy sailing, always take a bailer and paddle.
25   When canoeing, take buoyancy for the canoe and for yourself,
     and also use a spray cover.

Remember to 'Stay Safe'. If you need Rescue, dial 999 and ask for
Coastguard.

Cliff climbing

Climbing on the sea cliffs has only recently become popular. No more than a tiny handful of climbing enthusiasts were attracted to the cliffs for many years until the publication of Colin Mortlock's pioneering paperback in 1974, and from just over 300 routes then the number of climbs increased to over 800 in the 'golden year' of 1980 and over 1500 by 1985.

Some areas of the coastline are subject to restricted access for conservation or military reasons. There are also some large and important sea-bird colonies and in order to protect these and other cliff-nesting birds, certain restrictions must be observed during the nesting season. These restrictions have been the result of much patient negotiation involving the BMC, the NCC, the PNPA, the DWT, the NT, HM Coastguard and local climbers. Failure to stick to the terms of agreed access limits will strengthen the demand of ornithologists to have climbing in South Pembrokeshire banned completely. Climbers have already driven off the guillemot and razorbill population from Lydstep, so local opinion is strong. The following list gives the popular climbing areas and the limits of the restrictions:

Penbwchdy Head. No climbing between Pwll Deri YH and
 Penbwchdy Head 1 February–31 July.
St David's Head – Mur Cenhinen. Occasional seasonal ban
 1 February–31 July.
Stack Rocks. Cliffs between Range boundary fence on the W to
 Flimston Bay on the E, including the Cauldron and Stack
 Rocks. Seasonal ban 1 March–15 August.
Mewsford Point. Seasonal ban 1 March–15 August.
Mowing Word (W face). Seasonal ban 1 March–31 July.
Skomer and Skokholm. No climbing at any time.
Stackpole Head (E and S faces). Seasonal ban 1 March–
 15 August. W face seasonal ban 1 March–31 July.
St Margaret's Island. Seasonal ban 1 March–31 July.
 Permit from DWT at other times.

Cultural history

The Pembrokeshire coast everywhere bears the imprint of
successive generations of human occupation, and there is abundant
evidence to show that civilisations spread, from the earliest times,
by sea. The earliest known occupation occurred 50–20,000 years
ago, before the last advance of the ice drove man south. *Old Stone
Age (Palaeolithic) man* established his home in the limestone caves
in South Pembrokeshire – at Cat's Hole Cave at Monkton, at
Hoyle's Mouth near Tenby, and in Nonna's Cave on Caldey. 10,000
years ago, as the weather improved, Mesolithic man came
northwards. Mesolithic craftsmen fashioned flint tools near Solva,
on The Nab Head near St Bride's, on the banks of the Nyfer at
Newport, at Small Ord Point on Caldey, at Little Furzenip,
Castlemartin, at Fraynslake, and at Swanlake near Manorbier.

About 5000 years ago *New Stone Age (Neolithic) man* arrived
from the W, almost certainly by boat and probably in simple skin
craft not unlike the Welsh coracle and the Irish curragh of today.
Traces of his daily life have been found only at Clergyr Boia near St
David's and in caves on Caldey, but the most conspicuous marks of
his occupation are the burial chambers which have survived better
than the houses. These cromlechau – standing stones covered by a
capstone that may weigh as much as 28 tons – are concentrated on
the coast, along their trade routes, especially near sheltered
anchorages. Many of these are in the N of the county between
Newport Bay and St David's Head, and in the S Prescelly Hills. The
more dramatic are Carreg Samson on the coast at Abercastle;
Carreg Coetan Arthur near Newport and Llechy-yr-drybedd; and
the King's Quoit at Manorbier, South Pembrokeshire.

Bronze Age men came on foot about 3000 years ago from the E in
their search for copper in the Wicklow Hills. They used the crests of
the hills for their tracks, such as that followed by the Ridgeway from
St Clears via Laugharne, Tenby, Pembroke, and Hundleton to
West Angle Bay, and that across the Prescelly Hills to Whitesand
Bay. Their routes are marked by burial mounds and stone circles
and single standing stones, on hill-tops such as Foel Drygarn,
Prescelly, and by stone circles at Dyffryn and Garn Fawr.

The Bronze Age was followed about 2500 years ago by the *Iron Age*, whose people came by sea from Spain and Brittany via Devon and Cornwall. These people spoke languages which were the forerunners of Welsh and Gaelic: evidence of their settlements is widespread along the Coast Path and readily identifiable. They recognised the defensive potential of coastal promontories and headlands, building earthworks across the narrow necks of the coast. The first settlers built a single straight bank with a ditch outside, but by 100BC latecomers had developed complicated double-curving banks around the fort, sometimes with elaborate entrances. The names 'camp', 'promontory fort' or 'rath' have no archaeological significance: they were not military structures, but defended settlements inside the fortifications.

Later on, the other main type of defended settlement was developed: the hill-fort, which was built well into the Roman period. The hill-tops were surrounded by banks and ditches; below the summit of Carn Llidi near St David's, in the valley behind Porth Melgan, one can still see the stone walls which the Iron Age people built to enclose their fields. These fields show a continuity of 2000 years of agriculture, and there are similar traces on Skomer. On both St David's Head and Skomer there are also circular outlines of their round-stone houses. The fragmentary evidence taken from these sites still gives only a sketchy picture of how these people lived: the coast abounds in evidence and it is the interpretation that is so largely lacking.

On present evidence the *Roman military occupation* spread no further W than Carmarthen and during this period, which coincided broadly with the end of the Iron Age, Celtic tribal society evolved largely unmolested. In the post-Roman centuries, when the sea routes once more came into greater use, Pembrokeshire witnessed a period of intense activity. Contacts with Ireland had been maintained since Neolithic times, and in the 3c and 4c Irish tribes with their rulers settled here. Inscribed stones bearing Ogam script are important evidence for this contact with Ireland, and the earliest surviving archaeological evidence of *early Christianity* consists of these inscribed and carved stones: no buildings of the early period are known.

During the 5c, 6c and 7c the full force of the monastic movement within the early Celtic church was felt in Pembrokeshire. The early missionaries of the Celtic church came and went in their sea-going curraghs around the western seaboard, spreading the gospel between the scattered and emergent Celtic nations of Ireland, Wales, Cornwall and Brittany. The journeys were long and perilous but the faith of the wayfarers was strong. Probably the last thing they did before such a journey was to pray for delivery from danger and, the moment the journey was over, a thanksgiving was offered as they came ashore. Consequently shrines and chapels were established at points of landing or departure, and the names of the saints and missionaries are commemorated profusely around the coast – Saints Ann, Bride, Dogmael, Govan, Ishmael, Non, to name a few.

Inevitably a vigorous Christian community was centered in Pembrokeshire, as it commanded the largest intersection of the busiest sea-routes in western Europe. From the scattered landing places missionaries and pilgrims converged inland to the site of St David's ascetic community. Dewi Sant, the Patron Saint of Wales, was born about 500 and established his monastery and cathedral in **Glyn Rhosyn: according to tradition he died on 1 March 589 and his** reputed bones, with those of Justinian, his confessor, rest in the cathedral. The fame of the saint so resounded in Christendom that after his death the seaways were busy with pilgrims, and the sailors' chapels multiplied. Many missionaries sailed far inland up the numerous tidal creeks and estuaries to establish their little cells or oratories, which in due course became the churches of the countryside that still bear their names. The years 400–800, the Great Age of the Saints, marked a prodigious contrast with the darkness elsewhere and reached out to standards and aspirations that have perhaps not been exceeded by anything achieved since.

The *Vikings* dominated the western seas in 9c-11c, roving far and wide from their base in Scotland and from Dublin, Waterford, Wexford and the Isle of Man. St David's Cathedral was burnt no fewer than eight times during the 250 years of their reign, but their activities did not fundamentally affect the life of the people. The **Norsemen are now best** remembered by the names that they have given to places along the coast: '-holmen', a small island, and '-oy', a large island, as in Grassholm, Skokholm, Caldey, Ramsey, Gateholm and Skomer; '-vik', a safe anchorage, as in Gelliswick, Goodwick and Musselwick, and other names such as Angle and Dale, and such places in Milford Haven as Milford, Haverfordwest and Herbrandston.

It was the death of the last Prince of S Wales, Rhys ap Tewdwr, in 1093, that precipitated the most important event in the history of Pembrokeshire. The Welsh tribes, weakened by their own internal troubles, were no match for the *Norman armies* expanding westwards from England. Roger de Montgomery, Earl of Shrewsbury, with his army sailed up the Haven, landed at Pembroke in 1093 and quickly occupied the land to the S. It was their first foothold in Wales, and a stepping stone to Ireland. The Normans built one of their greatest castles at Pembroke, on a rocky ridge which is almost surrounded by the branches of the Pembroke River, one of the arms of the Milford Haven. They rapidly occupied the rich agricultural land to the S, and from this centre they erected a line of castles during the next 200 years which divided the N from the S.

This military frontier (the Landsker) became the demarcation line between two provinces that are sharply distinct from one another in language, place-names, ecclesiastical architecture and general culture, to this day. To the S the population is English-speaking: to the N the dominant language is Welsh.

It was William Camden, writing in *Britannia* in 1733, some decades after George Owen of Henllys (who wrote his *Description of Pembrokeshire* in 1603), who first styled the area S of the Landsker as 'Anglia Transwalliana', although there is some evidence that the term may have been used locally before that time. However this may be, the term used by Camden is the antecedent of the appellation given by Daniel Defoe, 'Little England beyond Wales'.

From *Norman times onward* the hinterland was devoted to agriculture and the coastal villages, particularly from the Elizabethan age, were busily occupied in trade around the Bristol Channel, the Irish Sea and the coasts of western Europe. In the 17c the county continued to flourish under the Stuarts, despite the

disturbing effects of the Civil Wars. The Welsh parts of
Pembrokeshire were, with few exceptions, strongly Royalist,
whereas the Anglicised parts produced enthusiastic Roundheads.
As a result of the rising of 1648 Cromwell ordered the destruction of
certain castles in Pembrokeshire, so that they could never again
become a challenge to the new regime.

Every coastal village was engaged in short- and long-distance
trade: landing stages, quays, piers, warehouses and even boats were
built in remote creeks like Abercastle, Porthgain, Solva and
Stackpole Quay. At the ports and creeks vessels discharged cargoes
of coal, limestone and other goods and took away grain and other
produce. No sheltered place on the coast where a cart road could
reach to the high tide was without a lime-kiln – the sour lands had
constantly to be sweetened with lime.

The great age of village seafaring came to an end when the
inventions of the *Industrial Revolution* and the coming of the
railways in the mid-19c gave commercial advantages to large
industrial units: fishing was concentrated in Milford Haven and
coasting passed from family schooners to the steamers of large
companies.

Slate and stone quarries rose to pre-eminence during the 19c. The
coal industry also had an early beginning: coal was probably mined
in the times of the Normans and the last colliery to work was closed
in 1939. Although Pembrokeshire produced very high quality
anthracite, the coalfield was beset by geological problems and the
industry declined rapidly during the early part of this century.

Milford Haven was for long an important station of the Fleet, and
now its natural deep-water anchorage has been developed to
provide the county with *trade in oil*. Tankers of up to 250,000 tons
use the Haven, and the shores have sprouted colonies of oil storage
tanks and other installations related to the petrochemical industry,
as well as an oil-fired power station. However, the decline in
importance of the importation of oil from the Middle East, and the
growing dependence on oil from within our own territorial waters
off Scotland which is imported into the country by pipeline rather
than by tanker, place a question mark over the future of this
industry.

Part one

St Dogmael's to Fishguard

1 St Dogmael's to Newport (Maps 1–7)   15.1ml/24.3km

Pembrokeshire, Cardiganshire and Carmarthenshire had been separate counties for centuries until 1 April 1974, when they were merged into one huge new county called Dyfed. Pembrokeshire ceased to exist as a county in its own right, yet the name still lingers on: the name of the National Park hasn't been changed to the Dyfed Coast National Park, and readers will already have noticed that I prefer to use the name Pembrokeshire, because that is the name that was used and always will be, no matter what our legislators will have us do.

The Pembrokeshire coast was designated as a National Park in 1952, but the Pembrokeshire Coast Path was not 'completed' until 1970. It must be realised at the outset that the Coast Path does not always follow the coastal boundary of the National Park, and it will be seen from the maps in this guide where the Coast Path enters and leaves the National Park.

Pembrokeshire's grasp of the estuary of the Afon Teifi is tenuous. The Lords of Ceredigion got early possession of most of both sides of the estuary, no doubt because Cardigan's castle was so near and so important, but St Dogmael's remained in Pembrokeshire because the Benedictine priory was an integral part of the Pembrokeshire Lordship of Cemaes (or Cemais). The Coast Path therefore begins on the county boundary at St Dogmael's, not on the side nearest Cardigan so as to permit a route through the village, but on the N edge of the village, so that the first 1.5ml/2.4km are in Cardiganshire, and on a road at that: nevertheless, as the Coast Path starts or ends at St Dogmael's, we might as well have a look at the village.

MAP 1

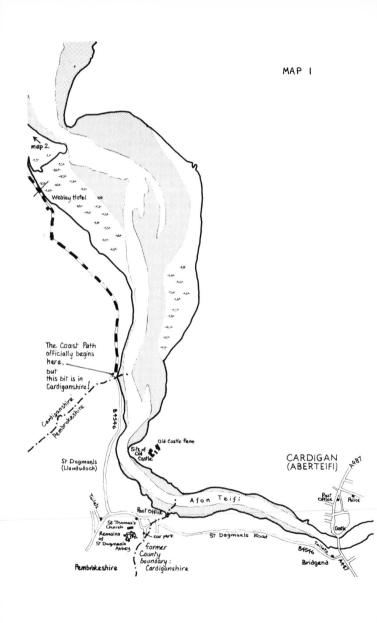

map 2

Webley Hotel

The Coast Path officially begins here, but this bit is in Cardiganshire!

Cardiganshire
Pembrokeshire

B4546

Site of Old Castle

Old Castle Farm

CARDIGAN (ABERTEIFI)

A487

St Dogmaels (Llandudoch)

Afon Teifi

Post Office

Police

Toilets

Post Office

St Thomas's Church

car park

St Dogmaels Road

Castle

Remains of St Dogmaels Abbey

former County boundary: Cardiganshire

Toilets

B4546

Pembrokeshire

Bridgend

A487

St Dogmael's (Llandudoch)

St Dogmael was the grandson of Ceredig – the prince who conquered Cardiganshire (Sir Ceredigion) and gave it its name. St Dogmael lived from about 450 to 500 and he founded a hermitage about 1ml/1.6km away from the present abbey. He also founded several other cells in Pembrokeshire, at Llandogwel in Anglesey, and also in Brittany.

The Abbey of St Mary the Virgin was the key to the early growth of St Dogmael's. It was founded in 1115 by Robert Fitz-Martin (Robert de Turribus), Lord of Cemaes and son of the Norman adventurer, Martin of Tours, for the reformed Benedictine order of St Bernard of Abbeville – the Order of Tiron – one of the rarer foundations in Britain. The rule was similar to that of the better-known Cistercians. St Dogmael's possessed two daughter houses in Wales, both in Pembrokeshire – one on Caldey Island, and the other at Pill, near Milford Haven – but they have never played the prominent part in Welsh history of abbeys such as Strata Florida or Valle Crucis.

Most of the building took place after 1200, but the greatest construction period was during the 14c. Today the fragmentary ruins consist of the outlines of various buildings, the most easily recognisable of which are the N transept and the N and W walls of the nave of the abbey church, which stand almost to their full height. The N transept is early 15c: the nave walls are 13c. Some interesting carvings are preserved, including a stone cadaver now placed in a recess in the N transept, and various fragments collected in the infirmary.

The site has been excavated and the ruins are being saved from continuing disrepair by the Department of the Environment. Guide-books are available from the nearby Post Office. Admission is free at all reasonable hours.

Part of the abbey site is occupied by the parish churchyard, with the church of St Thomas the Martyr standing alongside the abbey ruins. It was built in 1847, spacious and lofty, with daylight falling through tinted glass windows on to cream and white walls. Inside the church, on the W wall, is the important Sagranus Ogam stone: important in that its inscription provided the key to the successful interpretation of the Ogam alphabet in 1848. The stone, of 5c–6c date, and 7ft/2.1m high, has the Latin inscription SAGRANI FILI CUNOTAMI on one side, and the Ogam SAGRAMMI MAQU CUNATAMI on another. The inscription identifies 'Sagranus, son of Cunotamus'.

The High Street twists at the Cardigan end and sets itself to climb the hillside. There are many fine houses and villas, terraces and cottages, several of which are built in a distinctive way with layers of dressed slate between harder stones, forming attractive bands. Halfway up the hill the road to Poppit Sands turns off between the houses, and runs down to the tidal river.

St Dogmael's to Poppit Sands 1.3ml/2.1km
The Coast Path proper begins on the northern outskirts of the village, at the former county boundary where the road rises and turns away from the river front. There is no sign indicating the start of the Path, and you just have to follow the B4546 road all the way, for there is no alternative footpath. After 1.25ml/2km you enter Pembrokeshire again, and also enter the National Park, but there is still 0.25ml/0.4km to go before you come to the end of the road.

Poppit Sands is a very fine, large and sandy beach, both at high and low water, backed by sand dunes. The area is very popular in summer. The PNPA has acquired 50 acres/20 ha of dunes, freshwater marsh and grazing land under a management agreement, and the effects of this have been to restrict the access of cars to the beach and to control the passage of visitors through the fragile dunes area.

The River Teifi at Poppit is a dangerous place. Only bathe close inshore in the centre of the beach at slack water, or where the lifeguard indicates. The ebb tide creates strong currents and bathers should keep well away from the deep-water channels of the river at all times. The Teifi estuary bar – called the Cardigan Bar – can be dangerous to canoeists if there is a swell running, and can be a hazard to sailors if the sea is piled up when driven by a N or NW wind. High water is Milford time plus 1 hour 7 minutes.

Beyond the rocks at the W end of the sands, in an area below the youth hostel and reached by a faint path – not the Coast Path – from the end of the beach, can be found some fine examples of small-

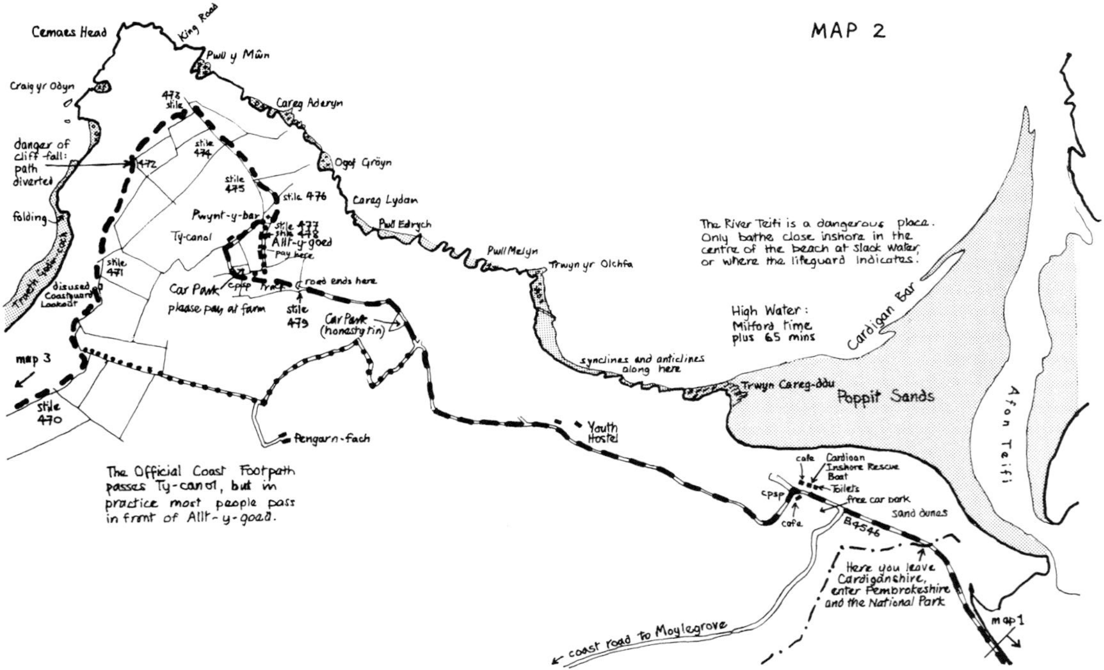

MAP 2

The River Teifi is a dangerous place. Only bathe close inshore in the centre of the beach at Slack Water or where the lifeguard indicates.

High Water:
Milford Time
plus 65 mins

Afon Teifi

Cardigan Bay

Poppit Sands

Ceibwr Bay

Twyn Carreg-ddu

café
Carlisan Inshore Rescue Boat
café — Toilets
free car park
café
cpark
Sand dunes
B4546

Here you leave Cardiganshire, enter Pembrokeshire and the National Park

← coast road to Moylegrove

Youth Hostel

synclines and anticlines along here

Trwyn yr Olchfa

Pwll Melyn

Pwll Edrych

Carreg Lydan

Ogof Grogin

Carreg Adarnyn

Ceibwr Bay

Pwll y Mûn

Craig yr Odyn

Cemaes Head

danger of cliff-fall: path diverted

folding

disused Coastguard Lookout

Pen-castell-bach

472 stile

473 stile

477 stile

stile 444

stile 478

stile 476
stile 472, 473
stile 478
Allt-y-goed
Pwyntyr

stile 471

stile 479

stile 470

map 3

Pwynt-y-rhos
Ty-canol
Car Park
please keep off farm

Car Park
(Nantrylin)

Car Park
(Nantrylin)

good roads here

stile 475

Pengarn-fach

map 3

The Official Coast Footpath passes Ty-canol, but in practice most people pass in front of Allt-y-goed.

map 1 ←

scale folding and faulting along the foreshore: a succession of simple synclines and anticlines in the blue-grey gritty sandstones and shales of Ordovician age can be seen from the path, or better still from the rocks and foreshore at low water.

Above the level of the folded rocks can be seen traces of a high inter-glacial sea level. During the Ice Age there were several warm intervals, known as 'inter-glacials', when the climate of western Britain was warmer than that of the present day. At such times mean sea level rose well above the present sea level, since there was a melting of the ice sheets of Greenland and Antarctica. As a result of these higher sea levels wave action was concentrated further inland in several locations than it is today, and wave-cut platforms and storm-beach deposits can occasionally be found above the present high-water mark. These deposits are referred to as 'raised beach platforms' and 'raised beaches'. They can be approximately dated by the glacial and other deposits which rest upon them; it seems that most of the raised beach features of Pembrokeshire date from the last inter-glacial period, which ended about 70,000 years ago.

The raised beach exposed in the low cliffs at Poppit Sands is a magnificent examples of this period. It is thickly covered with deposits from the last glaciation: the raised beach platform can be clearly seen cut across the bedrock, above which the pebbly raised beach and the overlying deposits are formed.

Poppit Sands to Cemaes Head 2ml/3.2km
The first 1.5ml/2.4km of this section are on a road, narrow and climbing steeply from the beach up past the youth hostel. At the end of the public road you come to the first of many stiles which you have to climb on your journey on the Coast Path. This one is numbered 479, and you have the satisfaction of counting down the numbers as you progress around the coast: by the end of the walk you will have become quite expert at climbing stiles!

The bold headland of *Cemaes Head* is the most northerly of the many fine headlands on the coast of Pembrokeshire. It guards the S side of the Teifi estuary and splendid cliffs rise to nearly 400ft/122m. On the tip of the headland Welsh gorse, sea-pinks, shags,

MAP 3

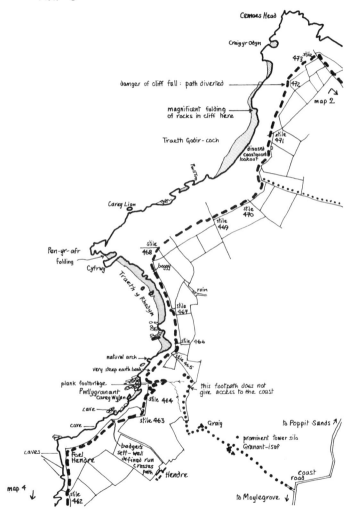

Cemaes Head

Craig yr Odyn

stile 473

danger of cliff fall: path diverted

472

map 2

magnificent folding
of rocks in cliff here

stile 471

Traeth Godir-coch

disused
coastguard
lookout

Twrra

Pen

stile 470

Careg Lion

stile 469

stile 468

boggy

Pen-yr-afr
folding

ruin

Cyfrwy

Traeth y Rhedyn

stile 467

stile 466

natural arch

stile 465

very steep earth bank

stile 464

this footpath does not
give access to the coast

plank footbridge
Pwllgranant
Careg Wylan

cave

stile 463

Graig

to Poppit Sands

cave

prominent tower silo
Granant-isaf

caves

badgers
sett-well
defined run
crosses
path

Foel
Hendre

Hendre

coast
road

map 4

stile 462

to Moylegrove

cormorants, fulmars and gulls abound. Some 40 acres/16ha of
Cemaes Head is a nature reserve of the DWT: the Coast Path
skirts the perimeter.

On a clear day there is a view of the entire sweep of Cardigan
Bay, with Plynlimon rising beyond Aberystwyth and the mass of
Cader Idris further to the L. Due N is Bardsey Island at the tip of
the Lleyn Peninsula, while in the foreground is Cardigan Island, a
40 acre/16ha reserve of the DWT. (Access to the island is
restricted, but boats from St Dogmael's and Gwbert-on-Sea take
occasional parties round the island during the summer months.)

Cemaes Head to Ceibwr Bay 3.8ml/6.1km
The path is good all the way on this section, well marked on the
cliff-top, but hard going: lots of ups and downs, strenuous but not
difficult. It is not for young children or the elderly, although the
return journey to the car at the end of the road from Poppit by the
path leading inland past the disused coastguard lookout makes an
easy short circular walk.

As you round the headland of Cemaes Head and face SW a new
vista opens up – Pencaer beyond Fishguard, with Strumble Head
lighthouse on the far R tip, and nearer to you, though still 10ml/
16km away, Dinas Head.

The high cliffs are wild and beautiful, rivalling those of the
coastline near St David's Head, and the complexity of the contorted
rocks is of particular interest. The cliffs are thrown into remarkable
folds on a large scale. The rocks exposed in the cliffs of Cemaes
Head, Pen-yr-Afr and Pwllygranant are grits and shales of
Ordovician age which were acutely compressed during the
Caledonian period into minor folds, some of which have fractured
into small faults. The outlines of the anticlines and synclines are
evident in the high cliff-faces. The cliffs are crumbling in places and
are not safe for climbing. The path on the top of Cemaes Head and
on the descent was made by bulldozer, one of several places around
the coast where the Coast Path had to be specially created.

Pwllygranant is a small, wild cove with a stream tumbling straight
into the sea. It is not a place for swimming when a sea is running.

Ceibwr Bay is a small rocky bay, an inlet with **a beach of shale**

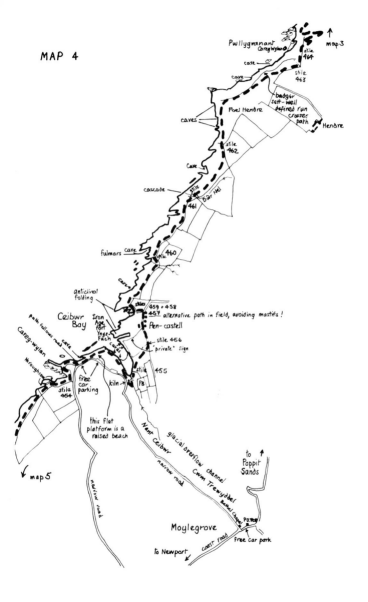

MAP 4

Pwllygranant
Careg Wylan
↑ map 3
stile 464

cave
stile 463

badger
sett - well
defined run
crosses
path
Hendre

Foel Hendre

caves

stile 462

Cave

cascade
stile 461
Bâr Môl

fulmars cave
460
stile

caves
anticlinal
folding

stiles 459 + 458
457 alternative path in field, avoiding mastifs!

Ceibwr Bay
Iron Age Fort
Ynys-Fach
Pen-castell
Careg-wylan
stile 456
"private" sign
Path follows road

Wroughton

stile 455
FB
free car parking
kiln
cave
stile 454

this flat
platform is a
raised beach

↙ map 5

narrow road

Nant Ceibwr
glacial overflow channel
Cwm Trewyddel
to
Poppit
Sands ↑

narrow road

Moylegrove
P.car
free car park

to Newport ↙
coast road

and pebbles. A small stream crosses some dirty sand at low water, but for most of the time shingle is exposed, making the place unattractive for swimming.

There is some doubt as to where the Coast Path runs at the head of the inlet. It appears that after crossing the plank footbridge you must keep to the shingle and flotsam to the N side of the bay, and then mount a steep muddy bank to a stile (no. 455). High spring tides may render the shore inaccessible.

At the N end of the bay alternating layers of grit and shale of Ordovician age were folded and faulted during the Caledonian period and are dominated by a sharp anticline. The 200ft/60m platform was excavated by waves of the late Tertiary period, and the present-day sea is cutting into this plateau and exploiting the zones of weakness, associated mainly with faults, to develop caves and small bays. The flat platform on the seaward side of the hillock, between the bay and the road, is a raised beach, with rounded stones embedded beneath the turf.

The valley of Cwm Trewyddel, carrying the Nant Ceibwr stream which feeds into the bay, is a glacial overflow channel, choked by glacial material. You can follow this valley inland for 1ml/1.6km along a narrow lane to the village of Moylegrove.

The small village of *Moylegrove* (Trewyddel) lies in the bottom of the valley, and you come to it suddenly when you travel by the coast road from St Dogmael's or Poppit Sands on your way to Newport. A number of colour-washed cottages cluster round the bridge over the Ceibwr stream, and two chapels – the Bethel Chapel, 1691, and the Tabernacle, 1894 – confront each other across the single village street.

The wide open fields on the stretch of coast around Moylegrove show a completely different pattern from the fragmented land of small farms further to the W. This must reflect the Norman influence of the nearby Marcher Lordship of Newport over what was probably within its domain. The place name – the grove of Matilda – comes from Matilda, the wife of Robert Fitz-Martin, the first Lord of Cemaes (d.1159). It was called Grava Matilda in 1291 and Molde Grove in 1326, names confirmed by the local historian Fenton.

Ceibwr Bay to Newport (Nevern Bridge) 8.0ml/12.8km
This is a lovely stretch of coastline, with no buildings anywhere, and
the first 4ml/6.4km remain chiefly in the memory for the great
changes in the vertical. Within a short while, on the Coast Path
created by a bulldozer, you come to Pwll-y-Wrach – the Witches'
Cauldron – a collapsed blowhole where an enclosed pool is
connected by a short tunnel to the sea. The stream running down
the valley suddenly breaks through the crust of the shales as it
passes under the footbridge carrying the Coast Path, and it forms a
gorge 10–12ft/3–3.6m deep. Instead of flowing straight into the sea
the stream plunges down a hole in the floor for a further 10–12ft/3–
3.6m and turns a corner to flow via an underground passage into the
Witches' Cauldron.

On the opposite side of the steep valley, overlooking the Witches'
Cauldron, is Castell Treruffydd, an Iron Age fort commanding a
peninsula above Traeth Bach. It has a single curved, low defensive
bank across a narrow isthmus, with a suggestion of a second bank
on the S side: the whole is not easily recognised in the confusion of
the eroded, slipping cliffs and the field banks. The site was
compared by George Owen to Tintagel.

Nearby, close to the confluence of the streams in Cwm Pen-wern
and Cwm Ffynnon-alwm is a chalybeate well, Ffynnon Alwas,
described by Owen as 'inferior to none . . . but the Tunbridge
Water'. Its site is much overgrown.

Further round the headland of Foel-goch is the small beach of
Pwll-coch, which can only be reached by the agile (near stile 444).
Seals breed in large numbers here, just as they do further along at
Godir-rhug and Godir-Tudor, beneath high, sheer and inaccessible
cliffs.

As you round the headland you see Newport across the broad
stretch of Traethmawr – the golden sands of Newport Sands – and
nestling under Mynydd Carn Ingli, one of the outliers of the
Prescelly Hills. From the edge of the lovely sand dunes of The
Bennett you may follow the official Coast Path to Newport Bridge
or, if the tide is out, you can walk across the sands and paddle across
the river – only a few feet wide, and shallow – to the old harbour at
Parrog.

MAP 5

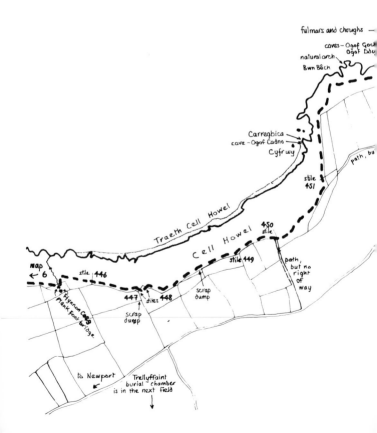

fulmars and choughs —

caves — Ogof Goch
Ogof Ddu

natural arch

Bwm Bâch

Carregbica

cave — Ogof Cadno

Cyfrwy

path, bu

stile 451

Traeth Cell Howel

Cell Howel

450 stile

map 6

stile 446

stile 449

path, but no right of way

Ffynnon Cadno

Plank foot bridge

447

stiles 448

scrap dump

scrap dump

to Newport

Trellyffaint burial chamber is in the next field

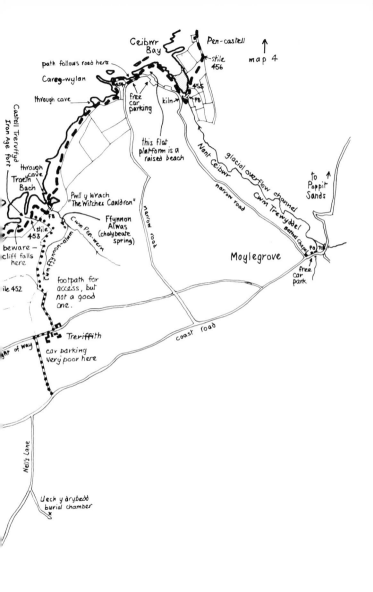

Ceibwr Bay

Pen-castell

map 4

stile 456

path follows road here

Careg-wylan

through cave

free car parking

kiln

PB

455

Castell Treruffydd Iron Age fort

this flat platform is a raised beach

through cave

Nant Ceibwr

glacial overflow channel

to Poppit Sands

Cwm Trewyddel

Traeth Bach

Pwll y Wrach "The Witches Cauldron"

PB

Cwm Pen-wern

narrow road

narrow road

Bethel Chapel

PO TCB

stile 453

Ffynnon Alwas (chalybeate spring)

Cwm Ffynnon-alwm

Moylegrove

beware – cliff falls here

free car park

footpath for access, but not a good one.

ile 452

coast road

Treriffith

car parking very poor here

ght of way

Nell's Lane

Llech y drybedd burial chamber

The official Coast Path crosses the River Nevern (Afon Nyfer) by Newport Bridge (Y Bont) which carries the road from St Dogmael's and Poppit Sands to the A487 at Newport. There was a bridge over the Nevern here, at the lowest bridging point of the river, in medieval times. It is said to have been demolished when an epidemic reached the town from Morfa in the 17c. Stepping stones were then used until the present bridge was built in 1894, and when the tide was high a ferry boat was used.

Some 30yd/31m upstream of the bridge a fragment of masonry marks the site of Ffynnon Curig – St Curig's Well – and nearby stood a 6c St Curig's Chapel, but all signs have now disappeared. At the same distance downstream of the bridge was the earliest known human settlement in the area, a Mesolithic site where some small flint implements were found in 1922. Further downstream, and still on the S side of the river, is a crescent-shaped earthwork beside the Coast Path called Hen Castell – the Old Castle – believed to be a defensive harbour of the Iron Age. Another ancient monument stands nearby: between the bridge and the main road is a fine cromlech, Carreg Coetan Arthur – a burial chamber whose capstone is balanced on two of its four uprights. It can be found behind the new holiday bungalows and former Cromlech Farmhouse, and is in surprisingly good condition.

Newport

Newport (Trefdraeth) was the capital of the Norman Marcher Lordship of Cemaes. William Fitz-Martin moved to Newport from Nevern in 1191 having been driven out of the latter place by Rhys ap Gruffydd. He built his castle on a spur overlooking the estuary and established a port. William conferred privileges on the borough: unique rights, which still exist, include the annual appointment of the Mayor of Newport, who presides over a Court Leet. The bounds of the town are beaten annually by the Lord Marcher, the Mayor of the town and the local Member of Parliament, all mounted on horses, with followers on foot. The 'Beating of the Bounds' takes place during August.

Ceibwr Bay from the Coast Path

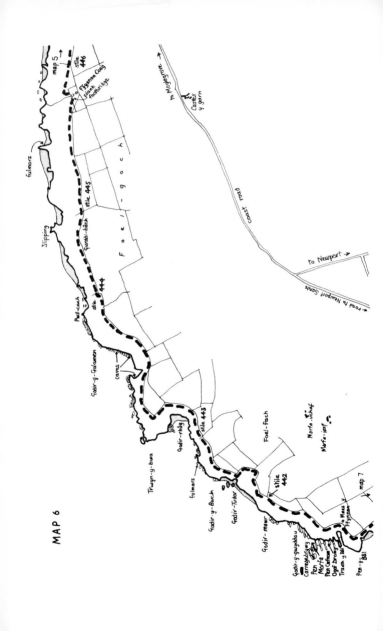

MAP 6

stile 446
map 5
Ffynnon Ceeg
plank footbridge

to Moylegrove
Castell
y garn

fulmars

Slipping

coast road

to Newport →

road to Newport Sands

Gwndwl-bâch
stile 445

Pwll-coch
stile 444

Godir-y-Golomen

caves

Trwyn-y-bwa

Godir-rhög
stile 443

fulmars

stile 442

Godir-y-Bwch

Godir-Tudor

Godir-mawr

Godir-y-gwylltau
Carreg-drwyn
Pen
Morfa
Pen Cerhwn
Ogof Brwyn
Traeth y Bâll
Pen-y-Bâll

Maes
Ffynnon

Morfa-uchaf

Morfa-iscf

map 7

Foel-fach

F a e l - g o c h

The castle was taken by Llywelyn the Great in 1215 and by Llywelyn the Last in 1257, and is said to have been damaged during the revolt of Owain Glyndwr in 1408. In 1497, when James Touchet (Lord Audley and Lord of Cemaes) was impeached and beheaded for high treason, the castle was forfeited to the Crown, but it was restored to his son in 1534. Ten years later the Lordship was purchased by William Owen of Henllys (up the valley) and in 1583 his son, George Owen, the Elizabethan historian, recorded that the castle had been 'in utter ruin for a long time'; so it remained until 1859 when Sir Thomas Lloyd of Bronwydd converted the gatehouse into a residence and restored the ruins beyond recognition.

The castle consists of two circular towers flanking the gatehouse – the Hunters' Tower on the NW, the Kitchen Tower on the SW (now a grass-grown mound), and the massive D-shaped Great Tower on the SE to protect the most vulnerable side. Adjoining this tower is a vaulted crypt which formed part of a chapel. The towers date from the end of the 13c, but the linking curtain walls were largely renovated when they were incorporated into the restorations of 1859 which created the mansion. The castle is occupied and is private.

St Mary's Church is massive, and retains the original Norman cruciform plan. The only part of the original structure is the bold, stepped buttressed three-storied tower, with a parapet and a fine weather cock on top. The church is unusual in having twin-aisled transepts. The walls are unplastered, but show excellent masonry in a local igneous stone in shades of pink, grey and pale brown. In 1835 the church was enlarged, and then in 1854 the rest was completely rebuilt in the Decorated style, only to be followed in 1879 by a thorough 'restoration'. The oak roof has been replaced by a plain deal one, which was subsequently whitewashed, a huge three-decker pulpit was built to obscure the chancel from the worshippers, and many relics were lost. The original Norman cushion-type font has been retained: it is one of the finest in Pembrokeshire, but it too was restored in 1854. The E window has four lights, depicting the Evangelists.

Across the road (Upper St Mary's Str) from the NE churchyard gate of St Mary's is a tiny chapel, now an adjunct to the parish church. The Methodist movement began in Newport in 1747 and in 1799 this Church Chapel was built for the Methodist and non-Methodist members of the parish church when some members demanded that the Sacrament should be administered by their own members rather than in the parish church.

Newport has some good, pleasant small houses, and one of the most distinguished-looking buildings is the Llwyngwair Arms. This hotel has been the meeting place of the Court Leet for many years: a copy of Queen Elizabeth's confirmation of the town's charter hangs inside. The streets and lanes below the castle walls are narrow and full of character, having some small Georgian houses and cottage rows with many windows.

The town was once an important sea port. In the 16c herrings were exported to France and Spain, and to Ireland to feed the Queen's militia there, and slates were 'sent by water to Haverford, Pembroke, Tenby and diverse parts of Ireland' (George Owen). By 1566 it was a woollen manufacturing centre and had a considerable trading with Bristol. George Owen described it (in 1603) as a once populous place having a brisk woollen trade, but it never recovered from a visitation of the plague in Tudor times, which diverted the market to Fishguard.

There is a long history of coastal trading, fishing and shipbuilding. The Parrog shipyards were famous for square-rigged vessels before 1830, and schooners afterwards. After the construction of the main quay at Parrog in 1825 there was a bustle of activity centered around local store-houses, coal yards and ship-repair yards. The coastal trade declined to the present century, but ships were still coming in with coal and culm until the mid-1930s. (Culm is an anthracite dust, which was produced in embarrassing quantities by the small mines of South Pembrokeshire. It was most useful when mixed with one part of clay to five parts of dust, rolled into balls by hand, and burnt on the fire, a cheap form of fuel.) The harbour is now silted up and the quay walls are in a poor condition. A double lime-kiln and a rubble-built warehouse (now converted into the Newport Boat Club HQ) are the only reminders of the days when most of Newport's trade was seaborne.

The town is now regaining some prosperity as a seaside resort, and many dinghy sailors now enjoy their sport in the estuary. There is a slipway for launching dinghies, but otherwise facilities are only basic.

The estuary of the River Nevern is relatively sheltered except from NW and N winds. Its sands are the biggest and best known in the N of Pembrokeshire, a splendid stretch of firm, yellow sand, both at high and low water, and backed by sand dunes. The sands are divided by the river: Traethmawr to the N and Parrog to the S, with Y Cwm to the W. Traethmawr is the main beach, 3ml/4.8km from town, and almost 1ml/1.6km long. Vehicular access is through the grounds of a nine-hole golf course (beware of flying golf balls!) to a large, free car park. Cars are allowed to park on the sands, and there is much argument as to whether this contributes to the erosion of the sand dunes. Until a car park twice the size of the present one is provided hundreds of cars would be turned away in summer, or would obstruct the road back across the golf course. As it is, all are absorbed, and there is still room on the beach for all who want to use it. Motorists venturing on to the beach should beware of soft sand.

Parrog Sands is the town beach. There is immediate access to the beach from the sea wall, and cars can be parked around the old harbour and almost on the beach. It is sandy at low water, shingly at high, except for the river estuary which is always a rather muddy sand. The sands are backed by rocks and there are many pools. Y Cwm is the name of the beach and cove at the far end of Parrog, where there is a diving-cum-landing place on the rocks to the W of the old lifeboat station, where the river enters Newport Bay.

Bathing is safe in the estuary except when the ebb tide creates fast currents. Newport Bar, the sandbank across the mouth of the river, has always been hazardous to shipping, except for a few hours on either side of high water.

MAP 7

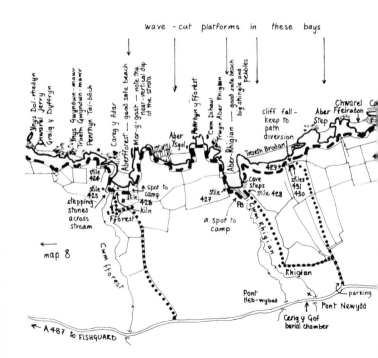

N E W P O R T B A

wave - cut platforms in these bays

Ynys Dol-rhedyn
Chwarel Jerry
Graig y Dyffryn
Ynys Gwyndwn-mawr
Traeth Gwyndwn-mawr
Penrhyn Tai-bach
Careg y Adar
Aberfforest — good safe beach
Mor-y-gest — note the near-vertical dip of the strata
Aber Ysgol
Pwllhyn y fforest
Cwm Dihewl
Trwyn Aber Rhigian
Aber-Rhigian — good safe beach shingle and pebbles
cliff fall — keep to path diversion
Traeth Brodari
Aber Step
Chwarel Ffeiradon

stile 424
stile 425
stepping stones across stream
Fforest
stile 426
a spot to camp
Kiln
stile 427
PB
a spot to camp
Cave steps
Stile 428
429 →
stiles 431 430

map 8 ←

Cwm Fforest

Cwm Rhigian

Rhigian

Pont Heb-wybod
Cerig y Gof burial chamber
Pont Newydd
parking

← A 487 to FISHGUARD

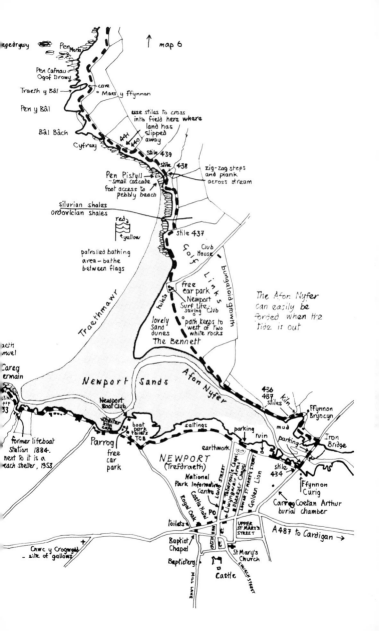

↑ map 6

egedrywy · Pen Morfa

Pen Cafnau
Ogof Drowy

Traeth y Bâl — · cove
· Maes y Ffynnan

Pen y Bâl

Bâl Bâch

Cyfrwy · use stiles to cross
into a field here where
land has slipped away

stile 439

Pen Pistyll — stile 438
— small cascade
foot access to
pebbly beach

zig-zag steps
and plank
across stream

Silurian shales
ordovician shales

red
yellow

stile 437

Golf Links

Club House

patrolled bathing
area — bathe
between flags

bungalow growth

The Afon Nyfer
can easily be
forded when the
tide is out

Traethmawr

free car park
Newport Surf Life
saving Club

toilets

lovely sand
dunes

path keeps to
west of two
white rocks

The Bennett

aeth
mwel

Careg
ernain

Newport Sands

Afon Nyfer

436
437 stiles

Kiln

FFynnon
Bryncyn

stile pip
33

Newport
Boat Club

boat
park
TCB

saltings

parking

ruin

mud

parking

Iron
Bridge

former lifeboat
station 1884.
next to it is a
beach shelter, 1953.

Parrog

free
car park

earthwork

stile 434

NEWPORT
(Trefdraeth)

National
Park Information
Centre

FFynnon
Curig

Golden Lion

Carreg Coetan Arthur
burial chamber

Royal Oak

Castle Hotel

PO

A487 to Cardigan →

toilets

Cnwc y Crogwydd
— site of gallows

Baptist
Chapel

Baptistery

Upper
St Mary's
Street

St Mary's
Church

Castle

2 **Newport to Fishguard** (Maps 7–10)   11.3ml/18.8km

Newport (Nevern Bridge) to Cwm-yr-Eglwys 4.3ml/6.9km
The condition of the Coast Path is good, but sometimes a bit
overgrown in summer. There is gorse, bracken and bramble, but
few trees, except in Cwm Rhigian and Cwm Fforest where
blackthorn, hawthorn, hazel, oak and ash grow. The walking is
easy, reasonably well marked, with a few gradients, but nothing
difficult. From the Nevern Bridge the Coast Path follows a track
beside the river estuary, skirting Newport to meet the road at
Parrog, where a row of delightful, colour-washed houses, protected
by a small but sturdy sea wall, have direct access to the beach at low
water. If the tide is out you can walk along the sands as far as Y
Cwm, where you have to regain terra firma.

The rocks exposed along this stretch of coast were originally
marine sediments deposited during the Upper Ordovician times.
The sea, exploiting weaknesses along both the bedding planes and
joint planes, has produced a striking and unusual rectilinear pattern
in the bays and headlands. At low water some of the best examples
of wave-cut platform in Pembrokeshire are exposed in the bays of
Traeth Samuel, Chwarel Ffeiradon, Aber Step, Traeth Brodan,
Aber Rhigian, Aber Ysgol and Aber Fforest. The platform is being
enlarged as each high tide cuts further into the cliffs. The platform
stretches out to sea, and if the sea level were to fall there would be
another stage in the cycle of marine erosion. Aber Rhigian, the
largest and most deeply indented of these bays, has been eroded by
the sea along a fault which runs inland along the foot of the eastern
cliff and which formed the wooded Cwm Rhigian. The shales to the
W of the fault dip very steeply seawards, i.e. to the N. The worn
edges of these rock layers trend, or strike, from E to W. At right
angles to this strike occurs a series of vertical cracks or joints which
developed as the rocks consolidated and were later subjected to
earth movements.

Aber Rhigian is a small cove, quite unspoilt, and sand is revealed

The Parrog at Newport

Pen yr Hwrdd
cave
Gadar Pen-y-fan
Llech Isaf
Stinking Hole
a flat but wind-exposed
spot for a tent
o.s. trig point No. S 5848
ruin of old coastguard lookout
cave
Pen y Fan
Llech Uchaf
Pwll-glas
dip of strata well-seen here
Aber Pen-clawdd
Pen Sidan
Cafnau
Pen-clawdd
Needle Rock
stile
418
steps
Trwyn Pen-dalfa
Ogof Pig-y-met
Ogof Pig-y-baw
Aberpensidan

Dinas   Island

path/track
bulldozed
along
here
Aber Trwyn
Aber Carreg
y Fran
Carreg-
y-Fran
Silurian shales
Ordovician shales
Island
Farm
Carreg John Evan
Y Trwyn
Aber Pig-y-baw
Pig-y-baw
419
stile
Catch y Mitiswr
stile 417
Pen Castell
Ogof Hen-castell
Castell
stile
Sailors'
Safety
Pwllgwaelod
— good safe beach
boat park
car
park (free)
f.b
cpsp
faike
church
Aber Gwyn
Bay Thomas Howell
Carreg
March
Cwm Dewi
stile 422
Cwm-yr-eglwys
path follows road
cpsp
what has happened to
stiles 415, 420 and 421?
422 is in Cwm Dewi
stile
423
Pwll Cwm
Pwll
Ffynnon-ovy
cave
boat park
cpsp
limekiln
car park (free)
steps
toilets and tap
cave
stile 414
stile 413
Methodist
Chapel
Bryn-henllan
Pwll Gway
cave
stile 412
path has been
bulldozed here
St Brynach's
Church
stile
411
Cwm Gwylog
plank
f.b
map 9
Ship Aground P.H.
Tcb
Dinas Cross
Dinas
Tabor
Baptist
Chapel
A487 to Fishguard

map 7 →

beyond the shingles and pebbles at low water. Access can be gained
on foot from the main road, where it is possible to park on the grass
verge. Aber Fforest is another small and unspoilt cove, which can
also only be approached on foot. Bathing is safe, and sand is
revealed at low water, below the shingle.

The Coast Path follows a road as it drops steeply down to *Cwm-
yr-Eglwys*, a small sea harbour sheltered from the prevailing SW
winds by Dinas Island, with its ruined church, and one of the most
popular small beaches on the N coast. The Welsh name for the
village is The Valley of the Church, but the only parts of the 12c
Celtic-type church to have survived the great storm during the night
of 25 October 1859 are the belfry and the W wall. (The storm
wrecked 114 ships on the coasts of Wales, including the *Royal
Charter* which went down off Moelfre, Anglesey, with the loss of
459 lives and gold worth nearly £5 million at today's values: most of
the gold was eventually recovered.) The ruined church, believed to
have been founded in the 6c, was dedicated to St Brynach, an
Irishman who is said to have talked with angels on the top of Carn
Ingli, 4ml/6.4km to the SE, behind Newport.

The small cove shows plenty of sand at low water, below some
shingle and pebbles. The swimming is good, and the grassy
churchyard makes a good picnic spot. It is an ideal setting – cottages
round the bay, with wooded, low cliffs on either side.

*Dinas Island circuit: Cwm-yr-Eglwys to Pwllgwaelod, via Dinas
Head 2.5ml/4km*
The big headland of Dinas Island rising seaward separates the two
bays of Newport Bay and Fishguard Bay, sheltering the former
from westerlies and the latter from easterlies. It has great cliffs and
large, well-drained fields belonging to its single farm, and is almost
separated from the mainland by a deep valley, an effect which
justifies the name 'Island'. The headland was once known as Ynys
Fach Llyffan Gawr – The Island of Llyffan the Giant – and it was for
centuries reserved as a grange for Pentre Ifan mansion. Ronald
Lockley's *Island Farmers* and *The Golden Year* and David Hay's
novel *Dinas Island* are all set here.

Part of Dinas Island is composed of black, marine shales and sandstone of Ordovician age, but the northern part is of younger rocks of the Silurian age, which include thick layers of pale-coloured grits. These grits offer greater resistance to wave erosion, and explain the continued existence of Dinas Island as a headland. These sedimentary rocks are well displayed in steep cliffs around the promontory, and the tilted and buckled layers are evidence of the great earth movements which affected Wales during the Caledonian period.

The magnificent cliff scenery and the sea birds are highlights of this excellent walk round the coast. Where the Coast Path leaves Cwm-yr-Eglwys inland wildlife predominates in the sheltered places. As the Path crosses the stream you can see Alexanders and fennel; scrub bushes of blackthorn, hazel and hawthorn shelter wild garlic, lords-and-ladies and hart's tongue fern, and the common polypody fern grows on sheltered trees. Speckled Wood, small Tortoiseshell and Peacock butterflies can often be seen. As the Path rises along the cliff edge the shrubs begin to be stunted by the salt-laden winds, and here, on the more open ground, bluebells, primroses and violets all add colour in spring.

The cove of Aber Pig-y-baw contains large, broad veins of white quartz, a hard mineral resisting erosion more effectively than the adjacent sedimentary rocks. It has crystallised from the hot igneous solutions intruded through the earth's crust during the earth movements.

The first landmark is soon reached when the gradient of the Path becomes a little steeper, as you cross from the Ordovician to the Silurian shales. Needle Rock is a massive sea stack sheltered from the winds and providing an ideal home for birds, and an interesting time can be spent observing them from the security of the Coast Path: outside the fence it is a straight drop to the sea.

Between April and July Needle Rock is particularly crowded and noisy. One or two pairs of great black-backed gulls nest on the top, from where they can watch out for and attack the unguarded eggs and chicks of other species. Herring gulls are numerous, and are the most common nesting gull in the area. Fulmars nest on the cliffs of the Island, immediately below the Path, as do jackdaws and rock pipits. The Needles bigger crevices are nesting places for shags.

Razorbills and guillemots also nest on the Rock: the razorbills occupy some crannies which may be seen from the Path, but the guillemots nest on ledges on the seaward side.

A little way beyond Needle Rock and again at Pwll Glas the graceful curves of the rock layers are evidence of the enormous pressures exerted on the earth's crust during periods of folding.

The gradual ascent of Dinas Head is marked by masses of bluebells, clumps of white sea campion and patches of wood anemone, birdsfoot trefoil and blue milkwort in late spring. Purple-pink thrift is abundant, and ling and bell heather flower in profusion in the summer. Two pairs of ravens may be seen around the Island throughout the year, and grey seals breed in the caves below the cliffs and in the inaccessible coves.

The OS triangulation point at 463ft/141m above sea level marks the highest point of Dinas Island. The view on a clear day embraces places up and down the coast of Cardigan Bay, from Cemaes Head to the E to Strumble Head to the W. The small ruin beside the pillar was once a coastguard lookout station. Strange depressions on a slab of rock nearby were pronounced to be the Devil's footprints.

Near the cliffs around Dinas Head you may see choughs, and stonechats and meadow pipits can be seen among the gorse bushes. The English stonecrop is common in the rocks, and lower down the slopes the wall pennywort is abundant. In May the flowering bluebells are everywhere and Early Purple orchids appear in groups here and there. Vernal squill decorates the short turf, and sheep's bit is striking in June and July.

One of the very few pubs to be found on the Coast Path is at *Pwllgwaelod*. The Sailors' Safety Inn has been an inn since 1593, and it has always displayed a light after dark to help guide vessels across the waters of Fishguard Bay, hence its name. The fact that this place has a pub and a café, a large free car park and immediate access to a good safe beach of grey sand makes it more popular than Cwm-yr-Eglwys.

Cwm-yr-Eglwys to Pwllgwaelod, via Cwm Dewi 0.75ml/1.2km
Not only does the official Coast Path go all the way round Dinas Island but it also makes a short cut across the neck of the headland

MAP 9

FISHGUAR

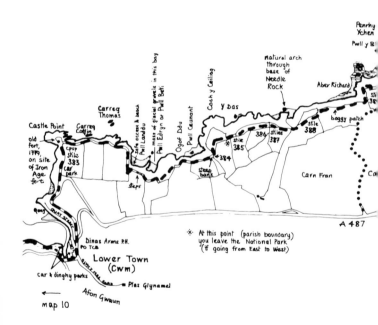

Penrhy
Ychen

Pwll y B

natural arch
through
base of
Needle
Rock

Aber Richard

Cach y Ceiliog

Y Das

stile
388

boggy patch

Carreg
Thomas

safe access & beach
Pwll Llanddu

mass of glacial gravels in this bay
Pwll Edryn or Pwll Befi

Ogof Ddu

Pwll Ceunant

stile
386

stiles
387

stile
388

Castle Point

Carreg
Coffin

old
fort,
1779,
on site
of Iron
Age
fort

cpsp
stile
383
car
park

stile
385

stile
384

steep
bank

Carn Fran

Ca

quay
quay slip

A 487

Dinas Arms P.H.
PO TCB

Lower Town
(Cwm)

car & dinghy parks

Plas Glynamel

← map 10

Afon Gwaun

☀ At this point (parish boundary)
you leave the National Park
(if going from East to West)

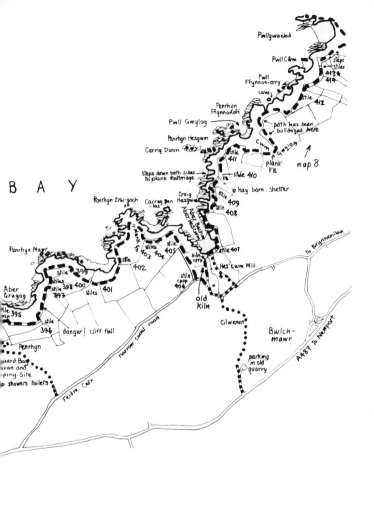

Pwllgwaelod

Pwll Carn

steps
413 stiles
414

Pwll
Ffynnon-ovy

caves

stile
412

Penrhyn
Ffynnonloft

path has been
bulldozed here

Pwll Gwylog

Penrhyn Hesgwm

Cerrig Duon   BAY

Cwm
Gwylog

stile
411

plank
FB

map 8

Steps down both sides
to plank footbridge

stile 410

to hay barn: shelter

B   A   Y

Penrhyn Enw-goch

Carreg Pen
-las

Craig
Hesgwm

stile
409

stile
408

Penrhyn Mawr

stiles
403

stile
404

stile
405

stile 407

to Brynhenllan

stile
402

kiln
crop

Hen cwm Mill

stile

stiles
399

stile
stiles 398 400
397

stiles

stile
401

stile
406

old
kiln

Aber
Grugog

stile
csp 395

danger! cliff fall

Cilwenen

Bwlch-
mawr

A487 to Newport

stile
396

Penrhyn

parking
'm old
quarry

uard Bach
avan and
ping Site
o showers toilets

narrow coast road

Feidre Cefin

through the valley of Cwm Dewi, saving 1.5ml/2.4km on the longer circuit round the coast.

Cwm Dewi is a shallow, flat-bottomed depression with steep wooded sides, and is poorly drained with no permanent watercourse. It was formed in the late Pleistocene times (about 20–17,000 years ago) when the remains of a large Ice Age glacier blocked what is now Newport Bay. Streams and meltwater were forced to flow westwards beneath the ice sheet, cutting through the marine Ordovician sandstones and shales, and the valley was thus formed, making Dinas a real island. This, and other similar landforms in Pembrokeshire – for example, the Dale-Westdale Bay valley – were infilled with boulder clay. Shells dredged from the floor of the Irish Sea have been found in these clays, pointing to the fact that these sub-glacial channels pre-date the advance of Irish Sea ice, which is usually regarded as belonging to the last glaciation.

A walk eastwards through Cwm Dewi shows how the open, windswept environment of Pwllgwaelod gives way to the sheltered conditions of Cwm-yr-Eglwys.

The marshy valley is a haven for wildlife. The marshland adjacent to the Path is the haunt of the sedge warbler, the grasshopper warbler and the reed bunting. The grasshopper warbler is difficult to see, but its continuous whirring song is easily heard. The bushy growth provides nesting sites for whitethroats, garden warblers, blackcaps and other small birds. The tall trees are favoured by a pair of buzzards, and there is a rookery. Several butterflies may be seen. The Orange Tip is common in May, as is its food-plant, lady's smock, and in the summer the Common Blue is frequently found. When the pink heads of the hemp agrimony are in bloom in August they attract Red Admiral, Tortoiseshell and Peacock butterflies. In the marshy area grow sphagnum moss, spotted heath orchids, marsh pennywort, marsh cinquefoil, bogbean, bog asphodel and cottongrass.

On the road from Pwllgwaelod to the A487 at Dinas you pass through the refreshingly unspoilt hamlet of *Brynhenllan*. St Brynach's Church was built here in 1860 in a plain and ordinary style at a cost of £789, to replace the destroyed church of Cwm-yr-Eglwys. The Methodist Chapel – Trefnyddion Califinaidd – was built in 1769, rebuilt in 1799 and again rebuilt in 1842. The main village of Dinas straggles along the busy A487 coast road. The church and chapel burial grounds of Brynhenllan and Dinas attest, in their tombstone inscriptions, to the importance of the villages as a nursery of deep-sea sailors.

Pwllgwaelod to Fishguard (Lower Town) 4.5ml/7.24km
There are several coves along this stretch of coast, most rather inaccessible; only one has access from a road, and a poor access at that. Pwll Gwylog is not that easy to get down to and it is a small cove, pretty well unknown, a contrast to its similarly named near neighbour. Aber Bach, or Aber Hescwm as it is also known, can be approached by a very narrow and rough lane. The cove is relatively deserted because of the limited parking: there is room only for a couple of cars on the verge where the Coast Path goes down a gated track. An alternative approach is by a footpath through Hes'cwm Mill. Aber Bach is a small cove, picturesque and unspoilt. It consists mainly of rock and shingle at high water, and only a little sand is revealed at low water. Bathing is safe.

Beyond Aber Bach and in the vicinity of the caravan site at the Penrhyn World War I lookout station the Path is overgrown in many places, which indicates that this stretch is little walked by the non-Coast Path walker.

At Castle Point there is a late 18c fort with double ramparts and three cannon – one dated 1785. From it there is a panoramic view of Fishguard harbour. A 5-minute stroll on an improved path brings you to a lay-by on the A487 at the top of the hill above Lower Town, and you follow the road down to Fishguard.

3 **Fishguard and Goodwick** (Abergwaun and Wdig)
(Plan A, Plan B, Map 10)

Lower Town to Harbour Village 2.5ml/4km
From Fishguard's Lower Town to Goodwick's Harbour Village is a walk of about 45 minutes, for the most part on a pleasant marine

parade, with plenty of seats for the views, otherwise all on the road. Most Coast Path walkers will wish to visit Fishguard and Goodwick for supplies and accommodation, and also to see what they offer.

Lower Town (Cwm) lies clustered at the bottom of a steep-sided valley where the River Gwaun (Afon Gwaun) enters the sea. The valley of the Gwaun is *the* classical example of a glacial overflow channel, a valley created by a roaring mass of meltwater, blocks of ice and boulders, about 15,000 years ago, deepening and widening a valley out of all proportion to the stream that it now carries. The valley also marks the change from the Ordovician shales to the E to the Ordovician volcanics to the W.

Lower Town has the air of a Cornish or Breton fishing village, with one narrow street and a quay. The picturesque setting of quayside, bridge over the river and row of cottages was chosen in 1971 for the setting of a film of Dylan Thomas's *Under Milk Wood*, starring Elizabeth Taylor and Richard Burton. Orson Welles' *Moby Dick* was also filmed here. The Fishguard Bay Hotel was a dilapidated house that was restored to accommodate stars and film crew.

In the Elizabethan era there was an important herring fishery here, then during the 18c the port increased in importance until it was second only to Haverfordwest in the volume of trade handled. The population grew to 2000, and most of the working men were mariners and fishermen. Corn, butter, cured herrings and pilchards (adult sardines), and slates were the main exports, and in 1792 there were about 50 coasting vessels based here. There was ship-building too, with peak production in the decade 1810–19. For many years the shipyard was famous for its schooners and square-rigged vessels.

The pilchards have now ceased to visit Welsh waters in shoals, and the fishery has died out. A tall, four-storey warehouse, once connected with the pilchard and herring industry, is now the Sea Scouts' HQ, called TS *Skirmisher*. After 1850 the coastal trade began to decline, and it was virtually killed off by the arrival of the railway at Goodwick in 1906. Nowadays the small harbour is the main sailing centre of the North Pembrokeshire coast. High water is Milford time plus 1 hour 3 minutes.

Lower Town, Fishguard

The pier and quayside were originally built by Samuel Fenton to service the then flourishing pilchard-fishing industry. During the **American War of Independence the privateer John Paul Jones** appeared off Fishguard and seized one of Samuel Fenton's ships. Jones then put an armed party ashore at Lower Town, and under threat of bombardment demanded 500 guineas from the people of Lower Town and Upper Town in return for the release of the ship. To hurry things along he fired two broadside warning shots into the town, one of which maimed Mary, the sister of one Richard Fenton, Samuel's neighbour, for life. The ransom was paid, the port saved.

Richard Fenton, a barrister, was a local character. He was a fine Greek and Latin scholar, a celebrated wit, and close friend of Oliver Goldsmith, Edmund Burke, Dr Samuel Johnson, Sir Joshua Reynolds, Garrick, and many others of their circle. He is best remembered for his topographical books, of which his *Historical Tour through Pembrokeshire*, published in 1811, is the most vivid. Later writers have delighted to quote from this guide, although modern historians treat it with caution. Much of what he wrote about is now in ruins or has disappeared. Some of the blame must go to him, for he attacked dolmen and tumulus with the eager vigour of the 18c amateur archaeologist. In 1850 Fenton built his charming house Plas Glynamel, which lies at the end of the Glan-y-mel Road, upstream of the Gwaun Bridge beyond some nice stone cottages: it is now an hotel. The house has a plain classical façade, with raised steps on either side of the front entrance, a design suggested by a French house, no doubt an influence of Fenton's French wife.

From the winding creek in Lower Town the road climbs steeply up to the square in Upper Town, but this approach can be avoided by taking the Coast Path via The Slade.

Fishguard (Abergwaun) is a picturesque little town, perched high above the old harbour. Prior to 1900 the main centre in Fishguard Bay was the old harbour of Lower Town, while Fishguard, or Upper Town as it was more usually known, was much smaller than it is today, and Goodwick was a not very successful fishing village. Its Welsh name means 'Estuary of the River Gwaun' whilst its other name is Scandinavian for a fishweir (*fiskrgard*).

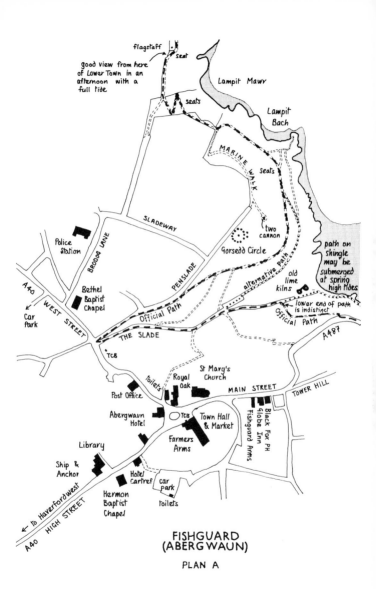

flagstaff

seat

good view from here of Lower Town in an afternoon with a full tide

Lampit Mawr

Lampit Bach

seats

MARINE WALK

seats

two cannon

Gorsedd Circle

path on shingle may be submerged at spring high tides

alternative path

old lime kilns

lower end of path is indistinct

SLADEWAY

BRODOG LANE

Police Station

PENSLADE

Official Path

Bethel Baptist Chapel

A40 WEST STREET

Car Park

THE SLADE

Official Path

A487

TOWER HILL

TCB

toilets

Royal Oak

St Mary's Church

MAIN STREET

Post Office

Abergwaun Hotel

TCB

Town Hall & Market

Black Fox PH Globe Inn

Fishguard Arms

Library

Farmers Arms

Ship & Anchor

Hotel Cartref

car park

← to Haverfordwest

A40 HIGH STREET

Hermon Baptist Chapel

toilets

FISHGUARD
(ABERGWAUN)

PLAN A

The hub of the town is The Square. On the S side is the simple pedimented Town Hall, a neat, classical, mid-19c building, brought into life by sensitive painting in greys and white. Today it houses the **Preseli District Council's Information Centre**. In the entrance hall **Fishguard's** seafaring life is enshrined in records of lifeboat rescues, **and** paintings of schooners, brigantines and smacks; of particular interest is the quayside scene of the *Gwaun Maid* of Fishguard, 119 tons, launched in 1846, with Vesuvius in the background.

On the other side of The Square, over the door of the Royal Oak, a sign says that within was signed the treaty following the French invasion of 1797. Lord Cawdor drew up the surrender treaty terms and signed them on the small table in the bar here on Friday morning, 24 February 1797, and General Tate subsequently countersigned the agreement at his headquarters at Tre Howel Farm. (For more of this story, see p.85.)

Next door to the Royal Oak is the parish church of St Mary's, built in 1857. It has nothing much to commend it except that its churchyard is the resting place of the redoubtable Jemima Nicholas, a Fishguard cobbler-woman, who went forth with a pitchfork and captured several Frenchmen in a field near Llanwnda during the invasion. Her gravestone stands against the S wall of the church, and can be read from the pavement in Main Street. Jemima died in 1832 aged 82 years.

The parish church is nothing when compared with the Hermon Baptist Chapel on the A40 Haverfordwest Road, just along High Street. It is the handsomest building in Fishguard and represents Nonconformist chapel architecture at its best. The façade is classical but almost top heavy with its grand portico and pediment and marbled columns. The interior is well lit naturally through clear glass on two levels, and has a gallery on four sides – three panelled in wood, the fourth having open-fretted painted ironwork. The pulpit, grained boxwood pews and decorated plaster ceiling are all very fancy, not in the low key one associates with religious dissent.

On the outskirts of Fishguard the Coast Path joins the main road and crosses a causeway over a marshy area at the head of Goodwick Beach. The Parrog provides immediate access to gently shelving but rather muddy sand at low water (shingle at high water) and bathing is safe. There are car parks at either end: some places are free, but the western end is a 'Trust the Motorist' park. Also some amenities.

On The Parrog there is a stone commemorating the capture of 1200 invading French troops by the 1st Baron Cawdor of Castlemartin (see p.86). The stone is of Carboniferous limestone and displays splendid fossils, notably solitary and colonial corals.

High water at Goodwick Beach is Milford time plus 1 hour 7 minutes.

Goodwick (Wdig), pronounced Good-ick, lies on the sheltered W side of Fishguard Bay, and was nothing but a small fishing village until the coming of the railway and the creation of Fishguard harbour. It then had high hopes of becoming a terminal for the Atlantic liners, but it is now a suburb and the terminal for rail and car ferry services to Ireland.

The official Coast Path follows the main road A40 up Station Hill, over the railway lines to a road junction, and then follows another road steeply uphill to the Harbour Village, taking in views of the harbour on the way up.

Fishguard Harbour is sufficiently deep to float the largest Atlantic liners, is free from shoals and sand bars, and is well sheltered. Moreover, it has the great advantage of offering the shortest crossing to Ireland from anywhere in England and Wales, the distance to Rosslare being only 54 nautical miles.

Prior to 1906, the small fishing ports of Fishguard and Goodwick were largely inactive. At the end of the 19c the North Pembroke and Fishguard Railway reached the town via Maeclochog and Rosebush: however, it was badly built and quite unsuitable for fast passenger and cargo traffic, and the final stages of reconstruction were not completed until 30 August 1906. Having thought earlier of Neyland as the ideal port for the Irish packet service and the trans-Atlantic passenger service, the management of the Great Western Railway company was now equally enthusiastic about Fishguard, and the Letterston to Fishguard link was completed. The cliffs beyond Goodwick were transformed by blasting operations: a completely new harbour was built, together with the North and East Breakwaters, and a passenger station, storage sheds and rail terminus were built on the quarry floor. The North Breakwater, built in 1907 from material from the quarry, runs out for 2500ft/ 762m across the bay from the Goodwick shore. It is a massive structure, containing 2 million tons of rubble topped with a concrete parapet. The Victorian Wyncliffe House was extended to become the GWR's Fishguard Bay Hotel, and terraces of houses were built on the hillside slopes for the railway and harbour workers.

The new harbour was opened in 1908 with the initiation of a steamer service on the short crossing to Rosslare, and at a stroke the hopes of New Milford (or Neyland) were killed overnight. The GWR port offices and staff were transferred to Fishguard, together with the vessels *Great Western* and *Great Southern* for the Irish Sea crossing. However, the expensive harbour works had been undertaken in the expectation that Fishguard would soon rival Liverpool as a great trans-Atlantic passenger port. In the intense rivalry between the shipping lines in the period prior to World War I the use of Fishguard as a terminus could save 40 miles on the New York-Liverpool route; accordingly Cunard Lines used Fishguard from six to eight times a month between 1910 and 1914, and vessels of the Booth and Blue Funnel Lines were also frequent visitors. Each needed 3 or 4 special trains to take the passengers to London.

A new breakwater constructed in 1913 caused silting of the harbour, and the Atlantic trade faded with the outbreak of war in 1914. Fishguard's heady days of success were short-lived. After the war the trans-Atlantic service was not revived. The little town suffered from the lack of an industrial hinterland, and so failed to entice business interests away from Liverpool, and as passenger vessels became larger the disadvantages of the harbour showed.

Since World War II Fishguard has been known best for its sea and trade links with Ireland. Gradually these have changed character, but they are still important. The Irish route is used considerably for livestock trade.

The Irish troubles hit the passenger trade drastically. Links with Waterford and Cork were discontinued and Fishguard became increasingly dependent on transport of containerised cargo to and from Wexford, and on the livestock trade. However, a new car-ferry service to Rosslare was re-introduced in 1987, and this makes Fishguard's future more secure.

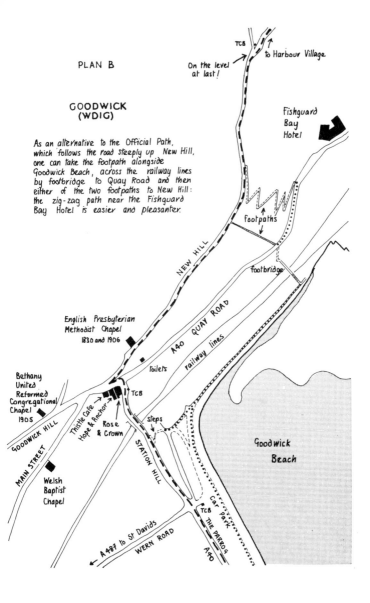

PLAN B

GOODWICK
(WDIG)

As an alternative to the Official Path, which follows the road steeply up New Hill, one can take the footpath alongside Goodwick Beach, across the railway lines by footbridge to Quay Road and then either of the two footpaths to New Hill: the zig-zag path near the Fishguard Bay Hotel is easier and pleasanter.

TCB

to Harbour Village

On the level at last!

Fishguard Bay Hotel

footpaths

New Hill

footbridge

A40 Quay Road

railway lines

English Presbyterian Methodist Chapel 1830 and 1906

toilets

Bethany United Reformed Congregational Chapel 1905

Goodwick Hill

Thistle Cafe
Hope & Anchor
Rose & Crown

TCB

Main Street

Welsh Baptist Chapel

Station Hill

steps

Goodwick Beach

Car Park

TCB

A487 to St Davids

Wern Road

The Parrog

A40

MAP 10

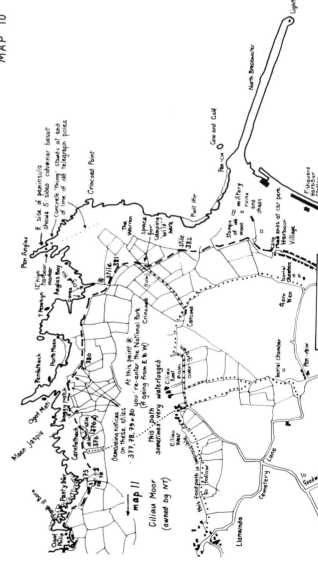

Lighthouse

North Breakwater

Cow and Calf

Fishguard Harbour Station

E side of peninsula shows 5-sided columnar basalt

Concrete 'thing' stands at end of line of old telegraph poles

Crincoed Point

Pen Anglas

Pwll Hir

Space for camping: wild mare

military ruins and sheds

car park

The Warren

car exits of car park

stile 382

Y Penrhyn

12" high harbour marker

Anglas Bay

Cerrig hill

(ruin)

stile 381

Stumps of old wood

Harbour Village

burial chamber

Garn Wen

Penkilvach

Porth Maen

At this point X you're re-enter the National Park (if going from E to W)

Crincoed

Catcoed

Carreg

Sgar Maen

baggy patch

380

Carnfathach

stile 376+376a

Demanding notices on these stiles - 377, 78, 79 + 80

this path sometimes very waterlogged

burial chamber

Maen Jaspis

Ciliau East

path over gate

Pen-rhiw

375

78

Pantybôr

Ogof Pilip

map 11

Ciliau West

Ciliau Moor (owned by NT)

this footpath is impossible to follow

Cemetery Lane

Llanwnda

to Goodw

Pan-cm-0

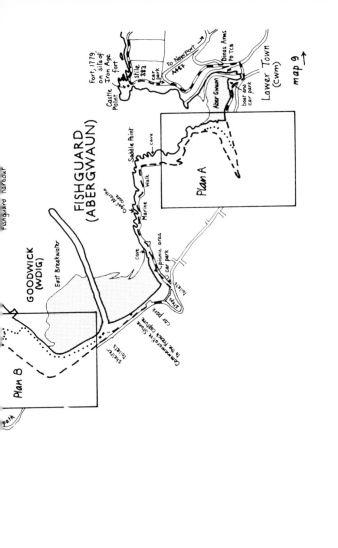

FISHGUARD (ABERGWAUN)

GOODWICK (WDIG)

Fishguard harbour

Plan B

Park

East Breakwater

Plan A

Commemorative Stone to the French Capture

car park

shelter toilets

toilets

picnic area
car park

Cave

Marine Walk

Ogof Marine

Cave

Saddle Point

Cave

Castle Point

Fort, 1779, on site of Iron Age fort

stile 393

car park

A487

to Newport

Dinas Arms Pb Tch

Aber Gwaun

boat and car park

Lower Town (Cwm)

map 9 →

Part two

Fishguard to St David's

4 Goodwick to Strumble Head (Maps 10, 11) 6.4ml/10.3m

To the W of Fishguard Bay the coast bulges northwards in a broad
headland called Pen Caer, with Strumble Head marking its most
northern tip. This land is different from the coast to the E as it is a
bold and mighty mass of Ordovician igneous rock with high and
magnificent cliffs, giving very few places where you can climb down
to the sea. Much of this stretch of the Path is hard and rough, and
sometimes it is difficult to trace through the scrub: it is best not to
wear shorts. This is not a stretch for young children.

Harbour Village to Carregwastad Point 3.5ml/5.6km
Leave Goodwick by going up the steep New Hill to Harbour
Village. Behind the houses here is Garn Wen, with the remains of
three burial chambers in a line running N-S. The most southerly is
the best preserved and is known as Carreg Samson – Samson's
Stone. A little further to the W at Pen-rhiw another burial chamber
comprises a fallen capstone partly resting on two of its three
uprights.
  The headland of Pen Anglas to the N of Goodwick is of dolerite,
characterised by columnar jointing, the rock mass having been
divided into basaltic columns, or prisms, which in cross-section are
often four-, five- or six-sided. They are popularly called, on account
of their appearance, 'torthau ceiniogau' (penny loaves). These
structures developed during the cooling of the molten rock: as it
cooled contraction led to the production of columns which are
perpendicular to the cooling surface – just as the drying and
cracking of mud under a hot sun leads to the development of a
similar pattern. This feature is best seen right down by the shore
line near the old harbour marker: the approach is through rough

grass and bramble by a faint path.

2ml/3.2km further on, past the coves of Anglas Bay, Porth Maen and Ogof Philip, you come to the larger cove of Aber Felin, where a path comes down to the coast from the village of Llanwnda, and beyond is the rocky headland of Carregwastad Point, famous for being the place where the last invasion of Britain took place in 1797. The story of the French landing is famous, not only because it was the last invasion on British soil but also because it was so short-lived and so unsuccessful.

The last invasion of England

The root cause of the invasion was the French hatred of England following the bitter wars of the 18c. The opportunity for revenge arose after the English had supported the French Royalists, by equipment and provisions, in an abortive landing at Quiberon in 1795. Lazare Hoche, a brilliant young general of the Republic, had driven the English back into the sea, and thereby captured a vast booty of stores, including British uniforms and rifles. He used this windfall to carry out a plan: to invade Britain with an expeditionary force, dressed in British uniforms, to land and foment a revolution, to encourage a sort of peasants' rising of the poor against the rich, and spread terror and civil war. There was to be a three-pronged attack: the main French force would be sent to Ireland, where there was a strong republican movement, another would go to Newcastle-on-Tyne, and the third attack would be on Wales. The expeditions to Ireland and Newcastle were dismal failures: the ships were forced to return to France after they had encountered storms, and some were wrecked.

Nevertheless, Hoche decided to go ahead with the third attack. He chose an Irish American named William Tate to command the invasion force. Tate had spent some time fighting for the Americans in the War of Independence and had become strongly anti-British, and was also in favour of America providing assistance for the French revolutionaries: it is assumed that he was chosen to command a French army because he could speak the language of the land that was to be invaded.

The invasion force, calling itself the Légion Noire, and consisting of 600 troops and 800 convicts, sailed in two frigates, the *Vengeance* and *Resistance*, under the command of Commodore Castagnier. They set sail from Brest on 16 February 1797. Tate's orders were to land in either the Bristol Channel or in Cardigan Bay, and strike inland. Obliged to choose the latter because the strong E winds prevented progress towards Bristol, Tate landed at Carregwastad on the night of 22 February 1797. Hoche had instructed Castagnier to sail to Ireland as soon as the landing was completed, to assist the French force which was supposed to be there. Tate was thus left to his own resources.

At daybreak on 23 February Tate set up his headquarters in Tre Howel Farm. The liberated convicts raided and ransacked neighbouring farms and cottages, for their food supplies were low, and they also got drunk in the process as most of the farms were well stocked with liquor from a recent shipwreck. The alarm was raised, and the first British commander on the scene was Colonel Thomas Knox, with his Fishguard Fencibles. He was too cautious, and he called upon the Lord Lieutenant of Pembrokeshire, Lord Milford, who in turn called in Lord Cawdor to command the various bodies of troops to counter the invasion. In the meantime Tate had been able to get his men in some sort of order and to advance towards Goodwick, but they were in no condition to offer much resistance to the energetic Lord Cawdor who had ridden up with his cavalry from Haverfordwest. The ensuing engagement, resulting in the ultimate capture of Tate's motley army two days after their landing, although it did nothing to alter the course of our history, gave the Castlemartin, later the Pembrokeshire, Yeomanry the battle honour 'Fishguard' which it carries on its cap badge.

Legend maintains that before Cawdor's arrival the French were discouraged by the appearance of a large force of several hundred on the hills around Fishguard, which was in fact a crowd of Welsh country-women in their national costume of red flannel cloaks and tall black beaver hats, walking round and round in a circle. The arrival of Cawdor's militia, believed by the French to be reinforcements, caused Tate to surrender. Tate's letter was

Carregwastad memorial

delivered to Cawdor at the Royal Oak in Fishguard, the French laid down their arms on Goodwick beach, and the 'last invasion of Britain' was over.

The story has been told many times and is vividly recounted in D K Broster's novel *Ships in the Bay!* and by Commander E H Stuart-Jones RN in *The Last Invasion of Britain*. There is a monument to the occasion on the top of the cliffs at Carregwastad.

Prior to the invasion it had been likely that Wales would develop a revolutionary movement between the Church and the Chapel, but the break was long in coming and the event of 1797 ended any chance. The invasion also had another important effect in Wales: the shock of it killed all sympathy with France and any taste that the Welsh might still have had for revolution against England.

Just inland from Carregwastad is the usual access point for visitors to the memorial stone, the tiny village of *Llanwnda*, consisting of a few farms and houses bordering a small piece of common ground scattered with large stones, some of which were probably part of a stone circle. There are no shops, no pub, no cafés, no Post Office: long may it remain unspoilt!

The church of St Gwyndaf is a well-known example of a 'Celtic'-type church. It is medieval in foundation, but was carefully restored in 1870, and partly rebuilt in 1881. It has a simple double sanctus bell-cote, and five stones incised with ancient crosses are built into the outside wall of the chancel. Retained in the roof of the nave are medieval timbers, on one of which is a rude boss of a human head. The chancel has lancet windows and plain vaulting, and there is a squint from porch to chancel. The interior is clear, with cream and white paint. Giraldus Cambrensis (qv) was one-time rector here.

Carregwastad Point to Strumble Head 2.9ml/4.6km
The Coast Path improves between the memorial stone and the coastguard station, possibly as a result of better access from inland, by rights of way through the farms of Tre Howel, Trenewydd and Tresinwen strung out along the narrow coast road. (Tre Howel is the farm which General Tate made his headquarters when he invaded with his troops in 1797.) Tresinwen farm was sold to Trinity House when it was decided to build the lighthouse on Strumble Head.

Pen Caer is the name of the headland jutting out W of Fishguard Bay and including Strumble Head, but there are two other headlands also named Pen Caer on this short stretch of coast: confusion! One juts out between Penrhyn and the small shingly cove of Porth Sychan, and just inland of the highest point of the coast here is the site of St Degan's (or St Tegan's) Chapel, no doubt an oratory built to commemorate a monk's safe landing. No remains are visible above ground, although in the 1750s the chapel was standing, with a roof.

Porth Sychan is a delightful cove with nice blue-green pebbles, but not really a bathing beach. Access to it is usually obtained from Tresinwen Farm, along an often wet footpath. In Porth Sychan and the neighbouring cove of Pwlluog examples of volcanic lava of a pillow-like structure are displayed. When the lava had been extruded under water as the result of a submarine volcanic eruption, or when it flowed into the sea from a land-based eruption, rapid cooling took place. This led to the formation of distorted or globular masses of lava which piled on top of one another to take on the appearance of a pile of pillows. The examples here are to be found low down in the cliffs.

Strumble Head is the magnificent culmination of a gloriously wild coastline. The wild and windswept cliffs make exciting scenery, especially when big seas spume in whiteness along their feet. On calm summer days the cliffs are beautiful, with their lichened rocks and many flowers and sea birds. The headland is an ideal place for 'sea watching' – looking out to sea for passing birds. During early morning and late evenings in summer Manx Shearwaters may be seen passing between Ramsey Island and Cardigan Bay, between nesting and feeding sites, but by far the greatest concentrations of birds may be seen in autumn and spring when migratory birds are passing.

Overhead may also be seen and heard high-flying aircraft, for at Strumble Head you stand underneath a main air corridor for London's Heathrow Airport. Just over the Garn Hills, 3ml/4.8km SE from Strumble Head, and seen from the Coast Path, is 'Green One', the homing beacon for Heathrow.

The cliffs of the headland, from Pen Caer to Strumble Head, and

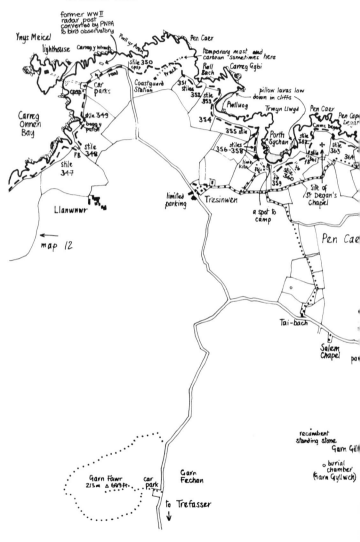

STRUMBLE HEAD

former WW II
radar post
converted by PNPA
to bird observatory

Ynys Meicel
lighthouse

Carreg y Wrach

Pen Caer

Pwll yr Auen

temporary mast and
caravan sometimes here

Carreg Ggbi

stile 350
cpsp

road

Coastguard
Station

track

Car parks

cpsp

Rail
Bach

351
stiles

pillow lavas low
down in cliffs

stile 349

boggy
patch

352 stile
353

354

Pwllwog

Trwyn Llwyd

Pen Caer

Pen Cae
Legar

Cnwc Degan

Carreg
Onnen
Bay

stile
FB 348

355 stile

Porth
Sychan

stiles
356-358

stile
357

stile 363

364

stile
FB

stile
347

lime
kiln

Llanwnwr

limited
parking

Tresinwen

stile
FB 360

FB
359

a spot to
camp

Site of
St Degan's
Chapel

map 12

Pen Cae

Tai-bach

Salem
Chapel

pa

recumbent
standing stone
Garn Gil

burial
chamber
(Garn Gyllwch)

Garn Fawr
215m △ 699ft

car
park

Garn
Fechan

to Trefasser

MAP II

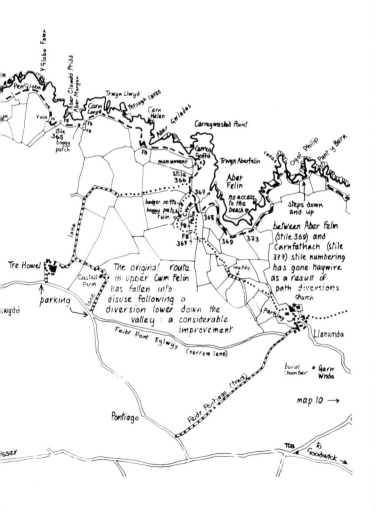

Y Globa Fawr

Pen Globa

ruin

FB

stile
365
boggy
patch

Aber Clawdd Prida

Aber Morgan

Trwyn Llwyd

Carn
Llwyd

through caves

Carn
Halan

Aber Gwladas

Carregwastad Point

FB

monument

stile
366

Carreg
Goffa

Trwyn Aberfelin

Aber
Felin

badger setts

boggy patch

ruin

FB

FB

367

367

368

369

373

no access
to the beach

cave

Ogof Philip

Pant y Barn

steps down
and up

between Aber Felin
(stile 369) and
Carnfathach (stile
377) stile numbering
has gone haywire
as a result of
path diversions

Tre Howel

Castell
Farm

lane

parking

lane

wydd

The original route
in upper Cwm Felin
has fallen into
disuse following a
diversion lower down the
valley: a considerable
improvement

muddy

church

Parking

Llanwnda

Ffordd Pont Eglwys (narrow lane)

burial
chamber

Garn
Wnda

map 10 →

Ffordd Pontiago (track)

Pontiago

sser

TCB

to
Goodwick

the island of Ynys Meicel are formed by a large intrusion of Ordovician dolerite, lava which was injected into the pillow lavas at a later date.

Strumble Head Lighthouse stands on the islet of Ynys Meicel, which is separated from the mainland by a very narrow gap through which the sea boils and froths in stormy weather. A small footbridge spans the gap and a long steep winding path leads to the station. The lighthouse was built by Trinity House in 1908 at a cost of £70,000 when the harbour works were going on at Goodwick, as it was an ideal position to guard the entrance to Fishguard Bay for the steamers that then came across the Atlantic. Today it serves the ferries that come across from Ireland. It is an important station as there is no comparable light further N in the whole curve of Cardigan Bay until Bardsey Island on the point of the Lleyn Peninsula is reached.

The station appears very squat and compact, although it is situated on the top of the islet. The tower is only 55ft/17m high, although the light is 148ft/45m above mean high-water mark. The white light is visible over a range of 31 nautical miles and flashes four times every 15 seconds. The fog signal sounds four times every 60 seconds, and can be heard over a distance of 5 nautical miles. It is sounded automatically when visibility falls below 2 nautical miles. The lighthouse is automatic, being operated by remote control and monitored from St Ann's Head lighthouse. Visiting is not allowed.

Also at Strumble Head is an important coastguard station, one of only two on the Pembrokeshire coast manned 24 hours a day. (The other is on St Ann's Head.)

5   **Strumble Head to Porthstinian** (Maps 12–20)   26ml/41.8km

There is a remote and wild stretch of coast between Strumble Head and St David's Head, a rocky waste of bracken, heather, coarse grass and precipitous cliffs, a superb stretch of quite rough going, although not for young children.

Westwards of Strumble Head the coastline becomes even more rugged and impressive than that which has gone before. The character of this section is typified by the gently undulating moorlands on the coast, truncated by rugged cliffs which make up in grandeur what they lack in height. On this windswept peninsula volcanic rocks come bursting up through the farmland: here is the highest point on the Pen Caer Peninsula, Garn Fawr, 699ft/213m, while the second highest, Garn Gelli, 625ft/190m, lies 2ml/3.2km further inland. Almost without exception the bays and inlets are cut in sedimentary rocks of Lower Palaeozoic age, while the headlands are of igneous rocks.

Strumble Head to Pwll Deri Youth Hostel 2.8ml/4.5km
The Path strikes SW along a delightfully rugged coastline, but it is not too well defined around Pwll Arian and Pen Brush, and is marked by cairns in parts. As you crest the rise at the high point above Pen Brush the magnificent cliffs of Penbwchdy form a solid wall 2ml/3.2km long across the bay in front of you. The cliffs of the mainland and the small islands are the nesting sites of sea birds, while the inaccessible beaches between Porth Maenmelyn and Pwll Deri are the breeding grounds of seals.

The prominent whitewashed house dramatically situated above the cliffs is Pwll Deri Youth Hostel. Opened on 6 July 1957 by the Lord Lieutenant of Pembrokeshire, Air Commodore J B Bowen CBE JP, it was established by generous financial assistance from the Pembrokeshire County Council, and was the first hostel to be provided in England and Wales as the result of co-operation between the YHA and a national park authority.

The youth hostel lies at the end of the road coming from Trefasser, a hamlet reputed to be the birthplace of Bishop Asser, the friend, counsellor and chronicler of the court of King Alfred. On the opposite side of the road from the youth hostel is the small farm of Tal-y-Gaer, in the yard of which is the corbelled crown of a beehive stone hut of the Irish 'clochan' type, described locally as a prehistoric pigsty.

Garn Fawr is a rock hill rising steeply behind the farm to a height of 699ft/213m. Its summit is crowned by a striking hill-fort of the

MAP 12

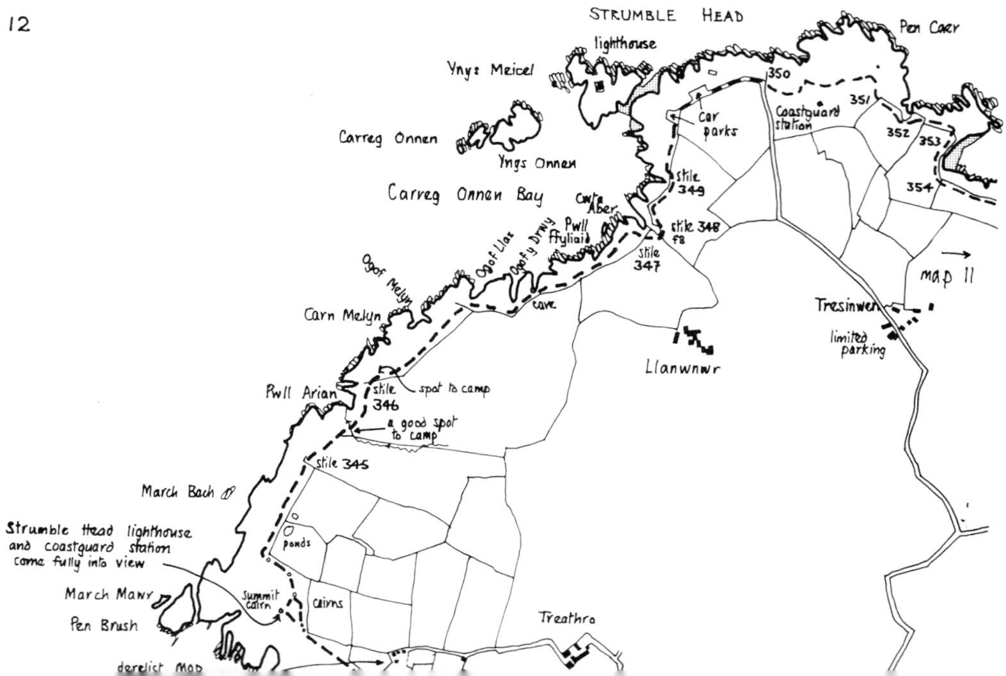

STRUMBLE HEAD

Pen Caer

MAP II

352 353

351 354

350

Coastguard station

Car parks

stile 350

stile 348

lighthouse

Tresinwen

limited parking

stile 349

Vnys Meicel

Ynys Onnen

stile 348 FB

Carreg Onnen

stile 347

Carreg Onnen Bay

Pwll Ffyliaid

Llanwnwr

Ogof Llong

cave

Ogof Golchfa

Ogof Melyn

spot to camp

stile 346

a good spot to camp

Carn Melyn

stile 345

Pwll Arian

ponds

Cairns

March Bach

Summit Cairn

Treathro

Strumble Head lighthouse
and coastguard station
come fully into view

March Mawr

Pen Brush

derelict Mab

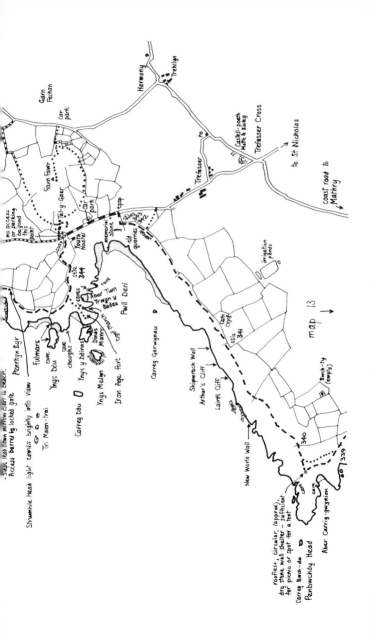

map 13

Garn Fechan

Harmony

Trehilyn

car park

Castell-poeth Motte & Bailey

Trefasser Cross

Po

Trefasser

to St Nicholas

Coast road to Mathry

Garn Fawr

Garn Fechan

Tal-y-Gaer

car park

cpp

cpp

Youth Hostel

Memorial Stone

Styles

old quarries

NO ACCESS or parking beyond this point

stiles 344

irrigation ponds

Carn Ogof

stile 344

Porthsychan

Porthsychan

caves

Aber Twrn Trwyn y Badau

Pwll Deri

Carreg Garwynau

Fulmars

cove

cove

cove

choughs

Ynys Dilu

Ynys y Dinasau

Dinas Mawr

Ynys Melyn

Iron Age Fort

Carreg Dau

Strumble Head light carries brightly into view

Porthlyn Bâr

Tri Maen-trai

— steep 120 down mellow steps to beach.
Access barrel by locked gate.

Shipwreck Wall

Arthur's Cliff

Laird's Cliff

Bwlch-ty (empty)

New World Wall

344

cpp

car

344

cpp

car

339

roofless, circular (approx),
drg stone, wall shelter – sufficient
for picnic or spot for a tent

Carreg Bach-dau

Penbwchdy Head

Aber Carrig-gwynion

Early Iron Age. It has three widely spaced ramparts connected to the natural outcrops of rock. Full use is made of the rocky crags, whose precipitous outward faces are linked by the walls, but so much stone has been removed over the years, and the site is now so overgrown, that the original layout is lost. It is one of the most remarkable Welsh hill-forts, with ramparts, ditches and hut-circles.

The hill is encircled by a public footpath from Tal-y-Gaer Farm, but the summit is best approached from the car park on the eastern side where a relatively easy slope leads to the main entrance in the ramparts. The view from the top is extensive, including on a clear day the Wicklow Mountains of Ireland to the W and Snowdon and the Lleyn Peninsula to the N.

Pwll Deri to Pwllcrochan 2.1ml/3.4km
The Path leaves the road not far from Pwll Deri and strikes along the ridge of the Penbwchdy cliffs. In places the Path seems barely wide enough for passage between the sheer cliff-face and the fields behind, as it winds in and out and over outcrops and pockets of rock arranged naturally to form a perfect rock garden. Flowers and lichens, butterflies and birds provide a year-round spectacle of beauty and interest as you walk this stretch, vying with the superb coastal scenery which stretches away towards St David's Head. The tall sea cliffs are developing rock climbing routes, impressive at close quarters, while on Penbwchdy Head itself there is a prominent black arch, not seen from the Path, which is a superb cave of columnar formation.

Pwllcrochan is a small shingle beach sheltered by 200ft/60m high cliffs. The cliffs are dangerous to climb, but the swimming is good, and sand is revealed at low water. Access to the beach is steep and difficult, but once there you can see a complete anticlinal fold in the rocks at the back of the cove. Pwllcrochan can be reached by a footpath over the fields from Velindre Farm on the coast road, but as there is no parking except on road verges, it is not recommended.

Pwllcrochan to Aber Mawr 1.5ml/2.4km
From Pwllcrochan to Aber Mawr the Path is good and walkable all the way, although it is rough at times. When you reach Aber Mawr

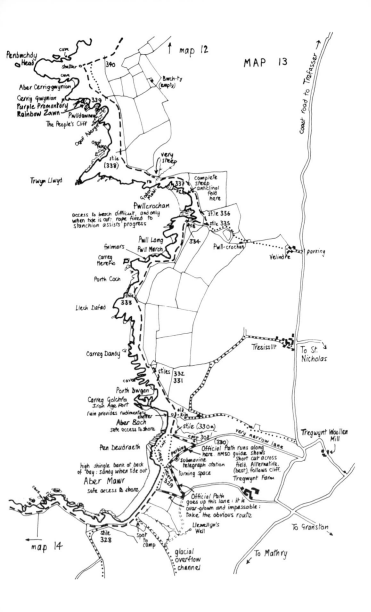

Penbwchdy Head

cave

shelter

340

↑ map 12

MAP 13

Bwch-ty (empty)

Aber Cerrig-gwynion

cave

339

Pwlldawnau

Cerrig Gwynion
Purple Promontory
Rainbow Zawn

The People's Cliff

stile (338)

Trwyn Llwyd

very steep

337

Complete sheep amticlinal fold here

Pwllcrochan

stile 336

access to beach difficult, and only when tide is out: rope fixed to stanchion assists progress

stile 335

fulmars

Pwll Long
Pwll March

334

Pwll-crochan

Velindre

parking

Carreg Herefio

Porth Coch

stile 333

Llech Dafad

Carreg Dandy

Tresissllt

To St. Nicholas

caves

stiles 332
331

Porth Dwgan

Carreg Golchfa
Iron Age Fort
ruin provides rudimentary shelter

alt kiln

stile (330a)

cairn 308?

Aber Bach
safe access to shore

Pen Deudraeth

330

Official Path runs along here. HMSO guide shows short cut across field. Alternative (best) follows cliff.

very narrow lane

Tregwynt Woollen Mill

high shingle bank at back of bay: sandy when tide out

submarine telegraph station

turning space

Tregwynt Farm

Aber Mawr
safe access to shore.

329

cave

Aber

Official Path goes up this lane: it is over-grown and impassable: take the obvious route

To Granston

stile 328

spot camp

Llewellyn's Well

← map 14

glacial overflow channel

To Mathry

Coast road to Trefasser

the Pen Caer Peninsula can be considered to end.

On the N coast of Pembrokeshire there are several localities where the glacial deposits of the Ice Age are preserved. During the last glaciation, about 20,000 years ago, the ice of the Irish Sea Glacier crossed the coast. It carried with it silt, sand, clay and stones dredged from the floor of the Irish Sea and Cardigan Bay, and deposited it as till in many coastal bays. The till is highly calcareous (which means that it reacts to dilute hydrochloric acid) and it has a dark-blue or purple colour. It is a stiff, plastic deposit which is extremely difficult to dig, and because of its high percentage of clay particles it waterlogs easily. It contains scratched or striated pebbles and stones, remnants of wood over 2 million years old, and fragments of marine shells. This till is called 'Irish Sea Till' and elsewhere there is a different till which is more stony and sandy, with a brown or red-brown colour.

At Pen Deudraeth, between Aber Bach and Aber Mawr, there is an exposure of Irish Sea Till. It is overlain by a thick deposit of sands, gravels and rounded boulders, and the low cliffs of crumbling earth and shale are gradually being eroded: the road from Tregwynt to Aber Bach and Aber Mawr once continued to Abercastle, but it was washed away less than twenty years ago.

Both bays are backed by storm banks of shingle, and a little sand is revealed at low tide; both are good swimming beaches. Aber Mawr, the larger, has a steeply shelving beach, with a high-low water range of less than 90ft/30m, and care is required in the surf at low water. At very low water a submerged forest may sometimes be seen in Aber Mawr, as at Whitesand Bay, Freshwater West and Amroth.

Between the two bays, looking like a locked-up holiday cottage, is a building from where the first Atlantic submarine telegraph cable was laid in 1873.

Both bays are accessible by car along a very narrow lane which leads through a tree-lined dingle to the Tregwynt Woollen Mill, an old mill that is still at work producing traditional Welsh weaves. Once water-, but now machine-driven, it attracts many visitors, and **is one of only two still working in Pembrokeshire.**

MAP 14

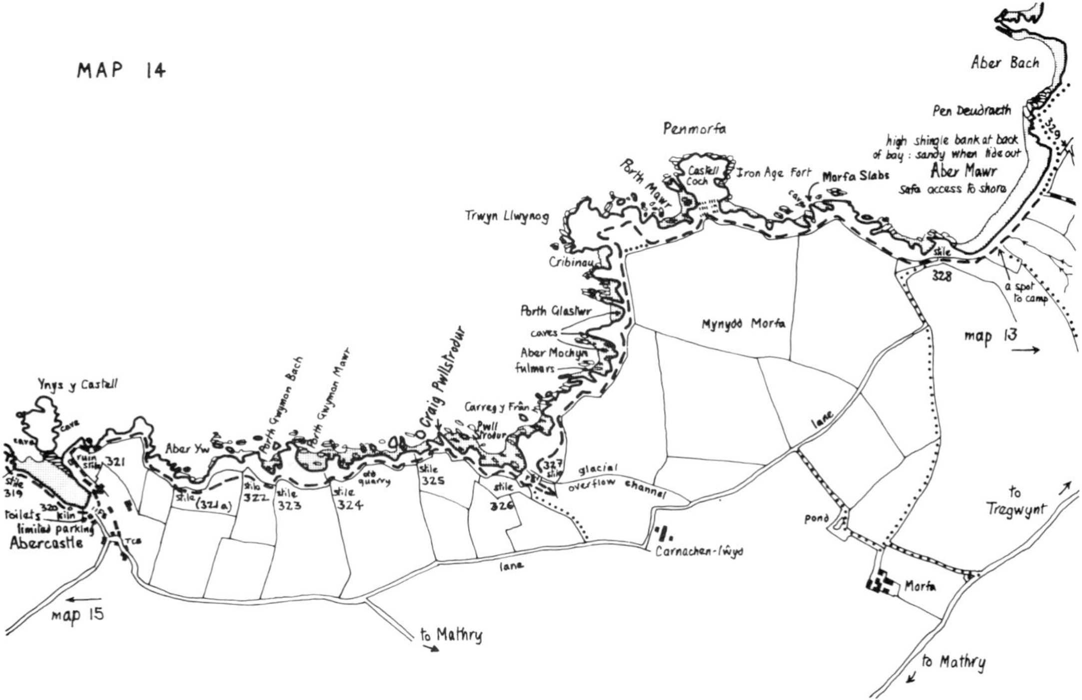

Aber Bach
Pen Deudraeth
high shingle bank at back of bay; sandy when tide out
Aber Mawr
safe access to shore
329
328
map 13
a spot to camp
to Trefasser
to Mathry
Morfa
pond

Penmorfa
Castell Iron Age Fort Morfa Slabs
cove
Mynydd Morfa
lane
Trwyn Llwynog
Porth Maur
Cribinau
Porth Glastwr
caves
Aber Mawbyn
fulmars
Carreg y Fran
Pwll Bwli
327
glacial overflow channel
stile
326
lane
Carnachen Wyd
Craig Pwllstrodur
stile 325
sea quarry
stile 324
Porth Gwymon Mawr
stile 323
Porth Gwymon Bach
stile 322
Aber Yw
stile (321A)
to Mathry
Ynys y Castell
Warren 321
320
stile 319
toilets limited parking
slip
Abercastle
map 15

Aber Mawr to Abercastle 3.25ml/5.2km

Glacial overflow channels running out into the sea are a feature of this part of the coast. The valleys feeding into Aber Bach and Aber Mawr are two examples, and there is one running into Pwll Strodur and another at Abercastle. Between them is the small headland of Penmorfa, which is a good site for the Iron Age promontory fort of Castell Coch. It has two ditches and three walls defending its landward side. The inner wall has a central entrance, and reveals masonry on its outer face. The outer bank has an 18c field-wall built on top of it, and comes right up close to the Coast Path.

Abercastle consists of a few houses at the back of a splendid little bay called Cwm Badau – The Valley of Boats. The place was known to have been an important and thriving harbour in 1566. Fenton says that corn and butter went out to Bristol in 1811 and general goods came back. Up to the 1920s anthracite and culm were coming in and oats going out. Lime was imported from West Williamston, and the anthracite was used to burn it in the kiln on the harbour: the kiln remains in particularly good condition and has not needed to be 'restored'. The gaunt greystone derelict warehouse that broods over the harbour was used by the coastal traders.

On 15 June 1876 the first man to sail solo across the Atlantic landed at Abercastle. He was Alfred Johnson, and his boat *Centennial* was only '20 feet long'.

The almost land-locked harbour reveals greyish sand at low water and the restricted foreshore is often crowded in summer as cars and boats and sub-aqua divers vie for space. The only amenities provided are some toilets: at one time there were three inns in Abercastle, but now there are none. Rocks and low cliffs shelter the inlet and there is good fishing from the harbour wall-walk (Coast Path) on the W side. Take care on the rocks on the N side, especially at low water.

Guarding the entrance to the harbour is the island of Ynys-y-Castell, supposed to be the burial place of Samson's finger, cut off when he erected the capstone on the burial chamber at Longhouse.

Abercastle to Aber Felin (Trefin) 2.8ml/4.6km

For the most part the going is easy, but the Path is quite narrow and dangerous at times as there are sheer cliffs and cliff-falls in places, so take care with children. This short stretch is quiet, unspoilt and has superb coast and cliff scenery.

0.5ml/0.8km from Abercastle, approached by road or from a path striking off from the Coast Path, at a farm called Longhouse (Ty Hir) there is an exceptionally fine dolmen, one of the most grandly situated of all Welsh burial chambers. Known locally as Carreg Samson, this Bronze Age burial chamber looks over the Abercastle inlet towards Strumble Head. The capstone, 15ft/5.2m long and 9ft/2.7m broad, stood on upright slabs. There are six uprights, only three of which support the capstone, and there is one slab on its side close by. The whole formed a polygonal chamber, but the covering mound has long disappeared. The engineering ability of those who built in the Megalithic period was remarkable, but even more so was the spirit of worship and of aspiration towards immortality that moved them. The story is that Samson placed the capstone in position using only his little finger, which now rests in its grave on the island within sight of the monument. Some believe that the name Samson may be a memory of the spiritual power of St Samson of Caldey and Dol.

Along the coast to the W of Abercastle there is an alternation of igneous and sedimentary rocks: the headlands are where the igneous rocks defy the sea and the many coves and inlets are where the softer sedimentaries have yielded. Three such coves are Pwll Whiting, Pwll Llong and Pwll Olfa, and it is best advised not to try climbing down to them as the steep slopes are dangerous when wet. On one of the igneous headlands, Pen Castel Coch, to the N of Pwll Whiting, is an Iron Age promontory fort. It has four ditches and three banks, the outer ditch seemingly hewn out of solid rock, but this may be simply skilled use of the local geology.

Aber Felin is the beach for Trefin, a small attractive cove, with rock pools and shingle. By the shore is the ruined Melin Tre-fin Mill, which closed in 1918. The mill dam was sited above the road bridge, but has now been filled in, but the leat which supplied the mill with water can still be seen. The mill has been restored and is maintained by the PNPA.

Trefin is the largest village on the coast between Fishguard and

MAP 15

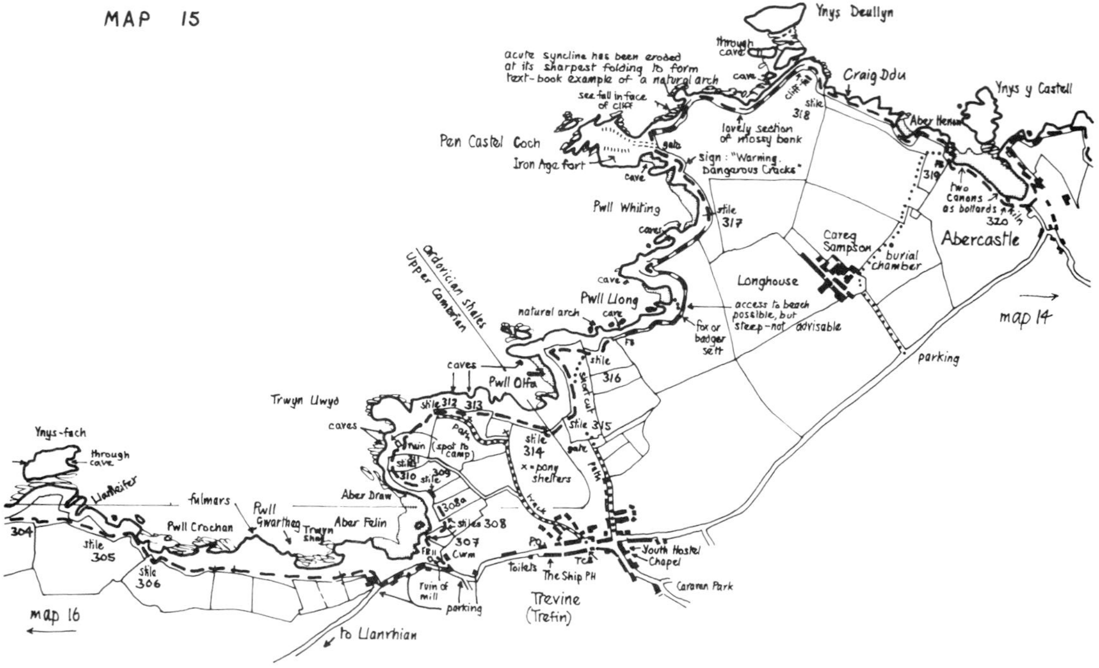

Ynys Deullyn

Ynys y Castell

→ map 14

Abercastle

Two caves
as bollards 320

Aber House

Craig Ddu

through cave

acute syncline has been arched
at its sharp folding to form
text-book example of a natural arch
see fall in face of cliff

Iron Age Fort

Pen Castel Coch

stile 318

lovely section of mossy bank

Carreg Sampson
burial chamber

parking

sign "Warning Dangerous Cliffs"

stile 317

cave

cave

caves

Pwll Whiting

Longhouse

access to beach possible, but steep - not advisable

caves

Pwll Llong

cave

stile

stile
pole path

short cut

stile 315

stile 316

natural arch

Pwll Offra

stile 312

caves

Ordovician shales
Upper Cambrian

stile 314

x-pong shelters

Pou

Trefin (Trefin)

South House
Chapel

Caravan Park

The Ship Ph

Trwyn Llwyd

stile

stile

Pwn camp B (camp)

stile

307 314 308

scale

Bell Cwm

Penn's mill

Aber Draw

caves

Pwll
Gwarthey
Trwyn Pwll
Ruin
Ruin

→ To Llanrhian

parking

Trwyn Llwyd

Fulmars

Pwll Crochan

stile 305

stile 306

→ MAP 16

Llangrove

through cave

Ynys-fach

stile 304

St David's, and a useful place for accommodation and supplies: there is a good youth hostel in the centre of the village. The village belonged to the bishops of St David's, and it was once the home of **Bishop Tully (1460–82) but nothing remains of his palace. The ruins of Trefin Mill inspired a former Archdruid of Wales to write his famous poem 'Melin Trefin'.**

Aber Felin (Trefin) to Porthgain 1.7ml/2.7km

This is a fairly easy short stretch of Path, and it isn't long before you crest a headland and descend to the small picturesque harbour of *Porthgain*, chiefly notable for its fascinating relics of industrial activity in quarrying and brick making. The little harbour, construction of which started in the 1860s, is overshadowed by the immense derelict shell of the former stone-crushing plant of the large quarries, which were the best-known quarries of roadstone in Pembrokeshire. A company called Porthgain Village Industries operated a thriving quarrying and brick-making industry between 1878 and 1914, although crushed igneous rock was being exported from the small harbour before 1878, and the plant was last used in 1932. The stone-crushing plant was built for the most part with bricks made on the spot from local shale.

Between 1902 and 1904 the harbour was rebuilt and longer quays were provided to cater for the sailing ships that called regularly for the export of stone from Porthgain and slate from Abereiddy. For a while business was brisk. Porthgain experienced a short-lived boom between 1904 and 1914, with the export of millions of tons of crushed roadstone to metal the streets of London, while at the same time the brickworks was in full production. However, in the Depression years following the end of World War I the company found it increasingly difficult to make profits, and it was forced to stop operations altogether in 1931: the last shipments of stone sailed away a year later.

Little remains of the brickworks, save the ruined stone building in the centre of the village 'green' on the edge of the habour. A long tunnel runs through the hill behind the storage hoppers into the quarry from which the shale was mined to make the bricks. This tunnel connected the works directly with the brick pit: you can still walk through the tunnel with the aid of wellies and a flashlight.

On the cliff-tops are the remains of some enormous quarries, and you can still see ruins and remains of various buildings and traces of railway tracks associated with the exploitation of the stone quarries out on the Penclegyr headland. The routes of other old railway lines can easily be traced to the slate quarry at Abereiddy.

The most prominent features of the stone-quarrying industry which remain today are the impressive array of tall, gaunt walls of the storage hoppers dominating the harbour, from which graded stone was loaded directly into moored vessels from five separate bunkers. These ruins are now scheduled Ancient Monuments by virtue of their industrial archaeological interest.

After Porthgain Village Industries ceased operating in 1936 the old works, the harbour, a row of six cottages (The Street) and two houses were taken over by a brickworks company, G R Stein Refactories of Sheffield, but they never reopened the stone quarry or the brickworks. The owners discovered their property was hardly profitable; in July 1980 the whole lot was put up for sale by private treaty as a single entity, but there was no buyer. The PNPA offered financial backing for the tenants and other members of the local community, which assisted them to buy the property. In return the villagers agreed to sell the harbour, quarry, brickworks, most of the village green and all the cliff land back to the PNPA. Now that the village is back in local ownership and control, one may expect some efforts being made to tidy the place up.

On the S side of the village green, adjoining The Street, is a small café, while on the opposite side, facing the sun, is the excellent and unspoilt Sloop Inn, a good pub, with old photographs of the harbour. Down by the harbour itself there are traces of an old water-mill and a well preserved lime-kiln.

Several small fishing boats are based on Porthgain harbour, mostly owned by part-time fishermen, and summer fishing trips for crab and mackerel can be arranged with them. The coast hereabouts is too dangerous for sailors who are unfamiliar with

local conditions: the harbour entrance – and it is the only one on the whole of this inhospitable coast except for Abercastle – is very tricky when there is a swell running. The entrance is so small and concealed that stone harbour-marker towers – which used to be painted white – were built as landmarks on the flanking headlands for the coasters which came in to load granite from the quay. Two breakwaters form a snug habour, which dries out completely at low water, leaving a sandy bottom. There is a slipway at the E end of the harbour near the lime-kiln, giving immediate access. High water is Milford time plus 50 minutes.

Llanrhian lies just inland from the harbour of Porthgain, at a crossroads on the coast road: a cluster of cottages, farm, school and the church of St Rheian. It is a place well worth visiting, because of the rare examples of a cruciform church and a ten-sided font. The grey church stands at the village crossroads surrounded by tall trees, and its tall tower commands a view of Porthgain harbour from where pirates and raiders might have been expected to approach.

The 13c stone tower has all the appearances of a stronghold – narrow slit-like windows, stepped gables of a low saddleback roof, and walls spread at the base. The tower once stood alone: slit-like windows are on the N, W, and S sides, but on the E there is an opening large enough to give access to the belfry, or upper storey of the tower. This opening has been partially filled in, since it is on the level of the ceiling of the present nave, and therefore completely inaccessible, and the slit in the N wall has been replaced by a door to provide a new means of entrance to the belfry. When access was originally gained through the opening in the E wall there must have been no nave adjoining, or else there was an extremely low building of which the apex of the roof was lower than the present eaves.

The walls of the tower are nearly 3ft/0.8m thick, and the slit-like apertures broaden out to about 3ft/0.8m on the inside. The church was entirely rebuilt, except for the tower, in 1836 and extensively restored in 1891. No evidence exists of the form of the church prior to 1836, although Fenton, writing in 1811, says, 'The church bears a sort of stunted tower and has the nave divided by a row of low pillars.' The 1891 restoration retains most of the 1836 features – stone flags in the nave, flat roof, stained pine-panelled walls – and it is well lit by clear glass diamond-paned windows.

An unusual feature is the decagonal 15c font in Perpendicular style, a style reflected also in the mullions of the windows. Each of the ten panels of the font contains an inverted shield, and on one there is the coat of arms of Sir Rhys ap Thomas – a chevron between three birds (choughs), technically described as 'Argent a chevron, sables, between three ravens proper'.

Sir Rhys, a supporter of Henry Tudor (Henry VII), had no known personal connection with Llanrhian, and he was buried in Carmarthen. Geologists have said that the stone bears a resemblance to the Stone of Solomon's Temple in Jerusalem. If this is so, a possible explanation is that Sir Rhys brought it to Carmarthen from the Holy Land, and it may have been presented to Llanrhian at a later date by the Archdeacon of Carmarthen, who was patron and rector of the parish of Llanrhian. The base of the font is modern and of local stone.

Porthgain to Abereiddy 2ml/3.2km
This is a fairly gentle walk on a good path, except for the rutted bit from Porthgain to Traeth Llyfn, caused by the repeated passage of cows.

The Llanrhian stream to Porthgain, and a similar stream flowing due W to Abereiddy, flow along glacial overflow channels through the Ordovician shales, creating Ynys Barry (Barry Island) in a similar manner to Dinas Island.

Porth Egr and Traeth Llyfn are two sandy W-facing bays which bite into the headland of Ynys Barry. The beach of Traeth Llyfn is flanked by 150ft/45m high walls of rock on which rock climbs have been recorded, and the sands are reached by steps and a narrow path. The steps were provided by Italian prisoners of war during World War II. On the descent you pass through an unusual thickness of glacial deposit. Traeth Llyfn was the scene of departure of two early Christians after a quarrel: from here Finbar (St Barre) sailed to found the city of Cork, while Columba sailed in penitence to Iona.

Abereiddy is another fascinating abandoned settlement. Here slate was quarried from the shaly rock, and traces of old quarry-

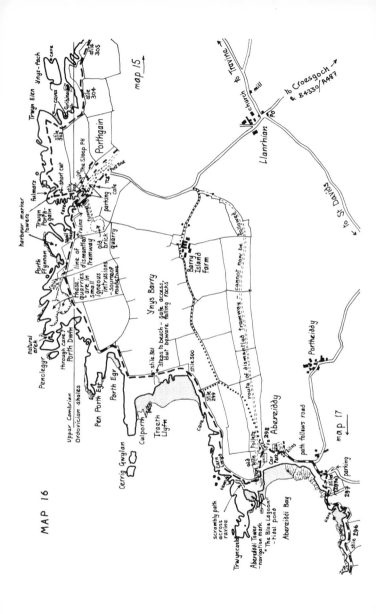

MAP 16

map 15

to Trevine

to Croesgoch & B4330/A487

to St David's

map 17

Llanrhian

church

mill

PO

Ynys-fach

stile 305   cave

caves

stile 304

Gribinau

Trwyn Elen

stile 303

The Sloop PH

Porthgain

Short cut

Fulmars

harbour marker towers

Trwyn Porth-gain

caves

Spoil

tunnel

ruins

Porth Flynnon

Red Bar

Natural arch

line of dismantled tramway

café

parking

Penclegyr

through cave? Porth Dwfn

old brick quarry

tunnel

Upper Cambrian Ordovician shales

these quarries are in small igneous intrusions – source of roadstone

Barry Island Farm

followed

cannot now be

route of dismantled tramway

Ynys Barry

Pen Porth Egr

Porth Egr

Culporth

stile 301

Steps to beach – Safe access, but beware falling rocks

stile 300

Cerrig Gwylan

Traeth Llyfn

stile 299

Abereiddy

Porthiddy

cave

old kiln

old limekilns

Car Park

stile 298

path follows road

toilets

ruins

Car Park

stile 297   parking

scrambly path across ravine

Abereiddy Bay

Trwyncastell

Abereiddi Tower & navigation mark

The Blue Lagoon – tidal pond

cave

stile 296

workers' cottages and quarry buildings and quay can still be seen.
Slate and shale flags became increasingly important for flooring and
roofing purposes after 1800. The 'slate' quarry at Abereiddy was
worked most extensively between 1850 and 1904 when slates were
exported not only to the rest of the county but also to the Bristol
Channel and English Channel ports. Because of the bay's exposure
to the W only small vessels (20–30 tons) could be loaded alongside
the quarry and consequently most of the later exports were hauled
along a narrow-gauge railway track to Porthgain, and sent from its
excellent harbour. Eventually the quarry was opened to the sea by a
narrow channel, making a deep harbour with an awkward entrance,
but the quarry closed overnight in 1904 when it became flooded in a
storm. The 'Blue Lagoon' is now a famous geological feature, and it
is still used by fishing boats, but the entrance is very narrow, and the
coast hereabouts is too dangerous to be sailed by people without
considerable local knowledge.

The rocks exposed in Abereiddi Bay and in Trwyncastell, the
headland to the N, belong to the Ordovician series. They were
originally mudstones which have been converted by pressure into
slates which split or cleave along planes coinciding with the original
mudstone layering. The Ordovician slates in the bedding planes
contain fossil graptolites, the delicate fossil *Didymograptus bifidus* –
the 'tuning fork' fossil, which lived about 500 million years ago. This
fossil was first discovered here, and the area is regularly visited by
field-parties in search of examples which may still be found in the
shale.

There used to be two lime-kilns working here, and there were
quite frequent landings of limestone on the open beach. In addition
assorted other cargoes were landed in the bay, for Abereiddy once
had a fine reputation for smuggling. Today there are a few part-time
fishing boats based here, used particularly for lobster and other
shellfish catches close inshore.

Abereiddy has a good-sized beach, and the pounding waves have
reduced parts of the slate cliffs into a beach of fine, clean but almost
black sand. Sand is revealed at low water, but the main impression
is of black stones, slate and shale, giving a foreboding aspect
sometimes. For all that it is a splendid beach. Surfing is possible at

low water from near the rocks at the S end of the beach, aided by
southwesterly winds. There are no amenities at Abereiddy except
for a toilet block at the N end among the ruins of quarry buildings,
and sometimes an ice-cream van calls. Cars are allowed to park
almost on the foreshore, without charge, and there is immediate
access to the gently shelving beach.

Abereiddy to Porth Coch 4.75ml/7.6km
The condition of the Coast Path is clear all the way, giving good
walking, even for children. This is a cliff-top walk along a majestic
and superbly impressive stretch of coast, with the dramatic hills and
St David's Head stretching away into the distance.

The condition of access paths from the farms to the S is doubtful,
though there are legal rights of way to the coast on foot through all
the farms marked on the maps. In the author's experience the paths
from Treleidr to Carn Penberry (stile 286) and Trefelly to Porth
Coch are the most useful and also the most possible. There is no
right to park a car at the farms and you ought always to ask for
permission, but parking is usually possible on the grass verges of the
highways approaching them.

You pass two Iron Age forts on this stretch of Path – first Caerau,
a fort that has a complicated defensive system added to an earlier,
*c*300BC, simple embankment on its NE side. This earthwork closely
resembles Castell Heinif (on the St David's Peninsula) in its
defensive arrangements. The second fort is at Castell Coch, where
an entrenchment cuts off a small peninsula, the size of which has
probably been diminished by slate quarrying. The outlines of a
double bank are visible, but access is impossible due to the
vegetation.

There is only one place where you can get down to the sea, and
that is at Aber Pwll, a small, wild cove, but it is not a place for
bathing.

Along this stretch of coast the scenery is dominated by several
upstanding hills – Carn Penberry (or Penberi), Carn Trellwyd,
Carn-ffald, Carn Perfedd, Carnedd-lleithr and Carn Llidi – which
assume impressive proportions when seen from a distance, and give
the coastline a monumental silhouette out of all proportion to their

MAP 17

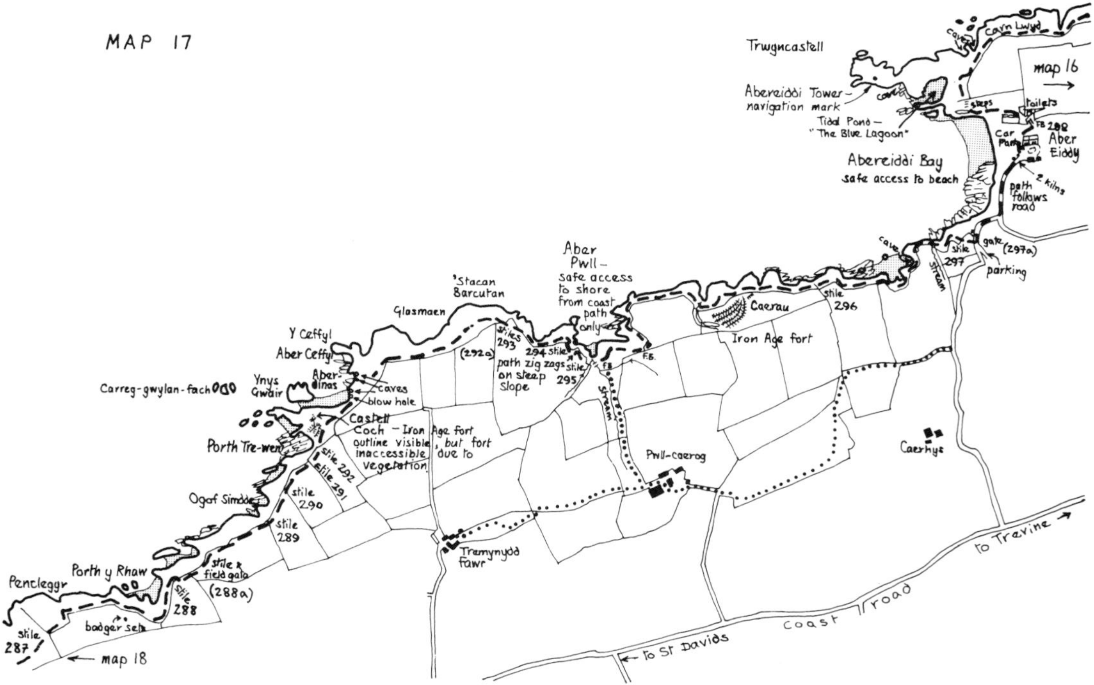

Trwyncastell

Abereiddi Tower — navigation mark

"Tidal Pond — "The Blue Lagoon"

Abereiddi Bay — Safe access to beach

Coch Llwyd

map 16

chalets

steps

Car Park

gate (298a)

parking

2 kilns

path follows road

Aber Eiddy

coast path

stile 297

stream

Caerau

296

Caerau

Iron Age fort

Pwll-caerog

Coast Road

to St Davids

to Trevine

Aber Pwll — Safe access to shore from coast path only

Sarn Barcutan

Glasfaen

(294a)

stile 295

stile 294

stile 293

path zigzags on steep slope

stream

Castell Coch — Iron Age fort visible in outline but fort inaccessible due to vegetation

Tremynydd Fawr

Y Castell

Aber Cyffig

Ynys Cyffig

Aber Pilins

hollow hole

caves

Porth Tre-wen

Carreg-gwylan-fach

Ogof Simdde

stile 292

stile 291

stile 290

stile 289

stile 288

stile 288a

stile & field gate

Penclegyr

Porth y Rhaw

badger sett

stile 287

map 18

MAP 18

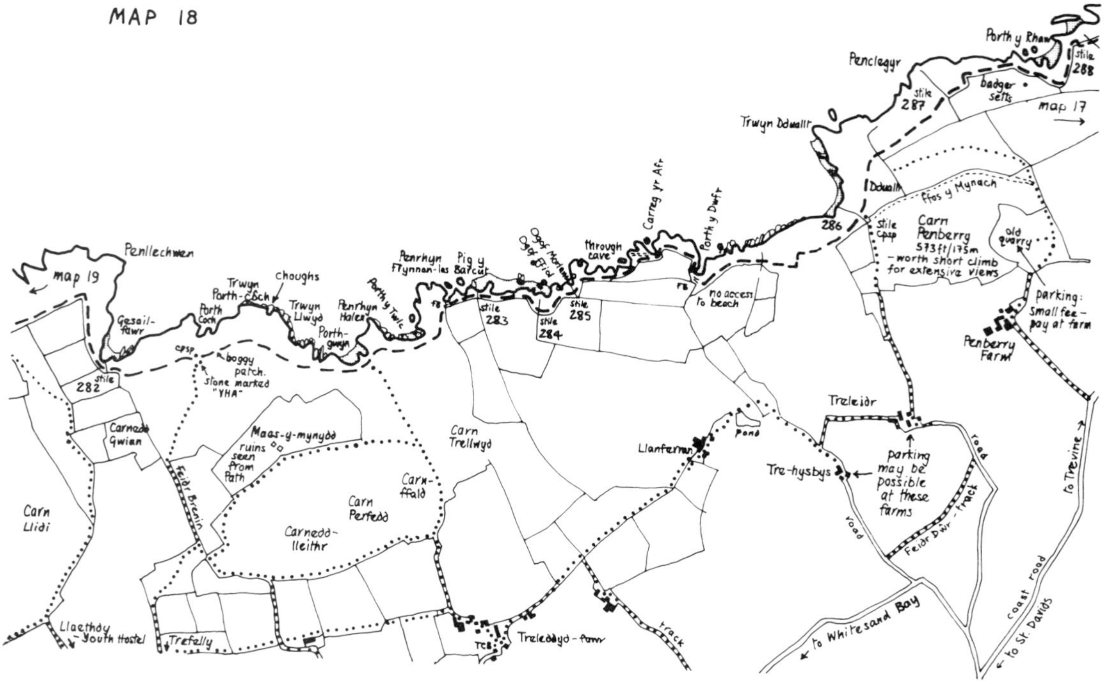

Porth y Rhaw
stile 288
Pencleger
stile 287
Trwyn Ddewllir
map 17
badger setts
Ddewllir / Foss y Mynach
stile 286
stile Cave
old quarry
Carn Penberry
513ft/135m
- worth short climb
for extensive views
parking:
small fee
pay at farm
Penberry
Farm
to Trevine
to St Davids
Coast Road
Trelewr
parking
may be
possible
at these
farms
Feidr-sand Road
to Whitesand Bay
road
Treflysbwys
Porth y Dwfr
no access
to beach
Carreg yr Afr
through
cave
Ogof Morfawr
Gap Ffald
Pig y Baw
stile 285
stile 284
stile 283
Llanferran
pond
Porthsychan
Porthmynawyd
Porthmynau-las Bellad
Porth y Twll
Porth-lleuog
Trelewr - Pony
track
Carn Trelwyd
Carn
Ffald
pond
Carnedd-
lleithr
Carn
Perfedd
map 19
Penllechwen
Ogaof-y-bower
stile 282
Carnach
Gwian
Carn
Llidi
Trwyn Llwyd
Porth Llong
Choughs
Trwyn Porth-llisky
cave
boggy patch
Stone marked
YHA
ruins 0
seen from
path
Maes-y-mynydd
Feidr Brenin
Trefelly
Llachdy Youth Hostel
track

height. It is sometimes not appreciated that even the highest of the group, Carn Llidi, is only 595ft/181m high. The deception of the mountainous dimensions of these hills results partly from the general flatness of the landform to the S and partly from the small number of familiar features such as trees or houses on their flanks which can be used to estimate scale.

These hills are formed of igneous rocks of Ordovician age. While the Cambrian and Pre-Cambrian rocks to the S have been worn down to the level of the 200–250ft/60–76m erosion surface, the outlines of the dolerite outcrops have been modified only slowly. These hills must have stood as islands at a time when sea level was some 200–250ft/60–76m higher than at present, perhaps similar in appearance to Ramsey Island today.

Around the W and N flanks of Carn Penberry runs the Ffos-y-Mynach (the Monk's Ditch) which was probably a boundary of the Lordship of St David's. It cuts across the peninsula from N coast to S coast, and although traces of a dyke or trench can be found its real origins and purpose are uncertain.

Porth Coch to Porth Mawr (Whitesand Bay) 2.85ml/4.6km
This short stretch encompasses the whole of St David's Head, the northern cliffs, the sandy beaches of Porth Melgan, Porth Lleuog and Porth Mawr, the magnificent hill of Carn Llidi, and the ancient earthworks of early settlers. It is a delightful area in which you can pass many hours looking at places of interest.

The rock of the St David's Head area is gabbro, similar in chemical and mineral composition to basalt, but whereas the latter cools quickly as a lava at or near the surface, the former cools quickly at depth, well below the surface of the earth. In this area this took place some 480 million years ago, in Lower Ordovician times. Unlike the fine-grained basalt, the gabbro consists of relatively large crystals, making the rock rough to the touch.

Not only in its rocks is the St David's Peninsula different. It is historically apart also, being from earliest Christian times a place of special significance for the Celtic church. From the Stone Age to the Iron Age, and from the Dark Ages to the Middle Ages, the area was a centre of power. The whole rock-strewn St David's Head is cut off from the mainland by the still-massive stone banks of an Iron Age promontory fort, containing within it a few hut-circles, while contemporary with them are the ancient fields traceable on the nearby slopes of Carn Llidi.

Gesail-fawr is a narrow rocky inlet defining the eastern end of *the northern cliffs* and has a small shingle beach reached by scrambling down a steep slope. Just beyond, on the Penllechwen headland, the Path turns a corner and runs SW for a full mile/1.6km, although over the open moor any line can be taken, hopping from one rock outcrop to another, or looking down deep zawns to the sea. On this rugged coast there is a splendour of flowers: in spring the ground is carpeted with pink, yellow and white, with thrift, orchids, lady's fingers, sea squill and sea campion, while in summer there are the deeper colours of the heather, sea-wort and knapweed.

Between Penllechwen and Trwyn-llwyd on the morning of 28 February 1860 the steamship *Nimrod* was driven ashore in a gale while on its way from Liverpool to Cork with 40 passengers and crew aboard. It was broken in two by the waves and there were no survivors. The *Nimrod* had earlier refused the offer of a tow into Milford Haven. These rocks have claimed dozens of shipwrecks over the years: the County Museum in Haverfordwest has a cannon and many other items brought up from an East India merchantman of around 1840.

These cliffs are the most important climbing grounds on igneous rock south of Scotland. The gabbro is not as rough as the famous rock of the Cuillin of Skye, but the frictional properties are better than the worn crags of the Lake District and Snowdonia.

Climbing possibilities on the headland were noted as long ago as 1900, but the cliffs weren't 'developed' until after 1966, when Colin Mortlock paddled up the coast by kayak and their potential was revealed. There are four main sea cliffs: from E to W they are Trwyn-llwyd (Grey Nose Cliff), Craig Carn Porth-llong (Coastguard Cliff), Mur Cenhinen (Black Cliff) and Craig Coetan (Red Cliff). Routes of quality are well represented in all grades and on all cliffs. One disconcerting aspect for the newcomer here is the seaweed and green slime within the tidal range – the granitic rock is therefore slippery because it does not have the self-cleansing properties of limestone. Trwyn-llwyd is the most complicated climbing cliff. Ridges are used to gain the climbs, but there are unpleasant chimneys and abseil descents needed to reach the centrally located routes.

Between Trwyn-llwyd and Carn Porth-llong the Coast Path goes through a gap in a ragged line of stones. This is the remains of an Iron Age wall, built to mark a field. There are many such 'enclosures' around Carn Llidi, and some are still in use after more than 2000 years.

Craig Carn Porth-llong looks the least attractive of the four main climbing cliffs. A coastguard lookout station on the top of the cliffs was built in 1956, but ceased to be manned in 1971 and was demolished soon after. The caravan sometimes stationed here is occupied by a shore party from the RN survey ships which often set up their beacons on this site when their vessels are working offshore.

The normal descent to the cliff of Mur Cenhinen is by the opening between Coastguard Buttress and the cliff, or by slippery, sea-washed ledges as a traverse from Craig Coetan. After scrambling down broken ribs, a smooth crescent-shaped glacis bends below the E wall and slides into the sea. The rock is often greasy and great care is needed to avoid spinning into the water.

Craig Coetan is the only cliff that can be seen and studied from the moor on top of the headland. However, the best view is obtained by descending into its steep flanking zawn, Ogof Coetan, down steep grass on to a spine of perfect gabbro jutting into the sea. The easy climbs on this cliff are particularly suitable for novices. Nearly all the climbs start from a slanting rake well above the sea, and below this the rock face drops directly into the sea.

Directly above Ogof Coetan and lying just off the Coast Path is Carreg Coetan Arthur – Arthur's Quoit – a New Stone Age burial chamber. It was built about 5500 years ago and the capstone, nearly 12ft/3.6m long and more than 1ft/0.3m thick, lies supported on one of its pillars. It occupies a position on top of the moor and is easily overlooked when passed at close quarters, although on the approach from Porth Melgan it is seen as a silhouette on the skyline.

As you near the tip of St David's Head the path veers to the S and descends slightly, and down to the R is the deep zawn of Ogof Crisial – Crystal Cave. Veins of yellow-white quartz can be seen running along the cliff on the far side of this deep rocky zawn and lead down into a virtually inaccessible cave under an overhang in the cliff-face. Erosion by the sea in storm conditions, when the water can reach up into the cave, has broken the fine quartzspar into fine fragments, known locally as 'St David's diamonds'.

St David's Head (Penmaen Dewi) is the glorious conclusion of the promontory, thrusting out into the open sea, but the Coast Path does not go right to the tip: you should.

The rugged promontory was once defended by the Clawydd-y-Milwyr – the Warrior's Dyke – to contain a small Iron Age fort, offering magnificent views of Ramsey Island, Whitesand Bay and the Sound between them. The Coast Path approaches the earthwork, before turning away E towards Porth Melgan. The fortifications of Clawdd-y-Milwyr consisted of a double rampart and three lines of ditches drawn across the neck of the headland, comprising a strong stone rampart with two outer banks. It is thought that the dyke was built about AD100, although the defences may not all be of the same age. The main wall was a formidable structure of dry-built stone and appears to have been originally about 15ft/4.5m high and about 12ft/3.6m thick at its base. It was probably the first part of the defences to be built. The other two walls are, like the main wall, defended by a ditch on the outer side, and these were probably of the second period of construction. The entrance was a causeway thrown across the ditches and a simple passage, 7ft/2.1m wide, through each wall.

Within the promontory fort itself there are about six or eight stone circles and rock shelters, remains of huts inhabited by the Iron Age people, forming a compact settlement on an otherwise almost barren rocky headland. Finds from excavations here suggest a mixed economy in which stock-breeding played an important part: they are displayed in Tenby Museum.

Although the headland is named after the saint who established Christianity throughout Wales in the 6c, the place was known to the Greeks before him: Greek navigators supplied the geographer Ptolemy with information which he used when mapping the western

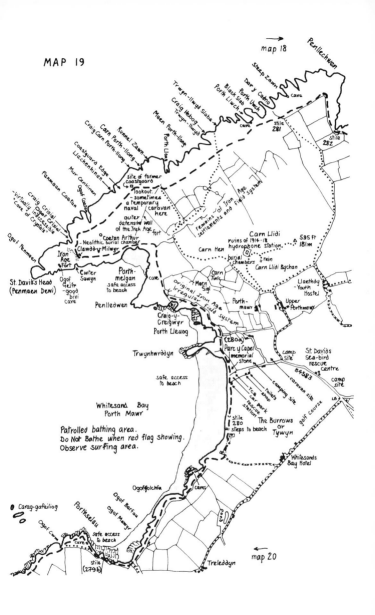

MAP 19

map 18

Penllechwen

Steep Zawn

Dan y Cadno

Trwyn-llwyd Slabs

Porth Lleuog

Black Slab

Porth Uwch

Porth Llwch

Trwyn-llwyd

Craig Hebog

Maen Porth-llong

Trwyn-llwyd

Craig Carn Porth-llong

Rumel Zawn

Carn Porth-llong

Maen Porth Llwm

Craig Carn Porth-llong

Coastguard Edge

Liechenhinen

Penmaen Coetan

Mur Cenhinen

Ogof Coetan

Craig Crisial

"Cave or Crystals"

-Virtually inaccessible

Ogof Penmaen

St. David's Head
(Penmaen Dewi)

Iron Age
fort

Ogof Geifr
- good
bivi
cave

Ewter
Sawyn

Coetan Arthur
-Neolithic burial chamber
Clawdd-y Milwyr

outer
defensive wall
of the Iron Age
fort

Lookout:
-sometimes
a temporary
naval caravan
here

site of former
coastguard

remains of Iron Age
settlements and field system

Carn Llidi

595 ft
181m

ruins of 1914-18
hydrophone station

Carn Hen

burial
chambers

cain

Carn Llidi Bychan

Carn
Twlc

Llaethdy
-Youth
Hostel

Upper
Porthmawr

Porth-
melgan

cave

safe access
to beach

Maen
Sigl

Porth-
mawr

original Iron Age
irregular field system

Penlledwen

Craig-y-
Creigwyr

Porth Lleuog

(280a)

Parc y Capel
memorial
stone

Trwynhwrddyn

St. David's
Sea-bird
rescue
centre

camp
site

B4583

caravan site

camp
site

safe access
to beach

Toll
Car park
rescue
station

camping site

golf course

Whitesand Bay
Porth Mawr

Patrolled bathing area.
Do Not Bathe when red flag showing.
Observe surfing area.

stile
280
steps to beach

The Burrows
or
Tywyn

Whitesands
Bay Hotel

Ogof Golchfa

caves

Ogof Barfau

Ogof Mawr

Careg-gafailiog

Porthselau

Ogof Cam

cave

safe access
to beach

stile
(279 b)

Treleddyn

map 20

stile
281

stile
282

shores of the (then known) world. He called the place the *Octopitarum Promontarium*, and it had for the Greeks as evocative a meaning as the Gates of Hercules that opened from the Mediterranean into the empty and shoreless waters on the edge of the world. The promontory has a close kinship with those other westward-pointing fingers of Europe – Land's End in Cornwall, Finistère in Brittany, and the similarly named Finisterre in Spanish Galicia. To the ancient world they all belonged to the same shore. Etruscans, Carthaginians and Romans had sailed into these unknown waters: each had named the coastlines they touched upon or navigated by in their days of ocean-going commerce and exploration – Belerion for Land's End; Thule for some northerly place, perhaps Norway or Iceland (although the Romans thought it applied to Shetland); and other names such as Erin, Albion and Liguria.

The powers of the Western Mediterranean jealously kept secret what lay out in the Atlantic until about AD200 when the Greeks managed to run the gauntlet and discover the islands off the NW coast of Europe. The translation of *Octopitarum* as the eight reefs and islets called the 'Eight Perils' is a convenient reference to the Bishop Rock (North Bishop) and its seven attendant Clerks that ride the waves beyond Ramsey Island and St David's Head, and the title may well be justified. However, early sailors ruled their navigation by the eight points of the compass, derived from the stars and the extreme points of the sun's movements from its rising and setting at winter and summer solstice. The eight points were taken to lie around the rim of the world: Ptolemy's informant may have meant that the promontory marked the edge beyond which men dared not travel.

The *Bishops and Clerks*, or the Eight Perils, were described by George Owen in 1603 in his study of Pembrokeshire as follows: 'A seaboord this Iland Ramsey rangeth in order the Bushop and his Clearkes being seven in number, all ways seen at lowe water who are not without some small choiristers who shewe not themselves but at spryng tydes and calm seas. They preach deadly doctrine to their winter audience, such poor seafaring men as are forcyd thether by tempest: onlie in one thing they are to be commended, they keepe residence better than the rest of the canons of that see are wont to do.'

The archipelago runs for nearly 4ml/6.4km from N to S, from the North Bishop (Carreg Esgob) 3ml/4.8km due W of St David's Head, to the South Bishop which is 5.5ml/8.8km SW of St David's Head, with the Clerks lying in between. The North Bishop has claimed (recorded) two ships – in 1854 the Crimea transport steamship *Morna* struck the rock and sank with the loss of twenty lives, and in 1910 the Houlder Line's 12,000 ton liner *Langton Grange* ended its days.

The South Bishop carries a lighthouse called Emscar, a corruption of its Scandinavian name. The foundation stone for the white round tower, 35ft/11m high, was laid on Queen Victoria's Coronation Day in 1838. The light, some 140ft/44m above the sea, was first lit on 14 February 1839. It is visible over a range of 24 nautical miles and flashes every 5 seconds. The fog signal gives three blasts of 5 seconds' duration every 45 seconds, and has a range of more than 5 nautical miles. The station was manned until 1983 but it is now automatic, being remotely controlled and monitored from St Ann's Head lighthouse.

The lighthouse was built in the path of migrating birds and the brilliance of its light often drew them on to its rays only to dash themselves against the lantern: thousands of birds were killed in this way. In order to save the birds from slaughter Trinity House, with the RSPB, erected special bird perches on the lantern for use during the migrating season, reducing the mortality rate considerably.

The lighthouse forms one of two landward points of a triangle, the other being Skokholm to the SE, and the apex being The Smalls some 14 nautical miles out into St George's Channel. These three lights are intervisible.

Back on the mainland, 0.25ml/400m E of the Clawdd-y-Milwyr, a strong but ruined wall is drawn obliquely across the promontory, towards the direction of Porth Llong. This outer defensive wall of the Iron Age fort is cunningly aligned along an abrupt change of slope in the ground in order to give added defensive height. It has two huts towards its northern end, and in defining the immediate territory of the promontory fort settlement perhaps also provided an enclosure for stock. Beyond that again, on the slopes of the valley that runs down to Porth Melgan, are the ruined walls and banks of an *ancient field system*. It is likely to be of two periods, with the more obvious stone rows probably marking an attempt at more recent (though still quite old) enclosure. The older fields are smaller, mostly on the S side of the valley, on the slopes of Carn Llidi, and not too easy to identify in the bracken.

The interest of the field-system complex as a whole lies in the picture that it presents of an Iron Age community with its related territory, where the outlying fields have been incorporated into cultivation patterns of later centuries. One cannot help but note that the 'modern' stone-walled fields immediately to the S of the ancient fields on Carn Hen and Carn Twlc retain the irregular 'early' pattern (or they may well be original), in contrast to the large straight-sided enclosures that today are characteristic of the remainder of the St David's Peninsula.

The stream which drains the moor and the shallow valley of the Iron Age field system runs down to Porth Melgan, a small, sandy and very attractive unspoilt cove, well worth the walk from Whitesand Bay to avoid the crowds. There is safe and easy access to the beach, which provides good swimming, but be careful of currents.

The bay and the shallow valley that feeds it have been eroded in slates of Lower Ordovician age. At the head of the bay there is a fine exposure of glacial deposits left behind during the last glaciation.

Carn Llidi, at a height of 595ft/191m above sea level, is one of the most impressive viewpoints on the coast. The top commands an excellent view of the storm-swept peninsula and of the splendid rocky coast: from it there is a good view of Ramsey Island and beyond it the South Bishop lighthouse. In exceptionally clear weather the hills of Wicklow, 85ml/136km away in Ireland, are visible across the water.

The hill consists of hard Ordovician igneous rock (gabbro) with Ordovician shales forming the lower slopes. The small peninsula of Trwynhwrddyn, between Porth Lleuog and Porth Mawr, at the foot of the slope, marks the line of a fault which runs out to sea between the shales and the Cambrian flagstones beyond. Veins of quartz associated with this fault impart to the rocks of this headland a greater resistance to marine erosion than that of the adjacent shales.

The tracks leading up Carn Llidi were constructed during World War I. Remains of brick and concrete buildings and foundations are old military installations. A hydrophone was built halfway up the hill and detected enemy submarines by the use of special microphones attached to cables running down the hillside and into the sea off Porth Melgan. The use of this equipment is said to have led to the destruction of fifteen German U-boats. In World War II the site was extended and became a radar station, with scanners perched on Carn Llidi. Fortunately they have all been demolished, and only the bases and paths remain, hidden in the dense gorse.

Whitesand Bay or Porth Mawr – Great Bay – is strictly speaking the bay between the headlands of St David's Head and Pencarnan, and the sands themselves are called Traeth Mawr, the Great Beach. It is a long, flat stretch of firm sand, backed by pebbles, the finest beach we have so far seen on this walk, with the possible exception of Newport Sands and Traeth Llyfn.

The bay faces W and onshore winds send white-capped Atlantic rollers thundering on to the sands, creating one of the best surfing beaches in Wales. Surfing is good all the year round, but it is at its best during spring and autumn. Bathing is safe S of the access road, but dangerous elsewhere because of strong currents: bathe only to the L of the lifeguard flag, and use surf canoes and Malibu boards to the R of the flag. In the summer months (i.e. July-September) lifeguards patrol the beach daily and they mark out the surfing area. Do not bathe when a red flag is flying. Bathing can be dangerous in surf and at low water, so have regard to all warning notices.

In summer the beach is crowded, but there is usually plenty of room at both ends where there are low cliffs and rocks. At low water you can walk the sands all the way to Porthselau, but apart from the access at the N end there is only one escape route, up the steps below the Whitesands Bay Hotel on to the Coast Path.

Whitesand Bay contains traces of a prehistoric forest: the antlers of a red deer and the jawbone of a brown bear which inhabited the forest have been found in the sand. Very low spring tides reveal a turf-like material, the remains of ancient tree trunks.

Inland there is an undulating study tract of land called The Burrows or Tywyn, which makes an ideal setting for a golf course. There is said to be a Roman settlement beneath the dunes called Menapia or Minervia, though this is probably legendary as no evidence has been found, although two Roman roads – the Via Julia and Fleming's Way – are supposed to have terminated here, and a settlement of some sort would be expected to mark the spot. A Bronze Age track from Salisbury Plain and Stonehenge, via the Prescelly Hills, also ended here, used by people who sailed by boat to the Wicklow Hills of Ireland for copper and, later, gold.

In the turf behind the dunes is the site of a chapel dedicated to St Patrick, who is said to have sailed from here to Ireland in the late 4c or early 5c. A rather inexpertly carved stone, partly covered with lichen, marks the site of St Patrick's Chapel (Parc y Capel) and says: 'Underneath lies a chapel dedicated to St Patrick. Built 6th–10th century. Excavated 1924.' A miraculous stone is said to have stood on this site, which St Patrick mounted to see Ireland. The outlines of the chapel, which was built around this stone, can now hardly be seen: they show that it was a very small building – only 30ft/9m long by 13ft/3.9m wide. It was used by sailors and Irish pilgrims to bring offerings and give thanks for a safe voyage. The chapel is now wholly destroyed, and the stone slab is all that is visible.

Whitesand Bay (Porth Mawr) to Porthstinian (St Justinian's) 2.2ml/ 3.5km

At the far end of Traeth Mawr the sands are linked at low water with the sandy cove of Porthselau, or Porthslee or Porthseli as it is sometimes spelt. Just offshore the paddle-tug *Guiding Star* went aground in 1882 and was wrecked: its remains can be seen at low water. Just inland of Porthselau is the farm of Treleddyn, where Thomas Williams lived. He was a retired sailor and was taking a walk that fateful February morning in 1797 when he saw a squadron of men-o'-war off the North Bishop. Although they were flying British colours, this did not deceive him: he gave the alarm, and the story goes that he kept the ships in sight all the way round to

Strumble Head – a considerable walk, especially for an old man. His wife was no less energetic, and won acclaim a few years earlier for rescuing the crew of a Swedish vessel off one of the Clerks. She put out in a boat alone from Porthselau, and having brought them safely ashore lodged them at her farm until they recovered.

The Pencarnan headland juts out to the W of Porthselau and where the Coast Path turns a corner Point St John guards the entrance to Ramsey Sound proper. This cliff and nearby Pencarnan Slabs provide some interesting rock climbs. It is a very easy path to Porthstinian and St Justinian's.

The little harbour of *Porthstinian* is generally referred to locally as St Justinian's, after the saint and his little chapel on the hilltop. St Justinian was a Breton hermit and martyr, who tradition says was the confessor of St David. Critical of the lax ways of his followers in St David's monastery he withdrew to Ramsey Island to devote himself to the service of God. But he was too strict a disciplinarian and eventually his followers rebelled and murdered him by cutting off his head. The story has it that Justinian picked up his head and walked over the sea to the mainland, where he was buried. A chapel was erected near the spot where he came ashore, and it became a place of pilgrimage. The chapel was rebuilt by Bishop Vaughan in the early 16c and the present ruins are the remains of his building. Bells from the chapel, stolen by Puritans, were lost in a wreck in Ramsey Sound, and they now chime only during great gales. The hermit saint now rests with St David in St David's Cathedral.

The harbour has one of the finest situated lifeboat stations in the kingdom. The home of the St David's lifeboat, the station, house and slipway, were erected in 1911–12 for £3000. The first lifeboat stationed here was the *Augusta* in 1869. The present boat, the *Joseph Soar*, was named at its launching in 1964 by Princess Marina after the organist at St David's Cathedral, who was also honorary secretary of the lifeboat station for 37 years. The lifeboats here have a great record of service, for the station is the only one for a long way on a very dangerous coast.

The harbour is intensively used, and all the boats have to be moored offshore in a very exposed situation. Four passenger boats are based here, mainly for supplying Ramsey Island and carrying day-trippers round the island.

MAP 20

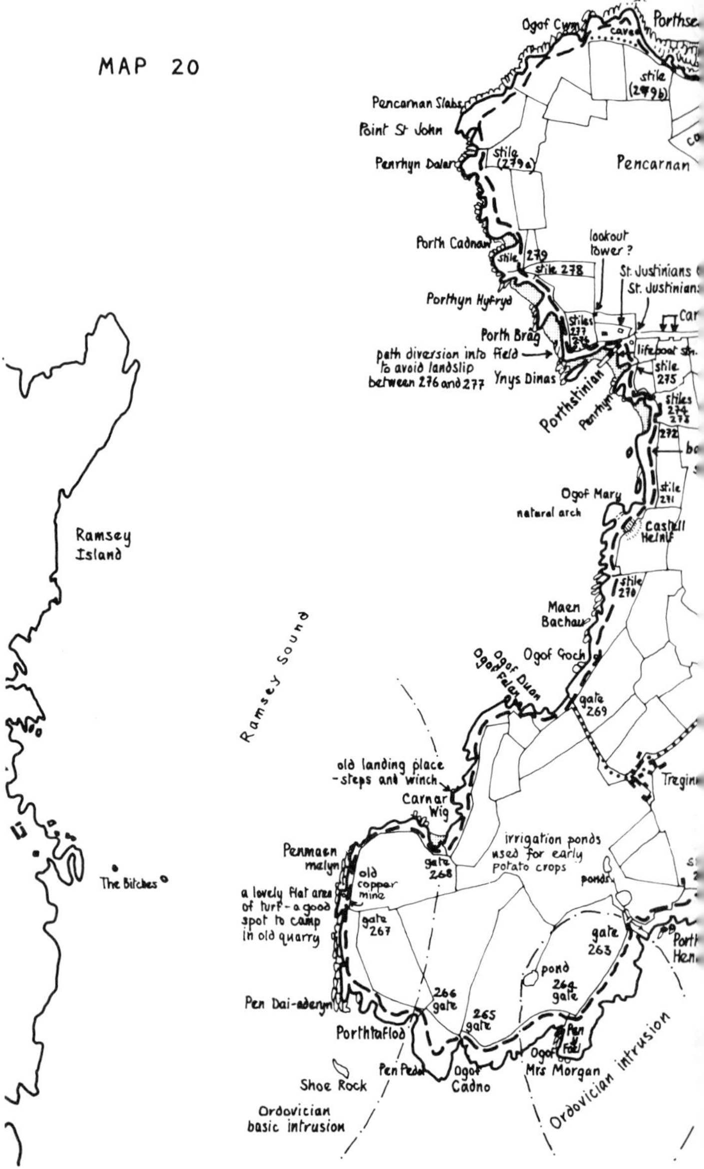

Ogof Cwm
caves
Porthse—
stile
(279b)

Pencarnan Slab
Point St John
Penrhyn Dalar
stile
(279a)
Pencarnan

Porth Cadnaw
stile 279
stile 278
lookout tower?
St Justinians
St Justinians

Porthyn Hyfryd
Porth Brâg
path diversion into field
to avoid landslip
between 276 and 277
Ynys Dinas
stiles
277
276
lifeboat stn.
stile 275
stiles
274
273
272
Car
Porthstinian
Penrhyn
stile
271

Ogof Mary
natural arch
Castell
Heinif
stile
270

Maen
Bachau
Ogof Goch
Ogof Dian
Ogof Faen
gate 269
Tregin

Ramsey
Island

Ramsey Sound

old landing place
– steps and winch
Carnar
Wig
irrigation ponds
used for early
potato crops
pond
Tregin

Penmaen
melyn
old copper mine
gate 268
gate 263
Porth
Hen

a lovely flat area
of turf – a good
spot to camp
in old quarry
gate 267
pond
264
gate

The Bitches

Pen Dai-adeyn
gate 266
gate 265
Porthtaflod
pond
Pen
roc
Ogof
Cadno
Mrs Morgan
Ordovician intrusion

Shoe Rock
Pen Pedn
Pen
roc

Ordovician
basic intrusion

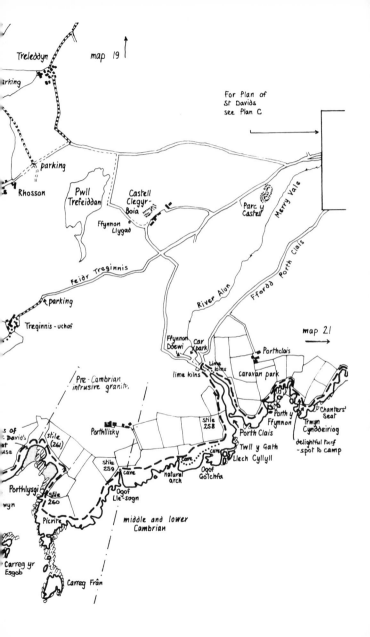

Porthstinian is a rocky cove and although it has a beach it is not good for bathing. There is a car park at the end of the approach road, but it is inadequate to cope with the traffic in summer.

The NT owns or protects several miles of the coastline and nearly 2000 acres/809ha of farm and common land between Carn Llidi and Porth Clais. Most of the land came into the Trust's control as a result of an appeal in 1939 with substantial help from the Pilgrim Trust, but other land was bought in the 1970s with Enterprise Neptune funds, or was given.

Lying just offshore, across the notorious Ramsey Sound, is the rocky Ramsey Island, which is described in the next chapter. The Coast Path walk continues in Chapter 7.

6   Ramsey Island

Ramsey Island, or Ynys Dewi – St David's Island – is guarded by sheer cliffs and treacherous seas. Nearly 2ml/3.2km long, and about 600 acres/243ha in extent, it is given shapeliness by two hills which rise no higher than 445ft/135m. Geologically this small island consists largely of Ordovician rocks: the southern half has extensive areas of intrusive igneous rocks, while much of the northern part consists of sedimentary rocks. The result is that the southern half is poorly soiled while the northern half is more fertile. At the N end some of the rocks are rich in fossils, particularly trilobites and brachiopods. The island forms a detached fragment of the late Tertiary marine platform, with hill-tops of igneous rocks which originally formed islands.

The island was a landmark for shipping and before the days of lighthouses the twin hills must have been the first glimpse of Wales for sailing craft coming E from Ireland or along the ancient trade routes from the Mediterranean. It is not surprising to find that two chapels or cells were built on the island, and a monastery founded here by St Devynog, traditionally in the 2c. It was here that St David and St Patrick are said to have met. Stone coffins have been dug up on its site. One of the cells was the home of the Breton hermit Justinian in 500.

It is probable that the island was formerly connected to the mainland, and it is said that, being troubled by many visitors wishing to do him honour, St Justinian took an axe and cut away at the rocks as he retreated towards his sanctuary. The axe became blunter with each blow so that The Bitches and Whelps remain as evidence of his failure to complete the job properly. The last cut of all is still known as The Axe. The Bitches and Whelps is a series of submerged or tidal rocks sticking up to trap the unwary, through which the tide runs at great violence at high water. The lifeboat *Gem* was wrecked here in October 1910. The great rock closest to the island, the bastion of the bridge known as the Great Bitch, is split apart, and through this axe-cut and a natural arch pours the N-going rising tide.

Although quite rocky the island was once a most productive farm, exporting corn, butter, cheese, sheep and wool to the mainland, and it could, like Caldey, support a considerable community. The island was farmed until 1968, then run as a nature reserve under an agreement with the RSPB until 1980. It is now farmed again.

The island abounds in sea birds, seals and rabbits – the latter, which are generally an intolerable pest, have no natural predators on the island. More than 30 species of bird breed on the island. It is a great place for choughs, peregrine falcons, ravens and buzzards. The W coast has splendid cliffs falling sheer into the sea and these are the breeding places in summer for guillemot, razorbill, kittiwake, fulmar petrels and various gulls. The coast has many caves and inlets, and on their beaches in September and October Atlantic grey seals come to drop their calves and breed.

Cliff climbing is not allowed, except by permit, and is best on the magnificent W coast. Otherwise there is no access to any beaches at any time.

The island is not generally open to the public, and in any case its splendours are best seen from the sea – by taking a boat on the 'Round Ramsey' trip if the weather is calm.

Boat trips around Ramsey
These are operated from St Justinian's Lifeboat Station by Mr F John (tel. St David's 438) on MV *Sea Vixen* which has approximately 30 seats. Departures are dependent on demand early in the season, and are at regular intervals at the height of the season. They depart from 1030 onwards. The time taken is 1½ hours. No individual advance bookings are taken, though special arrangements may be made for large parties. A minimum of ten persons is required for a trip.

   Ramsey landing trips: These may take place at the discretion of the owner from April until October, daily except for weekends, and weather permitting. Enquire at Porthstinian or PNPA Information Centres.

7   **Porthstinian to St Non's** (Maps 20, 21)   5.75ml/9.25km

This section of Coast Path takes you right round the southernmost tip of the St David's Peninsula, from Ramsey Sound round the corner to the N side of St Bride's Bay. The condition of the Path is everywhere good, for the most part on turf with heather, gorse and bracken around but not obstructing the route. It is suitable walking for the whole family and quite easy going. Apart from the road access points at Porthstinian and St Non's the only other access point by road is at Porth Clais, and there is only one right of way by foot, via the farms of Treginnis.

   This is a rocky coast with low but sheer cliffs, and indented with small bays. Ordovician and Pre-Cambrian intrusions alternate between the Cambrian shales, creating a great variety of rock-types and providing scenery of the highest quality, with offshore islands adding variety and interest. There are splendid views of Ramsey Island and across St Bride's Bay.

Porthstinian to Porthylsgi 3ml/4.8km
Just S of Porthstinian the Path passes alongside the double-banked

ramparts of Castell Heinif Iron Age fort, and you are soon on the extreme W tip of the peninsula at Penmaenmelyn, directly opposite Ramsey Island at the narrowest part of the Sound. It is only 0.5ml/ 0.8km across, but notorious waters lie between, and you can see and hear them swirling through The Bitches at the change of the tides. There are the remains of an old copper mine on the headland – just an old stone wall around a hole in the ground, into which the sea makes an entry at high tide: the mine was probably never worked.

Porthlysgi is named after Lysgi, Leschi or Lisgi, an Irish chief who landed here (although some say it was in Porth Clais) with his men and slew the local chieftain Boia, another Irish chief. Boia had his encampment on Castell Clegyr Boia, a small igneous monadnock beside the road to the W of St David's. The hillock had previously been occupied by a small group of Neolithic people, the remains of whose simple huts were found beneath Boia's settlement. Stone axes and round-bottomed bowls were found, indicating parallel cultures in Ireland and Cornwall, as well as some pottery and Neolithic flints in the hut foundations, when the site was excavated in 1943.

Boia's camp is Dark Age by tradition, but extensive excavations have failed to yield corroborative evidence of this period. The settlement was occupied by Boia in St David's time: Boia gave David some difficulty as he opposed his efforts to establish a monastery in the Merry Vale nearby – David built Parc y Castell (or Castell Penlan) on the edge of the valley, between Boia's stronghold and the monastery, in order to protect his church from the aggressive Boia – but he later became a convert and supported the church. Boia's fort is built in the earlier Iron Age tradition. Its stone-faced ramparts enclose the top of the hill, linking one crag with the next; its gate, looking down the slope to the W, was found to have flanking guard-recesses on its inner side.

St David's early defence of Parc y Castell later became the foundation of a ring motte and bailey, an early castle with two baileys which was probably built in 1115 by the first Norman bishop of the diocese.

Immediately to the W of Castell Clegyr Boia is **Ffynnon Llygad** –

the Eye Well – which may have been the source of water for the stronghold. Its waters are said to ebb and flow with the tide, which is a full mile/1.6km away and 200ft/60m below.

Porthlysgi is sheltered by cliffs and the rocky offshore islets of Carreg yr Esgob – The Bishop's Rock. The small shingle beach offers safe bathing in calm conditions, but it is completely covered at high tide. It is uncrowded, no doubt because the nearest car park and access point is at Porth Clais, 1.5ml/2.4km away by the Coast Path. On the N side of the bay are the foundations of the first St David's lifeboat house, built for the *Augusta* (1869–85).

Porthlysgi to Porth Clais 1.5ml/2.4km
In the vicinity of Porthlysgi there is supposed to be a meteorite, but more modern thinking is that it is 'Horneblende Picrite', an erratic boulder carried here during the Ice Age from N Wales. There is some doubt as to where it is situated: one guide says that it is at the head of the bay, protected from mutilation by a strong iron cage; another source says that it is on the E slope of the rock Carreg Fran; yet the 1:10,000 scale OS map shows an area marked 'Picrite' on the peninsula. The author has searched for the elusive boulder without success.

Off the E horn of Porthlysgi Bay is chain of islets, the largest and most distant being Carreg Fran – Crow Rock. The tide off the Fran has to be regarded carefully by small-boat sailors.

Porth Clais is a delightful long and narrow inlet, a valley deepened by glacial meltwaters and then drowned by rising sea level. The valley is now occupied by the diminutive River Alun, which flows past St David's Cathedral down the Merry Vale to the sea. Porth Clais has always been the port for St David's, although on this exposed coast any one of five bays would have been used to get access inland – Whitesand, Porthstinian, Porth Clais, Caerfai or Caer Bwdy – but none was suitable for the larger sailing vessels and steam vessels of the last 200 years.

In St David's time there must have been a considerable traffic of missionaries and saints through this narrow creek, setting out to and returning from Ireland, Cornwall, Brittany, N Wales and the Isle of Man.

St David was baptised in a spring just inland. Ffynnon Dewi – St David's Well – is said to have sprung up miraculously for the baptism of the saint by Elvis, Bishop of Munster. The well is on the site of the ancient Capel-y-Pistyll, which was demolished to make way for the town gasworks. The gasworks has now been demolished and is an enclosed car park for the visitors to Porth Clais. The spring is lost in the undergrowth at the far end of the car park.

The diminutive harbour was built in the 12c or 13c and forms a sheltered anchorage. The small breakwater, now in a sad state of disrepair, may date from Norman times, but it was extensively repaired in 1722. Because the narrow creek dries to a trickle at low tide, ships were always beached and unloaded into horse-drawn carts. There are records of coal imports here before 1400, and much cargo was carried in and out during Tudor and Stuart times: timber came from Ireland, and there were frequent exports of wheat, barley, corn and rye to Bristol and Barnstaple. Later there were imports of limestone and culm to supply the four lime-kilns, built in two double banks on the quayside: the kilns and the quays were renovated in 1975. In the present century, and up to the 1950s, coal was imported to supply the town gasworks.

There is a slipway at the head of the creek for the launching of boats, but the harbour and the adjacent coastline are not suitable for dinghy sailing, although good and popular for sub-aqua diving.

Porth Clais to St Non's 1.25ml/2km
From Porth Clais eastwards the southern flanks of the St David's anticline are formed by the steeply inclined and well-bedded purple sandstones of the Lower Cambrian series. These are easily seen on the Porth Clais headland, where the cliffs provide good rock climbing.

The small headland of Trwyn Cynddeiriog is also known as Mad Point, from the fury of the sea at its foot in a SW gale. Chanter's Seat, a ledge on the headland, commands a fine view of the inlet of *St Non's Bay*. St Non, Nun, or Nonnita, was the mother of St David and traditionally his father was Sant, a chieftain in Ceredigion (Carmarthenshire). St Non moved to a cottage on the site of the present chapel where St David was born in about 462. Shortly after the birth St Non went to Brittany. Dirinon, in Finistère, of which she is patron saint, has a chapel and well dedicated to St Non. The chapel there contains her tomb, which is one of the historic monuments of Brittany. In Wales St Non is venerated on 2 March, the day after St David's Day.

Tradition has it that St David was born on the site of *St Non's Chapel* during a great storm. Only the lower parts of the chapel walls survive, but it appears that the single-roomed structure measured only 20ft × 40ft/6m × 12m. It is not orientated in the usual Christian fashion, but is placed N–S. The earliest mention of a chapel here is a document of 1355. Of the chapels subordinate to the cathedral of St David's, St Non's was the principal – it was the most important of the seashore chapels in the area, and the offerings provided a steady income to Dean and Chapter. St Non's Chapel passed out of religious use at the Reformation when pilgrims ceased coming to St David's. It was converted into a dwelling-house, and later became a leek garden. Now in the guardianship of the Secretary of State for Wales, the monument is open at all reasonable hours without charge. Resting against the wall in the SE corner of the chapel is a rough stone marked with a plain, incised, linear, Latin Ring Cross, dating from 7c–9c. Although it was at one time built into a wall of the chapel there is no certainty that it had any direct connection with it, but it is the same type as one found at St Elvis, a few miles away, which is now in a porch of the parish church at Solva.

In the field around the chapel are five erect stones that are possibly part of a Bronze Age stone circle.

About 40yd/36m to the NE of the chapel, in the grounds of the modern retreat, beside the path, is the *Holy Well of St Non* which tradition says sprang up during a thunderstorm on the night St David was born. It was regarded as one of the most sacred and famous wells in Wales, and was visited by many pilgrims to St David's. The water was considered to have curing properties for eye diseases, and is said to rise and fall with the tide. Its popularity as a wishing well continued into the 19c when the present barrel

Artists at St Non's

vaulting, which perhaps replaced the ruins of a more extensive medieval structure, was erected. The well enclosure and the steps to it were restored in 1951 by the Passionist Fathers, who also built in the same year the Shrine to Our Blessed Lady adjacent to the well.

The Chapel of Our Lady and St Non was built at the expense of Cecil Hubert Morgan Griffiths, a Carmarthen solicitor and builder of the retreat, the foundation stone being laid on 1 March 1934. The style is based on that of the old chapels that were to be seen around the coast of Pembrokeshire as early as 500. The stones were gathered from the ruins of the Priory of Whitwell, which stood S of the cathedral on the road leading to St Non's from St David's (opposite the St Non's Hotel). Many of the carved and incised stones were let into the altar of St Non's.

The window above the altar depicts St Non and is by the William Morris school. Other windows represent St David, St Winifred, St Bride and St Brynach.

St Non's Retreat was built in 1929, and ten years later was taken over by the Passionist Fathers. The congregation was founded some 250 years ago, and specialises in the preaching of missions and retreats. For many years St Non's was a training centre for those studying to enter the Roman Catholic church, but it has more recently been adapted to serve as a centre for spiritual renewal for people from all walks of life.

St Non's Bay is the nearest point of the coast to the city of St David's, and as it has such close associations with the saint, it is here that we visit his cathedral city.

8   St David's (Tyddewi) (Plan C)

St David's ranks as a city through its possession of a cathedral, otherwise it would be described as a village, and a somewhat straggling one at that. It stands about 1ml/1.6km from the sea, on a wide, almost treeless and windswept plateau, overlooking the small **River Alun**, and doubtless owes its origin to the maritime pilgrim

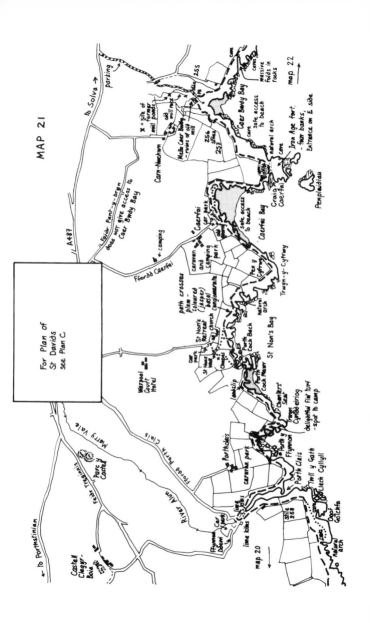

MAP 21

For Plan of
St Davids
See Plan C

← to Portmstinian

to Solva →

A487

parking

X = site of former mill pools

old mill race

255

253

256 stile

255

Melin Caer Bwdy – ruins of old mill

Carn Hamchan

Point-y-brynn does not give access to Caer Bwdy Bay

Caer Bwdy Bay

cave

cave

cave

map 22 →

massive folds in rocks

Safe access to beach

natural arch

cave

Iron Age fort – four banks. Entrance on E side

Penplaidiau

Castell Clegyr-Boia

Ffynnon Dewi

Merry Vale

Parc Castell

lime kilns

Ffordd Pound Clais

Warpool Court Hotel

path crosses plan – coloured (jasper) beds

St Non's Retreat

car park

St Non's Well

Chapel

Church

Porth Clais

Caerfai

camping

Fforld Caerfai

Caravan and Camping park

Porth y Cytnwy

Trwyn-y-Cytnwy

Craig Caerfai

Caerfai Bay

Safe access to beach

St Non's Bay

natural arch

Porth Coch Bach

handslip

Porth Coch Mawr

Chambers Seat

Trwyn Cynlo Ciriog

delightful fine turf – spot to camp

Porthclais

Caravan park

River Alum

Merry Vale

Ffordd Pen Clais

Porth y Ffyunnon

Twll y Garth

lime kilns

stile 258

Ogof Golchfa

Cogof Golchfa

map 20 ↓

Llech Cytlul

to natural arch

route from Ireland to Santiago de Compostella in Spain by way of Wales, Cornwall and Brittany. People throughout the Middle Ages, kings and commoners alike, streamed down the roads to St David's in pious pilgrimage. At various points around the peninsula on its seaward approaches chapels stood strategically at landing places where they could receive the thank-offerings of pilgrims who had arrived safely.

The Welsh name, Tyddewi – David's house – reflects its earliest origins as a semi-monastic religious settlement founded by the missionary saint. His church survived the Roman retreat and the Saxon and Viking raids, but it was a threat to the Normans, who set about reorganising the Celtic communities by imposing their own pattern of cathedral and diocese brought over from France.

The points of interest are of course the cathedral and the Bishop's Palace, and you make your way to these places of pilgrimage as you come up from St Non's. You enter the town by Goat Street, then come to Cross Square, the centre of the town. The ancient cross, its head-circle renewed, stands in the centre, forming a traffic island. Eastwards runs the main road A487, High Street, where the City Hall, having a reading room and a library, also houses an information centre of the PNPA, containing a lot of local material.

From Cross Square a street leads westwards, downhill. It is called The Pebbles, because originally it was surfaced with pebbles: today it is surfaced with tarmacadam. It would be far more attractive if the cars were removed, the street pedestrianised, and the pebbles replaced. You might pass through 'Britain's smallest city' and see no sign of the cathedral, or even the top of its tower, but as you pass down The Pebbles the big tower suddenly comes into view, with its pinnacles, surprisingly, near eye level.

You pass under the partly rebuilt 13c gateway called Porth-y-twr (Tower Gate) – the landward gate to the Cathedral Close for travellers arriving by road from the E. This gatehouse is the last survivor of four in the precinct wall. The gateway has on its N side an octagonal bell-tower, the relic of a structure built some 50 years earlier, and originally a detached campanile.

The Cathedral Close is an area of some 18 acres/7.2ha, still mostly surrounded by the Close Wall. The wall and its gatehouses

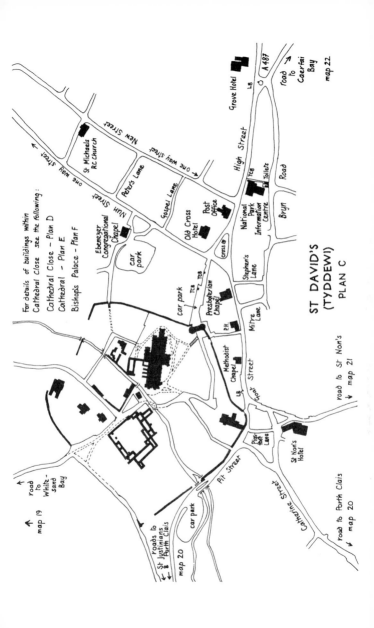

ST DAVID'S
(TYDDEWI)
PLAN C

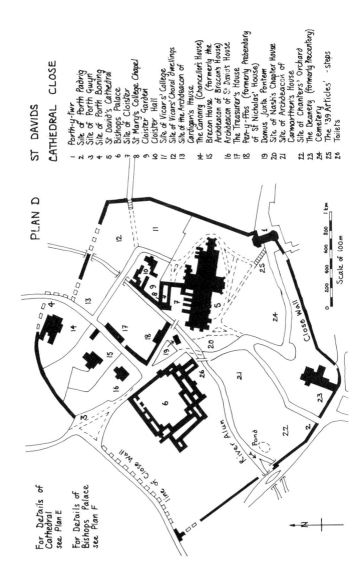

PLAN D ST DAVIDS
CATHEDRAL CLOSE

1 Porth-y-twr
2 Site of Porth Padrig
3 Site of Porth Gwyn
4 Site of Porth Boning
5 St David's Cathedral
6 Bishops Palace
7 Site of Cloister
8 St Mary's College Chapel
9 Cloister Garden
10 Cloister Hall
11 Site of Vicars' College
12 Site of Vicars' Choral dwellings
13 Site of the Archdeacon of Cardigan's House
14 The Canonry (Chancellors House)
15 Brecon House (Formerly the Archdeacon of Brecon's House)
16 Archdeacon of St David's House
17 The Treasurer's House
18 Pen-y-ffos (formerly Prebendary of St Nicholas' House)
19 Domus Juxta Pontem
20 Site of Nash's Chapter House
21 Site of Archdeacon of Carmarthen's House
22 Site of Chanters' Orchard
23 The Deanery (formerly Precentory)
24 Cemetery
25 The '39 Articles' - steps
26 Toilets

For Details of Cathedral see Plan E

For Details of Bishops Palace see Plan F

Line of Close Wall

River Alun

Pond

Close Wall

Scale of 100m

0 200 400 600 800 1 km

N

are attributed to Bishop Gower (1328–47). An enclosure was in existence at least as early as 1172. It was designed for the protection of the cathedral community and enclosed the Bishop's Palace and the canons' residences, as well as the cathedral church itself. The wall is visible at many points, but there is no access to the wall top.

The Cathedral Close is situated in the deep glacial meltwater valley carrying the River Alun (formerly known as Glyn Rhosyn) and the top of the cathedral tower is on the level of the plateau on which the town is built. The descent to the cathedral and the buildings within the close is by a flight of 39 steps, known as the 'Thirty-Nine Articles', and they bring you right to the S door of the cathedral.

The Revd Robert Francis Kilvert (1840–79, renowned for his diaries of 1870–9) arrived here in October 1871 (a good month to choose). 'And so we came to the end of the world where the Patron Saint of Wales sleeps by the western sea,' he wrote in his diary, with all the satisfaction of one who has travelled as far as is possible.

A brief history of St David's Cathedral (Eglwys Gadeiriol ty Ddewi) Little is known of St David, but certainly the idea of the saint has a powerful influence on men's minds. This great scholar and preacher is believed to have been born at nearby St Non's and, having spent some time as a pupil of St Paulinus and going on several preaching journeys, he returned here in about 550 to build his church and monastery. He died on 1 March 589.

St David's foundations have vanished. In 1081 William the Conqueror paid homage at the shrine of St David, but Viking raids became increasingly frequent in the 11c – in the first year of the reign of William Rufus (1088) the town was sacked by the Vikings and the church burnt. The Conqueror considered that the Celtic church needed to be thoroughly 'Normanised' and brought into the Province of Canterbury. This was not actually achieved until the death of Bishop Wilfred in 1115, when the Celtic monks were summoned to London and forced to elect Bernard, Chancellor of Queen Matilda, as their bishop. The cathedral was then organised on the lines of an English cathedral of non-monastic foundation with canons and chapter. David was canonised in 1120 by Pope

Calixtus II, and in 1123 the cathedral was rededicated to St Andrew and St David. It was to continue under Canterbury until the disestablishment of the Church in Wales in 1921.

The rebuilding of the cathedral was undertaken in 1180 and was not finally completed until 1522. It was begun during the episcopate of Bishop Peter de Leia (1176–98), the third Norman bishop: a large cruciform design of nave, nave aisles, transepts and a low tower. Giraldus Cambrensis gives a gossiping account of the see in 1188, in those times co-extensive with the original Principality of Dyfed. He himself was afterwards twice nominated to the bishopric, but failed to secure it (in spite of an historic struggle and three appeals to Rome), partly because of his connection with the Welsh royal line, and partly, no doubt, because he argued for the independence of the Church in Wales.

In 1220 the central tower collapsed, demolishing the choir and presbytery, although the Transitional Norman nave survived. In 1250 the choir, transepts, and presbytery were set up again, practically in the original design, although the wrecked presbytery was rebuilt in the Early English style. Massive rebuilding and modernisation took place in the first half of the 14c under Bishop Gower. Gower modernised the building completely: he heightened the aisle walls of the nave and chancel, enlarging the windows and inserting ones in the Decorative style. He vaulted Martyn's Lady Chapel, added two storeys above St Thomas Becket's Chapel for a chapter house and a treasury. He built the grand pulpitum and the S porch. He daringly added a second stage to the central tower (which was not completed until the third stage was erected in 1520 by Bishop Vaughan). Gower also rebuilt the Bishop's Palace: he was justifiably called the 'Wykeham of Wales'.

St David's, being a non-monastic foundation, suffered less than many cathedrals during the Reformation of 1538, but the holy relics disappeared, and Henry VIII ordered Edmund Tudor's tomb to be placed before the High Altar. In the 17c the interior was lime-washed and the cathedral suffered from neglect as well as from vandalism: the Cromwellians stripped lead from the roof and broke glass. In 1775 the Bishop's Palace was a romantic ruin.

John Nash commenced a restoration in 1793 by rebuilding Bishop de Leia's W front. In 1797 the cathedral roof was stripped of some of its lead so that the Yeomanry and Fencibles might have bullets to defend Pembrokeshire from the French who had landed at Llanwnda.

Parts of the church had become dilapidated and by the 1840s a thorough job of restoration was called for. In 1846 William Butterfield restored the nave aisle windows. Restoration continued in 1860 when Sir George Gilbert Scott was called in. He began in 1862 with the tower, then in a very dangerous state, and the reconstruction of its W arch. In 1870 Scott demolished Nash's W end of the nave, it being both unstable and 'incorrect' – he redesigned it, on what is thought to be its original design. Scott was also responsible for the timber vaulting in the N and S transepts and vestries. The choir and choir ceiling were restored, and the presbytery was restored and a new ceiling added.

John Oldrid Scott, younger son of Sir Gilbert, revaulted the Lady Chapel in 1902. William Douglas Caröe continued the restoration of the cathedral, followed by his son, Alban D R Caröe, and his grandson, Martin Caröe.

Tour of the Cathedral
St David's Cathedral is the largest, finest and most interesting church in Wales. Its core is a late 12c building, but alterations have given its exterior a style largely of the 14c. The total interior length is 298ft/90m, of which 130ft/40m are contained in the nave. The breadth of the nave and its side aisles is 68ft/20.7m. The transepts each measure 47ft × 33ft/14m × 13m, and the total length of the transepts and crossing is 131ft/40m. The the tower is 125ft/38m high.

The cathedral is open daily. An ascent of the tower may be made on application to the verger. A conducted tour of the cathedral takes place on Monday mornings in summer at 1100.

The restoration work of the late 19c has given the cathedral a somewhat harsh appearance, not enhanced by the dull, purple Caerfai sandstone. The lack of high-pitched roofs to the nave and choir – they are high-pitched over the transepts – induces a certain feeling of austerity, which, however, is in harmony with the bleak surroundings.

On entering the S door you plunge into de Leia's late Norman (Transitional) nave, and you are immediately struck by its contrast with the plain exterior. The 12c arcades, the 14c choir screen and the 16c oak ceiling combine in such a richness of decoration as to be overwhelming, and this is accentuated by the fact that the floor rises at an astonishing gradient – a rise of 3ft/1m from the W front to the High Altar.

Our tour through the cathedral follows the numbered sequence shown on the plan opposite.

The nave has six bays, with huge round arches on outward-leaning columns. The columns are alternately circular and octagonal, with detached shafts and traces of medieval painting, and the span between them is unusually wide for the height of the piers. These columns support another arcade, which is divided into a triforium with a simple pointed arcade and clerestory of single round-headed windows, an unusual combination. Typical Norman carving decorates the arches – chevron, zig-zag and lozenge.

An extraordinary ceiling of Irish oak was erected during the treasureship of Bishop Owen Pole (1472–1509), probably about 1500. A number of delicately fretted arches appear to carry the ceiling, but they are in fact pendants of it. Great decorative pendants hang down, tied back to the roof beams with elaborately carved struts, creating a very effective design.

Under the second arch (from the E) of the S arcade is the monument of Bishop John Morgan (1496–1505) with his recumbent effigy and sculptures round the base, including a vigorous panel representing the Resurrection at the foot. On the adjacent nave piers (2nd and 3rd from the E) are traces of ancient mural paintings.

The eastward view of the nave is terminated by a magnificent stone rood screen or pulpitum, an elaborate and beautiful work, one of the chief glories of the cathedral. It divides the nave from the choir under the crossing, and is of most unusual design, with niches arranged asymmetrically. On the N side of the opening are three dull, modern statues, while on the S side is the tomb of Bishop Gower, who built the pulpitum. In the Middle Ages a rood loft surmounted the screen.

The central passageway through the rood screen has unusual

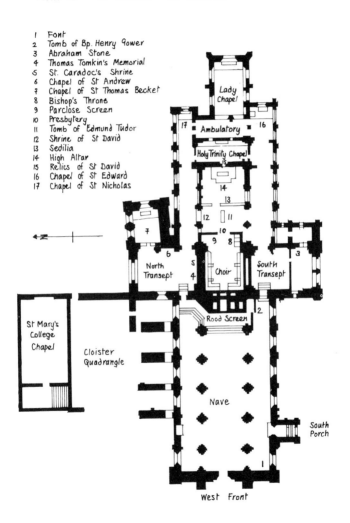

PLAN E   ST DAVIDS   CATHEDRAL

1   Font
2   Tomb of Bp. Henry Gower
3   Abraham Stone
4   Thomas Tomkin's Memorial
5   St. Caradoc's Shrine
6   Chapel of St Andrew
7   Chapel of St Thomas Becket
8   Bishop's Throne
9   Parclose Screen
10 Presbytery
11 Tomb of Edmund Tudor
12 Shrine of St David
13 Sedilia
14 High Altar
15 Relics of St David
16 Chapel of St Edward
17 Chapel of St Nicholas

Lady Chapel

17   Ambulatory   16

Holy Trinity Chapel
15

14

13

12   11

10

9   8

7

6

5
4

North Transept

Choir

South Transept

3

2

St Mary's College Chapel

Cloister Quadrangle

Rood Screen

Nave

South Porch

1

West Front

skeleton vaulting, and on its N side is a tomb with a lovely stone reredos with, on the vaulting above, the remains of some 14c paintings. The choir occupies the space under the tower, which rests on four massive arches. The circular-headed arch on the W is part of the original work of Bishop Peter de Leia, while the other three are pointed and date from the restoration after 1220.

A major programme of restoration was put in hand by Sir George Gilbert Scott in 1862–78; he afterwards regarded his rebuilding of the central tower as one of his greatest achievements. The tower ceiling is easily missed: a mirror on a table in the choir is used to illustrate the roof, which is painted with the names and coats of arms of some two dozen bishops associated with the building of the cathedral from the 12c onwards.

The transepts are entered from the nave aisles and both were largely reconstructed after the fall of the tower in 1220. The S transept was once the parish church, and is now partly screened off for the vestry. In the vestry is some spectacular 20c heraldic tiling recording the bishops, the work of Aida Lansdowne Miller and Basil Miller Williams, members of a local family who lived in Warpool Court. If there is no verger to show you into the vestry you can see more of their work in the Warpool Court Hotel.

In the N transept, at the back of the choir stalls, is the reputed shrine of St Caradoc, a monk from Llandaff who died in 1124. The two pierced quatrefoils in the base, like those in the shrine of St David, may have been intended for the insertion of a withered limb in hope of a cure, or for the reception of alms. Leading off the E side of the N transept is the vaulted chapel of St Thomas of Canterbury, built by Bishop Martyn. Used as a vestry until 1952 it has been restored as a memorial to Bishop Prosser, Bishop of St David's from 1927 until his death in 1950 and the third Archbishop of Wales between 1944 and 1949. The chapel contains a beautiful 13c double piscina on the R of the altar.

A room above the chapel of St Thomas is reached by a stair from the N aisle of the presbytery and was the original chapter house, but is now the cathedral library (shown, on application to the verger, but usually open to visitors on Thursdays, 1430–1630). Preserved in the library are some beautiful fragments of the original organ-case

(? by Grinling Gibbons), disastrously broken up in the course of the restorations. There are many interesting volumes and other antiquities, including original architects' drawings and scaled details of the fretted stonework and woodwork, and it is well worth a visit.

There is a dramatic contrast between the nave and the choir, heightened by the narrow passage through the deep rood screen. You leave behind the big, cool nave, with its mauve, purple and grey Cambrian sandstones, and enter the choir, with stone of a warmer colour, the warm glow of the oak stalls, traceried canopies and parapets, and a gaily painted timber roof, restored and copied by Scott from the medieval work.

The choir stalls, dating from about 1470, are famous for the carved misericords under the seats, and for the unique royal stall. The sovereign of England has been a canon of St David's since the Reformation, and is always its first prebend. The stall is in the SW corner of the choir, and is distinguished by painted and carved royal arms. The only times it has been occupied were when Queen Elizabeth II attended morning service on 7 August 1955 and the Maundy Service on 8 April 1982. The magnificent bishop's throne, nearly 30ft/9m high, dates from about 1500, and is one of the very few examples of this period left in Britain. It is an imposing structure, with three canopies: the bishop's seat is flanked by a seat on either side with a seat for a chaplain.

An open wooden parclose screen separates the choir from the presbytery, an unusual feature of the late Decorated period. The presbytery is composed of four simple Early English arcades, with chevron and other ornament, and lovely lancets. The lower row of lancets on the E formerly looked into the open space now occupied by Bishop Vaughan's Holy Trinity Chapel, and are blocked up, filled with glowing glass mosaics and dating from Scott's restoration. The jambs and arches of the lancets are more richly decorated than any others in the cathedral. The upper tier of four lancets was reconstructed by Scott in place of a poor (but genuine) Perpendicular window of Vaughan's. The richly painted roof, of 1461, was also restored by Scott.

In the centre of the presbytery is the large altar tomb of Edmund Tudor (d.1456), the Earl of Richmond and the father of Henry VII.

He was buried at the Grey Friars' church at Carmarthen, but at the Dissolution the remains were moved here on the orders of his grandson, Henry VIII. The tomb has a handsome brass, c1873, the original having disappeared in Cromwell's time. The placing of the tomb here may reflect not only the change in religious priorities brought about by the Reformation but also the political uncertainties of the age as felt by Henry VIII who set it here, before the High Altar and in front of the shrine of St David. Kilvert noted the dilapidated state of the tomb: '. . . the Dean and Chapter are hoping the Queen will restore it, so they have done nothing to it.' He stuck his umbrella through 'a huge rent . . . and stirred the kingly dust. It felt much like common earth.'

On the N side of the presbytery are the remains of the shrine of St David, a stone structure built in 1275. In the three arcades there were once panel paintings of Saints David, Patrick and Denis. In the back of the shrine, having access from the presbytery aisle, there were recesses for the receipt of offerings. The display of the saints' relics was one of the chief functions of the cathedral, and much of its prosperity depended upon the gifts brought by pilgrims. The shrine once had an ornamental wooden canopy, and a reliquary was placed on top of it, so that it could be seen by pilgrims processing round the presbytery aisle. Before then it had been placed either on or behind the High Altar.

The sanctuary is enclosed by a beautiful and rare oak sedilia dated between 1460–81, and the sanctuary floor is paved with some very old encaustic tiles. In the N wall of the sanctuary is the early 17c tomb of Treasurer Lloyd, one of the few of this date in the cathedral. His effigy has broken hands, broken R forearm and R foot, resting on couched lions.

In the S choir aisle, next to the recumbent effigy of Bishop Anselm le Gros (1230–48), is the tomb of Iorwerth, a Welshman appointed bishop from 1215–29, and then called Bishop Gervase, and next to him, further E, is the recumbent figure of a knight, assumed to be 'the Lord Rhys' or Rhys ap Gruffydd, the master of the south who died in 1196, the last true prince of S Wales. The

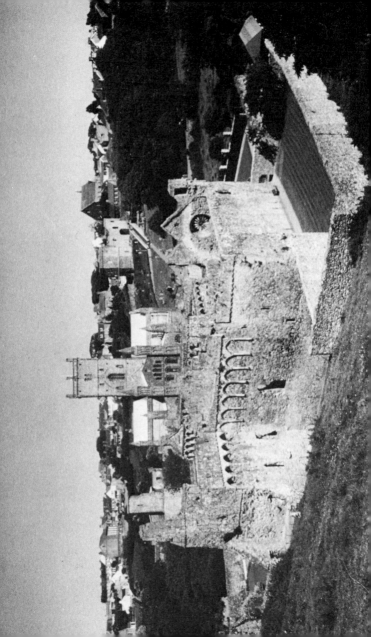

effigy next to this, still further E, has been suggested to be that of
Gerald de Barri (Giraldus Cambrensis), Archdeacon of Brecon,
who died in 1223.

In the N choir aisle is the tomb of Rhys Gryg (d.1234), fourth son
of Rhys ap Gruffydd. His effigy dates from the 14c and is similar to
his father's – both arms are broken, with his head supported on
pillars and his feet on a lion.

Adjoining the presbytery to the E and entered from the aisles is
Bishop Vaughan's Holy Trinity Chapel, a fine example of late
Perpendicular building, with splendid fan-vaulting tracery of the
Gloucester type in the roof. Originally this place was an open space
bounded by the presbytery on one side and the walks of the
ambulatory on the other three, a space left open to the sky for 200
years until Vaughan roofed it over.

An unexpected feature in the chapel is a recess immediately
behind the High Altar, with an opening that looks directly into the
sanctuary and presbytery. Scott found this recess walled up in 1866,
and when opened it revealed a quantity of bones, embedded in
mortar and probably hidden here at the time of the Reformation.
They are believed to be the remains of St David and his teacher St
Justinian. The bones are now enclosed in an oak casket placed in
the opening through which pilgrims used to view the reliquary
before the 1275 shrine was constructed.

The E wall of the Holy Trinity Chapel contains the altar and a
masterly amalgamation of medieval pieces. The altar is flanked by a
niche and a window on either side. The 14c altar reredos has a
central panel of the Crucifixion, flanked by Saints James, Andrew,
Peter and Paul, and is carved from Caerfai stone. On either side of
the Holy Trinity are two modern statues standing in 16c niches; on
the N is Bishop Vaughan, on the S Giraldus Cambrensis, the mitre
at his feet signifying the failure of his ambition.

The ambulatory and its ante-chapels date from the time of Bishop
Martyn, with the ante-chapels of Saints Edward and Nicholas
flanking the Lady Chapel.

The chapel of Edward the Confessor contains a large alabaster
monument to the benefactress, Lady Maidstone (d.1923). Lady
Maidstone was the grand-daughter of Bishop Jenkinson (1825–40),

whose robes used in the coronation of Queen Victoria are displayed in a glass case in the S choir aisle. Both this chapel and the chapel of St Nicholas show signs of attempts at stone vaults made at two different periods, but the intentions were never fulfilled, unlike the E walk of the ambulatory, which is vaulted.

The central Lady Chapel was built around 1300 in the Early English style, the work of Bishop Martyn. In 1775 Bishop Gower's vaulted roof fell in and the chapel lay open to the elements until it was revaulted in 1902. The tomb on the S side is probably that of Bishop Martyn, while that on the N was that of Bishop Bek. It was restored and subsequently used as a tomb for Bishop John Owen (1897–1926), a man famed for his fight against disestablishment.

St Mary's College

The ruins of St Mary's College are on the N side of the cathedral, and were once connected to it by a cloister. The college was founded in 1377 for secular priests by Bishop Houghton, Lord Chancellor to Edward III, with the aid of John of Gaunt, to ensure that the divine services should be sung properly. The chief feature remaining is the Perpendicular style chapel above a pointed barrel vault, with a plain tower at its SW corner. The college must have been a fine building, with its high walls and large windows, but John Nash was allowed to use it as a source of building stone during his restoration of the W front of the cathedral in 1793. The preservation of the building was secured in 1933 through help from the Pilgrim Trust. During work on the conversion of the buildings into a cathedral hall in 1966 a tomb, believed to be that of Bishop Houghton, was uncovered.

The Bishop's Palace

After the cathedral the next most important place of interest is the magnificent Bishop's Palace, one of the finest ecclesiastical buildings in Wales. It stands immediately opposite the cathedral, on the other side of the River Alun. For the location plan, see Plan D, p.138, and for details of the building, see Plan F, p.151. The ruins are in the care of the Department of the Environment, on behalf of the Secretary of State for Wales. They are open throughout the year at the 'standard' hours of admission – 0930–1600, or 1730, or 1900, depending on the time of the year, and on Sundays from 0930–1400. There is an admission fee.

The superb ruins convey the immediate impression of having been built as a whole, but the palace was mostly built between 1280 and 1350 and is usually referred to as Bishop Gower's work. The building was begun by Bishop Bek, continued by Bishop Martyn and adorned by Bishop Gower. That the construction should be regarded as Gower's work suggests what a great builder he must have been. He built only about half the palace but he gave the whole building his own stamp of individuality by crowning all the buildings, whether his own or his predecessor's, with a richly ornamented, arcaded parapet wall, unparalleled elsewhere except in his own work at Lamphey Palace (E of Pembroke) and at Swansea Castle.

The palace occupied three sides of a large single quadrangle (c180ft × 150ft/55m × 45m), the N and W sides of which have largely disappeared. The S side is occupied by the Great Hall and chapel, with the Bishop's Hall, Bishop's Chapel and kitchens on the E side. All the chief rooms are at first-floor level, carried on vaults.

Tour of the Palace, following plan F, opposite
The entrance to the palace is through a vaulted gateway in the N wall, a plain building two storeys high. The oldest parts of the palace are the N wall extending to the R, and the range on the W: the style of the vaulted late 13c work indicates part of the rebuilding carried out by Bishop Bek. It is probable that these rooms served as apartments for guests staying at the palace, as a similar example exists at the episcopal castle of Llawhaden.

Straight across the quadrangle from the gateway is Gower's Great Hall, with a projecting hall at one end and a chapel at the other, occupying the whole of the S side of the courtyard.

The Great Hall is a large building, 119ft × 31ft/36m × 9m, approached by a marvellous porch up a flight of steps to a striking ogee archway enriched by canopied niches containing the remains of statues. Inside, the hall proper, 88ft/27m long, reveals a beautiful rose window of trefoiled lights at the E end. The size of this building

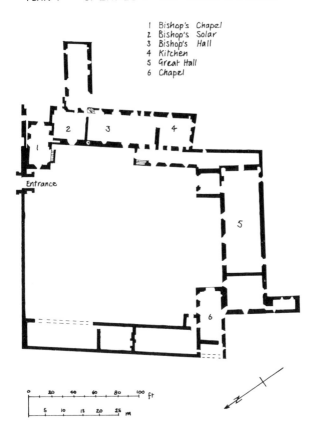

PLAN F   ST DAVIDS : THE BISHOP'S PALACE

1 Bishop's Chapel
2 Bishop's Solar
3 Bishop's Hall
4 Kitchen
5 Great Hall
6 Chapel

Entrance

makes you realise the scale of Gower's hospitality, or the strength of his urge to build – the Bishop's Hall is only half the size.

The halls built by Bishop Gower at the episcopal palaces of St David's, Lamphey and Swansea all have a structural feature which calls for special attention, especially as that here at St David's is the earliest in which the characteristic features of Gower's work are to be found. The excellence of this work and the absence of any local prototype are evidence that the bishop imported skilled workmen to carry out his building at St David's, while at Lamphey local builders imitated the style, with crude results.

Gower achieved a harmony of design by constructing open arcaded parapets extending around the tops of the walls of the main buildings. Slender columns rising from carved corbels are embedded in the wall for part of their height, and from these spring the moulded arches. Above these was a wall-walk, finished with battlements. That the arcades are not machicolations is clear from the position they occupy in relation to the roof: any missiles thrown down them would ricochet far beyond the base of the walls and well away from any sappers mining there. The arcades provided outlets for the rainwater falling on the roof. The pattern of the arcaded parapet is continued round the gable of the Great Hall in a decorative manner with purple and cream stone.

The decay of the Great Hall dates from the time of Bishop Barlow (1536–48), the last to live in the Palace and an active suppressor of pilgrimages and destroyer of relics. He stripped the lead from the roof when he removed from St David's to Abergwili near Carmarthen. According to local tradition he removed the lead to provide dowries for his five daughters, for whose successful marrying-off he would naturally make any sacrifice: all married bishops.

Immediately following Gower's death in 1347 a new chapel was built at the N end of the E range – the Bishop's Chapel. Like the rest of the palace it is built on a series of vaults which provided basement rooms and storage space.

Occupying the centre of the eastern range is the late 13c Bishop's Hall, also built on vaults. The entrance to the hall is by an external stair, covered by a porch exhibiting the semi-octagonal head characteristic of Gower's work on the Great Hall. At the S end of the Bishop's Hall a new kitchen was built c1350, conveniently sited to serve both halls, with a passage linking it to them.

The Reformation began the decay and destruction of the medieval palace. By the turn of the 18c the buildings stood derelict and roofless, and it wasn't until the 19c that repairs were carried out to halt its complete destruction.

Part three

St David's to St Ann's Head

9 **St Non's to Solva** (Maps 21–23)   5.05ml/8.1km

The Coast Path is in good condition for most of the way, but
landslips at Aber Llong cause walkers to go on to neighbouring
farmland.

St Non's to Caerfai Bay 0.75ml/1.2km
Following the coast eastwards you soon come to Caerfai Bay,
having rounded the headland of Pen-y-Cyfrwy (Saddle Head). A
flight of steps and a rough path lead steeply down to flat sands with
shingle and rocks at the back below high cliffs. The bay is a lovely
and sheltered spot, the closest beach to St David's, and as a
consequence usually very busy. Nevertheless, it is a beautiful
bathing place, a favourite with children, having firm sand and rock
pools. From Caerfai was obtained some of the stone used in
building St David's Cathedral. It is chocolate-coloured, redder than
that from Caer Bwdy, but streaked with bands of green, purple and
red. The quarries below the car park were reopened in 1972 when
enough stone was taken to restore the cathedral for another 50
years.

Caerfai Bay to Caer Bwdy Bay 1ml/1.6km
The eastern headland of Caerfai Bay is Penpleidiau, with an
offshore island of the same name. There is a good view of this
headland from Pen-y-Cyfrwy across the bay. Stretching across the
Penpleidiau promontory, from cliff to cliff, is a promontory fort,
one of the best on the coast. The earthwork is unusual in that it
consists of four parallel ramparts and ditches, with an entrance on
the E side, and it has a fine view of a line of magnificent cliffs.
   Caer Bwdy had a quarry from which some of the purple

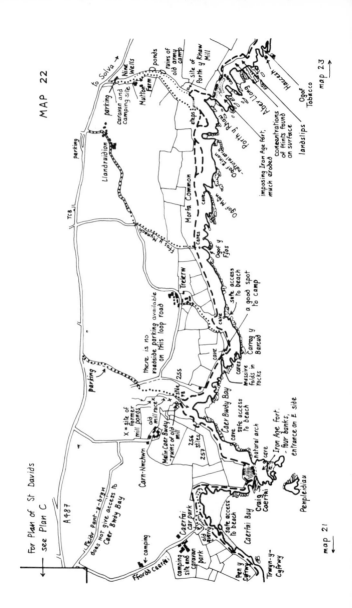

MAP 22

For Plan of St Davids
see Plan C

A487

Ffordd Pant-y-bryn
does not give access to
Caer Bwdy Bay

Parking

X = site of former
mill ponds

there is no
roadside parking
available
on this loop road

to Solva

Nine Wells

ponds

ruins of
old army camp

site of Porth y Rhaw Mill

Multoot
Farm

caravan and
camping site

Parking

Tca

Llandruidion

steps

Morfa Common

ruins of old
mill

255

256

257

stiles

Caern-Newchwn

Malin Caer Bwdy
- ruins of old
mill

camping

Caerfai
Car Park

camping
site and
caravan
park

old quarry

Pen y
Cyfrwy

Trwyn-y-
Cyfrwy

Ffordd Caerfai

Caerfai Bay

safe access
to beach

Craig Caerfai

cave

natural arch

cave

Iron Age fort
- four banks,
entrance on E side

Pembleidiau

cave

Caer Bwdy Bay

safe access
to beach

massive folds
in rocks

cave

cave

Carreg y Barcud

a good spot
to camp

safe access
to beach

Trefeirw

cave

caves

caves

Ogof y Ffos

Ffos y Mynach

Ogof Mawr

national trail

Ogof Emlon

Porth y Rhaw

imposing Iron Age fort,
much eroded

concentrations
of flints found
on surface

landslips

Aber Llong

Ogof
Tabacco

site of Porth y Rhaw Mill

map 23

map 21

sandstone was quarried to build and maintain St David's Cathedral, but signs of it are now being lost in the undergrowth. There is a huge square lime-kiln and remains of an old mill site. Caer Bwdy is a small, rocky bay, but a little sand is revealed below the shingle and pebbles at low water. It is attractive and unspoilt, and much quieter than Caerfai, probably because there is no direct access by car.

Between 1940 and 1943 the NT bought some 111 acres/45ha of rough coastal land from Caerfai to as far E as Porth-y-Rhaw, and it also protects 367 acres/148ha of farmland.

Caer Bwdy Bay to Porth-y-Rhaw 1.3ml/2.0km

Between Caer Bwdy and the headland of Carreg-y-Barcud there is a wide and deep zawn where there is a massive fold in the purple Caerfai sandstone of the Lower Cambrian, faulted against the green-grey sandstones of the Solva Beds of the Middle Cambrian.

Just beyond the headland you come to another zawn, Ogof y Ffos, which marks the southern end of the Ffos-y-Mynach, the Monk's Dyke. This earthwork starts on the coast here and cuts off St David's Peninsula from S to N: its slight banks are still traceable in one or two places where it crossed Dowrog Common and on the W side of the hill called Carn Penberry where it reaches the N coast. Its real origins are uncertain and its purpose unknown.

The Path runs straight over Morfa Common and drops down to Porth-y-Rhaw, a rocky inlet similar to Caer Bwdy, but smaller. Access to it is only from the Coast Path, or by a path from Nine Wells on the main road: there is car parking near the farm. There are many ruins above Porth-y-Rhaw – an old stone-built mill, and more recent brick buildings which look as if they might have been the sewage works for the St David's airfield, Brawdy's wartime satellite.

Porth-y-Rhaw to Solva 2ml/3.2km

There is a splendid Iron Age promontory fort immediately E of the cove, much eroded, with interlocking banks forcing the approach path into S-turns. A blowhole, Ogof Castell, marks its eastern

Porth-y-Raw Iron Age fort (previous page)

defence. From the fort there is a superb view back along the wild cliffs to the islands off the southern tip of Ramsey.

Inland is Llanunwas where it is said locally that there is a tunnel from the farmhouse down to a cave in the cliffs. One can guess for what purpose; Ogof Tobacco, no doubt, partly tells the tale. The peninsula 'The Cradle' was named after the sailing ship *Cradle* which took emigrants from Solva to the New World in the 1840s.

The early Palaeozoic Cambrian rocks around here and Solva are folded and faulted shales and they contain a variety of trilobites, one source being halfway up the cliffs in Aber Llong. Access to the cliffs here and in other places is difficult, and access to Gewni Beach is only for the adventurous.

At Sterling Hock you turn a corner and enter a long and fjord-like narrow valley – the Solva estuary. From the top of the cliffs there is a magnificent view up the winding creek to the little village at its head, and the Path drops down to the quayside where there is usually a bustle of activity.

Solva is today one of the most popular villages on the coast of Pembrokeshire as it provides a first-class harbour for yachtsmen, although it was for a long time a centre of coastwise trade.

Solva's seafaring history goes back to the 14c when it was a small port, and in 1603 George Owen described it as 'a portlet for small shipping'. Solva was the best of the many small harbours in use around St Bride's Bay, although its difficult entrance retarded its development. Nevertheless, by 1811 there were 36 ships in the port, and there were as many as nine warehouses in Lower Solva – some of which you can still see today. Oats, barley, butter, timber and other agricultural products were shipped out to Bristol, and coal, culm, limestone and general merchandise came in from Bristol, the Irish ports and further afield. But by 1856 the trade was beginning to dwindle, like that of most small coastal settlements, as a result of competition from the new railway network.

In 1848 emigrants sailed from here to America. The fare was £3 for adults, 30 shillings for children under fourteen and infants were free. Water, fuel and bed places were provided, but passengers had to take their own food with them. The journey took between seven and seventeen weeks. Solva's Trinity quay was built in 1856 to handle stone for the construction of the second Smalls lighthouse.

For centuries the farms of the St David's Peninsula were renowned for their cereal production, and lime was widely used for the soil once its agricultural benefits had been appreciated. Much of the lime for use on the peninsula was burnt at Solva, where there were once twelve kilns in operation. There is a fine group of four round ones on the S shore of the creek. There were still eight kilns in operation at Solva in 1908, and a *Bristol Trader* continued to run a regular service until 1914. Examples of the wooden ketches and schooners used to transport this lime may be seen as stranded hulks at Angle. The kilns soon ceased operating at the outbreak of war.

Solva is an attractive boating centre, much used by dinghy enthusiasts and cruiser owners. Boats can be hired for fishing and sight-seeing trips along the coast. However, the coastline is dangerous, with an onshore swell most of the time, and rocks off the entrance make the harbour a difficult one. There are dangerous twin rocks – the Black Rock, which is situated in the centre of the entrance and has outlying reefs to the W side, and St Elvis Rock, close inshore on the E side – which make the harbour difficult to enter without local knowledge. For inexperienced sailors the SE corner of St Bride's Bay, sheltered from the prevailing south-westerlies, is much safer.

The long sheltered inlet dries out almost completely at low water, and sailors should be aware that at half-tide, when there is a strong southwesterly sea running, half of the harbour can become dangerous as it alternately dries and fills with each large swell. This phenomenon is called the 'Solva bore', but it is only rarely encountered. High tide is Milford time plus 12 minutes.

10   **Solva to Little Haven** (Maps 23–28)   11.6ml/18.6km

The Coast Path is a good cliff-top walk all of the way to Newgale, much of it created by bulldozer, although you wouldn't think so seeing it today, now that the scars have healed. The walking is

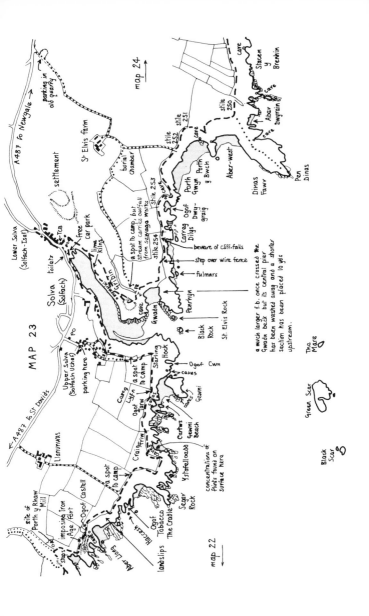

MAP 23

A487 to St Davids

A487 to Newgale

Lower Solva (Solfach-Isaf)

Solva (Solfach)

Upper Solva (Solfach-Uchaf)

parking in old quarry

St Elvis farm

settlement

burial chamber

Tea

Free car park

lime kilns

toilets

PO

parking here

Llanunwas

site of Porth y Rhaw Mill

imposing Iron Age fort

landslips

Ogof Cadno

Ogof Tobacco

The Cradle

Scar Rock

Ystrad Rock

Aber Llong

concentrations of flints found on surface here

a spot to camp

a spot to camp

Craig Triw

Gwrhyd Beach

Carfas

caves

Gwmi

Ogof Cwm

Slating Hook

Ogof Cwrw

Caerg Lyfn

Black Scar

Green Scar

The Mare

St Elvis Rock

Black Rock

Gwadn

caves

Parrhyn

fulmars

step over wire fence

beware of cliff-falls

a spot to camp, but stream carries outfall from sewage works

Carreg Dilys

Ogof Dwig-graig

Porth y Bwch

Porth Gwyn

stile 254

stile 253

stile 252

stile 253

cave

cave

Aber-wast

Dinas Fawr

Pen Dinas

cave

Aber Bwgrain

cave

cave

stile 250

stile 251

Staeen y Brenin

map 24

a much larger f.b. once crossed the Gwadn beck but its central pier has been washed away and a shorter section has been placed 10 yds upstream.

mostly easy, with one or two exacting gradients to Newgale, and then as you bear southwards you notice a distinct softening of the landscape as you make the change from the older rocks of the St David's Peninsula to the geologically softer rocks of St Bride's Bay.

The coastline between Solva and Newgale, including large areas of farmland inland, is owned by the NT. The Gribin Point was given in 1937, but other areas were bought in 1967 and 1973 from Enterprise Neptune funds.

Solva to Porthmynawyd 3ml/4.8km
The valleys of the Solva and the adjoining Gribin, which unite as they enter St Bride's Bay, were eroded by streams of meltwater issuing from and flowing under an ice-sheet which covered the area during the last glaciation. That of the Solva was worn deeper than that of the Gribin, so that when later sea levels rose the Solva was created as a ria, and the Gribin was not. The Gribin is the name of the tongue of land between the two valleys, the walk to the top of which is an easy stroll from Solva, and which provides a good viewpoint of the village and the harbour. On the top is an Iron Age earthwork, with the original walling still visible on the N face of the defensive mound.

The Gribin stream runs into the sandy cove of the Gwadn, and provides Solva with a bathing beach. It is a very pleasant and unspoilt spot, but be warned that the stream comes down past a sewage works! A path leads inland to St Elvis Farm, passing the remains of two cromlechs, and to the remains of St Teilo's Church, which is a pile of ruins in the farmyard.

The headlands of Dinas Fawr and Dinas Fach to the E provide magnificent prospects of coastal scenery. Dinas Fawr is a wide headland, colourful in September when the heather, Welsh gorse, golden rod and wild carrot are all in flower. Dinas Fach is narrower and more imposing, with its pinnacles and offshore island.

Dinas Fach, the bay of Porthmynawyd and the area E to Cwm-bach consist of Pre-Cambrian volcanic ashes which have been slightly folded at the end of Pre-Cambrian times, and subsequently overlain by rocks of succeeding systems. During the Caledonian Earth Movements these rocks were all compressed to form a large

MAP 24

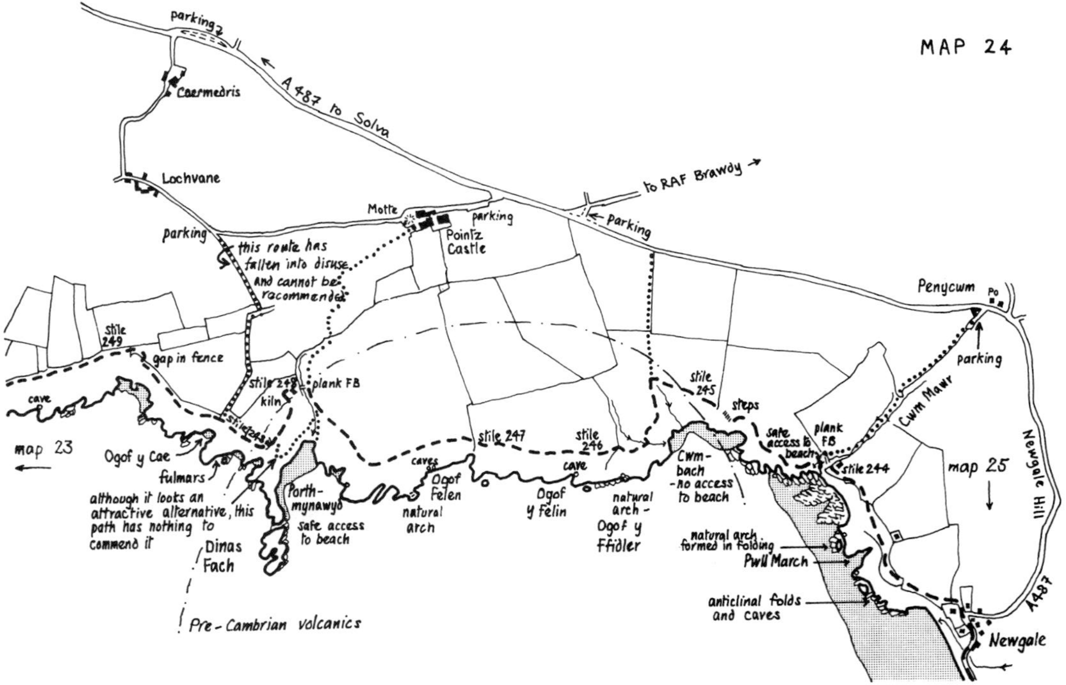

A487 to Solva →

Parking 2

Caermabris

Lochvane

← Parking

to RAF Brawdy →

Parking

Parking

Pengwm Pt.

Newgale Hill

A487

Newgale

map 25 →

Parking

Cwm Mawr

stile 244

plank FB

safe access to beach

stile 245

steps

Cwm-bach – no access to beach

natural arch, formed in folding

Pwll March

anticlinal folds and caves

stile 246

natural arch
Ogof y Ffidler

cave

Ogof y Felin

stile 247

Pointz Castle

Parking

Motte

parking

this route has fallen into disuse and cannot be recommended

kiln

plank FB

stile 248

gap in fence

stile 249

cave

map 23 →

Ogof y Cae

fulmars

although it looks an attractive alternative, this path has nothing to commend it

Porth-mynawyd safe access to beach

Ogof Polen
caves

natural arch

Dinas Fach

Pre-Cambrian volcanics

anticline, with its axis running from Newgale to Trefgarn. The crest of the upfold was subsequently removed by erosion and has revealed the old volcanic rocks which formed its core.

Porthmynawyd is a small sandy cove at the head of a deep valley, pleasant and uncrowded. It can only be reached by walking the Coast Path from Solva or Newgale, or by footpath from Pointz Castle. (Pointz Castle is a grand name for what is now only a grassy mound next to some farm buildings. It was named after Ponce, a tenant knight of Bishop de Leia, Bishop of St David's from 1176–98. The present farm takes the name of the former 'castle'.)

The peace of the coast is often shattered by the noise of low-flying aircraft landing and taking off from nearby *Brawdy Airfield*. The RAF Tactical Weapons Training Unit has one helicopter flight and squadrons of Hawker Hawks jets based here, and you frequently see the bright yellow rescue Sea King helicopters of 202 Search and Rescue Squadron patrolling the coast on training exercises or real-life emergencies. A recent addition to the airfield is an Oceanographic Research Station, set up by the US Navy. A cable from the Research Station runs into the sea at Porth Mawr (Whitesand Bay), but it is a more sophisticated system than that used by the hydrophone station on Carn Llidi 60 years earlier.

Porthmynawyd to Newgale 1.75ml/2.8km
From these cliffs there are magnificent views southwards along the line of Newgale Sands, and where the Cambrian shales give way to the rocks of the Coal Measures, at the mouth of Cwm Mawr, there is access to the beach if the tide is out. Otherwise you have to continue to a bend in the A487 main road, and follow the road through the village, a generally chaotic collection of new bungalows, gift shops, beach cafés, summer kiosks, pub, petrol station, toilets, caravan and camping sites – a mess of unplanned buildings and uses. In 1882 the Duke of Edinburgh called and gave his name to an inn that was to be washed away during a great storm in 1896: the pub was subsequently rebuilt on the landward side of the road.

Newgale Sands

On the great long sandy stretch of *Newgale Sands* W and SW winds produce impressive surf, and even in the calmest offshore breezes the surf rolls majestically. Swimming is safest in the middle of the beach, but too many people gather at the N end, too close to the rocks for safety, where there are tidal undertows. Swimmers need to take care at low tide and in surf. Surfing is good at all stages of the tide, and throughout the year, and there is direct access to the beach from the road across a steep pebble bank.

It is strange that these extensive sands, though exposed to the prevailing winds, have produced no dunes at their rear unlike those, for example, at Freshwater West. Instead the sands are backed by a steep and huge bank of pebbles thrown up by the tide. This tremendous pebble bank, 1ml/1.6km long, is one of the most spectacular features to be seen on the Coast Path. It is a true storm-beach, constructed largely by storm waves to a height of about 17ft/4.5m above the beach. The top bank is storm level; successive lines on the seaward side mark gradations of high-tide levels. At high tide during severe storm conditions pebbles are thrown by waves over the crest of the ridge and on to the main road, which runs behind it for part of its length, indicating that the pebble beach shows a tendency to migrate inland.

Most of the stones in the pebble beach are of local grey, green and blue sandstones from the St David's Peninsula, but there are also many far-travelled glacial erratics. Probably the beach has been built from boulders and shingle sorted out of the boulder clay which was deposited during the various Quaternary glaciations on the floor of St Bride's Bay. The coast is assaulted by waves which, together with the tidal currents, have gradually driven the stones eastwards. The storm-beach obstructs the natural outlet of the **Brawdy Brook to the sea, and has resulted in the formation of a** marshy area behind the barrier, a very common feature on those parts of the coast exposed to the open sea.

After heavy storms at low tide the stumps and debris of a great submerged forest are occasionally revealed by the scouring tides. Giraldus Cambrensis passed up this coast of 'Niwegal' in 1172 and likened the forest to 'a grove of ebony'.

The Brawdy Brook marks the boundary of 'Little England

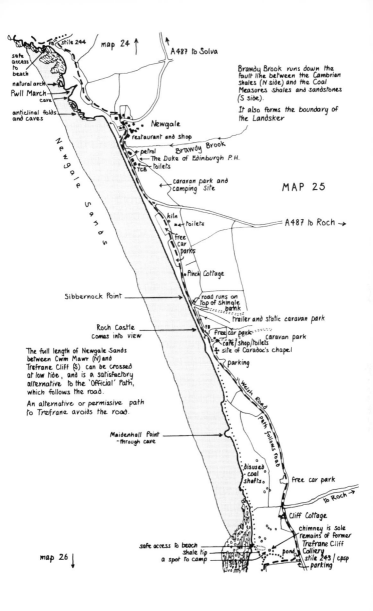

stile 244

map 24 ↑

A487 to Solva

Brawdy Brook runs down the fault line between the Cambrian shales (N side) and the Coal Measures shales and sandstones (S side).

It also forms the boundary of the Landsker

safe access to beach

natural arch

Pwll March cave

anticlinal folds and caves

Newgale

restaurant and shop

Brawdy Brook

petrol

The Duke of Edinburgh P.H.

toilets

TcB

caravan park and camping site

MAP 25

kiln

toilets

A487 to Roch →

free car parks

Pinch Cottage

Sibbernock Point

road runs on top of shingle bank

trailer and static caravan park

Roch Castle comes into view

FB

free car park

caravan park

café/shop/toilets

site of Caradoc's chapel

parking

The full length of Newgale Sands between Cwm Mawr (N) and Trefrane Cliff (S) can be crossed at low tide, and is a satisfactory alternative to the 'Official' Path, which follows the road.

An alternative or permissive path to Trefrane avoids the road.

Welsh Road

Path follows road

Maidenhall Point – through cave

disused coal shafts

free car park

To Roch

Cliff Cottage

chimney is sole remains of former Trefrane Cliff Colliery

stile 243/cpsp

parking

safe access to beach

shale tip

a spot to camp

pond

map 26 ↓

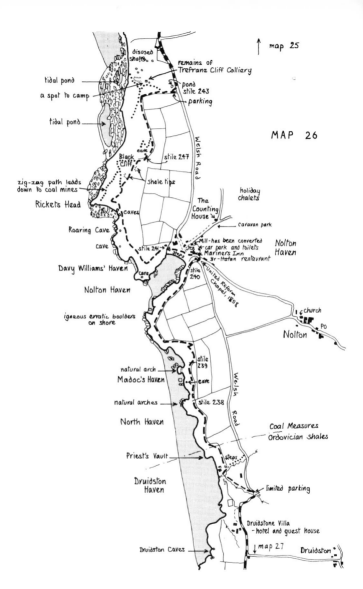

map 25

MAP 26

disused shafts

remains of
Trefrane Cliff Colliery

tidal pond

pond
stile 243

a spot to camp

parking

tidal pond

cave

stile 247

Welsh Road

Black Cliff

shale tips

holiday
chalets

zig-zag path leads
down to coal mines

The
Counting
House

Rickets Head

caves

caravan park

Roaring Cave

cave

Mill-has been converted
car park and toilets
Mariners Inn
Yr-Hafan restaurant

Nolton
Haven

stile 241

steps

Davy Williams' Haven

cave

Nolton Haven

stile
240

United Reform Chapel 1858

church

PO

igneous erratic boulders
on shore

Nolton

natural arch

stile 239

Madoc's Haven

cave

natural arches

stile 238

North Haven

Coal Measures

Ordovician shales

Priest's Vault

Welsh Road

steps

Druidston
Haven

limited parking

Druidstone Villa
- hotel and guest house

Druidston Caves

map 27

Druidston

Beyond Wales', the boundary which even today separates Welsh-speaking from English-speaking Pembrokeshire. George Owen, the historian, has discussed this division in some detail, and sometimes used the old legal term 'land-scar' (that is, boundary) to express himself. Unfortunately some later writers interpreted this as a proper name and have tried to impose the name 'landsker' on this dividing line.

The western end of this boundary was defended by a castle, Roch Castle, the last in a line of castles that the Normans built right across Pembrokeshire, effectively dividing the county between the N, which was left to the Welsh, and the S, which was settled by the Normans. The other castles in the chain, beside Roch, were at Haverfordwest, Picton, Wiston, Llawhaden, Narberth and Laugharne.

Newgale to Nolton Haven 2.5ml/4km

For the next 1.5ml/2.4km the official Coast Path follows the narrow coast road, called Welsh Road, but if the tide is out, *and has not turned*, it is easier to walk right along the beach and scramble up the cliff at Trefrane Cliff. Midway along the Newgale Sands the Bathesland Water stream runs down a valley to the coast, and from the coast road you can look up the valley, past the caravans, and see Roch Castle picturesquely sited on the skyline, nearly 2ml/3.2km inland. At the foot of the climb of the Welsh Road away from the beach is the site of St Caradoc's Chapel, the scene of a miracle. In 1124 when the body of St Caradoc was being carried along this road to St David's Cathedral for burial, 'a prodigious fall of rain inundated the whole country' but the pall 'miraculously remained dry and uninjured by the storm'.

At the S end of Newgale Sands the shore merges geologically into the Coal Measures Series, and the coastal area to the S was once the centre of much mining activity. The Newgale and Nolton coalfield had six main collieries and many 'levels' and 'slants' exploiting the coal seams beneath St Bride's Bay. Several levels can be seen in the coal seams in the cliffs between Newgale and Nolton Haven, reminders of a local industry dating back to at least 1439. The Trefrane Cliff Colliery was worked from about 1850 to 1905, and coal was exported in small vessels which were beached on the sands at Nolton Haven. There were plans to reopen the colliery after 1915 with a railway line to Milford Haven to export the coal, but the plans came to nothing.

Nothing but the ruins of the Trefrane Cliff Colliery now remain. Standing at the bottom of a short but steep valley overlooking the sea, they lie silent and often undiscovered by the visitor driving along the coast road. A ruined chimney stack, together with the foundations of the engine house and other buildings, a vegetated spoil heap and overgrown shafts are all that remain of a once-thriving industrial activity. It is estimated that at least 230 million tons of unworked coal reserves still lie under the sea in the Newgale-Nolton area.

The Welsh Road comes down to sea level at *Nolton Haven*, where a deep and narrow inlet, formed by the ice sheets, breaks through the coastal cliffs. The hamlet of the Haven consists of a farm with a sprawling, untidy farmyard, a few cottages, the inevitable cafés, caravans and pub, and a classic United Reform Chapel of 1858.

The line of a tramway which brought the coal mined up-valley to the coast is still visible, and the Counting House still stands alongside the old track-bed: it was from here that the number of wagonloads of coal transported to the quay were recorded. The quay, built at the head of the inlet on the N side of the beach in 1769 by Abel Hicks for the Folkestone Colliery Company to export anthracite and coal mined locally, has long disappeared, but the man-made embankment on the seaward side of the road where coal was stocked preparatory to shipping can still be seen.

Nolton Haven has a sandy beach, backed by pebbles, between high cliffs. There is immediate access from the road: there is a good car park, but despite this summer visitors still inconsiderately take their cars on to the beach blocking access for boats. The high-low water range is over 100yd/100m. Bathing is safe, except when the ebb tide is more than halfway out, as then strong currents are created near the headlands.

Nolton Haven to Druidston Haven 1.25ml/2km

There is a short stretch of road to follow as you climb up out of
Nolton Haven to the stone-built chapel at a road junction, and then
the Path turns to the coast again. Off the headland on the S side of
Nolton Haven there are several igneous boulders, erratics dropped
from the melting ice, and there are numerous others to be found
along this coast.

Madoc's Haven has some fine caves in its cliffs, some of which
have joined to form natural arches. Its beach, together with
neighbouring North Haven, marks the N end of Druidston Haven, a
fine stretch of flat sand backed by sheer cliffs 150ft/45m high.
Because of restricted parking on the coast road the beach is never
over-crowded.

Druidston had nothing to do with druids, in spite of what the
name of the hotel and guest house would have you believe. Locally
pronounced 'Drewston', it was called Drue's Town after Alfred
Drue or Drew, a knight of Henry I who first settled in this locality
(*c*1110).

Druidston Haven to Broad Haven (Hotel) 2.5ml/4km

At Druidston Haven the Coast Path leaves the cliffs and you follow
the Welsh Road for 0.5ml/800m, and then there are 1.75ml/2.8km
of lovely cliff path and a final 0.25ml/400m of road into Broad
Haven.

The road passing through Nolton Haven, Druidston Haven and
past the Harold Stone is the line of the original Neolithic or Bronze
Age track linking landings at Monk Haven (St Ishmael's) and Porth
Mawr (Whitesand Bay). This 'Welsh Way', or Welsh Road as it is
now known, cuts off the dangers of voyaging round the headlands,
islands and promontories, and across the open, windswept St
Bride's Bay. The Harold Stone marks the legendary site of victories
by Harold, Earl of Wessex, over the Welsh. It is more likely to
be of the Bronze Age period: it stands in a field next to a building
plot between Stiles 232 and 233, but is so small it cannot be seen
from the Coast Path.

The Druidston Chins and Haroldston Chins are fine cliffs of the
Coal Measures, and Haroldston Bridge is one of the finest natural

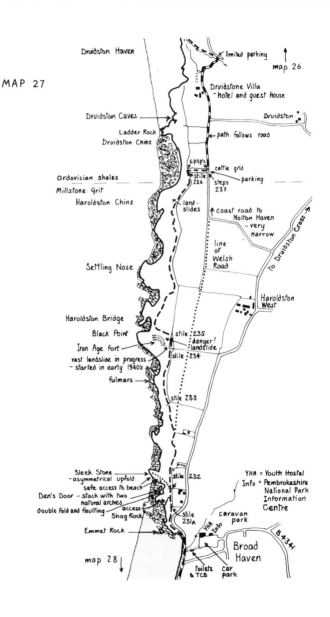

MAP 27

Druidston Haven

limited parking

map 26

Druidstone Villa
- hotel and guest house

Druidston Caves

Druidston

Ladder Rock
Druidston Chins

path follows road

cpsp's

cattle grid

stile
236

steps
237

parking

Ordovician shales

Millstone Grit

Haroldston Chins

land-
slides

coast road to
Nolton Haven
- very
narrow

line
of
Welsh
Road

Settling Nose

To Druidston Cross

Haroldston
West

Haroldston Bridge

Black Point

stile 235

Iron Age fort

danger!
landslide

vast landslide in progress
- started in early 1940's

stile 234

fulmars

stile 233

Sleek Stone
- asymmetrical upfold

stile 232

safe access to beach

YHA = Youth Hostel
Info = Pembrokeshire
National Park
Information
Centre

Den's Door - stack with two
natural arches

Double fold and faulting

access

Shag Rock

stile 231a

caravan
park

Emmet Rock

YHA
Info

Broad
Haven

B4341

map 28

toilets
& TCB

car
park

arches on this stretch of coast. On nearby Black Point is an Iron
Age fort displaying the usual defensive characteristics, but access to
it is now protected by modern landslides. The Point was subject to
an enormous landslide in 1944: some local people say it was
triggered off by a mine being washed ashore and exploding on the
rocks, but more recent landslides of the early 1960s suggest that the
headland is suffering from erosion by the sea. It may not be long
before the Coast Path will need to be diverted inland hereabouts.

At the N end of the Broad Haven beach there are some
spectacular examples of folding, sea stacks and natural arches. The
light-coloured sandstone layers interbedded with blue-black shales
belong to the Coal Measures Series, and were subjected to
movements during the Hercynian mountain-building era, so that
the upper parts of slightly folded anticlines were forced to over-ride
the lower part along slightly inclined thrust-fault planes.

The Sleek Stone, jutting out of the cliffs like a huge stranded
whale, is a magnificent example of a reverse or thrust-fault
disturbing the folded strata. The cliff is about 50ft/15m high, and
when the tide is fully out you can scramble over it and study the
anticlinal structure in three dimensions.

Immediately S of the Sleek Stone are three stacks – Den's Door,
Shag Rock and Emmet Rock, the former being undermined by two
natural arches, while the cliffs at the back of the Door display
double folds and faulting. These examples cannot be properly
appreciated from the Coast Path, and they can only be seen at close
quarters when the tide is out.

Broad Haven became fashionable as a bathing place at the
beginning of the 19c, and has retained its popularity ever since.
There are lots of new bungalows up on the hill and caravan sites up
the side valleys. The place seems rather depressing, even in the
summer season, in spite of there being an all-the-year-round
community. The Broad Haven Hotel dominates the sea-front and
has direct access to the beach across the road.

The only buildings of interest to the Coast Path walker are in the
car park at the N end of the village – the information centre and the
youth hostel. The information centre – formerly the Pembrokeshire
Countryside Unit, opened in 1970, whose director was John Barrett

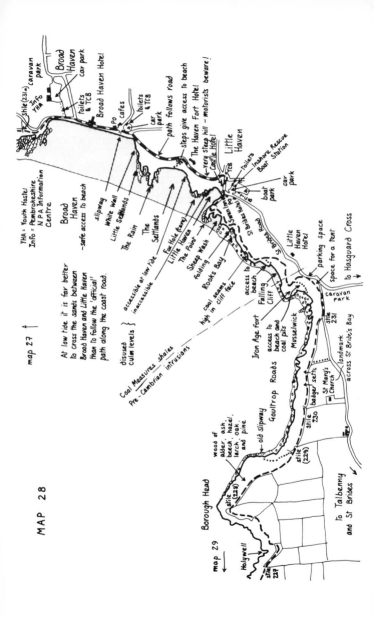

MAP 28

map 27 ↑

YHA = Youth Hostel
Info = Pembrokeshire
N.P.A Information
Centre

At low tide it is far better
to cross the sands between
Broad Haven and Little Haven
than to follow the 'official'
path along the coast road.

Broad Haven car park
Broad Haven Hotel
stile (23¤) caravan park
Info YHA
toilets & TCB
cafes
P.O
toilets & TCB
car park
path follows road
steps give access to beach
The Haven Fort Hotel
very steep hill – motorists beware!
Castle Hotel
Little Haven
TCB
toilets
Inshore Rescue Boat Station
car park
boat park
St Brides table

slipway
safe access to beach
White Wall
Little Sandlands
The Rain
The Sandlands

Broad Haven
– safe access to beach

Fox Hole (cave)
accessible at low tide
inaccessible
Little Haven
The Point
Sheep Wash
folding cliffs
Rooks Bay

disused Culm levels
Coal Measures shales
Pre-Cambrian intrusions

high coal seams in cliff face
access to beach
Falling Cliff

Iron Age fort
access to beach and coal pits
Musselwick

Little Haven Hotel
parking space
space for a tent
to Hasguard Cross
caravan park
stile 231

St Mary's Church
badger setts
stile 230
landmark
across St Bride's Bay
to Talbenny and St Brides

Gaultrop Roads
wood of alder, ash, beech, hazel, larch, oak, and pine.
old slipway
stile (229)

Borough Head
stile (228)
Holywell
map 29 →
stile 227

– is now in the hands of the PNPA, and is open for business from the beginning of April to the end of September. The PNPA also began the construction of the nearby long-awaited youth hostel in 1978. It opened its doors on 27 June 1980, and is operated on a long-term lease by the YHA.

Broad Haven has a splendid beach, a broad expanse of firm sand which is safe for bathing. The best time for surfing is at high water, and winter is the best season.

Broad Haven to Little Haven 0.6ml/960m
The beach at Broad Haven unites with that of Little Haven at low tide, enabling access to The Settlands and also providing a convenient walk to Little Haven, as the official Coast Path follows a narrow and busy road, to be avoided if possible. If the tide is out it is preferable to walk along the sands as this gives you an opportunity to see some good examples of folding in the rocks of the cliffs. In a small cove, The Rain, to the N of a small promontory of the same name, the thinly-bedded Carboniferous sandstones and shales have been intensely folded, giving rise to a series of small-scale anticlines and synclines. The strata of the headland between The Settlands and Little Haven have been folded up into a large anticline, and some of the softer mudstones in the core of the anticline have been removed by wave erosion to form a cave known as the Fox Hole.

Little Haven, formerly an important harbour for the shipment of coal mined in the neighbourhood, is a lovely little village squeezed into the mouth of a small valley. Three narrow roads, each of them descending steep hills, provide difficult access, and as a consequence there is severe congestion during the height of the holiday season.

At high tide the sea laps a bank of shingle right beside the road, and in spring tides and storms washes over it. A path along the sea wall past the Swan Inn on the S side of the rocky bay (the Coast Path) takes you quickly to The Point, where there are many rock pools and magnificent views of St Bride's Bay.

At Little Haven the sandy beaches of St Bride's Bay are left behind. The coast turns a corner, and you find you are going W instead of S. The Coast Path rises from the level of the beaches to run along the top of red and black cliffs that form the peninsula defining the S side of St Bride's Bay.

Little Haven to St Bride's Haven 5.6ml/9km
There is a good path all the way providing quite easy walking, but there is only one intermediate access from the coast road between these two points, at Mill Haven. The walk is especially attractive because you have the unusual experience of walking through a wood, one of the very few on the coast.

The church of St Mary the Virgin, Talbenny, stands just off the Coast Path, overlooking St Bride's Bay. Here, as is also the case with the churches of Haroldston and Walton, the tower would have served as a beacon for ships in St Bride's Bay. These three, together with the tower of the now ruined church of St Elvis, would have covered the outlook into the whole bay.

The church is characteristically Celtic in style – rectangular, with a chancel and a nave, and a double bell-cote above the W wall – but it is an example of the Early English style introduced by Bishop Peter de Leia about 1180 and merged into the Decorative style of *c*1328.

There are two features of interest in the church: halfway up the wall separating the nave from the chancel, on the N side, is a small square doorway, which led originally to a rood-loft, now disappeared. This was a platform built across the chancel arch to carry the rood or crucifix, and from it the sermons were preached, and the Gospel read at Mass. The second feature is the continuous stone bench around the sides of the chancel. This dates from the time when there was little or no seating for the congregation: worshippers would remain standing throughout the service, though the elderly and infirm 'went to the wall' to sit.

St Mary's Church overlooks Goultrop Roads, a sheltered corner of St Bride's Bay. Down by the shore is an abandoned sailing lifeboat station, and only the old slipway is now left. The station closed in 1922 after 40 years' service, owing to the difficulty of obtaining a crew. Although a path leads down from the Coast Path it is no longer possible to reach the shore here, since a cliff-fall in the late 1940s blocked the path.

On the way to Borough Head you pass through a pleasant woodland of oak, ash, hazel, beech and larch, all the more pleasurable in May when the bluebells are in flower and the blackthorn in bloom.

Beyond Borough Head the Path leads through bracken and bramble to another headland where the offshore islands of Stack Rocks come into view. Otherwise known as St Bride's Stacks – to avoid confusion with the other Stack Rocks, the Elegug Stacks at Castlemartin – these small rocky islets are the home of cormorant, gull and grey seal.

An Iron Age fort above Brandy Bay encloses 0.5 acre/0.2ha with two lines of banks, its inner bank continuing far down the slope. Brandy Bay and Dutch Gin are two small coves which give in their names a clear indication of their purpose on this coast. Between Foxes' Holes, another narrow creek, and Mill Haven there is another Iron Age fort, called Broadmoor or Mill Haven Camp. The 1.5acre/0.6ha fort is enclosed by a single bank and ditch, and has a central entrance.

Mill Haven is a small pleasant cove of shingle and large dark red boulders: there is inland access by footpath from Lower Broadmoor Farm. At Mill Haven there is a dramatic change from the Pre-Cambrian intrusive rocks to the N and the Lower Old Red Sandstone rocks to the S. On the Path near Brandy Bay Iron Age fort the colour of the rocks and the soils in the fields and of the Path itself suddenly changes into a rich deep red.

Between Warey Haven and The Falls grey blocks lodged in the cliff-top were deposited by the melting ice of the last Ice Age.

St Bride's Haven is a charming spot, one of the most attractive coves in the bay, and unlike those coves opposite it across the bay – Porth Clais, Caerfai and Caer Bwdy – relatively quiet. It has the added attractions of a church, the remains of an old lime-kiln, an early graveyard, and a little landing-place among the rocks.

MAP 29

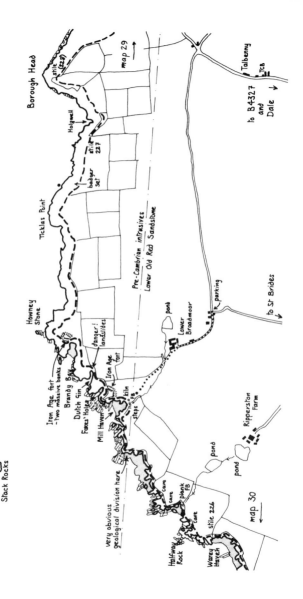

Stack Rocks

Borough Head

stile (228)

map 29

Holgwell

stile 227

badger set

Ticklas Point

Pre-Cambrian intrusives
Lower Old Red Sandstone

Howney Stone

Iron Age fort
- two massive banks

Brandy Bay

Dutch Gin

Foxes' Holes

Mill Haven

Iron Age fort

kiln

steps

pond

Lower
Broadmoor

parking

to St Brides

to B4327
and Dale

Talbenny

Tea

Very obvious
geological division here

Halfway Rock

cave

cave

plank FB

cave

stile 226

Warey Haven

pond

pond

Ripperston
Farm

map 30

The low cliffs of the Old Red Sandstone drop low into the Haven and give a warm colour to the rocks. Boulders and rocks give way to an inlet of gently shelving sand, an ideal safe bathing place for children, although only fit for bathing in fine weather. The Haven is sheltered from the prevailing southwesterly winds, but is open to the northerly gales, and in some winds and swell the sea is treacherous.

St Bride, otherwise known as Bridget or Brigid of Kildare, was the contemporary of St David. She lived from c450 to 525 and prepared Ireland for its Golden Age. She never actually left Ireland to set foot on the Welsh shore, but her cult was widespread: she was the first to become an abbess with authority over a bishop in running jointly a nunnery and a monastery for corporate work and worship. Her devout followers spread widely in the 5c and 6c: they set up a chapel here; sixteen more are dedicated to St Bride in Wales alone, with others in Cornwall, Brittany, Cologne, Italy and Czechoslovakia. St Bride's feast day is 1 February.

The early chapel is said to have stood in the Haven near to where the old lime-kiln now stands, and was swept away in a storm, together with much of its graveyard. Some 20yd/18m to the E of the lime-kiln in the eroded cliff you can see the ends of two stone coffins dating from early Christian times, uncovered by progressive erosion. The present medieval church was thoroughly restored in the 1860s.

St Bride's once formed part of the estate of the Barons of Kensington, whose lands, before the advent of death duty, stretched unbroken for the 12ml/19km from their residence here to Haverfordwest. During the 19c the Edwardes family from Sealyham, near Wolf's Castle, added the Barony of Kensington to their title: they had land in London, where Philbeach Gardens, Edwardes Square and Marloes Road commemorate their interests.

When the estate was broken up, the late Victorian baronial 'castle' became Kensington Hospital which, because of the clear atmosphere, specialised initially as a convalescent home and treatment centre for tubercular children. For some twenty years, c1950–70, it was Pembrokeshire's geriatric hospital, but it became redundant with the opening of the new Withybush Hospital at Haverfordwest.

Early in 1979 the AHA offered to sell the hospital, other buildings and adjacent land to the PNPA. The opportunity to acquire the hospital and its tenanted farmland was declined by the PNPA, but they did however acquire the rest of the estate – the cliff-top land outside the farmland boundary wall from the Haven to The Nab Head, the Haven itself, the slipway and boat houses (since demolished), the ruins of the medieval abbey of St Bride's, and other land between the church and the crossroads.

The PNPA already leases the foreshore from the Crown Commissioners, and ownership of the Haven and adjacent land now enables them to introduce a comprehensive management scheme to ease the problems of congestion, and to reconcile conflicting recreation interests, particularly between different users of the beach. A new car park is proposed, hidden in the woodland, and cars are now kept off the beach. There are two walled gardens: one is set aside for Scouts and Guides and similar organised groups, and the other is intended to become a camp site for those walking the Coast Path.

St Bride's Haven to Musselwick Sands 2.3ml/3.7km
The Path is good all the way, flat but exposed around the cliff top of The Nab Head. This is the site of a Neolithic flint-chipping factory dating from *c*5000BC. Flint is not indigenous to Pembrokeshire and it was probably imported from Ireland. Polished axe- and arrow-heads were made here and traded through St Bride's Haven and along the prehistoric trackways to other parts of Britain. The site has been excavated and chipped flints, pierced beads and flint implements have been found: some are exhibited in Tenby Museum. 'Nab' derives from 'knap', the process of flint chipping.

The neighbouring headland of Tower Point has two sides of precipitous cliffs, and supports a big Iron Age promontory fort on its top. The fort has two ditches and two banks, the inner bank massive. The entrance is on the E side, slightly N of centre. What look like circles within the fort are in fact small stone quarries,

St Bride's Church

probably worked for the purpose of building the wall around the Kensington estate.

From The Nab Head to Musselwick Sands the cliffs get more and more colourful. Steeply tilted strata of near-black rocks alternate with beds, some of pale grey and some of rich purple-red. Then the bedding-plane changes and for a short distance the rocks are tidily horizontal, but then suddenly they buckle in chaos. At New Quay there is a dramatic change in the rocks where suddenly, right on the Path, they change from the beautiful red-purple rocks of the Lower Old Red Sandstone on the N to the black Middle Ordovician shales on the S.

At the parish boundary between St Bride's and Marloes, at Stile 219, you come on to the site of a former MOD installation. This was an RAF bombing range of World War II, used by Halifaxes in particular. The target was about 400yd/400m out to sea, and on the cliff-top there was a system of concrete strips 10yd/9m long × 1yd/0.9m wide, with trap-doors and mirrors let in, and arrows pointing towards the target. The lookout hut was supplemented by another over the other side of Musselwick Bay, by East Hook Farm, to take cross-bearings on the strikes.

Musselwick Sands is a wide, sandy beach, accessible at low water. It is backed by high, sheer, black cliffs, too steep to be climbed, and as there is only one means of access visitors should beware being cut off by the tide: don't go N of Black Cliff on an incoming tide, and never stay down on the sands waiting for high water. The beach has flat sands, and is safe for bathing at low water. The cove is remote and unspoilt, with footpath access from the Marloes road, where there is good parking space on the grass verges.

Marloes is the most westerly village in Wales, and its church, cottages and council houses suggest a village on the English pattern. Its name, Moelrhos (bare moor), resembles Morlais in Cornwall and Morlaix in Brittany – similar-sounding settlements on three peninsulas that would have been familiar to ancient mariners.

St Peter's Church is a sturdy little cruciform church standing on a knoll at the S end of the main village street. It has the local characteristics of hagioscopes and a barrel-vaulted chancel, like St Bride's, and was restored in 1874. In the main street is the Victorian

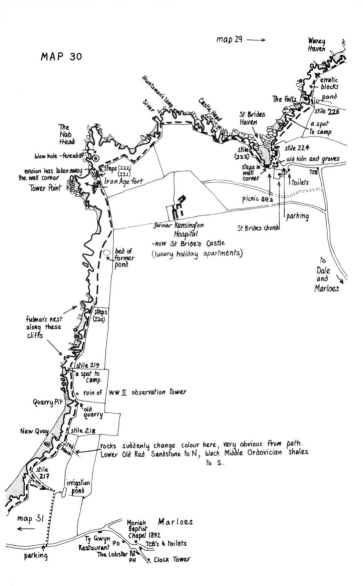

map 29 →

MAP 30

Warey Haven

erratic blocks

The Falls

pond

stile 225

a spot to camp

Huntsman's Leap

Silver

Castle Head

St Brides Haven

stile 224

old kiln and graves

stile (223)

steps in wall corner

The Nab Head

blow hole - fenced off

steps (222) (221)

Iron Age fort

erosion has taken away the wall corner

Tower Point

TCB

toilets

picnic area

parking

St Brides church

former Kensington Hospital

-now St Bride's Castle (luxury holiday apartments)

to Dale and Marloes

bed of former pond

steps (220)

fulmars nest along these cliffs

stile 219

a spot to camp

ruin of WW II observation tower

Quarry Pit

old quarry

New Quay

stile 218

stile 217

rocks suddenly change colour here, very obvious from path. Lower Old Red Sandstone to N, black Middle Ordovician shales to S.

irrigation pond

map 31 ←

parking

Marloes

Moriah Baptist Chapel 1892

Ty Gwyn Restaurant

Po

The Lobster Pot

PH

TCB's & toilets

Clock Tower

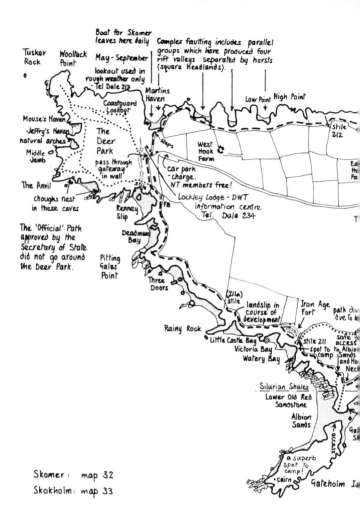

Tusker Rock

Woolfack Point

Boat for Skomer leaves here daily May - September

Complex faulting includes parallel groups which have produced four rift valleys separated by horsts (square headlands).

lookout used in rough weather only - Tel Dale 212

Martins Haven

Low Point   High Point

Coastguard Lookout

Mouse's Haven

Jeffry's Haven natural arches

Middle Jamb

The Deer Park

pass through gateway in wall

West Hook Farm

stile 212

car park - charge. NT members free!

Lockley Lodge - DWT information centre Tel. Dale 234

The Anvil

choughs nest in these caves

The 'Official' Path approved by the Secretary of State did not go around the Deer Park.

Renney Slip

FB

Deadman's Bay

Pitting Gales Point

Three Doors

(211a) stile

landslip in course of development!

Iron Age Fort

path div ove to k

Rainy Rock

Little Castle Bay

Victoria Bay

Watery Bay

stile 211

camp

safe access spot to re Albio Sands and Ho Neck

Silurian Shales

Lower Old Red Sandstone

Albion Sands

Ga Sh

a superb spot to camp!

cairn

Gateholm Is

Skomer: map 32

Skokholm: map 33

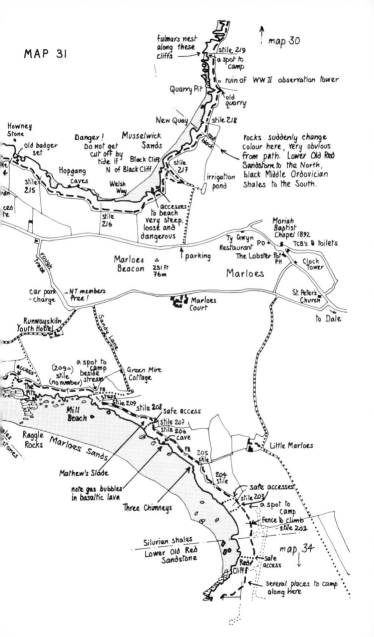

MAP 31

↑ map 30

fulmars nest along these cliffs

stile 219

a spot to camp

ruin of WW II observation tower

Quarry Pit

old quarry

New Quay

stile 218

Howney Stone

old badger set

Danger! Do not get cut off by tide if N of Black Cliff

Musselwick Sands

red black

rocks suddenly change colour here, very obvious from path. Lower Old Red Sandstone to the North, black Middle Ordovician shales to the South.

Hopgang caves

Black Cliff

stile 215

stile 217

Welsh Way

irrigation pond

stile 216

accesses to beach very steep, loose and dangerous

Moriah Baptist Chapel 1892

Ty Gwyn Restaurant

PO

TCB's & toilets

↑ parking

The Lobster Pot

PH

Clock Tower

Marloes Beacon △ 251 ft 76m

Marloes

car park - charge

NT members free!

St. Peter's Church

to Dale

Runwayskiln Youth Hostel

Sandy Lane

Marloes Court

access

(209a) stile (no number)

a spot to camp beside stream

Green Mire Cottage

The Pit

FB steps

stile 209

stile 208

safe access

Mill Beach

stile 207

Raggle Rocks

Marloes Sands

stile 206

cave

Little Marloes

Mathew's Slade

FB

205 stile

note gas bubbles in basaltic lava

204 stile

safe accesses

Three Chimneys

stile 203

a spot to camp

fence to climb

stile 202

Silurian shales Lower Old Red Sandstone

map 34

Red Cliff

safe access

several places to camp along here

shales stones

clock tower, commemorating the local landowner, William, fourth Lord Kensington, who died in 1896. It was built by his widow in 1904 as a reminder of his punctuality. The villagers once had a flourishing trade gathering leeches from Marloes Mere and sending them to Harley Street for the traditional blood-letting.

Musselwick Sands to Martin's Haven 2ml/3.2km
This is a delightfully easy stretch of Path, the northern sector of a very easy circular walk around the Marloes Peninsula: there is only a short stretch of road to walk across the neck of the peninsula between Musselwick and Marloes Sands.

Part of the coast between Musselwick Sands and Martin's Haven is a nature reserve of the DWT, opened by R M Lockley in May 1970 not long before he emigrated to New Zealand.

The coast to the N of West Hook Farm displays four rift valleys, including Martin's Haven, separated by horsts (square headlands), caused by complex parallel faulting of the Silurian shales in the Skomer Volcanic period.

Martin's Haven is sheltered and remote, the last cove along the southern arm of St Bride's Bay. It is a shelving, shingly inlet, with low cliffs and rocks around. The beach has no sand, and it is not a good swimming place for small children, but there is diving off the rocks at high tide, where steps lead down to a landing place. The cove is a haven for small fishing boats and has long been used by local people for fishing and lobster-potting. These activities have been replaced by pleasure craft, in particular those used by sub-aqua divers, who sometimes completely obstruct the slipway and beach access. The high tide is Milford time plus 10 minutes.

Just above the beach is the Lockley Lodge Information Centre of the DWT, which is normally open daily from Easter to late October. It sells guide-books, nature trail leaflets and a wide selection of gifts, as well as giving information about the Trust's nature reserves on the offshore islands and their visiting arrangements (tel Dale 234). Formerly a keeper's cottage and boat store, it has been converted by the NT with MSC labour. It opened in 1986, and replaced the little hut at the end of the public road opposite the NT car park.

Martin's Haven is best known as the departure point by boat for the islands of Skomer and Skokholm. (The Coast Path walk continues in Chapter 15.)

12   **Skomer** (Map 32)

Skomer is the largest island off the Pembrokeshire coast and it lies 1.5ml/2.4km off the mainland, separated by the turbulent and treacherous waters of Jack Sound. It is a windswept grassy plateau of some 722 acres/292ha and is internationally known for having the finest sea-bird colonies in NW Europe. The island is a National Nature Reserve which is leased by the DWT from the Nature Conservancy Council.

Geologically Skomer consists largely of hard, resistant volcanic (mainly basaltic) rocks of the Skomer Volcanic Series. The rocks were thrust northwards along an inclined plane of fracture, probably during the Hercynian Earth Movements, to rest upon younger and, in this instance, less resistant Old Red Sandstone rocks to the N. The Skomer Volcanics outcrop over a distance of over 25ml/40km from The Smalls and Grassholm Island to the W, through Skomer, Midland Isle, and the Marloes Peninsula, through to St Ishmael's in the E.

Relics of hundreds of hut-circles and enclosures, principally in the S of the island, and seen from the path from High Cliff to The Wick, around Skomer Head, and in the N, suggest that the island had a population in Iron Age times much larger than its resources could ever have supported. The island settlement does not seem to have been engaged in the usual activities of tool-making or copper or gold prospecting, but it may have been a harbour for navigators in the dawn of seafaring. Whatever the purpose of settlement, the island must certainly have been, as it is today, a great breeding ground for sea birds, making it attractive to human colonists with its

opportunities for unlimited bird-meat which could be eaten fresh in the summer or dried and preserved for the winter. In the absence of rabbits – a pest introduced by the Normans – the island would also have yielded a rich pasture, manured by the sea birds, and it would therefore have been ideal for primitive agriculture.

The settlers had a walled defensible camp known as South Castle on The Neck where there is a great fallen rampart across the SW isthmus. On the most easterly isthmus there still stands a small stone circle where the settlers doubtless carried out the rites and ceremonies of their pagan religion. There is also on the island a standing stone, traditionally called Harold's Stone, of unknown origin, although it probably marks a Bronze Age burial.

Skomer, like Skokholm, Grassholm and many others to be found around the coast, is a name of Scandinavian origin dating back to the later Dark Ages when the Vikings, centered on Dublin, were supreme along the Irish Sea coasts. After the Vikings came the Normans, who spurned the island agriculturally; like the other islands, Skomer appears to have remained uncultivated for many centuries. It is possible that it was only occupied in summer when sheep and cattle were grazed and the sea birds exploited. The farmhouse was built in the early 18c, but it was only in the 19c that the island was extensively farmed and its produce exported. In 1959 it was bought jointly by the NCC and the DWT, and established as a National Nature Reserve.

The National Nature Reserve
The island is particularly famous for its sea-bird colonies, its seals, and its spring and early-summer flowers, and each deserves special mention.

There are some 30 *bird species* on the island, and the most famous inhabitants of all are the Manx Shearwaters, probably numbering over 100,000 pairs! They nest all over the island, and wherever there are burrows the birds will not be far below the surface: the paths on the island are carefully laid out so that the sleeping birds are not disturbed by carelessly placed feet. The birds are nocturnal,

Skomer from the Deer Park

so usually only visitors who spend a night ashore will see them.

Among the other species of breeding birds there are: kittiwake, 17,000 pairs; puffins, 6500 pairs; lesser black-backed gull, 5000 pairs (among the bluebells, away from the cliffs); guillemot, 3000 pairs (the largest colony in Pembrokeshire); herring gull, 2000 pairs (on niches on the cliffs); storm petrel, 500 pairs (nesting amongst loose stones and field walls); great black-backed gull, 80 pairs (on the rock outcrops of the Mew Stone and Garland Stone); cormorant, twelve pairs (mostly on the S side of the Mew Stone); and shags, seven pairs (mostly on The Neck). Land birds include buzzard, peregrine, raven, chough, little and short-eared owl, jackdaw, meadow and rock pipit, skylark, wheatear and curlew. In addition, across the island in spring and again in autumn, there are the floods of migrant birds moving along the Atlantic coasts of Britain.

Skomer has no predatory *animals*, and no trees, so some birds which on the mainland would nest in trees here nest on the ground. Rabbits are common, but they are usually driven out of their burrows by Manx Shearwaters looking for nesting sites, and no rabbit – or puffin for that matter, which also nests in holes in the ground – would argue with the sharp beak of a Shearwater! There are only five species of mammal on Skomer (various voles, mice and shrews) and one of these is a species of vole unique to the island – the Skomer Vole (*Clethrionomys glareolus skomerensis*).

Grey seals can normally be seen, basking on the Garland Stone and other rocks at low tide. In autumn up to 150 animals may be present on the Garland Stone on some days. After Ramsey, Skomer is the second most important breeding site for seals in SW Britain.

In their way the *flowers* on Skomer outshine the beauty and wonder of the birds – great carpets of colour blaze in spring and early summer, and are particularly marvellous in early June when, as a bonus to the nesting birds, fields of bluebells and red campion cover the ground. Nearer the cliffs are ox-eye daisy, sea campion and scurvy grass, while on the cliffs themselves the thrift is massed in tussocks ranging from the palest pink to the deepest crimson. Later in the summer thyme, birdsfoot trefoil, cinquefoil, speedwell, lady's bedstraw, knapweed and cat's ear shine purple and yellow amongst the grasses.

MAP 32

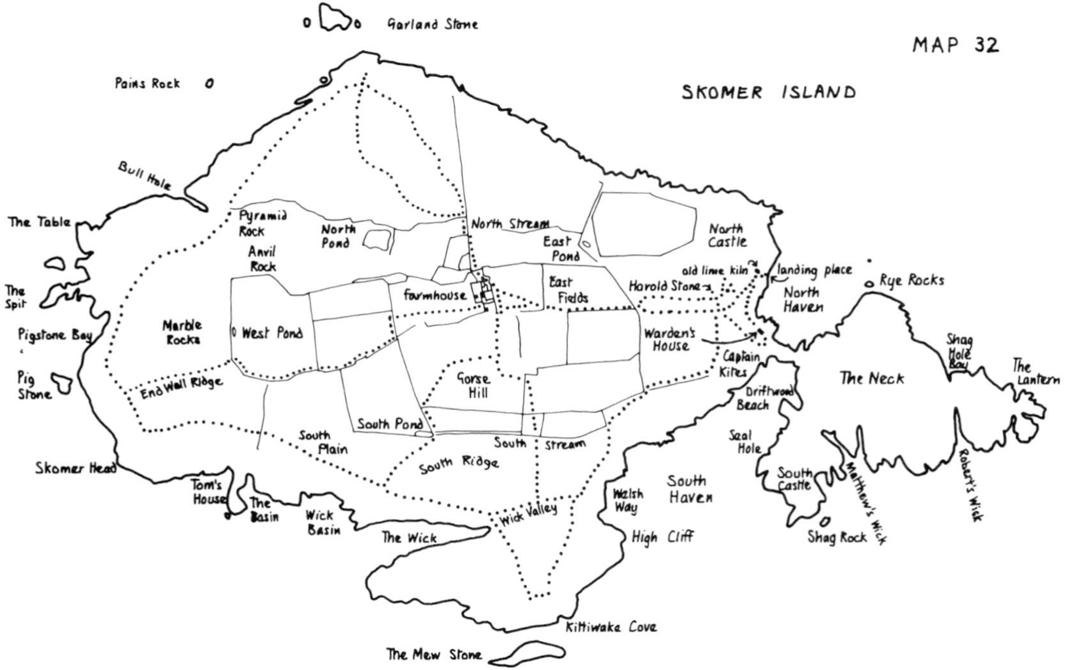

SKOMER ISLAND

Garland Stone

Pains Rock

The Table

The Spit

Pigstone Bay

Pig Stone

Skomer Head

Bull Hole

Pyramid Rock

Anvil Rock

North Pond

West Pond

Marble Rocks

Endwall Ridge

Tom's House

The Basin

Wick Basin

The Wick

North Stream

East Pond

East Fields

farmhouse

Gorse Hill

South Pond

South Plain

South Ridge

South Stream

Wick Valley

North Castle

old lime kiln

Harold Stone

Warden's House

Captain Kites

Driftwood Beach

Seal Hole

landing place

North Haven

Rye Rocks

The Neck

Shag Hole Bay

The Lantern

Robert's Wick

Matthew's Wick

Shag Rock

South Castle

South Haven

Welsh Way

High Cliff

Kittiwake Cove

The Mew Stone

Access arrangements

Skomer Island has a resident warden and the island is open daily from April until late September except Mondays (Bank Holidays excepted), between 1000 and 1800. Except for the Spring Bank Holiday week the number of visitors landing on any one day up until the end of July is restricted to 100: but there are no toilets or other facilities for day visitors. No dogs are allowed on the island, and camping is not permitted. There is limited self-catering **accommodation for members of the DWT.**

Guide-books are available on the island and at the Lockley Lodge Information Centre at Martin's Haven. A self-guiding trail follows marked paths allowing visitors to the principal breeding cliff sites: please stay on the footpaths at all times in order to minimise disturbance to the sea-bird colonies.

The island is accessible by boat from Martin's Haven, but visitors are reminded that the landing places at both Martin's Haven and Skomer can at times be difficult; depending on the tide, passengers may have to be ferried to and from the boat by large inflatable dinghy: this is an important consideration for the very young, the infirm and the elderly.

Weather and tides permitting, the boat crosses from Martin's Haven to Skomer at 1000, 1100 and 1200, provided that the maximum number allowed on the island is not exceeded. The crossing takes about 20 minutes, and the first visitors of the day normally have about five hours ashore. It is strongly recommended that, during periods of unsettled weather (which can include fog), and at the beginning and end of the season (April–May and September), intending visitors check with the boatman regarding sailings. No advance bookings are taken for ordinary day visits.

The official boat to land visitors is the *Dale Princess* operated by the Dale Sailing Company, Dale (tel. Dale 349), to whom all enquiries regarding the boat service should be directed.

Round trips of the island on the *Dale Princess* depart from Martin's Haven at 1300 on Sun, Tues, Wed and Thur; evening cruises organised by the National Park Information Service (tel. Saundersfoot 812175) on Tues and Fri – advance bookings only.

13   **Skokholm** (Map 33)

Skomer's near neighbour to the S is the 240 acre/97ha island of Skokholm, whose fine dark-red sandstone cliffs contrast with Skomer's dark rocks, which are some 40 million years older in the geological timescale. The island lies some 2ml/3.2km off the mainland coast, and is just over 1ml/1.6km in length. It is owned by Mr Hugh Lloyd-Philipps of Dale Castle, into whose estate it passed in 1740, and is leased from him by the DWT. Like the other islands – Skomer and Ramsey – it is a splendid sea-bird sanctuary.

The flat, level top of the island is a remnant of the late Tertiary wave-cut platform truncating steeply dipping and folded rocks. It has been isolated from the mainland by marine erosion along zones of weakness possibly following faults on the present-day sea bed.

The rocks continue those of St Ann's Head and Gateholm Island: the red marls and the purple, grey and red sandstones, all belonging to the Old Red Sandstone Series, were compressed into folds with E–W axes. A downfold or syncline is clearly seen in the southern half of the island. The strata along the S coast can be seen to dip steeply inland and to strike into a direction parallel to the cliff edge; the strata in the headland to the NW of The Head, on the other hand, dip gently to the S. There is a parallel upfold or anticline along the W coast.

One would have thought that Skokholm would have held the same attraction for settlers as Skomer, but its size, comparative inaccessibility, and the savage tide-races that surround it no doubt deterred permanent occupation.

The Normans introduced rabbits to the island in the 12c, and managed the island as a warren. The island was farmed between 1750 and 1900, and was made famous by Ronald M Lockley's two books of the 1930s, *Dream Island* and *Island Days*. Lockley lived on the island from 1927 to 1939 and extensively renovated the original 18c farm buildings. He established Britain's first bird observatory here in 1933 and thousands of migratory birds were ringed on the island each year. Farming finally ceased in 1940, since when the island has been managed as a nature reserve. Lockley, aged 84, returned from his home in New Zealand for the Jubilee

Anniversary celebrations of the DWT on Skokholm and Skomer, on 24 June 1988, when he was introduced to HRH The Prince of Wales.

The Nature Reserve

The former farmhouse is now a place where you can stay and learn about the birds of Skokholm. Full-board accommodation is available on a weekly basis and there are also some courses on birdwatching and on the history and natural history of the island. Enquiries about visiting, accommodation and courses should be addressed to the DWT.

The range of breeding *birds* on Skokholm is smaller than on Skomer: there are no kittiwakes, and few guillemots breed simply because the cliff-faces do not provide suitable nesting ledges. The balance is to some extent restored by the storm petrel, a nocturnal species, of which about 6000 pairs nest on the island, and a population of about 35,000 pairs of Manx Shearwaters. These birds are present from March to early October, with peak numbers occurring in July when non-breeding birds visit the island. Late August and early September are particularly exciting, for the chicks are then emerging from their burrows in preparation for a journey which will take them to South American waters. Cloudy, preferably moonless, nights are best for observing the nocturnal and noisy Shearwaters.

Other sea birds include about 5000 pairs of puffins, several hundred pairs of razorbills, guillemots and fulmars, and the three large gulls; while gannets, shags, cormorants and kittiwakes, which breed on nearby islands, can usually be seen offsore. Land birds include oyster-catchers, lapwings, ravens, wheatears, rock and meadow pipits, and choughs.

During the peak migration periods of spring (April-May) and autumn (August-September) a large number of different species may arrive on the island, and in some years there are spectacular 'falls' of common British breeding birds – larks, thrushes, warblers, flycatchers, pipits and finches, depending on season and weather.

Access arrangements

Skokholm is open from early April until late September on a weekly

MAP 33

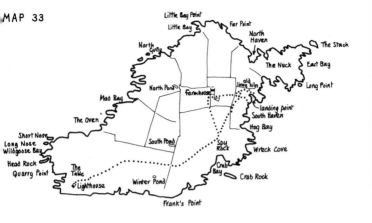

SKOKHOLM ISLAND

basis, and full, if simple, facilities are available for visitors. Accommodation is limited, and there are similar restrictions to those on Skomer concerning dogs and camping. There are no daily visits, although special visits may sometimes take place as part of the programme of guided walks run by the National Park Information Service.

The official boat to land visitors is the *Dale Princess* sailing from Dale at about 1300 each Saturday, or as soon as tides or weather permit. All enquiries regarding the boat service should be directed to the Dale Sailing Company (tel. Dale 349).

Skokholm Lighthouse
A Trinity House lighthouse stands at the W end of the island. The white octagonal tower, 60ft/18m high, and adjacent two-storey dwellings, were built in 1916. The red light, some 178ft/54m above the sea, is visible over a range of 17 nautical miles, and flashes once every 10 seconds. The fog signal sounds every 15 seconds, and has a

range of 4 nautical miles. The station was manned until 1983, but it now automated and remotely controlled and monitored from St Ann's Head lighthouse.

The lighthouse forms the landward corner of a triangle of lights, the others being South Bishop and The Smalls. These lights keep ships well clear of this extremely dangerous coast and guide them safely into Milford Haven or the Bristol Channel. During the long period of warm clear weather in July 1983 the loom of Tuscar Rock, the Irish lighthouse, could be seen from Skokholm light at a distance of 46 nautical miles.

14   Grassholm and The Smalls

Grassholm
Grassholm is the outermost of the offshore islands of the Pembrokeshire coast, lying some 6.5ml/10.4km W of Skomer and 10ml/16km off the mainland of the Deer Park. A submarine reef of basalt, stretching from the Marloes Peninsula and through Skomer, throws up to create the 22 acre/9ha islet of Grassholm, and also forms the reefs of The Smalls. The island is waterless and has never been inhabited by man for more than a few days at a time.

The island is renowned worldwide for its vast colony of gannets, which cluster so thickly on the NW side that they make a white patch visible from the mainland on a clear day, while birds flying around the island produce a corresponding white cloud.

The gannet colony is the only one in Wales and the third largest in the British Isles. The birds are believed to have come here in the 1860s from the much persecuted Lundy colony in the Bristol Channel. The population has been fast increasing ever since 1883. In 1872 there were twelve breeding pairs; in 1924, 1000 pairs; in 1964, 15,500 pairs; today there are 28,500 pairs. Allowing for one nestling and at least one immature bird to each adult pair, this

Grasshom from The Wick, Skomer

makes a total of 114,000 gannets by the middle of the summer.

Grassholm was purchased by the RSPB in 1948 and is managed by them as a National Nature Reserve. Access is difficult: the voyage takes about 1–2 hours, depending upon the departure point from the mainland, the boat, and the tide, and can only be done in any case in really calm weather. No landing is permitted before mid-June, and after then only one boat per day is allowed to land passengers. The official boat for landings and round trips is the *Dale Princess*, operated by the Dale Sailing Co, (tel. Dale 349). Sailings depart from Martin's Haven on Mon and Fri (except on Bank holidays) – advance bookings only. Evening cruises organised by the National Park Information Service (tel. Saundersfoot 812175) take place on Thurs – advance bookings only. There are no facilities on the island, and no dogs are allowed.

If you can manage a landing you will witness the most magnificent mass bird spectacle in all Wales.

The Smalls and the Hats and Barrels

Grassholm is not the furthest land W. Some 3ml/4.8km beyond Grassholm are the low-tide reefs of the Barrels, while a further 2.5ml/4km beyond them is the reef of the Hats. Even further out, some 8ml/12.8km W of Grassholm, beyond the tide races and shoals, are two rocks projecting only 12ft/3.6m above the highest tides – The Smalls, the most westerly land in Wales.

The Smalls and the Hats and Barrels have no doubt been known to west-coast mariners for many centuries: they appear as dangerous reefs in early charts, and have been the cause of many shipwrecks. On 12 October 1978 the Greek oil tanker *Christos Bitas* ran aground on the Hats and Barrels reef, spilling some 35,000 tons of oil, part of her cargo. She was finally sunk 340ml/547km W of Ireland on 31 October 1978. Rapid response ensured minimal damage to bird life but it was the suffering of sea birds caused by this incident that prompted the idea of a Centre for Oiled Birds: it was subsequently set up by the DWT at West Williamston on the Daucleddau, and it received a Prince of Wales Award in 1982. On 16 June 1985 the 1,321-tonne tanker *Bridgeness* went aground on The Barrels, spilling 400 tonnes of her cargo, and an entire puffin colony of 5000 birds was destroyed. It is now likely that the Department of Transport will get the approval of the International Maritime Organisation for an official 'Navigational Area to be Avoided' off the Pembrokeshire coast.

The Smalls Lighthouse

The reefs were such a terrible danger to shipping that in 1765 a certain John Phillips, a Cardiganshire man who was docks manager at Liverpool, called public attention to them when he set about obtaining a lease from the Treasury with the idea of erecting a lighthouse on The Smalls and profiting from the revenues from the dues. A lease was not granted until 1774, and Phillips advertised for designs, choosing one submitted by Henry Whiteside, a musical-instrument maker from Liverpool.

Whiteside had designed an octagonal house or hut of timber, 15ft/4.5m in diameter, perched on nine legs or pillars, five of wood and three of cast iron, spaced around a central timber post. At the rock surface the legs spanned 23ft/7m and the overall height was 65ft/19.8m. The hut had two apartments, a living-room below divided into compartments for sleeping berths and stores, and a lightroom and lantern above.

Whiteside sailed from Solva on 17 June 1775 with eight Cornish miners, a blacksmith and two labourers to erect his lighthouse, but at the first attempt the wind and sea rose so suddenly that the cutter had to sheer off to avoid being wrecked, and five men were left stranded on the rock for two days and nights before they were rescued.

During the winter of 1775–6 Whiteside erected the whole structure temporarily on the Gamlin at Solva. This was a fortunate decision as the iron legs proved to be faulty and had to be replaced with wood. When work was resumed in the spring of 1776 iron rings were fixed into the rock to which the workmen tied themselves for safety. On 1 September 1776 the oil lamps were first lit, and before leaving the rock the workmen excavated a large hole to hold coals, and fresh water in a wooden tank.

By December it was obvious that the structure was incapable of withstanding the forces of the sea and drastic repairs and alterations became necessary. Phillips had no funds to carry them out; he discharged the keepers, extinguished the light, and made over his interest to a committee of Liverpool traders. These men induced Trinity House to obtain an Act of Parliament in 1778 which authorised them to rebuild and maintain the lighthouse, and to levy reasonable dues. Trinity House eventually bought the lease in 1836.

The crew of the lighthouse has always been three since the tragic experience of Thomas Howell. In a storm in the winter of 1780–1, one of the two keepers on duty – Joseph Harry – died. His companion Howell, fearing that he might be suspected of foul play if he committed the body to the deep, and unable to attract attention, used the interior woodwork panels of the house to make a coffin, and lashed it to the lantern rail of the tower. Passing ships noticed this strange object but raised no alarm. Keeper and coffin remained on the rock for three weeks before the usual relief boat came from the mainland, by which time Howell was almost mad.

The lighthouse dues became very valuable as shipping increased. Whiteside's astonishing structure stood for more than 80 years against the tremendous gales of the Atlantic, and his principle of raising a superstructure on piles so that the sea could pass through them with 'but little obstruction', adopted since on hundreds of sea structures, is best illustrated today by the oil rigs in the North Sea.

In 1856 the Board of Trade sanctioned the building of a new lighthouse in stone. This, the present structure, was completed and lit by 7 August 1861. The circular tower, 141ft/43m high, cost £50,125 to build. It is painted with red and white horizontal bands, and can be seen from the mainland on a clear day with powerful glasses. The white light, some 125ft/38m above high water spring tides, is visible over a range of 26 nautical miles in normal conditions, and flashes three times every 15 seconds. The fog signal sounds twice for two seconds every 45 seconds; the range is 3 nautical miles and it is controlled by an automatic fog-detector. A lower fixed light on the E side of the tower is so masked as to cover only the dangerous shoals and reefs of the Hats and Barrels and the islands to the E.

During the long period of warm clear weather in July 1983 an interesting case of extreme visibility was reported to Trinity House.

Bardsey Island lighthouse (off the Lleyn Peninsula) could be seen by day from The Smalls at a distance of 69 nautical miles, and after dark Strumble Head light (38 nautical miles) and Tuscar light (35 nautical miles) were both visible. The usual ranges of these lights are published at 28, 29 and 28 nautical miles respectively.

According to the Meteorological Office, Bracknell, when the sea temperature is relatively cold and the density of the air is decreasing rapidly, caused by a layer of low air in contact with cooled water, light rays from objects low down near the horizon are bent down and the effect is to render objects that are normally below the horizon visible. Thus, lights may be 'raised at night' at much greater distance than one would normally expect. This phenomenon is known as abnormal refraction.

15   **Martin's Haven to St Ann's Head** (Maps 31, 34, 35)

6.8ml/10.9km

The 'official' Path approved by the Secretary of State did not go around the Deer Park, and it is difficult to understand why this decision was made. After all, the Deer Park is part of the mainland Pembrokeshire coast, and there is a footpath around it. As at Dinas Island and Lydstep Head there is a short cut across the neck of the promontory, but this is no excuse for not designating a long-distance footpath around the coastline proper.

The Coast Path is in good condition all the way, but in one or two places there are diversions into the adjoining fields because of landslips, and there is a steep climb up to Great Castle Head from Westdale Bay.

The Deer Park Circuit 1ml/1.6km
The Deer Park is the most westerly part of the Dale-Marloes Peninsula which separates St Bride's Bay from Milford Haven. The coastguard lookout at its highest point, 189ft/58m above the sea, provides a fine vantage point: to the N lies the broad expanse of St Bride's Bay bounded on its N side by the St David's Peninsula and Ramsey Island; to the W lies Midland Isle and Skomer; while to the

SSW is the island of Skokholm across Broad Sound.

The small valley marking the landward boundary of the Deer Park is excavated along a zone of weakness in the rock, leaving headlands of resistant igneous rock at its seaward ends. The rocks of the Deer Park, Midland Isle and Skomer are all of the same volcanic series, and they outcrop along the southern coast of the Deer Park between The Anvil and Renney Slip, where the igneous rocks are magnificently exposed in the sea cliffs. These cliffs are for the greater part over 100ft/30m high and are dangerous, so you are urged to keep well away from all cliff edges. However, the character of the lavas can be examined in safety at the coastguard lookout and at Wooltack Point. The rock is typically dark grey to black in colour and finely crystalline, and is similar in composition to basalt.

As with other headlands and promontories around the coast, the defensive potential of the Deer Park was recognised by Iron Age man. The steep E-facing valley slope above Martin's Haven forms a natural defensive element, and running due S the remains of an Iron Age defensive bank and ditch become more evident, so that on the cliff above Renney Slip the embankment is clearly visible. A promontory fort occupied the whole of the area to the W, but was a defended settlement rather than a military one.

During the late 18c to 19c the promontory was enclosed for a second time. The high stone wall from Martin's Haven to Renney Slip, which follows the valley, was built to enclose the Deer Park as a planned embellishment of the Edwardes estate. There is no evidence that deer were ever introduced, less still that they would have survived.

Martin's Haven to Marloes Sands 2.2ml/3.5km
It is but a few minutes' walk to cross from one side of the peninsula to the other, and you soon get views of different horizons. We leave behind the broad expanse of St Bride's Bay and turn in a different direction, gradually making our way eastwards around South Pembrokeshire.

Renney Slip is a small and very attractive sandy cove. Adjoining Deadman's Bay is another secluded cove with a beach of pale grey sand and rock, which can be reached by a steep and winding path.

The Path continues SE following the contortions of cliffs and inlets to the triple embankments of an Iron Age fort above Victoria Bay. It is one of the few Iron Age forts around the coast having water conveniently to hand: a stream immediately E runs down the cliffs to Watery Bay. At this point a path runs inland to Runwayskiln – the youth hostel – and a NT car park.

Albion Sands is a fine, small sandy beach, curving round to link up with Gateholm Island at low tide. The *Albion* was the first paddle steamer to be bought for a Welsh shipping company, and she was beached here in April 1837 after having been damaged in Jack Sound. Two rusting iron shafts project from the sand at low tide, all that is left of the wreckage.

Horse Neck is the promontory overlooking Gateholm Island, and on the steep descent, if you wish to gain access to the sands, you pass the transition from Silurian shales to Lower Old Red Sandstone rocks. From here you get a splendid view along the length of Marloes Sands, backed by cliffs clothed in wind-pruned blackthorn, privet and bramble. The steep bedding of the rocks forming the cliffs is particularly evident. These less resistant Silurian shales were up-ended 440–400 million years ago just before the more resistant Old Red Sandstone rocks deposited on top of them. The Silurian rocks are for the most part inclined towards the sea and traversed by innumerable faults which follow a general N-S direction. The cracks and faults were created during the Armorican Earth Movements *c*240 million years ago. Waves now exploit the cracks, eating away the layers of shale from between the sandstone, forming caves and arches which collapse to leave large detached 'stacks'. The resulting rocks and boulders form sheltered sun-traps on the beach. Silurian fossils are relatively common.

Gateholm Island is a small island, accessible at mid-tide, consisting of resistant rocks of the Old Red Sandstone series. Similar rocks that once adjoined the headland of Horse Neck were faulted down on either side and replaced by the less resistant Silurian rocks, which have been subsequently removed by comparatively recent erosion by the sea. The island was once intensively inhabited: archaeologists have found the remains of 130 hut-circles. The huts are set end-to-end or grouped around

MAP 34

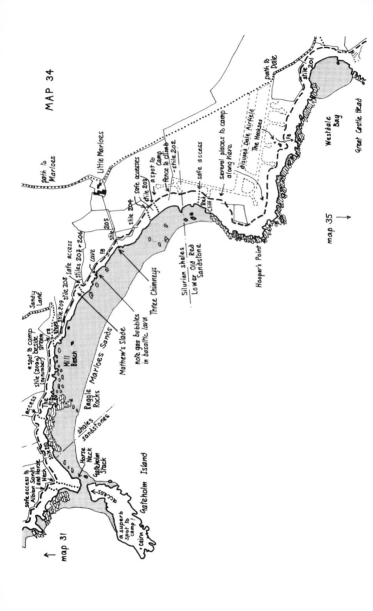

path to Marloes

Little Marloes

Sandy Lane

a spot to camp (take number?)

stile (209) beside stream

access

The

Mill Beach

safe access

stile 208

stile 209

safe access

stiles 207 + 206

cave

stile 205

stile 204

stiles 203

safe access

fence to climb

a spot to camp

stile 202

safe access

stile 201

path to Dale

The Hooses

disused Dale Airfield

several places to camp along here

Westdale Bay

Great Castle Head

map 35

Hooper's Point

Red Cliff

Silurian shales
Lower Old Red Sandstone

Three Chimneys

note gas bubbles in basaltic lava

Mathew's Slade

Marloes Sands

Raggle Rocks

shales
sandstones

Horse Neck

stile 200

Gateholm Stack

Gateholm Island

access

cairn

a superb spot to camp

map 31

safe access to Albion Sands and Horse Neck

courtyards, unusual for an Iron Age settlement in this area, and were occupied in the 3c and 6c. Evidence for the first period of occupation comes from Roman pottery and a coin of Carausius (AD287–293), while from the second period there is a ring-headed bronze pin of the Irish type. It has been suggested that Gateholm might have been a monastic site in the early Christian tradition of other island communities, such as Caldey.

Back on the mainland the Path runs along the top of the cliffs, although there is access to the sands from Horse Neck at low tide. (There is also access at the E end of the bay, beside Stile 203, and to the beach centre by Sandy Lane, the usual access from inland.)

Marloes Sands vie with Freshwater West as the finest and most picturesque beach on the Pembrokeshire coast. 1ml/1.6km of flat sands make a gentle curve between rocky headlands of Old Red Sandstone. SW winds create impressive surf, which gives good surfing, and bathing is safe between the shelter of the headlands.

In the middle of the bay is Mill Beach, where a stream and path come down from Marloes. Traces of an old mill leat may be seen down near the beach, but there are no signs of the mill which it served. Sandy Lane is a sunken path running inland between high banks of blackthorn and bramble, and emerging on the Marloes road near the NT car park. Nearby is Runwayskiln, a former farm and now a youth hostel. The YHA obtained a long lease from the NT and conversion work on the farm was carried out by local contractors and volunteers from Milford Haven schools. Opened in January 1978, it is the best simple hostel in Wales.

Runwayskiln and its land, and the adjoining Trehill and West Hook Farms, totalling 524 acres/212ha, are owned by the NT. A further 73.5 acres/30ha of coastal land, including the Deer Park, Midland Isle and Gateholm Island, were bought by the NT in 1981 with money from Enterprise Neptune funds and a Countryside Commission grant, and thereby the NT has complete ownership of the Marloes Peninsula.

Marloes Sands to Westdale Bay 2.1ml/3.3km
From the Sandy Lane access point to Marloes Sands the Coast Path continues along the top of the cliffs, but if the tide is out it is more

worthwhile to walk along the sands to the end of the beach, if only to better appreciate two interesting geological features in the cliffs. Near Mathew's Slade basaltic lava exposed in the cliffs displays vesicular structure – gas bubbles given off during the cooling of the lava within molten or semi-molten rock became trapped on solidification, thereby producing cavities or vesicles.

Just beyond, the Three Chimneys show how landforms can be strongly influenced by geological factors. Here beds of Silurian sandstone and mudstone are standing vertically. The extremely high angles of dip were caused by the intense pressures exerted during the Armorican Earth Movements. A fourth chimney disappeared in a gale in November 1954: the anemometer at Kete went off the scale in a gust of 130mph/210kmph.

The bay of Marloes Sands ends at the transition from the Silurian shales to the Lower Old Red Sandstone, and the Path runs around the edge of the disused Dale Airfield. Dale Airfield was a Fleet Air Arm station named HMS *Goldcrest*, which subsequently moved to Brawdy. The Hookses was formerly Hook Vale Farm before it was 'submerged' by the aerodrome.

Westdale Bay is an exposed beach pounded by breakers in high winds from the SW. It lies on the line of the Ritec fault, which runs straight up the length of the Milford Haven, down the Ritec valley from which it is named, to Tenby, and eventually across the neck of the Gower Peninsula W of Swansea. In pre-glacial times the sea ran through the Dale valley and the Dale Peninsula was another offshore island. The fault line was exploited by the ice during the last Ice Age, and a channel was cut deep into solid rock by the watercourse excavated beneath the ice sheet by the meltwater issuing from it: the orientation of the channel suggests that the ice was moving from the land towards the W. The strait was then plugged by material released from the melting ice, and now these unconsolidated glacial and periglacial deposits are being eroded by the action of the sea, winds and rain. We have already noticed similar features at Dinas Island.

Westdale Bay has a sandy beach backed by shingle and high

The Three Chimneys, Marloes Sands

crumbling cliffs. Bathing is safe except when the tide is ebbing and in heavy surf, which creates strong undertows. There is access to the bay direct from Marloes by footpath, and by footpath from Dale through fields past Dale Castle. Alternatively there is vehicular access along a narrow lane from Dale church to the top of the cliffs on the edge of the former airfield.

From Westdale Bay you can make a short cut into Dale village (0.75ml/1.2km) as the circuit of the Dale Peninsula is a further 6.25ml/10km. The complete circuit Westdale-St Ann's Head-Dale-Westdale is 7ml/11.2km.

Westdale Bay to St Ann's Head 2.5ml/4km
At Westdale Bay the line of the cliffs turns S, and there is a good stiff but short climb up to Great Castle Head. A late Iron Age promontory fort (*c*100BC) occupies the top, having massive banks and ditches, and a ramped entrance on the E side. The approach path into the fort was defensible by clever use of an abrupt change of level caused by geological faulting.

The Path levels out and continues S past Kete. This was the site of HMS *Harrier*, the Royal Navy Air Direction Centre, a radar and meteorological school, which was closed in 1960. In 1967 the NT purchased 168 acres/68ha of land here, including 1.5ml/2.4km of coastline, out of money raised by Enterprise Neptune. They have removed all traces of the radar station, opened up the coast to the public, provided a free car park for access to the coast, and restored the land to its former agricultural use.

The Coast Path joins the public road coming up from Dale, and you are soon out on to the headland. The high cliff-top of *St Ann's Head* is known for its gales, its virtually frost-free climate, and the wild tide-races that fret the sea below. The Head guards the approach to Milford Haven, one of Britain's finest deep-water harbours, long recognised by merchants and shipowners for its sheltered position. It was at nearby Mill Bay that Henry Tudor, Earl of Richmond landed in 1485 on his way to become the King of England; and from the Haven that Henry II led his army into Ireland in 1172. Today large fleets of oil tankers gather in its anchorage.

Just beyond the end of the public road you come upon the coastguard's magnificent lookout, converted in 1910 out of one of the original lighthouses, which in turn was built on the site of St Ann's Chapel, a building which was probably erected by Henry Tudor in thanks for his landing at Mill Bay in 1485. The coastguard station – the Milford Haven Maritime Rescue Sub-Centre – is the main reception point for all '999' calls relating to coastal and marine emergencies in Pembrokeshire. It has direct contact with all maritime search and rescue facilities in the country, and is also in constant contact with the MHCB's Signal Station to ensure safe passage of the supertankers into the Haven.

Dangerous reefs lie just below the surface of the sea off St Ann's Head, almost in mid-channel of the approach into Milford Haven, and in two groups which shipping must pass through. The greatest dangers, some 7 nautical miles SE of St Ann's Head, are the dreaded Crow Rock and The Toes lying off Linney Head, which have claimed many more vessels than the reefs within the harbour. Today two usable channels are marked clearly by many sets of leading lights, all vital to safe navigation within the Haven.

There has been a lighthouse on *St Ann's Head* for centuries, perhaps right back to the time when a chapel dedicated to St Ann stood here, a chapel whose custodian had the job of keeping a nightly beacon flaming.

Trinity House was granted a patent on 15 March 1713 to build a lighthouse at St Ann's Head. They in turn, as was their policy at the time, leased it to the owner of the land, Joseph Allen, who agreed to build two lighthouses and keep them in good repair. To help maintain the lights Allen was permitted to collect dues amounting to one penny per ton cargo on British vessels, and two pence on foreign vessels. Allen established two towers, and coal fires were lit in them in June 1714.

The front light of the two, endangered by cliff erosion, was rebuilt in its present position in 1841 some 30ft/9m from the cliff edge. When the rear light was closed in 1910 – it later became the coastguard station – the front light was modernised, and in 1958 was put on to mains electricity. The light, some 157ft/48m above the sea, is visible over a range of 23 nautical miles. The light flashes every

5 seconds, white in most of its arc, but with a red sector towards
Crow Rock and The Toes. The fog signal, contained in the curved
tower that replaced the old square fog-horn house, sounds twice
every 60 seconds. The nearby helicopter pad is used to transport
engineers to the lighthouse on The Smalls, South Bishop and
Skokholm.

Visiting may take place from 1300 until one hour before sunset
every day except Sunday. Visiting is free of charge and without
prior permission from Trinity House, but may not take place during
foggy conditions, and there may be times when visitors are
inconvenient, for example, when work is in progress. To avoid
disappointment you are strongly recommended to telephone the
keeper to advise of the expected time of arrival and size of party:
The Principal Keeper, St Ann's Head Lighthouse, Dale,
Haverfordwest, Dyfed, SA62 3RS (tel. Dale (064 65) 314).

A new lighthouse has been erected by the MHCB in the mouth of
the Haven off St Ann's Head. The Mid-Channel Rocks Lighthouse
is a prefabricated steel tower secured by 20ft/6m bolts to the sea
bed. Its stem is a steel tube filled with concrete, which had to be
carried to the site in 600 loads by helicopter. Mid-December was
(rightly) chosen as being likely to produce a calm day for the tricky
operation of lowering the tube from a helicopter on to its exact
position. The lantern is powered by 77 dry batteries which need to
be replaced each year. The light, completed in 1966, indicates the
entrance to the deep-water channel into the Haven.

At St Ann's Head gale-force winds (i.e. of at least 39mph/
63kmph) are experienced on about 32 days in an average year, and
gusts of up to 90mph/145kmph are not uncommon. The Head
shelters the entrance of the Haven from westerly gales and provides
a magnificent viewpoint to watch the pilot launches going out to
meet incoming oil tankers.

Trinity House helicopter at St Ann's Head Lighthouse

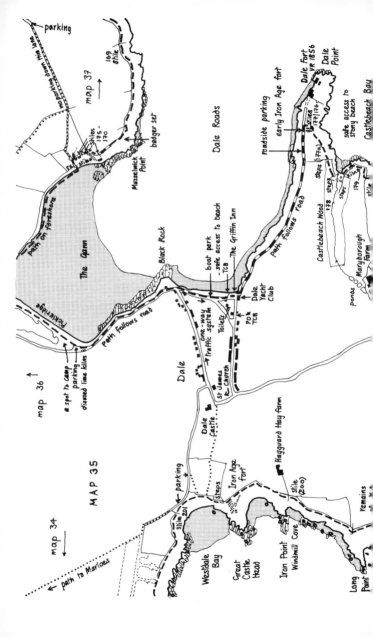

MAP 35

← map 34

parking →

path to Marloes

Westdale Bay

Great Castle Head

Iron Point

Windmill Cove

Long Point

Steps

Iron Age fort

stile 201

remains

Haggyard Hay Farm

stile (Zoo)

Dale Castle

St James Church

one-way traffic system

Toilets

Dale

P.O & T.C.B

Dale Yacht Club

boat park – safe access to beach

The Griffin Inn

T.C.B

Black Rock

Path follows road

parking

a spot to camp parking

disused lime kilns

The Gann

map 36 ↑

Path follows road

Path on foreshore

Musselwick Point

stiles 175 – 176

T.C.B stile

stile 169

map 37 →

no parking down this lane

parking →

badger set

Dale Roads

roadside parking

early Iron Age fort

Path follows road

Dale Fort VR 1856

stiles 177 & 178

Dale Point

Castlebeach Bay

safe access to stony beach

stile 179

steps

kiln

steps

Castlebeach Wood

Ponds

Maryborough Farm

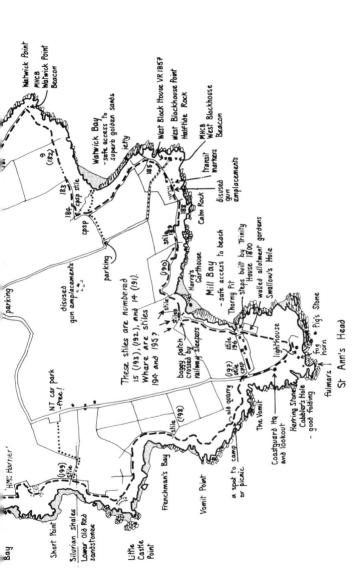

Bay
HMS 'Harrier'
Short Point
Silurian shales
Lower Old Red sandstones
Little Castle Point

Watwick Point
MHCB Watwick Point Beacon

(182) 9

Watwick Bay
— safe access to superb golden sands
icky

183
cpsp stile
184
cpsp

parking

disused gun emplacements

parking

NT car park — free!

These stiles are numbered 15 (193), (192), and 14 (191). Where are stiles 194 and 195?

stile (190)

stile (189)

boggy patch crossed by railway sleepers

West Block House VR 1857
West Blockhouse Point
Hatfide Rock
MHCB West Blockhouse Beacon

Transit markers

disused gun emplacements

Calm Rock

188

Mill Bay
— safe access to beach

Harry's Garthouse

Thorny Pit

Steps built by Trinity House 1800

walled allotment gardens

Swallow's Hole

stile (196)
cpsp

Franchman's Bay
stile (198)

Vomit Point

old quarry

a spot to camp or picnic

stile (197)
cpsp

The Vomit

Coastguard Hq and lookout

Herring Stone
Cobbler's Hole
— good folding

lighthouse

fog horn

Pig's Stone

fulmars

St Ann's Head

Part four

The Milford Haven

16 The Milford Haven Waterway

The natural harbour of Milford Haven has been considered by many to be one of the finest deep-water anchorages in the world. It is some 20ml/32km long: from its 2ml/3.2km wide mouth between St Ann's Head and the Angle Peninsula it runs for some 11ml/17.6km to Mill Bay near Burton, at which point the waterway swings northwards to the Daucleddau – the common estuary of the Rivers Western and Eastern Cleddau. Almost as far inland as Neyland the Haven* maintains a width of about 1ml/1.6km and allows access to vessels of up to 55ft/16.7m draught at all states of the tide. Silting is not a severe problem, and the only real disadvantage of the waterway is its entrance, which is relatively shallow and exposed to the prevailing southwesterly swell, but the dredging and marking of a channel makes the waterway accessible.

The Haven is a submerged and sunken river valley, an arm of the sea enclosing over 70ml/112.6km of coastline. Its fluvial origin is demonstrated in its branching pattern and its tributary tidal creeks. It is a ria, or drowned river system, similar to those of southern Ireland and the S coasts of Devon and Cornwall. The inlet was originally a river valley excavated along the Ritec fault in the wave-cut plateau of Pembrokeshire when the sea level was at least 100ft/30m lower than at present, possibly during an inter-glacial period in the early part of the Ice Age, about 10,000–7000 years ago. The Haven has been filled and emptied by seawater on at least

---

* Where reference is made to Milford Haven confusion may arise in the mind of the reader as to whether the waterway or the town of the same name is meant. In this guide I shall refer to the waterway as 'the Haven' and to the town as 'Milford'.

two occasions since then, as sea level has fluctuated in step with the occurrence of glacial and inter-glacial stages. With the final disappearance of the ice and the return of the sea, sea level rose appreciably and flooded the lower reaches of the valley, converting it into a deep inland harbour. The greater part of the southern shore of the Haven consists of the southward dipping Old Red Sandstone rocks of the northern edge of a syncline. The sea has broken through this ridge of hard rock and developed bays along the axis of the syncline where the overlying Carboniferous limestone occurs at the surface: the two embayments are the estuary of the Pembroke River and Angle Bay.

The natural harbour of the Haven was described by Defoe on his 17c tour as one of the greatest and best inlets of water in Britain. 'Mr Camden', he recalls, referring to the visit of the earlier traveller and antiquarian, 'says it contains 16 creeks, 5 great bays, and 13 good roads for shipping, all distinguished as such by their names; and some say a thousand sail of ships may ride in it and not the topmast of one can be seen from another; but this last, I think, merits confirmation.'

> Say, and speak thick,
> . . . how far it is
> To this same blessed Milford; and, by the way
> Tell me how Wales was made so happy as
> To inherit such a haven.

(Imogen, in *Cymbeline* (Act III, Scene 2) by William Shakespeare)

Milford Haven Oil

The unique advantages of the Milford Haven as a deep-water port were recognised by the major oil companies. At the beginning of the 1950s, demand for oil was growing; tankers grew too, to meet the economics of the long haul round the Cape of Good Hope, the Suez Canal then being closed. The Haven was the only natural harbour in the southern half of Britain that could cope with ships of the size then existing or envisaged: over 150,000 tons. The Haven has a deep-water channel of 53ft/16.4m for the first 6ml/9.6km to the Texaco berth, and thereafter 42ft/12.8m for the next 2ml/3.2km as far as Wear Point, and then a minimum of 34ft/10m as far as Pembroke Dock. In addition, it was within relatively easy reach of the great market of the Midlands.

The first refinery was built on the N shore of the Haven near Hubberston by the Esso Petroleum Company. Opened in November 1960, it heralded the most industrial phase in Pembrokeshire's history. Esso was followed by the Texaco refinery at Rhoscrowther in 1964, and by the Gulf refinery at Waterston in 1968. Amoco, slightly inland, commenced operations in 1973. Another important installation is the British Petroleum Angle Bay Ocean Terminal at Popton Point and its tank farm at Kilpaison, opened in 1960. Oil is pumped from here to the BP refinery at Llandarcy near Swansea.

Vessels of 75,000 tons (Esso's 'County' class) were at one time considered to be large, but since the completion of the £7.5 million dredging and blasting scheme by the MHCB in 1970, the Haven has handled VLCCs (Very Large Crude Carriers) of up to 260,000 dead weight tons (dwt) – vessels like the enormous *Esso Scotia* and *Esso Cambria*. The *Esso Scotia* was the first 250,000 tonner ever to enter a British port, and arrived in the Haven in October 1969 on her maiden voyage.

All of the vast oil refineries and tank farm complexes on or near the shores of the Haven were designed to mar as little as possible the beauty of the landscape: all but one of them (Gulf) and the Pembroke Power Station are in the Pembrokeshire Coast National Park, but despite expensive and extensive earth-moving and contour-shaping the visual impact is widespread and corrosive. By day the tall towers and stacks punctuate the distant skyline; close at hand the security fencing, the unnatural earth banks and the steel shapes are oppressive; and sometimes the smell is very nasty. Only at night, when the sites are lit up with a multitude of lights, do they make an awe-inspiring sight.

Britain's major oil port, Milford Haven handles some 35 million tons of crude oil and oil products annually. Before the oil companies started operations approximately 700,000 net register tons of commercial shipping used the Haven. In 1961, the first full year of operations as an oil port, some 4.7 million tons were handled. The figure rose steadily up to 1974, when it reached 59.1 million tons. Since then imports of petroleum and lubrication oils have declined, and crude-oil imports are now half the 1974 peak. Recession and North Sea oil have further reduced the Haven's traffic.

Only about 5 per cent of the refined products from the Haven refineries leave by road and rail, the rest being re-exported by tankers and by the *3 M's Pipeline*. Of the vast network of pipelines which are essential to the workings of the refining complexes, none is more important than this one, linking Milford Haven with the Midlands and Manchester (hence the 3 M's). It was built at a cost of £15 million in 1972–3 by a consortium of the Esso, Gulf, Amoco and Texaco companies, and carries petrol, kerosene, diesel fuel and other refined products in a pipeline from Waterston (on the N side of the Gulf refinery) to Seisdon, W of Birmingham. From Seisdon there are smaller pipelines to Birmingham, Nottingham and Manchester. The pipeline has a capacity of 9 million tons per annum.

In the 1958 Milford Haven Conservancy Act the government recognised that a new civil port authority would be needed to control the enormous volume of shipping that would be using the Haven. The *Milford Haven Conservancy Board* (MHCB) was appointed to meet this need and is charged with the task of maintaining, improving, protecting and regulating the navigation, and in particular the deep-water facilities. It has jurisdiction over all the tidal water of the Haven and its approaches, and its five major responsibilities are shipping control, inspection and maintenance, aids to navigation, improvement, and anti-oil pollution control.

All vessels entering and leaving the Haven are in constant radio contact with the Signal Station at Hubberston. The Station provides vessels with information on weather, tidal levels, visibility and shipping movements within the Haven, as well as arranging for pilots to meet vessels at the entrance: the MHCB's five green-and-white patrol and pilot launches are a familiar sight on the Haven, taking pilots to and from the ships. The MHCB provides and maintains a complex system of buoys, lights and navigation beacons to facilitate safe passage, and day and night transit lights have been put up at West Blockhouse Point, Watwick Point, Great Castle Head and Little Castle Head.

In Britain's major oil port it is perhaps inevitable that human error sometimes results in oil polluting the waters of the Haven: although such pollution does not only come from the operations of the oil industry. Individual oil companies each maintain the most stringent regulations, strictly enforced, for ensuring that oil spillages do not occur at their terminals. The Board, in close collaboration with the five resident oil companies, has developed a unique, and now world-renowed, anti-oil pollution service. This responds immediately to pollution regardless of source of responsibility, the protection of the Haven being of over-riding concern. A special oil dispersal vessel, the *Seaspray*, is equipped and constructed for the most efficient treatment of floating oil with emulsifying chemicals. For dealing with major oil spillages a floating boom, together with an oil-skimming apparatus, is held in constant readiness. In addition, the *Seaguard* is specially designed to clean up heavy oil spills. Developed in France following the *Amoco Cadiz* disaster off the Brittany coast, it is the only craft of its type currently in use in Britain, and was first used to help deal with a minor spill in the Haven in May 1983. Fortunately oil pollution is a rare phenomenon, but it is rigorously prosecuted.

17   The defence of Milford Haven

After the period of Anglo-Norman settlement, the strategic importance of Milford Haven appears to have passed unnoticed. Apart from the landward-orientated Iron Age forts, the Dark Age encampments, and the Norman castle at Pembroke, no attempt was made to construct permanent fortifications, in spite of the fact that Milford Haven was a point of departure for Ireland, and in addition was the landing point for Henry Tudor in 1485 when he returned from exile to establish the Tudor dynasty after the Battle of Bosworth Field. It was the great scare of 1538–40 which led Henry

VIII to embark on an elaborate scheme of coastal defence, and Henry's castles are conspicuous features of the English shore. The whole scheme extended from Hull to Milford Haven.

The advent of the Spanish Armada in 1588 caused further uneasiness leading to an examination of the Haven's possibilities for defence, which was conducted efficiently by George Owen (1552–1613), the Pembrokeshire historian and Deputy Lieutenant of the County. Owen recommended a plan for the fortification of the Haven based on the triangle of Thorn Island, Dale Point and Stack Rock, but it was not implemented until nearly 300 years had elapsed! In 1757, following the outbreak of war the previous year, Lieutenant Colonel Bastide, the Director of Engineers, was sent to survey and advise as to where forts or batteries might be built round the Haven. His suggested plan of six forts was thought to be too expensive and therefore it was reduced to three. The necessary land was purchased and the Ordnance Department put in charge of construction, but only one fort, at Paterchurch Point (Pembroke Dock), was started. It was not completed, the danger of invasion having passed by 1759.

During the first half of the 19c the value of the deep-water anchorage of the Haven increased with the advent of steam shipping and the building of the Admiralty dockyard (moved in 1814 from Milford to Pembroke Dock) and this, coupled with a general fear of France and the invention of the rifling of gun barrels, resulted in much thought being given to defending the Haven. A committee was formed, which in 1817 appointed Major General Sir Alex Bryce to look into the defence of the Haven. He made a number of far-sighted proposals, and suggested two lines of defence behind the entrance fortifications.

The first was to be five forts built near the mouth of the Haven, crossing it at a strengthened Stack Rock, and the second line to consist of another four forts in the area to the W of Milford, from a fort to be built at Hubberston via a floating battery, due S to Popton Point. This would prevent steamships from approaching within 3.45 nautical ml/6.4km of the naval dockyard. Four other forts (including a defensible barracks) were to be built around Pembroke Dock, each battery also to be protected from landward attack.

Among other proposals, Bryce suggested for the outer defence of the entrance to the Haven the provision of a nine-gun battery on Stack Rock, a six-gun on Thorn Island, and a twelve-gun near Chapel Bay, as well as a chain of forts across the peninsula E of Pembroke Dock to protect these batteries from landward attack.

Nothing was done at the time, but works were carried out on Bastide's 1757 plan of Paterchurch Fort in 1830. The fort was garrisoned in 1831; in 1837 it was dismantled and replaced by a battery, built by the Admiralty in 1840–42 to protect their new dockyard at Pembroke Dock. The importance of the naval dockyard was then again stressed, and an army garrison was declared necessary in addition to the marine garrison. Construction was commenced in 1844 of the Defensible Barracks on Barrack Hill, above Pembroke Dock, and was completed on 25 November 1845. The two 'Martello towers' on either side of the dockyard were constructed in 1849–57, and were intended for coastal defence, but were obsolete for military purposes by 1905.

The growth in importance of the dockyard and Haven anchorage, together with the aspirations of France and the 'Liberal Awakening' under Palmerston, led to yet another reappraisal of the defences of the Haven. Lengthy negotiations over the purchase of the land at Dale Point and Thorn Island had been taking place, and work commenced at Stack Rock in 1850 and at Thorn Island in 1852. Dale Fort was completed in 1856, followed by West Blockhouse Fort in 1857.

It was imperative that steamships should be brought to a standstill at the entrance to the Haven, and in a report by the Royal Commissioners on the defences of the United Kingdom in 1860, six forts were proposed: of these only Scoveston and the fort on St Catherine's Island, Tenby, were actually constructed, and by 1867 Stack Rock Fort, South Hook Battery, Hubberston Battery and Popton Battery were in various stages of completion.

Of the forts which can still be seen around the shores of the Haven, some could accommodate more than 200 men and were armed with about 30 guns. In all, the forts could accommodate a total garrison of about 1900 men, defending the Haven with 200 heavy guns. The cost of constructing these defences was about £1 million. Had the plan been implemented in total the forts would have required a garrison of between 7000 and 8000 men in time of war to man some 300 or more guns. The total cost of all the works would have amounted to several millions of pounds even at that time.

With the completion of these fortifications in the early 1870s little more was attempted in the Haven. The design of permanent fortifications was becoming rapidly outmoded during 1875–1900 with the increasing range and effectiveness of artillery. The defences were never put to the test and were largely obsolete by World War I, when they were garrisoned for coastal and later air defence. They were again garrisoned during World War II, mainly carrying anti-aircraft batteries for defence against the frequent German air-raids. Since 1945 nine of the forts and batteries have been abandoned and are in a derelict and often dangerous state. Some are very eerie indeed and those who explore them should be aware of unexpected holes and drops in their floors. Taken as a group these 19c forts, sometimes called 'Palmerston's Follies', remain a unique example of their kind, and of the military thinking of the period in which they were constructed.

Milford Haven is one of the few defended ports in the British Isles where the fortifications are virtually all of one date – eleven out of the fourteen forts were constructed within a twenty-year period. Despite the closeness of date, there is considerable difference in design and each fort has distinctive features. The mid-19c concept of permanent fortification, governed as it was by the invention of rifled, long-range artillery, can be seen here in isolation. Beside their architectural fascination all now convey an impression of a dream quite out of scale with life. Their very nature makes them now almost indestructible. Construction was of a high standard: for the most part external facing is in limestone masonry, with the forts of the 1850s using fine quality ashlar and some fine granite. Internally, particularly for vaulting and piers, brick is used extensively, cast iron is used for stairs, and many of the steel shutters in the casements remain. The timber used in floors and partitions has suffered with the passage of time, but the carving of the ashlar details is of extraordinary precision.

One final point of interest lies in the fact that this system of forts was one of the last to be designed for defence against attack from the landward side, and each fort incorporated a substantial defensible barrack accommodation and military garrison, making each self-supporting and organised for all-round defence, although as a group the forts were sited to cover one another. This vital concept was apparently forgotten in the 20c when, for instance, the absence of a suitable defensive network to defend the landward approaches to the naval batteries and port of Singapore facilitated its rapid capture by the Japanese in 1941, with disastrous results.

18   Haven North Shore: St Ann's Head to Milford (Hakin Point)
(Maps 35–39)   13.05ml/21.5km

The Path around St Ann's Head to Dale is good, but although the stretch from Dale to Hazelbeach is not as good as that around St Bride's Bay, it is better than the path on the opposite shore of the Haven.

St Ann's Head to Dale 3.6ml/5.8km
The E side of St Ann's Head and the Dale Peninsula faces into the Haven and has three attractive beaches with red-speckled, off-white sand – Mill Bay, Watwick Bay and Castlebeach Bay. Access to all is by the Coast Path only, although cars can be driven to near West Blockhouse Point to reach the first two, and to near Dale Point to reach the last. All three beaches shelve steeply, and swimmers should stay close inshore because currents swirl in and out of the Haven.

As you turn your back on St Ann's Head lighthouse you pass the end of a row of Trinity House cottages and come to the coast again at Thorny Pit, a place where Trinity House built steps in 1800 so that materials for the building of the lighthouse might be landed: it was easier to sail stone down the Haven than to carry it by road overland.

Mill Bay is famous for being the landing place at sunset on Sunday, 7 August 1485 of the Earl of Richmond, on his way to become Henry VII, King of England. In the Wars of the Roses the Lancastrians suffered a number of crushing defeats, the worst of which was the Battle of Tewkesbury in 1471, when Henry VI was captured and subsequently stabbed to death in the Tower of London. That left Henry Tudor, Earl of Richmond sole Lancastrian claimant to the throne, and he and his uncle, Jasper Tudor, fled to Pembroke Castle where Henry had been born. The Yorkists besieged the castle, but Henry and Jasper were rescued and Henry sailed to France.

At that time the most powerful figure in S Wales was Rhys ap Thomas, Lord of the South, and in 1483 he swore allegiance to Richard III of England vowing that Henry would only return to Wales 'over his body'. On 1 August 1485 Henry Tudor was recalled from his exile in Brittany, and he returned with his uncle Jasper to reclaim the Lancastrian crown. Henry landed at Mill Bay with 2000 men and Pembrokeshire rose to greet them with open arms, seeing at last a chance to have a Welshman on the throne of England and Wales. The Bishop of St David's was as enthusiastic as the rest, and absolved Rhys ap Thomas from his oath to Richard III since Richard himself was perjured, being 'a usurper and a murderer' (of the Princes in the Tower). Rhys, with all his following, went to meet Henry, and thought it as well to make his own interpretation of the oath by lying on the ground before him and inviting Henry to step over his body. Rhys became one of Henry's most powerful allies and the army of liberation moved in a two-pronged march northwards, one part under Rhys through Brycheiniog (Breconshire) and one under Henry through Ceredigion (Cardiganshire), Henry pausing a night at Machynlleth on 11 August. The two parties joined up at Shrewsbury on 15 August with a gathered army of 5000. They were in Stafford on 17 August, and from there the way to Bosworth was short.

Henry's campaign was a lightning one if ever there was one: within two weeks of his landing he had raised and organised a large army, and after his extraordinary march to Bosworth, where he killed Richard III in the Battle of Bosworth Field on 22 August

1485, he was proclaimed king: with Henry VII the Tudor age began and an era of peace came to Wales.

The present wreck on the sands in Mill Bay has nothing to do with Henry's landing in 1485. It is the remains of a boom defence vessel which broke away from the tug towing it off for scrap in 1964.

West Blockhouse Point is the headland between Mill Bay and Watwick Bay, and on its tip the West Blockhouse was built in 1857 for a garrison of 80 men. It took five years to build, cost £45,000 and had twelve guns, and an open battery was added in 1900. It was manned throughout the two World Wars when it was used mainly for anti-aircraft defence. It was abandoned in 1950 and is now owned by the Landmark Trust. West Blockhouse formed the outer defences of the Haven together with the East Blockhouse across the Haven at Angle and Thorn Island, Dale Fort and Stack Rock.

New navigation towers were erected in 1970 on West Blockhouse Point – the MHCB West Blockhouse Beacon (teamed up with the Watwick Point Beacon) and three transit markers – to enable the colossal tankers to find and keep to the dredged deep-water channel. These lights are very modern and powerful, having a range of 5ml/8km by day and 19ml/30km by night. Their brilliance can be increased or decreased as required by poor visibility and day or night operation. The forward light, West Blockhouse Beacon, has outriggers with red lights indicating the entrance to the Haven's deep-water channel. The back light, the Watwick Point Beacon, is 159ft/50m high, and is the third tallest lighthouse in the world.

Castlebeach Bay has a stony beach, and the remains of an old lime-kiln and lime-burner's cottage are at the mouth of the valley. The valley leading down from Maryborough Farm is delightfully wooded, being one of the few places on the coast where trees grow. Trees survive on the Pembrokeshire coast only in the shelter of E-facing valleys, and sycamore are more numerous because other species hardly ever regenerate naturally.

The easternmost headland of the Dale Peninsula is the narrow promontory of Dale Point, an ideal place for Iron Age man to build a fort overlooking the Haven: its single defensive bank spans the narrow neck of the promontory, and has been excavated by students from the Dale Fort Field Centre.

On the very tip of the Point is Dale Fort, a solidly built battery, similar to that of West Blockhouse Point Battery. It was built between 1852 and 1856, cost £45,000, had twelve guns and a garrison of 80 men. Since 1947 it has belonged to the Field Studies Council, and from it the Dale Fort Field Centre runs courses in branches of natural history, including biology, and geography and archaeology; but the Centre is chiefly notable as a leader of marine biology study, for which it is ideally situated.

For the next 0.75ml/1.2km the Coast Path follows a road through a sycamore wood down to Dale, a charming village sheltered from all but E winds, said to be the sunniest place in Wales. On the descent from Dale Point you can look across the sheltered anchorage of Dale Roads. Dale village has had a long seafaring tradition. In 1566 it was one of the main villages of the Haven and was as large as Fishguard. In the 18c and early 19c the historian Fenton (who was not always reliable) records that the village was ruinous and poor. In 1841 the population was 382, including many shipwrights, apprentices, fishermen and merchant seamen. Lime was imported to be burnt in the lime-kilns around the village, and cargoes of all types were loaded and unloaded on the beach with horses and carts approaching the vessels at low tide.

There are now no fishing boats registered at Dale, but it is possible to arrange fishing and sightseeing trips along the coast and to the islands. Dale slipway is the departure point for trips to Skokholm, but for landings on Skomer you must go to Martin's Haven. Because of the sheltered waters of Dale Roads, free from tidal currents and off the main shipping lanes, Dale is an ideal sailing centre. There is often severe congestion in the holiday season because of the inadequate car-parking facilities. Motorists wanting access to the coast for walking around the peninsula would be well advised in high season to park out of Dale, and leave the village-centre parking places to those towing and manoeuvring dinghies.

The church of St James is on the N side of the village, well away from the centre of activity. It has a small tower and is typically 'English' but has nothing much of interest in it. Beyond the church, on the way to Westdale Bay, is Dale Castle, a largely modern residence which may well stand on the site of an early defence. The manor of Dale was held in the 13c by Robert de Vale, whose family had been established in Pemrokeshire since about 1130. Later sales resulted in the occupancy of John Lloyd in 1776, whose descendants still live there, the Lloyd-Phillips surname appearing in 1823.

Dale to Sandy Haven 5.75ml/9.25km
Before setting out from Dale it is important to consult the tide tables, remembering that high tide is Milford time plus 5 minutes. Roughly speaking, you can get across The Gann 'bridge' from Pickleridge (0.5ml/800m N of Dale) 2 hours before low water; you can cross the 'bridge' at Sandy Haven up to 2 hours after low water; and you should allow 2 hours to walk between the two. It is possible, particularly at spring tides, to get across 3 hours before or 3 hours after low water at both places, but don't count on it. Therefore, depart from Dale on an outgoing tide.

At high water – and this may span a period of 8 hours – the Gann Diversion necessitates a detour via Mullock Bridge, and the Sandy Haven Diversion necessitates an even longer detour via Rickeston Bridge. Neither of these diversions forms part of the Coast Path, but it is well worth knowing that they exist. Each may take up to 2 hours to walk, and you have to ask yourself if it is worth waiting a minimum of 2 hours to cross the river estuaries in order to save the extra miles.

The crossing of The Gann from Dale to Musselwick is 1.5ml/ 2.4km, while the Gann Diversion via Mullock Bridge is 3.5ml/ 5.6km, an extra distance of 2ml/3.2km. The Sandy Haven Diversion from one bank of the Sandy Haven Pill to the other via Rickeston Bridge and Herbrandston is 4ml/6.4km. The distance between Musselwick and Sandy Haven on the Coast Path is 4.25ml/6.8km: therefore, if the journey between Dale and Sandy Haven is done at high water via both the Gann and Sandy Haven Diversions, then you will have walked 11.75ml/18.8km.

We have already seen that the ice of the last glaciation extended only as far S as the Milford Haven. Nevertheless, the ice was active enough to transport glacial erratics from far afield. When the ice began to melt, about 17,000 years ago, vast quantities of meltwater

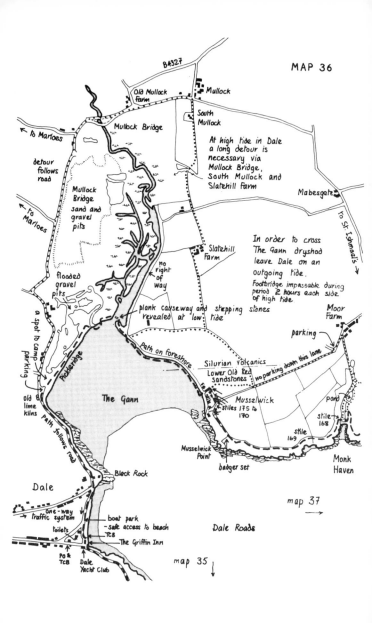

MAP 36

B4327

Mullock

Old Mullock
Farm

South
Mullock

to Marloes →

Mullock Bridge

At high tide in Dale
a long detour is
necessary via
Mullock Bridge,
South Mullock and
Slatehill Farm

detour
follows road

Mabesgate

to Marloes →

Mullock
Bridge
sand and
gravel pits

to St Ishmael's →

In order to cross
The Gann dryshod
leave Dale on an
outgoing tide.
Footbridge impassable during
period 2 hours each side
of high tide.

Slatehill
Farm

flooded
gravel
pits

no
right
of
way

plank causeway and stepping stones
revealed at low tide

Moor
Farm

parking

a spot to camp
parking

Path on foreshore

Silurian volcanics
Lower Old Red
sandstones

no parking down this lane

pond

old
lime kilns

Picklebridge

The Gann

Musselwick
stiles 175 to
170

stile
168

stile
169

Path follows road

Musselwick
Point

badger set

Monk
Haven

map 37

Dale

Black Rock

one-way
traffic system

boat park
-safe access to beach
TCB

Dale Roads

toilets

The Griffin Inn

PO &
TCB

Dale
Yacht Club

map 35 ↓

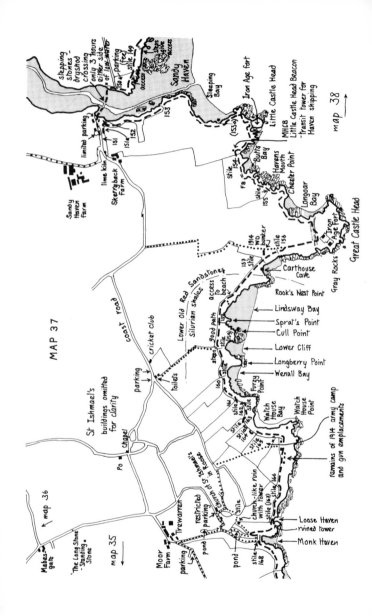

MAP 37

map 38 →

St Ishmael's
buildings omitted
for clarity

← map 36

Mabes's
gate

The Long Stone
– Standing
Stone

map 35 ↓

coast road

cricket club

parking

toilets

chapel

Po

Moor
Farm

parking

pond

Trewarren

restricted
parking

Church of St Ishmael's
in Roose

church-like ruin
with tower

pond

pond

stile
168

Monk Haven

Loose Haven
ruined tower

stile (167)

stile 166

remains of 1914 army camp
and gun emplacements

Watch
House Point

Watch House
Bay

stile 165

stile 164

stile & stile

stile 163

Furzy
Point

stile 162

Wenall Bay

Longberry Point

Lower Cliff

Cull Point

Sprat's Point

stile 161

Lindsway Bay

good path

steps

Access
to beach

Rook's Nest Point

Carthouse
Cave

Gray Rocks

stile 157

stile 156

Iron Age Fort

Great Castle Head

1914 WD bunker

stile

Lower Old Red Sandstones

Silurian shales

Longoar Bay

Chaster Point

Havens Mouth

stile 155

FB

stile 154

Butts
Bay

MHCB
Little Castle Head Beacon
–Transit tower for
Haven shipping

Little Castle Head

Iron Age fort

Sleeping Bay

Sandy Haven

stone slip-
way access

car
parking

stile 149

crossing
only 3 hours
either side
of low water

stepping
stones/
drybshod

use

stile 150

limited parking

stile 151

stile 152

153

(1536)

154

155

156

157

Sandy
Haven Farm

Skerryback Farm

lime kiln

deposited sands and gravels. Some of the fluvio-glacial deposits are laid down in The Gann valley, close to the limit of ice in the last glaciation. The gravels contain shells radiocarbon-dated as being about 38,000 years old, thus showing that these marine creatures were alive in the Irish Sea before the onset of the Ice Age, and must have been carried here by the ice as it moved SE towards Wales.

During 1941–2 substantial airfield construction in the area produced heavy demands for sand and gravel, and the deposits in The Gann provided an ideal source of material. However, the contractors left too narrow a barrier on the seaward side of the gravel workings and the sea subsequently broke through the Pickleridge and flooded the pits. Since then the shoreline has been gradually moving inland; since 1947 two lagoons have been filled up with stones pushed in by the tide.

The remaining lagoons are now an important wildlife habitat, the area behind the Pickleridge having been designated a Site of Special Scientific Interest. In winter the lagoons are the haunt of the little grebe or dabchick as well as goldeneye, scaup, smew, Slavonian grebe and red-breasted merganser. Also in winter are wigeon, Brent geese, greenshank, green sandpiper and little stint.

Beyond The Gann you pass Musselwick and soon come to Monk Haven, a small sheltered cove at the mouth of a thickly wooded valley. Gently shelving, shingly sand is revealed at low water. One can well imagine this place as a landing for an early Celtic missionary, and indeed in the days of the saints and even more so during the medieval pilgrimages, this cove was a busy place. The landing was also used in Neolithic times, as a road – the 'Welsh Road' – ran from here to St David's, removing the dangers of sailing round the coast through the reefs and tide races around the offshore islands.

The head of the cove is blocked off by a high wall of local red sandstone, dating from the 18c when the valley was part of the great Trewarren Estate. There are two other interesting remains nearby: the watch-tower on the headland to the E of the cove is a folly built c1860 and known as the 'Malakov', its architect having been a serving officer in the Crimean War; the other remains are of religious buildings in the woodland beside a path leading inland.

The charming little wooded valley behind Monk Haven runs up

past the secret little church of *St Ishmael's* to the village of the same name, and is well worth a detour. A steep-sided wooded valley leads you first to the small church of St Ishamel's in Roose, set in isolation from the village amongst trees. The building is a simple cruciform shape, in red and purple sandstone, with a bell-cote probably in the place of an earlier small tower. Inside it is dark and cool because the trees exclude the light and the walls are plain-coloured wash, typical of 19c 'restoration'.

The church was founded in the middle of the 6c by St Ishmael, who also helped St Teilo and St Aidan in founding a monastery at St David's. He was a disciple of St David and is believed to have been appointed Bishop of St David's by his uncle, St Teilo, on the death of St David in 589. The church's festival is celebrated on 16 June.

The original 6c building was reconstructed by St Caradoc about 1100. The chancel and transepts, added in the 13c and 14c, are of different dates and they are not symmetrical. Both transepts have hagioscopes through the chancel for a view of the altar.

St Ishmael's beach is Lindsway Bay, reached by a good path from the village cricket field. A steep path and steps lead down to flat sands with rocks and cliffs at either end. The beach is shingle at high water, sandy at low water, and quite safe for bathing. The bay occupies an embayment in Silurian shales between the sandstones of Watch House Point and Great Castle Head. HRH Prince Charles, the Prince of Wales, first set foot on Welsh soil here in 1955. In 1973 the tanker *Dona Marika* was aground for thirteen weeks in the bay.

Great Castle Head has an Iron Age promontory fort with a single embankment dating from *c*300BC, and it provides good views of the vast oil refineries to the E and of tanker traffic in the Haven. Nearby Little Castle Head also has an Iron Age fort, also with a single bank and ditch. The MHCB has two buildings as forward markers on Great Castle Head, with an 85ft/26m tower on Little Castle Head as a back marker. The tanker pilot has to line these up, in order to maintain his position in the Haven channel.

When the Coast Path was originally designated it ran inland a little between Little Castle Head and Skerryback Farm (as shown in

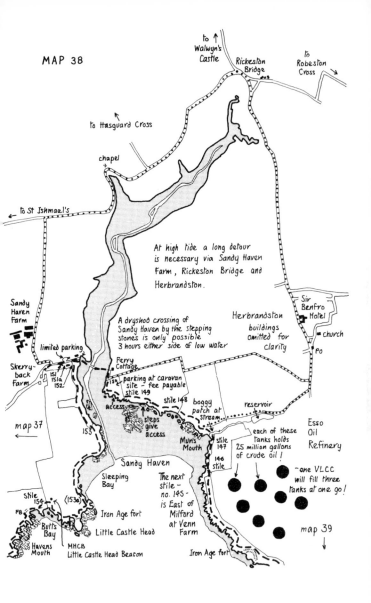

MAP 38

to
Walwyn's Castle

Rickeston Bridge

to
Robeston Cross

to Hasguard Cross

chapel

to St Ishmael's

At high tide a long detour
is necessary via Sandy Haven
Farm, Rickeston Bridge and
Herbrandston.

Sandy
Haven
Farm

limited parking

Skerry-
back
Farm

151
151a
152

Ferry
Cottage

154

153

map 37

access

A dryshod crossing of
Sandy Haven by the stepping
stones is only possible
3 hours either side of low water

parking at caravan
site - fee payable
stile 149

stile 148

150

steps
give
access

Mun's
Mouth

Sandy Haven

Sleeping
Bay

The next
stile -
no. 145 -
is East of
Milford
at Venn
Farm

stile
154

(153a)

FB

Butts
Bay

Havens
Mouth

MHCB
Little Castle Head Beacon

Iron Age fort

Little Castle Head

boggy
patch at
stream

reservoir

stile
147

146
stile

Herbrandston
buildings
omitted
for
clarity

Sir
Benfro
Hotel

church

PO

Esso
Oil
Refinery

each of these
tanks holds
25 million gallons
of crude oil !

- one VLCC
will fill three
tanks at one go !

map 39

Iron Age fort

the 1974 edition of the HMSO guide). The footpath has since been diverted around the coast proper via Sleeping Bay and Sandy Haven. Thickly wooded banks overlook the picturesque creek of Sandy Haven, where trees overhang the water at high tide. Flat, firm red sands are revealed at low water, but the estuary is flooded at high tide. The bay is not really a good place for swimming, but the low cliffs and rocks provide ideal spots for sunbathing.

Access for vehicles is limited on both sides of the Sandy Haven Pill, but is better on the E side where a lane comes down from Herbrandston. This approach gives access to the largest expanse of sand, on the E side of the creek.

The causeway and stepping stones across Sandy Haven Pill give a dryshod crossing only 2 hours either side of low water, otherwise a 4ml/6.4km detour has to be made around the Pill via Rickeston Bridge and Herbrandston. Consult the tide tables, and remember that high tide is Milford time minus 5 minutes.

Sandy Haven to Gelliswick Bay 2.5ml/4km
This is not the wild coast of the N of Pembrokeshire nor of the Dale Peninsula, but one of the attractions of the scenery along the Coast Path is its variety. The change from the quiet solitude of Monk Haven and the sylvan beauty of Sandy Haven to the open and man-made landscapes around the oil refineries is striking. The Path is quite adequate, and for the last 1ml/1.6km from the Esso jetty to Gelliswick Bay it is on a road, but there is no alternative way.

The vast complex of the Esso oil refinery dominates the coastal scene, and we can get a good look at this from South Hook Point, the next headland up the coast. On the way, between Mun's Mouth and Kilroom, the Path passes an Iron Age fort: the outer of its two banks is very small.

South Hook Fort now stands within the security fence of the Esso oil refinery, and is utilised by the oil company as a store. It was built between 1859 and 1863 at a cost of £48,154 and had a garrison of 180 men within the defensible barracks, which had guns mounted on the roof. The main guns were in two batteries, and are outside the security fence, alongside the Coast Path: fifteen guns faced W and five guns faced E, their arcs of fire interlocking with the guns of

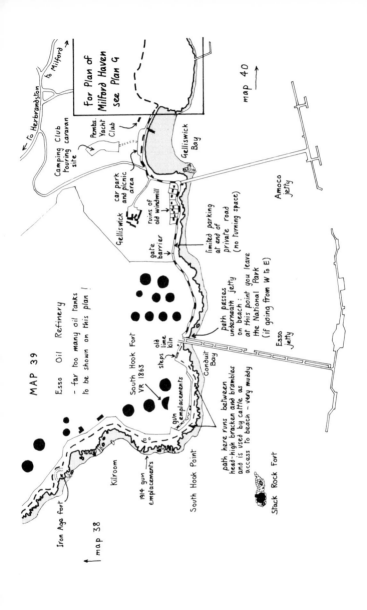

MAP 39

to Milford →

to Milford →

to Herbrandston →

Camping Club touring caravan site

Esso Oil Refinery
– far too many oil tanks to be shown on this plan!

Iron Age fort

map 38 →

Kilroom

1914 gun emplacements →

South Hook Point

South Hook Fort
VR 1863

steps
old lime kiln

gun emplacements

Conduit Bay

path here runs between head-high bracken and brambles and is used by cattle as access to beach – very muddy

Stack Rock Fort

path passes underneath jetty on beach : at this point you leave the National Park (if going from W to E)

Esso jetty

limited parking at end of private road (no turning space)

gate barrier →

Gelliswick

car park and picnic area

ruins of old windmill

For Plan of Milford Haven see Plan G

Pembs. Yacht Club

Gelliswick Bay

map 40 →

Amoco jetty

Stack Rock Fort. The battery was substantially altered in 1900.

Stack Rock lies just 0.5ml/800m offshore, and is dominated by the Palmerstonian *Stack Rock Fort* built upon it. A tower was built in 1850–52 at a cost of c£6000 and carried three guns, but in the period 1859–67 it was substantially altered. The fort was developed to support an armament of 26 turret guns and a garrison of 168 men, though only 23 guns were installed. The fort has 50 rooms and is on two levels, with floors and roof of concrete. Water was collected from the roof and stored in underground tanks. The fort cost £96,840 to build and was the most expensive construction of the whole of the Haven's defences.

Stack Rock is one of the few remaining privately owned forts and is a listed ancient monument. The 1870 Pallister cannon remain, as do the tremendous iron doors and shutters of their emplacements. The whole property was offered for sale in October 1978 at £20,000, which seemed a bargain, but this could only have been because it will take so much money to make it habitable.

Construction of the *Esso oil refinery* started in July 1958 and was completed two years later at a cost of £60 million. It came 'on stream' when it was officially opened on 3 November 1960 by HRH Prince Philip, Duke of Edinburgh. Just over twenty years later the refinery was closed down: in March 1983 the plant stopped processing crude oil, but it continues as a distribution terminal for petroleum products.

The original design capacity of the refinery was 4.5 million tonnes of crude oil a year, which steadily increased over the years until in 1973 a major expansion programme was completed increasing the capacity to some 15 million tonnes a year. But this big surge in new capacity came into operation just as UK oil demand sagged: at the end of 1974 the UK oil industry had capacity to process more than 140 million tonnes of oil a year, but throughput – the amount of feedstock of crude oil and partly refined products fed into the refineries – during 1975 was less than 94 million tonnes, a utilisation rate of only 65%.

The oil industry was wrong-footed: there was a massive over-

Esso oil refinery from Little Castle Head

supply of refining capacity in the UK and throughout Europe.
Between 1973 and 1981 UK oil demand dropped by 30 per cent.
During 1981 utilisation was down to 60 per cent, and it seems
unlikely that it will be higher than 70–75 per cent during the mid-
1980s.

Excess refinery capacity was also linked with the changing pattern
of demand. Oil demand for transport, chemical feedstock and non-
energy uses, such as lubricants and bitumen, has remained
relatively static compared with the 1973 level: for heating uses and
for electricity generation the story is very different. Big price
increases and economic recession have encouraged both energy
saving and the substitution of other fuels for oil, so that the annual
demand for fuel oils, used in large boilers and electric power
generation, slumped in the decade 1972–82 from 40 million tonnes
to about 15 million tonnes.

Heavy fuel oil products also happen to be the products needing
the least intensive refining and the fewest number of supplementary
processes to prepare them for the final customer. Most transport
fuels and lubricants, and lighter fuels such as petrol, gases and
naphtas for chemical feedstock, need more intensive treatment, but
their value in the market place is very much greater. The changing
mix of demand therefore dictated the need for new or revamped
plant to produce those higher value products. In the three years
1980–82 Esso spent some £130 million on new facilities at Fawley,
and it no longer needed two refineries, so in the autumn of 1982 the
company announced their drastic decision to close down the
Milford Haven refinery.

Esso was the first refinery in the Haven, and was the largest: the
site occupies 1270 acres/515ha. It accounted for 25 per cent of the
Haven's oil traffic. Although the refinery has closed very little of
the plant has been demolished. Included in a total of 122 tanks,
spheres and propane drums are five crude oil tanks of 25 million
gallons/112,600 cubic m capacity, some of the largest in the world,
with a diameter of 282ft/85.4m and a height of 64ft/19.5m. These
largest tanks are around the western edge of the site. The smaller
tanks hold petrol, diesel oil and jet fuels.

The marine terminal – the jetty reaching out into the Haven – is

3000ft/914m long, and has five berths. Tankers of 250,000dwt can enter and berth at every tide, while substantially larger vessels can only berth on spring tides. At maximum capacity this terminal could handle 28 million tonnes of oil a year.

The Coast Path passes underneath the Esso jetty and follows a private road to Gelliswick, where you reach the *Amoco jetty*. This also stretches out into the Haven for 3000ft/914m, but it is smaller than Esso's in that it has only three berths. Thirteen buried pipelines connect the jetty to the refinery at Robeston, about 1.5ml/2.4km inland. The Amoco refinery site cannot be seen from the Coast Path: only if you take the Sandy Haven Diversion (see p. 230 and Map 38) can you see its coloured tanks on the inland plateau skyline.

From Amoco's jetty the Coast Path swings down and around Gelliswick Bay, a beach of dull red shingle and low-tide sand overlooked by the grey walls of the derelict Victorian Fort Hubberston. Gelliswick is the 'town beach' of Milford Haven, but it is not a good bathing beach, being better, and more popular, for sailing. There is immediate access from roadside parking, and a slipway for launching boats. Water skiers and sailing dinghies contrast with the supertankers that can often be seen moored at the nearby Esso and Amoco jetties.

Gelliswick Bay to Hakin Point 1.25ml/2km (Plan G)
At Gelliswick, beneath the dark ramparts of Fort Hubberston, the Coast Path enters the urban fringe of Milford Haven, passing inland through the housing estates of Hubberston and Hakin, before coming out on to Hakin Point along a promenade path beside the Haven. Walkers on the Coast Path may be tempted to cut corners and pass straight through on their way to Milford, but there are two places of interest just off the route which are worth more than a passing glance – Fort Hubberston and the Hakin Observatory.

Fort Hubberston is the most accessible of the Palmerston forts around the Haven and has consequently suffered from vandalism as well as dereliction from old age. Nevertheless one can carefully explore the ruins to gain an impression of the strength of the Victorian defences. The fort was built between 1860 and 1865 at a cost of £87,894 for a garrison of about 250 men. The garrison was housed in a two-storied, D-shaped, bomb-proof barracks, and this is the part of the fort which is most accessible. The gun emplacements were sited further down the headland, closer to the sea. There were 28 guns: casements for eleven guns, plus eight in open battery and nine in battery to eastwards. The cartridge magazine was sited below the casements, with the powder magazine cut into the rock behind. The open battery was included in the alterations of 1900.

The Hakin Observatory is an octagonal ruined dome near the playing-field entrance in the council estate, and is the only relic of Greville's projected 'mathematical college'. The Observatory was built by Charles Francis Greville, the builder of Milford Haven, in 1811. The building is a two-storied octagonal tower, topped by a small observation dome having an internal diameter of 19ft/5.8m. It was designed with narrow slit openings continuing up from the side walls, leaving only a narrow ring of masonry round the central 'eye' at the top. There is no record of the tower ever having been used as an observatory, nor of the two single-storey wings having been used as a school of navigation as intended. The building is in a semi-ruinous state. For permission to view, ask at Observatory House, Acton Road.

At Hakin Point the Coast Path officially comes to an end, or rather there is a break in continuity because urban Milford intervenes. The Coast Path recommences on the far side of Milford, but there is 1ml/1.6km in between which has to be covered on foot: I shall call it the Hakin-Milford Link, and there is no reason why the route that has to be followed could not have been designated as the official Coast Path or even a Town Trail. After all, the Coast Path is designated through Fishguard and Goodwick, so why not here?

The Hakin-Milford Link is described as a town trail through Milford in the next chapter, following a description of the town, and the resumption of the Coast Path between Milford and Hazelbeach follows that, on p. 251.

Fort Hubberston, Milford Haven

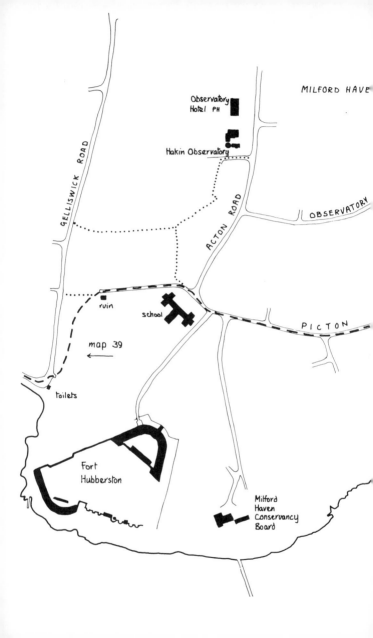

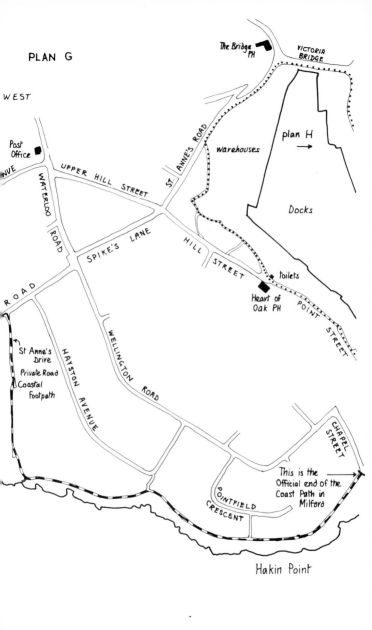

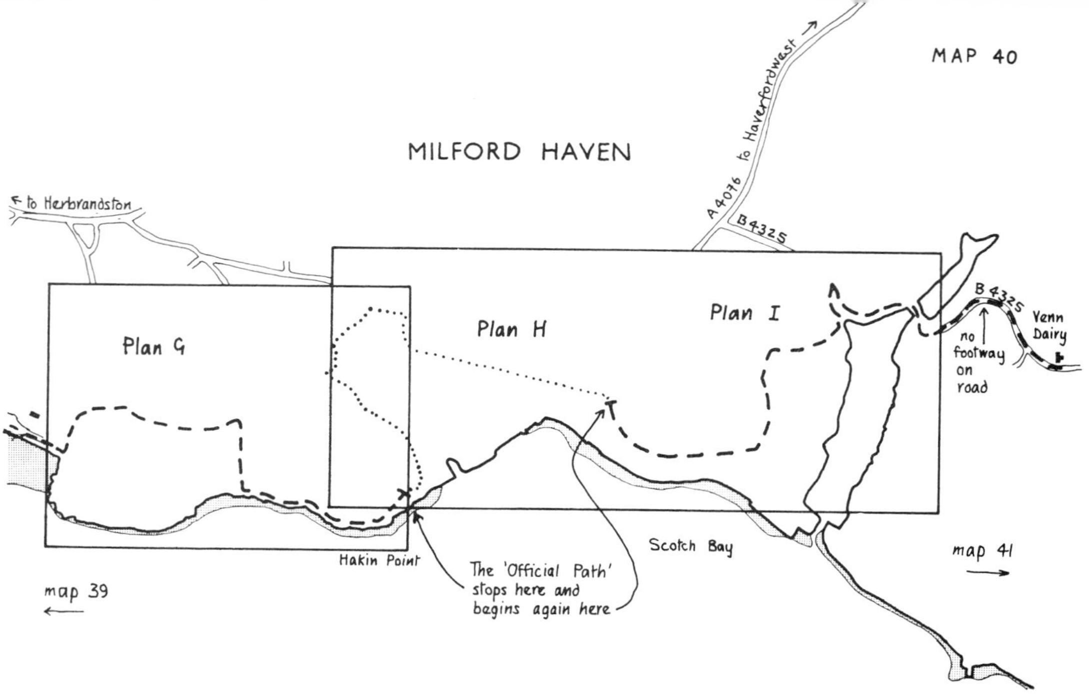

MAP 40

MILFORD HAVEN

Plan G

Plan H

Plan I

Venn Dairy

B 4325

no footway on road

A 4076 to Haverfordwest

B 4325

Scotch Bay

The 'Official Path' stops here and begins again here

Hakin Point

To Herbrandston

map 39

map 41

19 **Milford Haven (Hakin Point to Hazelbeach)**
   (Maps 40, 41)   4.75ml/7.6km

Milford is an interesting town having historical naval and military
associations and important fishing and petroleum industries; it is
also a popular holiday resort. Situated on the N side of the splendid
natural harbour of the Haven it enjoys a mild climate at all seasons,
thanks to its southern aspect and sheltered position.

   This chapter traces the growth of the town from its early days as a
fishing village to its planned development as a fishing port, naval
dockyard and trans-Atlantic terminal, and concludes with a Town
Trail on the 'missing link' between the two terminal points of the
official Coast Path on either side.

   Throughout this guide reference has been made to high tide as
'Milford Time' plus or minus a number of minutes: the tide is
measured from the entrance to Milford docks.

The growth of the town

Milford was originally a hamlet set on a hill separating Castle Pill to
the E and Priory Pill to the W. At the Dissolution of the
monasteries the lands came into the possession of the Barlow family
of Slebech. The wealthy heiress Catherine Barlow married Sir
William Hamilton (1730–1803), who outlived her and enjoyed her
fortune. He inherited the Manors of Pill and Hubberston from her,
and in 1791, at the age of 61, he married the 26-year-old Emma
Hart, to whom he had been introduced by his nephew, the Hon.
Charles Francis Greville, son of the Earl of Warwick.

   The enterprising Sir William secured an Act of Parliament in 1790
– the Milford Haven Harbour Act – to enable him 'to make and
provide Quays, Docks, Piers and other erections' at Hubberston
and Pill in order to develop a port. Sir William was at that time
British Envoy at the court of Naples and he had visited 'Old
Milford' with his energetic nephew, who had Emma living under his
protection. Greville recognised the enormous capabilities of the
Haven and impressed upon his uncle its potential as a port for Irish
traffic. Greville was entrusted to act for Sir William in the
enterprise when Hamilton returned to Naples: buildings were laid

out and docks planned, but very soon Greville was being pressed for money by his creditors. Sir William, who had evidently been more impressed by Emma than by his nephew, promised to act as security for the debts, provided the reluctant Emma was sent to Naples.

Greville canvassed several Quaker families engaged in the whaling trade who had taken refuge in Britain from Nantucket, Massachusetts, during the American War of Independence. He negotiated their transfer to Milford to help him set up an Atlantic whaling industry: they settled and they made their livelihood by providing spermaceti oil to light the lamps of London, and that industry flourished until the 19c. The Quakers' Meeting House, a small building with big windows, was finished in 1811.

Shortage of money delayed progress but in 1793 the Navy Board gave Greville a contract to build warships. A site for shipbuilding was leased to the Navy Board and two naval men-of-war were laid down. About this time a French refugee, Jean-Louis Barrallier, appeared on the scene. Barrallier's technical skills as an engineer and draughtsman attracted Greville's attention, and the Frenchman constructed the dockyard for Greville. Barrallier also laid out the town on a grid-iron plan, with three principal streets running parallel to one another across the hillside, intersected by side streets at right angles: the three main streets are called Hamilton Terrace, Charles Street and Robert Street, and some of the other streets commemorate the Quaker connection; for example Starbuck Road and Nantucket Avenue.

Money continued to be very short and the shipbuilder went bankrupt, but Greville was not to be daunted. Sir William inspected progress in 1801 – his wife had by now become deeply involved in her romance with Hamilton's friend Lord Nelson. Greville persuaded the Hamilton household to celebrate the fourth anniversary of the Battle of the Nile by another visit to Milford: in July 1802 all three – Sir William, Lady Hamilton and Lord Nelson – attended the celebrations, which included a grand fair, an agricultural show and a regatta. Nelson laid the foundation stone of St Katherine's Church, and he made his famous speech extolling the virtues of the Haven – he praised it as the best natural harbour in the world apart from Trincomalee in Ceylon (Sri Lanka) – at a dinner in Peter Cross's Inn (thereafter named after him – The Lord Nelson) in Hamilton Terrace.

Sir William died in 1803, Greville in 1809, both failing to realise their hopes for the town. The early flourish of prosperity was short-lived. Greville was succeeded by his brother Roger Fulke, who refused to renew the lease for the shipyard. The Admiralty abandoned plans for a naval dockyard at Milford in 1814, and transferred to a site across the Haven, thus giving birth to Pembroke Dock. The Irish Mail packet service moved in 1836 from Milford to Hobbs Point (Paterchurch), and the whaling industry declined.

Milford docks were not completed until 1888, almost a century after the founding of the town, its hopes of attracting trans-Atlantic trade unrealised. The Priory Pill was enclosed, Milford was set up as a trawler port, and a small local fishing industry established itself. Between 1900 and 1914 the discovery near Milford of rich fishing grounds, the excellence of the Haven as a port, and the size of the docks themselves led to a remarkable growth in the fishing industry: Milford was in the top league of fishing ports – the sixth largest in Britain. The fish market was expanded and new dock facilities were built.

The fortunes of the industry fluctuated violently between the wars as a result of national economic factors, and over-fishing of the western grounds was evident by 1931. By 1946 Milford occupied only fourth place in the fishing league, after Grimsby, Hull and Fleetwood. A slow decline started: gradually catches became smaller and smaller, and the numbers of trawlers fell drastically. The chief fishery was hake, which proved too easy to catch, and international over-fishing destroyed the grounds. The decline was spectacular: by 1972 there were only twelve trawlers registered at the port, compared with 97 in 1950.

In the 1960s and 70s Milford went back to an old trade again – oil, only this time not from sperm whales but from underground. The dramatic growth of the oil-refining capacity around the Haven led to an appreciable expansion in the local labour force but failed to generate a significant expansion in downstream activities. In the early 1970s the Haven went to great lengths to prepare for a major

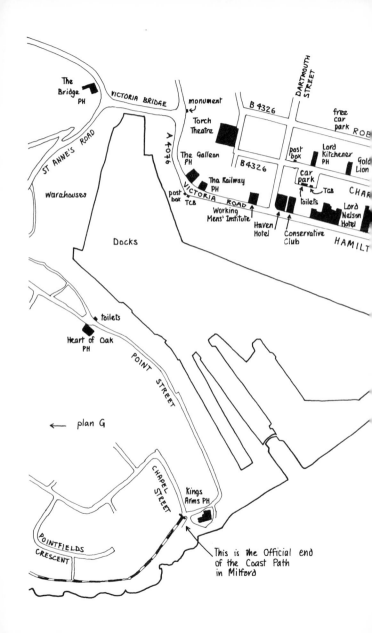

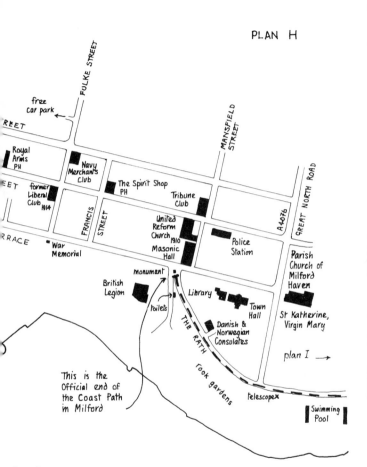

FULKE STREET

free
car park ←

...REET

Royal
Arms
PH

Navy
Merchant's
Club

The Spirit Shop
PH

...EET

former
Liberal
Club 1914

Tribune
Club

MANSFIELD
STREET

A4076

GREAT NORTH ROAD

FRANCIS STREET

United
Reform
Church 1910

...RRACE

War
Memorial

Masonic
Hall

Police
Station

Parish
Church of
Milford
Haven

monument

British
Legion

toilets

Library

Town
Hall

St Katherine,
Virgin Mary

THE RATH

Danish &
Norwegian
Consulates

plan I →

This is the
Official end of
the Coast Path
in Milford

rook gardens

telescope✕

Swimming
Pool

...cotch Bay

MILFORD HAVEN — CENTRAL

Celtic Sea oil exploration effort, but following disappointing early drillings interest evaporated and, with it, the prospect of jobs.

Milford's recent economic record has been one of dashed hopes and unfulfilled promise, but it was designated an Enterprise Zone in February 1984. The EZ theory is that business will prosper and the economy grow faster if business is not constrained by a nexus of planning and other bureaucratic regulations. One of the benefits is a ten-year period of rates relief. Plans were made to take advantage of deep-water access, and some thirteen sites mainly around Milford and Neyland, and around Pembroke Dock, have been earmarked for new industry. However, the economy now is too dependent on chance construction-work for future prosperity to be anything but uncertain.

The Hakin-Milford Link: a town trail 1ml/1.6km
We have seen that the official Coast Path stops at the Kings Arms on Hakin Point and recommences at the E end of the town on Hamilton Terrace, not far from St Katherine's Church. The ground between these two points must be covered on foot, so I shall describe a route past the docks and through the town which, in conjunction with Plans G, H and I, should make it easy for walkers to find their way.

Priory Pill defines the western side of the town but it was enclosed in the 1880s to create the docks, and you have to walk inland to Victoria Bridge, which marks the termination of the A4076 Haverfordwest-Milford road. The bridge was opened on 12 October 1933 by Sir Euan D Jones, Baronet, Lord Lieutenant of the County of Pembroke, and Lady Jones. Facing the E end of Victoria Bridge is a huge memorial tablet set into a wall, commemorating 'the memorable and interesting event, of Milford Haven having through the blessing of providence, twice afforded refuge and security to King George the Fourth and to his attendant squadron, from violent and succeeding tempests which beset them in St. George's Channel, on his majestys return from Ireland in September 1821,' and giving details. The tablet was placed there by Roger Fulke Greville.

Victoria Road climbs up from Victoria Bridge and becomes

Hamilton Terrace, and Greville's grid-iron plan becomes evident –
the broad, long, tree-lined street is Milford's most desirable, having
unrivalled views out across the harbour. Gleaming stucco and
colour-washed houses and hotels sun themselves above the inland
sea, watching the gigantic tankers go gliding by. The Lord Nelson
Hotel occupies this frontage to the sea, and at the E end of
Hamilton Terrace is the Town Hall, containing a stained glass
window that depicts Nelson's flagship *Victory* with the figures of
Nelson and a fellow officer.

Charles Street is the town's principal shopping street, lying
parallel to and behind Hamilton Terrace, and Robert Street behind
that has the least pretentious housing of the three streets. Old
buildings are not, of course, numerous in a town founded only at
the end of the 18c.

The town's War Memorial is a magnificent affair on the Hamilton
Terrace promenade, but there is another more unusual monument
of the same period a little further along the road. A marble obelisk
is inscribed in English on its W face and in Belgian on its E face,
recording the gratitude of the people of Ostend who lived in Milford
Haven during the Great War. This monument, standing at the
junction of Hamilton Terrace and The Rath, marks the
recommencement of the official Coast Path, and we shall return to
this point after we have visited the parish church of Milford, the
Church of St Katherine.

The architect was in all probability Jean-Louis Barrallier. Popular
tradition in Milford has long maintained that Lord Nelson laid the
foundation stone of the chapel in August 1801, but Nelson did not
make his first visit to the town until August 1802, and the
foundations were not dug until September 1802. It is more likely
that the 'first stone' was laid by Sir William Hamilton himself.

When completed in 1808 the chapel stood in splendid isolation at
the E end of the town. It was a squarer building than it is today,
since it had a nave and four bays only. It is now a rather
commanding structure in the Gothic revival style, with a chancel, N
and S aisles, and a soaring W tower with ornamental battlements,
all being added in 1902–7.

The church was consecrated on 14 October 1808 and dedicated to

PLAN I

MILFORD HAVEN - EAST

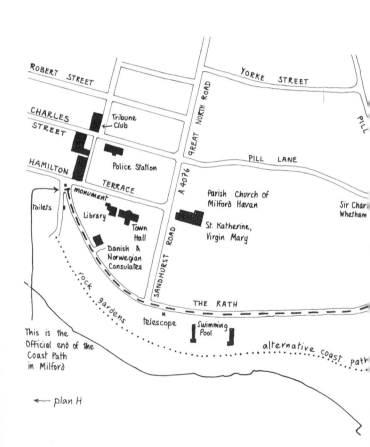

ROBERT STREET

YORKE STREET

CHARLES STREET

Tribune Club

HAMILTON

Police Station

TERRACE

PILL LANE

GREAT NORTH ROAD

Parish Church of Milford Haven

Sir Char
Whetham

toilets

monument

Library

Town Hall

St. Katherine, Virgin Mary

Danish & Norwegian Consulates

A 4076

SANDHURST ROAD

rock gardens

THE RATH

telescope

Swimming Pool

alternative coast path

This is the Official end of the Coast Path in Milford

← plan H

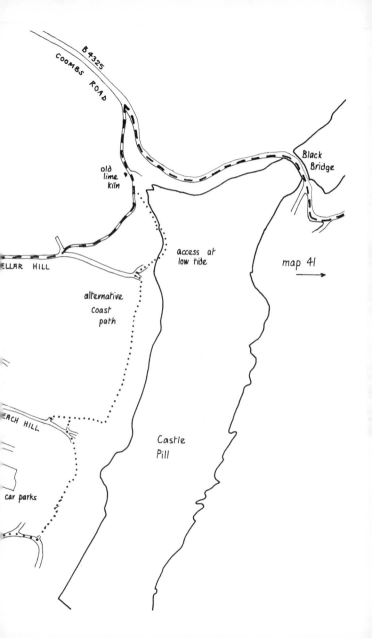

St Katherine of Alexandria, Virgin and Martyr. The choice of this patron saint is said to have been acknowledgement to William Price, a friend of the Greville family, who held the insecure office of Master of the Royal Hospital and Collegiate Church of St Katherine near the Tower of London. St Katherine is portrayed in the centre light of the E window, and is flanked by St Bride, St Botolph, St Nicholas and St David.

Greville's proposal to use a porphyry urn which had been brought back from Egypt as a font was objected to by the Bishop of St David's as it had been used 'for unholy purposes' and was therefore most unsuitable for the purpose of a baptismal font. It is still in the church, but removed to the porch. It is inscribed to the memory of Nelson.

There are various other oddments of Nelsoniana preserved in the church. Nelson presented a Bible and a prayer book which can still be seen, and another reminder is the truck of the mainmast of the French battleship *L'Orient*, which was blown up in the Battle of the Nile in 1798. The flagship of Admiral Brellys, it was the vessel on whose burning deck the legendary boy is said to have stood (in the poem 'Casabianca' by Felicia Dorothea Hemans, 1793–1835). The relic was presented in memory of Nelson by his lady-love Lady Hamilton. The original relic was removed to the Royal United Services Institute in London's Whitehall, and that on display in the church is a replica. Sir William Hamilton lies buried in the **church at Slebech, N of Milford.**

Milford to Hazelbeach 3.75ml/6km
The E side of Milford is defined by Castle Pill and the Coast Path has to run inland around this creek, but because of a defence establishment and the Gulf oil refinery does not reach the coast again for another 3.5ml/5.6km. It is perhaps one of the most disappointing stretches of the Coast Path (another is the stretch between Pembroke Dock and Pembroke) and one can well understand why walkers leaving Milford will take public transport all the way to Pembroke, particularly as the Haven has to be crossed

The War Memorial, Milford Haven

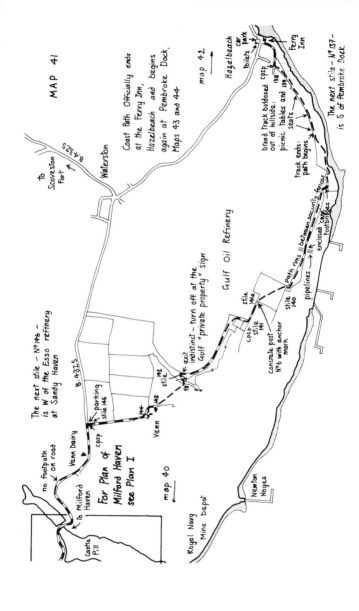

MAP 41

The next stile – N°146 –
is W of the Esso refinery
at Sandy Haven

to Scoveston
Fort

to B·4·325

Waterston

Coast Path officially ends
at the Ferry Inn, Hazelbeach
Hazelbeach and begins
again at Pembroke Dock,
Maps 43 and 44.

map 42 →

B·4·325

no footpath
on road

to Milford Haven

Castle Pill

For Plan of
Milford Haven
see Plan I

cpsp
Venn Dairy

parking
stile 145

← map 40

M2
stile

143
Venn

exit
indistinct – turn off at the
Gulf "private property" Sign

Gulf Oil Refinery

stile
144a

cpsp
stile
144

Concrete post
N°6 with anchor
mark

stile
140

pipelines

Path runs
between security fences

enclosed concrete
footbridges

track ends:
path begins

broad track bulldozed
out of hillside:
picnic tables and
seats

138

139

cpsp

Hazelbeach
car
toilets Park

Ferry
Inn

The next stile – N°137 –
is S of Pembroke Dock.

Royal Navy
Mine Depot

Newton
Noyes

by the Cleddau Bridge in any case.

The Coast Path restarts in Milford on Hamilton Terrace at the junction with The Rath and this road is followed through the Pill housing estate to Cellar Hill and the B4325 Milford-Neyland road and the crossing of Castle Pill by Black Bridge. There is an alternative path, closer to the coast and running behind the back of the housing estate, but this was not designated, perhaps because it gives views over the derelict Thos Ward's ship-breaking yard, which was established in 1934 and closed in 1956.

On the opposite side of Castle Pill is the Royal Navy Armament Depot, set up in 1934, which exports mainly mines explosives from Newton Noyes.

The Coast Path follows the B4325 for a short distance before heading towards the coast around the Gulf oil refinery, but if this road is followed past Waterston to Neyland you pass the vast Scoveston Fort, one of Palmerston's defences of the Haven. Its six-sided form is protected by a huge dry moat and inner bank, cut by heavily-guarded entrance tunnels. The security afforded by its defences would make it ideal for conversion into a nudist camp.

Following a two-year construction programme the *Gulf Oil Refinery* and petrochemical complex came on stream and was officially opened by HM Queen Elizabeth II on 10 August 1968. The site covers 460 acres/186ha.

The Gulf plant was the only one in the Haven which produced chemicals as well as fuel products: the petrochemicals complex annually produced about 200,000 tonnes of high-purity benzene and cyclohexane for use in the plastic and nylon industries. Due to competition from Europe, benzene production was curtailed in April 1981 and in March 1982 the petrochemicals complex was finally closed down and subsequently demolished.

The company supplies one-third of the heavy fuel oil for the CEGB's Pembroke Power Station, and this is pumped across the water in a pipeline passing under the bed of the Haven. It has a 35 per cent share in the Fluid Catalytic Cracking Unit (Cat Cracker) adjacent to Texaco's refinery on the opposite side of the Haven, to which it is also connected by pipeline.

Hazelbeach to Neyland 1ml/1.6km

The 'official' Coast Path stops at the Ferry Inn, Hazelbeach, and recommences again S of Pembroke Dock, and the Countryside Commission leaves walkers to their own discretion for the stretch in between. That was all right when the Neyland-Hobbs Point ferry ran, but now walkers have to make the crossing of the Haven by the Cleddau Bridge, not a very encouraging prospect. The Hazelbeach-Pembroke Dock Link via the Cleddau Bridge is a minimum distance of 4.5ml/7.25km, and having come as far as Hazelbeach you have to walk to Neyland in order to get transport to the opposite side of the Haven.

The coast road between Hazelbeach and Neyland passes through the village of Llanstadwell, whose English-style square-towered church is almost washed by the tides of the Haven. The church is dedicated to St Tudwal, a Welsh monk revered also in Brittany, where he died in 564. The church was extensively and vigorously restored in 1876.

20   **Neyland** (Map 42)

Neyland owes much of its origins to Sir Isambard Kingdom Brunel, who founded the port when he made it the terminus of his South Wales Railway, which reached the N shore of the Haven in 1856. The huge Great Western Hotel was built on the waterfront, a pier was constructed, and at once the Waterford steamer service was transferred to the new port from Hobbs Point on the opposite side of the Haven. A thrice-weekly service was run to Waterford and then a twice-weekly run to and from Cork.

The place was called Milford Haven until 1859, and when the new town was created it was renamed New Milford. It enjoyed a period of prosperity as the packet port for Ireland; it became a fishing port; there was some shipbuilding; and a railway wagon works was

Propane spheres at the Gulf oil refinery

established on the edge of the town. However, the prosperity was short-lived; Pembroke Dock acquired its railway link in 1864 and was rapidly developed as a naval dockyard. Then in 1906 a blow fell from which recovery has never been complete: the Irish traffic was transferred to Fishguard. The town was then named Neyland. The fish trade died and the wagon works closed in the same year. Further distress came when the town lost its rail service as Lord Beeching wielded his famous axe in 1955. Neyland lost its car ferry link with Pembroke Dock when the Cleddau Bridge opened in 1975, and it now finds itself increasingly isolated as the Haven's centre of gravity has shifted.

Neyland is a pleasant, upretentious town. Long terraces of 19c cottages line the hillside. The Atlantic route is commemorated in a terrace named after Brunel's *Great Eastern*, now the only reminder of more hopeful days. The *Great Eastern* was the world's biggest ship when she was launched in 1858, and she had special berthing facilities at Neyland.

Neyland to Pembroke Dock 3.5ml/5.6km
Walkers have to go through the town to the A477 to get access to the road for the Cleddau Bridge. My map No.42 shows a route up to the roundabout at Great Honeyborough, and another way, involving less road-walking, is along The Promenade and Picton Road – look for the unusual octagonal Victorian letter-box – and then by Cambrian Road and a path above Neyland Wood direct to the Cleddau Bridge road. Maps No. 42 and 43 and Plans J and N show a route which I suggest is the best means of reaching the recommencement of the 'official' Coast Path on the southern side of Pembroke Dock. My suggested Pembroke Dock town trail is described in the following chapter, followed by the short section of the 'official' Coast Path between Pembroke Dock and Pembroke town.

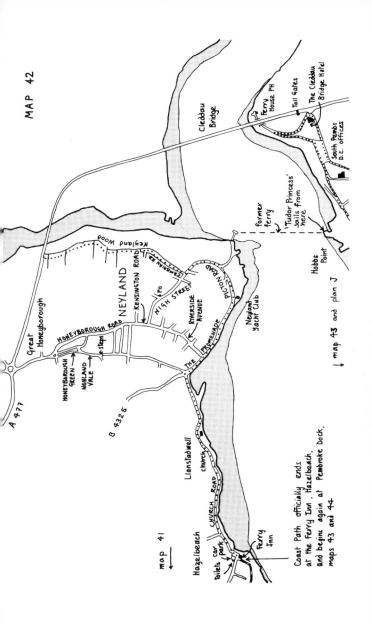

MAP 42

Cleddau Bridge

Ferry House PH

Toll Gates

The Cleddau Bridge Hotel

South Pembs D.C. offices

former ferry

'Tudor Princess' sails from here

Hobbs Point

↓ map 43 and plan J
→

Neyland Wood

Kensington Road

CAMBRIAN RD

NEYLAND

PO

HIGH STREET

RIVERSIDE AVENUE

PICTON ROAD

THE PROMENADE

Neyland Yacht Club

Great Honeyborough

HONEYBOROUGH ROAD

HONEYBOROUGH GREEN

NEYLAND VALE

←steps

A 477

B 4325

Llanstadwell church

CHURCH ROAD

Coast Path officially ends at the Ferry Inn, Hazelbeach, and begins again at Pembroke Dock, maps 43 and 44.

map 41

Hazelbeach

toilets

car park

Ferry Inn

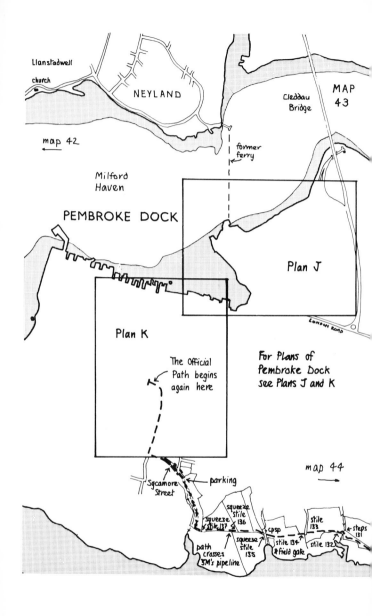

Llanstadwell
church

NEYLAND

Cleddau
Bridge

MAP
43

map 42

former
ferry

Milford
Haven

PEMBROKE DOCK

Plan J

Plan K

The Official
Path begins
again here

For Plans of
Pembroke Dock
see Plans J and K

map 44

Sycamore
Street

parking

squeeze
stile 136

squeeze
stile 137

squeeze
stile 135

path
crosses
3M's pipeline

cpsp

stile 134
& field gate

stile
133

stile 132

steps
131

21   Pembroke Dock

Pembroke Dock was the second of the new towns to appear on the shores of Milford Haven. Paterchurch had been selected by the Admiralty to replace their earlier dockyard at Milford, and the Royal Naval Dockyard was established here in 1814. The first ships built were the *Valorous* and *Ariadne*, both being launched on 10 February 1816, and as the dockyard grew so did the town, becoming the only real industrial town in Pembrokeshire.

The dockyard gained a great reputation for innovations in naval shipbuilding and for its excellent workmanship. It is not often realised that for most of the century Pembroke Dock was the most advanced shipbuilding yard in the world. It introduced major technological developments in naval shipbuilding – there were experiments with steam propulsion, with paddles and with screw propellers, and with iron cladding.

The Irish Mail Packet Service was transferred from Milford to Pembroke Dock in 1836, and between 1850 and 1865 the dockyard was a hive of activity. The Haven assumed strategic importance as a result of the disturbed political situation on the Continent, and a large military garrison was established at the dock. After the arrival of the railway line to the dockyard in 1864 raw materials were easier to import, and the town prospered, its fortunes based largely upon both civilian and naval shipbuilding. By 1875 the town was one of the chief industrial centres of W Wales, and up to 3000 men were employed.

The dockyard was abruptly closed by the Admiralty in 1926, causing great local distress. The whole community suffered much hardship, and as the unemployment rate approached 25 per cent the borough was classed as a Distressed Area. Between 1926 and 1931 a population of about 15,000 declined to 12,000.

During World War II the town was established as the main Atlantic base for the RAF Sunderland flying-boats, and part of the dockyard was used as a naval base. The Atlantic Patrol of reconnaissance and anti-submarine missions of RAF Coastal Command was organised from here, and innumerable Atlantic

PEMBROKE DOCK

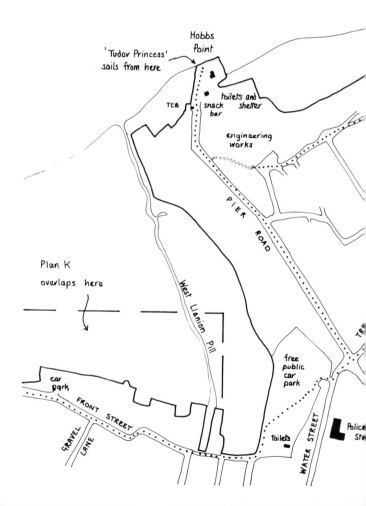

Hobbs Point

'Tudor Princess' sails from here

toilets and shelter

TCB

snack bar

engineering works

PIER ROAD

Plan K overlaps here

West Llanion Pill

free public car park

car park

FRONT STREET

GRAVEL LANE

WATER STREET

toilets

Police Sta

TRE

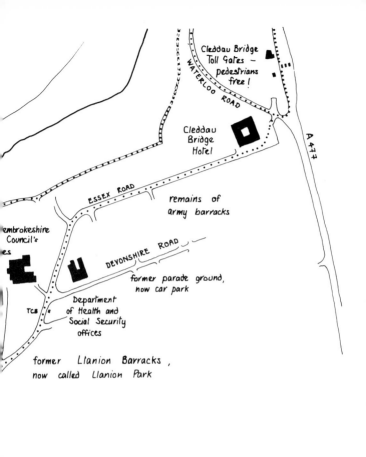

Cleddau Bridge Toll Gates — pedestrians free!

WATERLOO ROAD

A 477

Cleddau Bridge Hotel

ESSEX ROAD

remains of army barracks

embrokeshire Council's es

DEVONSHIRE ROAD

former parade ground, now car park

Department of Health and Social Security offices

TCB

former Llanion Barracks, now called Llanion Park

LONDON ROAD
to PEMBROKE →

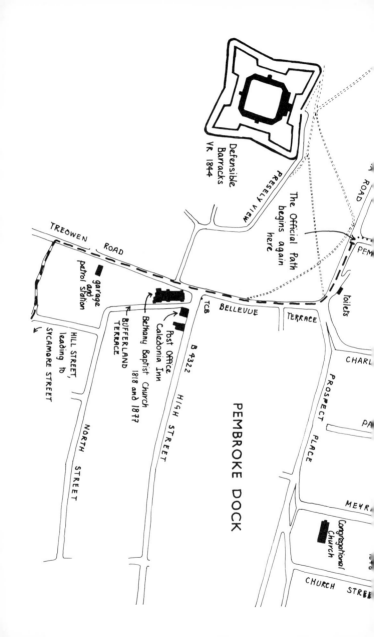

Defensible Barracks VR 1844

The Official Path begins again here

PRESELY VIEW

TREOWEN ROAD

garage and patrol Station

Post Office
Caledonia Inn
Bethany Baptist Church 1818 and 1877

BUFFERLAND TERRACE

BELLEVUE TERRACE

TCB

B 4322 HIGH STREET

PEMBROKE DOCK

HILL STREET, leading to SYCAMORE STREET

NORTH STREET

SYCAMORE STREET

toilets

PEM

ROAD

CHARL

PROSPECT PLACE

PA

MEYR

Congregational Church

CHURCH STREE

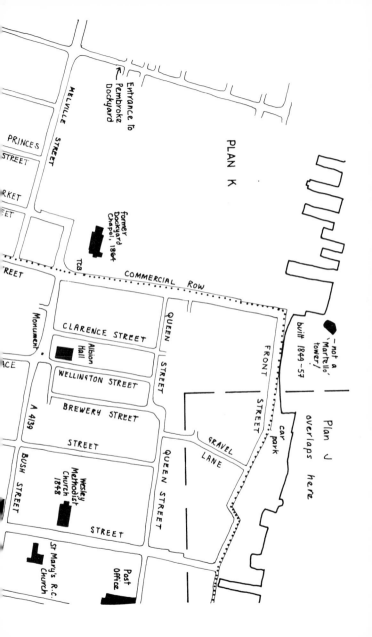

PLAN K

Entrance to
Pembroke
Dockyard

MELVILLE STREET

PRINCES STREET

RKET EET

former
Dockyard
Chapel, 1864

TCB

COMMERCIAL ROW

Monument

CLARENCE STREET

Albion Hall

WELLINGTON STREET

ACE

A 4139

BREWERY STREET

STREET

BUSH STREET

Wesley
Methodist
Church
1848

STREET

St Mary's R.C.
Church

QUEEN STREET

QUEEN STREET

FRONT STREET

GRAVEL LANE

Post Office

— not a
'Martello'
tower!

built 1849-57

CAR park

Plan J overlaps here

convoys were assembled in the sheltered waters of the Haven.
Much mine-laying, mine-sweeping and escort work was co-
ordinated from the dockyard headquarters. The town became an
important fuel-storage depot, and there was a sizeable garrison.
However, the wartime activities were a mixed blessing, for the town
attracted enemy bombing attacks and suffered greatly from air
raids, particularly in July 1940 and June 1941.

The main naval base closed in 1946 (although the Navy still
maintains a presence) and the flying-boat base closed in 1959, when
flying-boats were abandoned by the RAF. The last Sunderland
flying-boat was taken in pieces from Pembroke Docks to the RAF
Museum at Hendon in 1971, where it is on permanent display. The
dockyard has since been used by only two relatively small private
shipbuilding and repairing concerns, although a small part of the
dockyard was subsequently created as the new base for the B & I
ferry company's operations to Eire, but this was short-lived.

A Pembroke Dock town trail

This tour of the town starts at the Cleddau Bridge, visits Hobbs
Point, takes us along the town's 'promenade' to the edge of the
dockyard and terminates at the Defensible Barracks and the
recommencement of the 'official' Coast Path. It is a distance of
about 1.5ml/2.5km, and is shown on Plans J and K.

For many years the people of Pembrokeshire looked forward to a
direct road link between the opposite shores of the Haven. The long
road journey between Milford and Pembroke Dock took the
motorist through Haverfordwest, Canaston Bridge and Carew, a
journey of some 27ml/43.4km. This problem of access presented a
severe barrier to social and economic integration between the main
towns of the county, and was particularly highlighted by the growth
of the oil industry in the late 1960s.

The precarious Neyland-Hobbs Point ferry maintained a daily
schedule of some 30 crossings each way, but it was no real
compensation for the lack of a direct road link. At long last, with
the industrial development of the Haven well under way, a £3-
million project was commenced to build a box girder bridge from

Barnlake, between Neyland and Burton, to Pembroke Ferry, with associated roadworks.

Tragically there was a collapse of one of the sections of the bridge during construction, on 2 June 1970. One of the two 252ft/76.8m spans on the S bank fell, killing four workmen and injuring five others. Following the government investigation of box girder bridges the project was much delayed: work only recommenced in February 1972.

The *Cleddau Bridge* consists of four 252ft/76.8m spans, two 490ft/149m spans, and a 700ft/213m river span, which is about 120ft/36.5m above high-water level of the Haven. It was the largest single unsupported span in Europe at the time, now superseded only by the Humber Bridge. The official opening was performed by the Secretary of State for Wales, the Rt Hon. John Morris QC MC, on Friday, 23 May 1975, by which time the cost had quadrupled to almost £12 million. Tolls are levied on users in an attempt to recoup the cost, but pedestrians go free!

As you cross the Cleddau Bridge you can look down on the upstream side to see the oil-storage depot at Waterloo. There are other oil tanks at Llanreath, at the mouth of the Pembroke River, seen from the Coast Path at Hazelbeach. These two depots were established between the two World Wars and were of vital importance to the Allied shipping which used the Haven as a convoy assembly and departure point. During the course of World War II some 17,000 ships sailed from the Haven, and they all had to be fuelled from these depots, which were supplied by tankers making the dangerous journey through the enemy-patrolled waters of the Atlantic and St George's Channel.

The tank farm at Waterloo is still used for oil storage, principally for the Navy. Waterloo and Llanreath are connected by tunnels to the dockyard. They have a comfortable old-fashioned air: note the contrast between these old concrete-encased tanks and the larger steel tanks which have been built fairly recently around the Haven refineries.

From the Cleddau Bridge toll-gates a route may be found alongside or through the former Llanion Barracks to *Hobbs Point*. This was formerly the ferry-crossing point to Neyland, and the importance of this link can be judged from the huge car park on Pier Road which was used for the marshalling of road traffic waiting to cross the Haven.

The only interest that Hobbs Point has for the visitor today is that steamer excursions are operated from the landing, both upstream into the Daucleddau and downstream into the Haven. Coast Path walkers having the time for a cruise could take both sailings, observing the contrast between the sylvan banks of the reaches and pills of the Daucleddau and the busy shipping lanes and oil refineries of the Haven. The downstream cruise is to Thorn Island and back, and a commentary is given over the public address system identifying the landmarks and shipping.

Tudor Princess Cruises operate every day throughout the summer from the beginning of May until the end of October. The 80ft/24m twin-diesel launch *Tudor Princess* sails upriver at 1200 and 1600, and downriver at 1000 (party bookings only) and 1400. Each cruise lasts approximately 1 hr 40 mins. Moonlight evening cruises lasting approximately 3 hours sail, subject to advance bookings, in June, July and August only, and are a good way of seeing the illuminations of the oil refineries and the navigation lights of shipping (tel. Pembroke 685627).

In 1979 the British & Irish Steam Packet Co. Ltd (the B & I Line) moved their services from Fishguard to a new ferry terminal at Pembroke Dock, the Line's new flagship, MV *Connacht*, arriving on 23 May on her inaugural sailing from Cork.

The new ferry terminal, costing £8 million, was formally opened on 16 October 1979 by Nicholas Edwards, Secretary of State for Wales 1979–87 and MP for Pembroke (now Lord Crickhowell).

Services were operated between Pembroke and Cork, and on 23 May 1980 a new service between Pembroke and Rosslare was inaugurated. A regular ferry service promised to produce considerable spin-off benefits, but in 1985 the service was abandoned, another victim of the recession. The Rosslare service began again in 1987, but this time from Fishguard, to which it returned after eight years.

The 'Martello Tower', Pembroke Dock

The town of *Pembroke Dock* was planned on a grid-iron pattern with wide streets, similar in concept to that of Milford. From Hobbs Point go along Pier Road, across the Water Street car park, and along Front Street, the town's 'promenade'. At the far end is the NE 'Martello tower': it is not anti-Napoleon, but was built as an inner defence of the dockyard. This one had three guns and a garrison of 12 men. There is another one – the SW 'Martello tower' at the end of Melville Street. This had five guns and a garrison of 24 men. Both towers were built between 1849 and 1857, at a total cost of £9,230.

The dockyard is still surrounded by its grand wall, and Commercial Row flanks its perimeter. The gloomy-looking dockyard chapel, built in 1834, was once converted into a motor-car museum, but that closed around 1980.

If you turn E at the junction of Commercial Row with Pembroke Street you will come into Albion Square, which has an appropriate Victorian monument adorned by functional ornament and inscriptions. It takes the form of a small obelisk, a marble column on steps, topped by a lamp standard. The foot of the base is dated on each of its sides 1814–1914, and the column has separate inscriptions on each main face commemorating major events in the town's history.

On a hill immediately above the dockyard, at the end of Pembroke Street, are the Defensible Barracks. The barracks were built in 1844–5 at a cost of £80,000 and were intended to house a garrison of 500 men. The building is square in plan but is surrounded by stellar-shaped fortifications consisting of a deep dry moat and a huge wall, revetted to allow no dead ground around it. The barracks were not themselves defended by any armaments, but were purely to accommodate the 'defencibles' or troops who would act as reinforcements to the inner Haven's forts and defences. have acted as reinforcements to the inner Haven's forts and defences.

At the end of Pembroke Street, below the Defensible Barracks, we come to the end of the Hazelbeach-Pembroke Dock Link and the Pembroke Town Trail and rejoin the 'official' Coast Path.

Pembroke Dock to Pembroke 2ml/3.2km

The 'official' Coast Path at first follows Bellevue Terrace and Treowen Road and then descends a rough track following a shallow valley leading towards the muddy shores of the Pembroke River. The Path follows through fields giving occasional glimpses of the river and Pembroke Castle through the trees, and emerges on to an area of open ground, once a quarry. There is a full frontal view of the castle from here, and one's appreciation of its fine setting will depend on the state of the tide, because the river is still tidal up to this point.

The Path soon emerges on to the A4139 Pembroke-Pembroke Dock main road and here ends, only to restart on the far side of Pembroke at Monkton. This short stretch of Path between Pembroke Dock and Pembroke is the only stretch of the 'official' Coast Path between Hazelbeach and Monkton, a distance of 7.5ml/12km. The continuation of the Coast Path is described in Chapter 23 but we make a break here to look around Pembroke and its magnificent castle.

22 **Pembroke** (Map 44, Plan L)

Pembroke is built on a limestone ridge which culminates at its western end in a great mass of rock, the sides of which descend precipitously to the tidal waters of the Pembroke River, an almost land-locked inlet of Milford Haven. Finely situated on the rock is Pembroke Castle, one of the most imposing ruins in the kingdom. In the whole of Wales perhaps only Caernarvon and Harlech Castles can compete in the magnificence of their sites and the strength and style of their buildings.

The castle is to Pembroke as the Cathedral is to St David's, and the growth of the town was dependent upon the fortunes of the castle. The layout of this chapter follows a similar format to others in this guide where the coastal towns are described: firstly a brief history of the town, followed by a description and tour of the castle, and finally a Pembroke town trail.

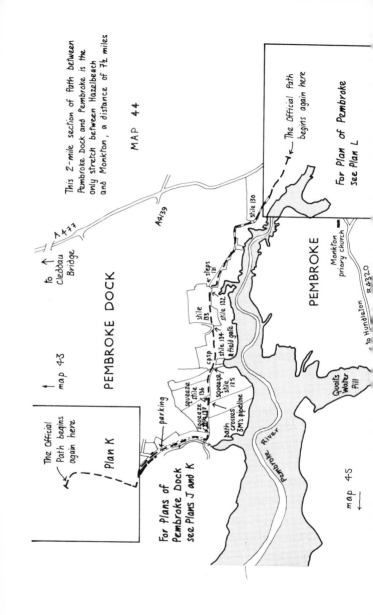

MAP 44

This 2-mile section of Path between Pembroke Dock and Pembroke is the only stretch between Hazelbeach and Monkton, a distance of 7½ miles

PEMBROKE DOCK

map 43

to Cleddau Bridge

A477

A4/39

The Official Path begins again here

Plan K

The Official Path begins again here

parking

Squeeze stile 117

Path crosses 3M's pipeline

squeeze stile 136

squeeze stile 135

stile 134

a field gate

CPSP

stile 132

stile 133

steps 131

stile 130

For Plans of Pembroke Dock see Plans J and K

PEMBROKE

Monkton Priory church

For Plan of Pembroke see Plan L

to Hundleton

B4320

Quoits Water Pill

Pembroke River

map 45

Brief history

The site for the castle was chosen by the Normans very soon after the Conquest as their base against Ireland and the Welsh. The first castle was built in 1100 by Arnulf de Montgomery, son of the Marcher Lord of Shrewsbury, in the reign of William II. It consisted of a palisaded fort of stakes and turf, with a ditch dug across the headland from cliff to cliff. When the Montgomery family fell from grace in 1102, as a result of their unsuccessful rebellion against Henry I, the king granted the castle to Gerald de Windsor, Montgomery's steward, who rebuilt it in 1105 and justified the king's trust by long and faithful service.

The Earldom of Pembroke was created in 1109 and Gilbert de Clare, better known as Strongbow, was created the first Earl. In 1138 the Earldom was raised to become a County Palatine; Strongbow was the first Earl Palatine and he was followed by the Fitzgilberts of Clare, the Marshalls, de Valences, the Hastings and the Herberts. The Earl maintained his independent position, exercising rights of sovereignty within the boundaries of the Palatinate, until it was abolished in 1536.

Gilbert Strongbow was succeeded by his son Richard Strongbow in 1148, and in that year Richard sailed with a force of Welsh archers for a further conquest of Ireland. Henry II sailed from Pembroke too for Ireland in 1172. When Richard Strongbow died in 1176 his infant daughter, the heiress Isabel, passed with his estates into the charge of the king, who held the Earldom until Isabel was married to William Marshall. The present castle is largely the work of William Marshall and his five sons: William held the Earldom from 1189 until his death in 1219, and was succeeded by his five sons in succession until 1245 – William Marshall II, Richard, Gilbert, Walter, and finally Anselm, all of whom were to die childless.

During the peace of Edward I's reign (1272–1307) William de Valence built a strong wall around the town which had grown up outside the castle walls, strengthened by bastions and entered by three main gates. The gates have long since gone, but parts of the walls still remain.

In 1453 Henry VI granted the castle to his half-brother, Jasper Tudor, and in January 1457 his nephew was born here, afterwards

stile 129
cpsp

stile 128
cpsp

parking

sluice

CASTLE VIEW

to Pembroke Dock

A 4139

ROCKY PARK

THE GREEN

map

This is the Off
of the Coast P
in Pembroke

For Plan of Castle
see Plan M

Castle

site of Old
Mill

Town Quay
Car Park

toilets

National Park
Information
Centre

WESTGATE HILL

Westgate
Presbyterian
Church

Car park

CHURCH

TERRACE

BRIDGEND TERRACE

Pembroke River

car park

Lion
Hotel

THE PARADE

Town
Hall

car park

toilets

B 4320

to Angle

map 45

Lower Common Park

Watermans Arms
Mill Bridge
Royal George Hotel

St Mary's
Church

MILL POND WA

A 4139

MAIN STREET

Mo
Wa

P
O

COMMON RO

PEMBROKE

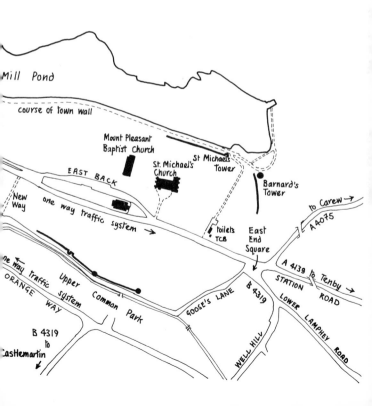

Mill Pond

course of town wall

Mount Pleasant Baptist Church

St. Michael's Church

St Michael's Tower

EAST BACK

New Way

one way traffic system →

Barnard's Tower

toilets TCB

East End Square

to Carew →

A 4075

one way traffic system

Upper Common Park

ORANGE WAY

A 4139 to Tenby

STATION ROAD

Goose's Lane

B 4319

WELL HILL

LOWER LAMPHEY ROAD

B 4319 to Castlemartin

to become Henry VII. When Henry VI was defeated at the Battle of
Tewkesbury brother Jasper Tudor and young Henry fled to France,
only to return fourteen years later by landing in Mill Bay in the
Haven. After the Battle of Bosworth Field Henry became Henry
VII. His son, Henry VIII, abolished the County Palatinate in his
Act of Union of 1536, and the castle reverted to the Crown.

The next time Pembroke found itself so involved in the affairs of
the nation was during the Civil War of 1642–9. Pembroke, alone of
all the Welsh towns, was not held for Charles I and the Royalists;
the Puritan mayor of Pembroke, John Poyer, with Major General
Rowland Laugharne of St Bride's and Lieutenant Colonel Rice
Powell, defended the castle for Cromwell's Parliamentarians, and
the town remained untaken throughout the campaigns.

However, when Parliament was dissolved early in 1648 and the
second stage of the Civil War broke out, Poyer changed his
allegiance and went over to the dying Royalist cause, supporting
also the dissension between the Independents and the
Presbyterians. Poyer's insurrection against Parliament was a serious
matter for Cromwell, since it was a Parliamentary stronghold that
had turned against him.

Cromwell personally took charge of the siege of Pembroke
Castle, but the defences and the garrison were stubborn enough to
hold off the Parliamentary assault for seven weeks, from 24 May to
11 July 1648. The 48-day siege was one of the longest in the Civil
War and only came to an end as a result of the betrayal of the
castle's water supply.

During Cromwell's siege damage was done to the Barbican Gate,
the By-gate Tower, the Henry VII Tower, the West Gate Tower
and the North Gate Tower. After capturing the castle Cromwell
ordered that the fortress be dismantled to prevent any recurrence of
the trouble, but there is no evidence that anything was done.

The three renegade leaders – Poyer, Laugharne and Powell –
were sent to the army headquarters at Windsor, tried by court
martial, found guilty of treason and condemned to be shot. They
were held in the Tower of London until the following spring, but
then the Army Council resolved, as a gesture of clemency, to
execute only one of them, and lots were drawn for the victim. On

two pieces of paper was written 'Life Given by God', and the third was left blank. The blank piece was drawn by Colonel Poyer and he was shot in the piazza at Covent Garden a few days later, nine months after his surrender, on 25 April 1649. Thereafter his descendants bore the motto 'Destiny is against me', in memory of the fate of their ancestor.

After the Commonwealth the castle was neglected for nearly 250 years but in 1880 it was partly restored by J R Cobb of Brecon. Joseph Richard Cobb (1821–97) – lawyer, antiquary, promoter of the Brecon & Merthyr Railway, and restorer of castles (he restored Caldicot, Manorbier and Pembroke) – spent three years on excavations and reconstruction.

The castle was again neglected between 1883 and 1928, when it was purchased by Major General Sir Ivor Philipps KCB DSO of Cosheston Hall, Pembroke, who carried out extensive restoration. On his death his daughter, Mrs Basil Ramsden, became the owner and in 1959 she leased the castle to trustees, which included the former Pembroke Borough Council. Although the castle is still **privately owned and administered by trustees, the Welsh Office has undertaken restoration work on the great keep.**

Pembroke Castle

The Castle is built on a well-chosen site that is almost a fortress itself, a mass of rock with precipitous sides plunging down to the tidal waters of the Pembroke River. The rock, with the formidable defences of the castle itself, makes Pembroke almost impregnable, and one of the largest and strongest fortresses in Wales. The best general view of the castle is obtained from the W, on the opposite bank of the pill, at high tide, from where the walls and towers are seen grouped with magnificent effect, backed by the town wall and the tower of St Mary's Church.

The irregular shape of the castle follows the natural shape of the rock, and consists of an outer curtain wall protected by five large round towers and a gatehouse. The S side of the outer curtain – the inland side, away from the river, and therefore the most vulnerable – was double-walled, and an extra 8ft/2.4m was added to the inside giving it a total thickness of 15ft/4.5m. The towers on this side are connected by passages through the thickness of the walls.

There are two baileys – the inner bailey on the point of the promontory, built about 1190–1200, and the outer bailey, added during the early 13c. The inner bailey is triangular, with its apex at the point of the promontory. Its buildings, with the great keep in the middle, are ranged around the S curtain and were formerly defended by a ditch which ran along between the baileys from one face of the cliff to the other. The inner gateway and a considerable portion of the inner curtain wall have been destroyed. The outer bailey is defended by a curtain wall with strong towers at the angles: the tower next E from the gatehouse – the Barbican Tower – is crowned with a stone dome.

Hours of admission
Easter-30 September: Monday-Friday 1000–1900, Saturday 1000–1800, Sunday 1100–1900.
1 October-Easter: Monday-Saturday 1030–1700. Last admissions 1 hour before closing time.

Tour of the Castle
The main approach to the castle is still up the Westgate Hill below the Bygate Tower, then turning at an acute angle beneath the Barbican Tower, through the Barbican Gate to the main gatehouse.

The Barbican Gate is noteworthy because it compels an oblique approach to the gatehouse, and for its internal semi-circular angle-towers connected by a flying arch. This last feature is found externally at Neath and Llawhaden, but is unique on the inner face as here.

The magnificent gatehouse shows the development of defences of the gateway becoming more numerous and more scientifically disposed. In the gateway passage are two systems of barriers in succession, each system consisting of a portcullis, a machicolation, and a two-leaved door, while behind the inner door there is a third machicolation. All the machicolations are wide openings spanning the passage from side to side. Projecting from the inner face of the gatehouse, immediately above the passage, there was a fighting

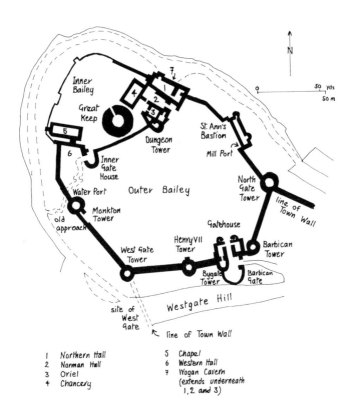

PLAN M PEMBROKE CASTLE

- Inner Bailey
- Great Keep
- Dungeon Tower
- Inner Gate House
- Water Port
- Monkton Tower
- old approach
- West Gate Tower
- St. Ann's Bastion
- Mill Port
- Outer Bailey
- North Gate Tower
- line of Town Wall
- Gatehouse
- Henry VII Tower
- Bygate Tower
- Barbican Tower
- Barbican Gate
- Westgate Hill
- site of West Gate
- line of Town Wall

1	Northern Hall	5	Chapel
2	Norman Hall	6	Western Hall
3	Oriel	7	Wogan Cavern
4	Chancery		(extends underneath 1, 2 and 3)

gallery, built as a bridge between two stair turrets. The gallery was entered by a doorway in the inner wall of the gatehouse and had battlements towards the bailey. It provided for the event of the gateway being taken by assault, as from this commanding position an enemy rushing into the bailey could be attacked from the rear.

The gatehouse was one of the important residential parts of the castle. The upper rooms, large and numerous, are entered from the stairs in the towers on each side of the entrance and have passages on each floor through the thickness of the outer curtain connecting them with the Barbican Tower on the E and the Henry VII Tower and Westgate Tower on the W.

Once through the gatehouse you enter the broad green sward of the outer bailey. Here we can visit the towers that protected the curtain on the vulnerable town side before visiting the inner bailey. By going straight ahead across the grass, bearing slightly right, we can follow the wall in a clockwise direction, visiting first St Ann's Bastion.

St Ann's Bastion consists of a long rectangular hall with a turret at each end and commanded the approach to the castle from the old mill by the river by a gateway known as Mill Port leading through the wall and cleverly hidden from attack (although why this entrance was never found and breached during Cromwell's 1648 siege I don't know).

Coming back towards the gatehouse you next reach the North Gate Tower where the town wall was attached to the castle.

The Barbican Tower stands at the SE angle of the castle adjoining the gatehouse, and has a basement and two floors. A circular stair in the thickness of the wall ascends from the basement to the first floor, while another stair on the opposite side leads from the first floor to the curtain wall and on up to the second floor and roof, from which steps rise to a turret. The tower has a wall connecting it to the gatehouse, and a narrow passage through it gives access to the first-floor rooms in the gatehouse.

The gatehouse has already been described, and from its residential rooms a mural gallery leads into the rooms of the Henry VII Tower. A mantelpiece over a fireplace in a room on the second floor at one time had a central ornament or coat of arms: this room was the birthplace of Henry VII in 1457.

The Westgate Tower commanded the old West Gate of the town, and was almost entirely destroyed after the Civil War. Next comes the Monkton Tower, so called because it looks SW across the Pembroke River to the early defences in the village of Monkton.

Next along the wall is the old approach and the Water Port. In the early days when the castle consisted only of the inner bailey and great keep the approach from the river was by a twisting path up the cliff to the inner gatehouse. When the castle was extended by the addition of the outer bailey this pathway was filled in and the curtain wall built over it and a new entrance built at a higher level, known as the Water Port. A water supply was brought into the castle through this archway by earthenware pipes from springs on the hill about 1ml/1.6km S of the castle. In 1880 the filling was cleared out to reveal the original approach.

If we follow the old approach we come to the inner gatehouse, the original and only entrance to the inner bailey. On the L is the Western Tower, Western Hall and the castle chapel, and on the R, at the far end of the inner bailey, is the Dungeon Tower. Beyond the Dungeon Tower the curtain wall continued to the outer curtain wall at the Northern Tower, but this was subsequently incorporated into the later additions of the Northern Hall.

The Northern Hall is the great hall of the castle, its outer wall projecting beyond the outer curtain, overlooking the river. Both its ground-floor 'basement' and its upper main floor are divided by the line of the old inner curtain wall. There is a narrow access into the basement at the W end, and a staircase leads down from it into the Wogan Cavern below. In the small E chamber of the basement a narrow staircase in the thickness of the wall leads up to the hall above. The main approach to the hall is from an outside staircase at the W end. There are two doorways from the Northern Hall leading into the adjoining Norman Hall.

The Norman Hall consists of a basement with a hall above, and was probably one of the first buildings to be erected within the inner bailey. There is no direct access to the main floor of the hall from outside, entrance being obtained either from the Northern Hall or the ante-chamber on the S side known as the Oriel.

Beneath the Northern and Norman Halls is a large cavern, 80ft long and 60ft wide (24m × 18m). A winding stair, dark and often slippery, leads down to it from the Northern Hall. The cavern, known as the Wogan Cavern, was probably used as a storehouse and boathouse, and its opening to the cliff doubtless had a gate, to be used for the reception of supplies.

The crowning glory of this fine castle is the great keep,

architecturally the castle's most imposing feature, built by William Marshall about 1200. The keep is a fully developed cylindrical tower over 100ft/30m high, standing apart from other buildings and on the highest ground in the inner bailey. It is without buttresses, vaulting, arcading or gallery and is regarded as the finest medieval round tower in the British Isles.

A keep was still considered of value as a last resort in defence until into the 13c and round towers were almost universal until the influence of cannon caused great modification in the form of fortification. The great keep at Pembroke is the best surviving example from this era.

The tower had a basement and four storeys, built of undressed limestone, and rises with two offsets from a widely spread plinth. The floors of the rooms have disappeared, and the tower is now open from ground level to its dome-shaped stone roof, and the view upward from inside is most impressive.

The tower has an internal diameter of 24ft/7.3m, and the walls at its base are 19ft/5.8m thick. Even at the first floor the walls are 15ft/4.5m thick, and the wall is 20in/500mm thicker at the point where the spiral staircase occurs than on the opposide side. The staircase, in the thickness of the wall, provides access to the floors and to the roof, and to the basement.

The main entrance to the keep was at the first floor and was reached by a flight of steps up to a drawbridge which spanned a gap in front of the doorway. The entrance floor had a fireplace but no windows, other than two narrow loopholes and, like all the other rooms, is circular and there are no wall-chambers.

A spiral stairway led from the first floor down to the basement. The basement had no well, latrine or drain within it, and it had no openings other than two loopholes, now blocked. The wall was pierced at a later date and this rough opening, now the entrance to the keep, has been driven in through the plinth to the foot of the stairway: this new entrance clearly relates to post-military times.

The third storey was the principal room of the keep; it has a fireplace, two loopholes and a two-light window, richly decorated

Pembroke Castle: the keep and great hall

on the outside with dog-tooth ornament and a carved head. The fourth storey has a similar two-light window and four loopholes, but no fireplace. This top storey is covered by a stone dome, rising at its crown 30ft/9m above the floor of the room; the dome is 7ft/2.1m thick at the haunches and 4ft/1.2m thick at the crown, and is strongly built. A ledge 9in/228mm wide for the support of the timber centre on which it was built runs round the level of its springing line, and corbels for the main truss of the centre still remain in the wall.

On the summit of the keep there were two fighting terraces, one round the base of the dome and the second, behind and above the first, round its haunches. The spiral staircase emerges from under a stair hood into the outer rampart. The outer parapet is about 4ft/1.2m high and has holes in its foot for the escape of rainwater from the roof. At the time of siege a wooden platform was erected outside the wall on which archers could stand to shoot, and holes for the brackets of this temporary structure are to be seen all round the parapet immediately below the arrow-loops. The arrow-loops have no cross-slots, but are square-cut at the base. This enlargement gave the archer greater range when shooting low. This style of arrow-loop dates the keep from c1200 – later in the 13c arrow-loops were usually terminated both at head and foot by circular holes, and if there was a cross-slot that also had a circular hole at either end.

The height of the keep enabled the watchers on the top to command an extensive view. The ramparts are so much above the tops of the surrounding castle walls that nearly all the ground outside was under observation. The top of the keep provides a fine view of the castle, and of Pembroke, and we can look over the town before taking our leave of the castle to follow the Town Trail.

A Pembroke town trail

Pembroke's castle is justly famous, but the remarkable survival of the town walls, and of a town almost entirely confined within them, is surprisingly little known, perhaps because the three town gates have disappeared.

In the early 14c a wall was thrown from the West Gate of the castle, and another from the North Gate, to take in both sides of the long narrow ridge to a point about 0.5ml/800m from the castle. There were three town gates, through which the entrances to the town still pass: the North Gate at Mill Bridge, the West Gate on Westgate Hill on the road to Monkton, and the East Gate at the junction of roads to Carew, Tenby and Lamphey. The remaining parts of the walls on the S side give the town a picturesque appearance.

The limestone ridge separates two streams, one of which ran through marshland on the S side, and the other on the N; they joined at the headland to form the Pembroke River. That on the N was dammed to form the tidal mill pool to work the mill which fed the castle garrison, and this is a good place to begin a tour of the town.

We enter the town on the A4139 from Pembroke Dock at Mill Bridge, which is the site of the old corn mill. The original rights for a mill were granted by King John to the Knights Templars of St John of Jerusalem. The last mill building was destroyed by fire on 7 September 1955.

On the downstream side of Mill Bridge is the old town quay. An old warehouse, the Royal George Hotel and the Waterman's Arms across the other side of the mill pond are reminders that Pembroke was once a port. The North Gate was behind the Royal George, and was demolished in 1820: a remnant of the adjoining town wall survives behind the antique shop opposite, at the foot of Northgate Street.

From the dam follow the new esplanade – Mill Pond Walk – beside the pool, immediately below the town wall. An alley – Morgan's Way – leads up to Main Street, but we will continue along the whole length of the walk to St Michael's Tower and Barnard's Tower. A pathway turns to join Main Street at the E end of the town, close to East End Square, where stood the East Gate. The East Gate was destroyed on Cromwell's orders in 1648 after the surrender of the town and its castle.

Main Street runs the length of the ridge, but not in a straight line, and towards the E end it briefly divides before joining again. The pattern of the town today is still one of a long medieval thoroughfare, but the curse of a one-way traffic system and parked cars spoil the atmosphere. The buildings are not individually remarkable, but collectively they make a good street scene and their survival is important. Mostly Georgian in flavour, many are 19c, presumably with medieval foundations. Their irregular roofline is emphasised by a slight dip in the ridge, and the houses, hotels and shops are all rather grey in tone, from the predominant use of limestone and Welsh slate; as the ridge is only one street wide the houses have plenty of sun and views.

If we walk down Main Street towards the castle we see some of the larger town houses and the formidable façade of the Methodist Chapel. Close by on the N side is Mount Pleasant Baptist Church and the church of St Michael and All Angels. This was built in 1832 but in 1887 it was extensively renovated and partially rebuilt. St Michael's has some interesting memorials, including a brass tablet in the nave giving in confusing detail the family history of Joshua Allen.

At the far end of Main Street the Lion Hotel with its human-faced lion looks down Northgate Street, and on the opposite corner is the entrance to the church of St Mary the Virgin. St Michael's and St Mary's are Pembroke's two parish churches, and services alternate between them: architecturally St Mary's is the better, although neither is very interesting.

The church of St Mary the Virgin was built in 1350 but was thoroughly Victorianised in 1879. A blocked doorway in the ringing chamber of the square tower is evidence that the E end of the nave would have had a gallery similar to that which can still be seen at Manorbier. The corbelled structure over the organ probably supported another gallery, for there is another blocked doorway to this in the ringing chamber.

If when you leave St Mary's you go down by the side of the Lion Hotel on the S side of Main Street behind the houses and shops you will come to the remains of the medieval wall that ran along the line of The Parade. Viewed from Common Park or the Orange Gardens estate opposite the wall, town gardens, trees and park are an attractive feature of the town. Orange Gardens has a grid-iron layout of attractive, mostly single-storey town cottages built in terraces, similar to those in Pembroke Dock.

As we are now on the S side of the town we are in a position to make our journey on the south shore of Milford Haven to the Angle Peninsula, and this next stage is described in the following chapter.

23   Haven South Shore: Pembroke to Angle
(Maps 45–48)   14.7ml/23.6km

The coastline of the S shore of Milford Haven seems at first sight, with a glance at the map, to be a most unpromising one, since much of it is round the muddy bays of the Pembroke River and Angle Bay, and around the Pembroke Power Station and the Texaco refinery. It would appear that because of this, and also because a large part of the coastline to the SW is denied to the walker as it lies within the Castlemartin Artillery Range, a number of Coast Path walkers on leaving Pembroke go directly on the B4319 road to Bosherston and St Govan's Head, missing completely the walk around the Castlemartin Peninsula.

This is to be regretted because the S shore route is in fact quite enjoyable, especially between Monkton and Lambeeth, as the Path passes through delightfully unspoilt countryside. Unfortunately they are two places where the Path is uncared for or doesn't seem to exist – to the W of the Texaco jetty, and on the S side of Angle Bay – and the walking is surprisingly hard going. However, unless more walkers use this Path the route will become more overgrown and perhaps fall into disuse, which will make it even harder going for those true Coast Path walkers who want to walk all of the way.

The 'official' Coast Path does not begin again until you are well out of Pembroke, on the edge of Monkton village, and you have to walk out on the B4320 road for 1ml/1.6km to get there. This section is the Pembroke-Monkton Link, and it gives us an opportunity to have a look at Monkton Priory Church.

The Pembroke-Monkton (Quoits Mill) Link 1ml/1.6km
From Pembroke Castle go down Westgate Hill and over the Pembroke River bridge, and up the road on the far side, called

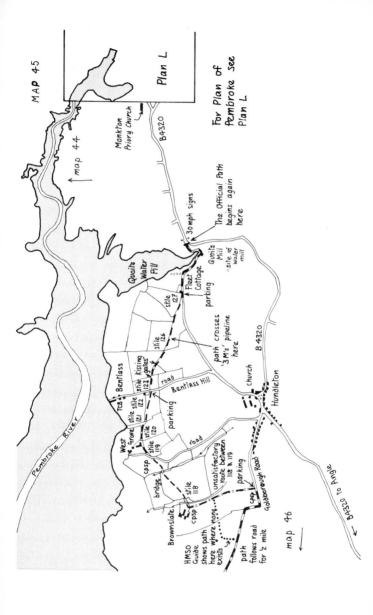

MAP 45

map 44

Plan L

For Plan of Pembroke See Plan L

Pembroke River

Monkton Priory Church

B4320

30mph signs

The Official Path begins again here

Quoits Water Pill

Quoits Mill -site of water mill

Fleet Cottage

parking

stile 127

path crosses '3 M's' pipeline here

stile 126

B 4320

Bentlass

Tea

stile 122

stile 121

kissing gates

stile 123

road

Bentlass Hill

parking

church

Hundleton

West Grove

stile 120

stile 119

road

cpsp

stile 118

bridge

cpsp

unsatisfactory route between 118 & 119

parking

Brownslate

HMSO Guide shows path here where none exists

Galborough Road

cpsp

path follows road for ½ mile

map 46

B4320 to Angle

Bridgend Terrace. Instead of following the B4320 around the corner turn R up the narrow Church Terrace, which leads directly to the *Priory Church of St Nicholas and St John, Monkton*. A good distant view of Pembroke Castle can be enjoyed through the trees in the churchyard.

A church and some monastic buildings were built within a large defensive earthwork which pre-dates Pembroke Castle. By about 1090 Arnulph de Montgomery came and occupied this earthwork and the Welsh are said to have attacked it in 1092 and again in 1094, but without success, so it must have been a very strong defence. In 1098 Arnulph was so well established in the district that he made a gift of the church of St Nicholas 'within his castle' to the Benedictine foundation of Seez in Normandy, which was transferred to St Albans in the reign of Henry VI in 1473.

The original church was a double church, the long aisleless nave being used as the parish church, while the services of the monks were held in the chancel. After the Dissolution the monastic church was allowed to fall into ruin. The choir and sanctuary became roofless, and only the long narrow nave remained. The church has a big tunnel-like barrel-vaulted nave, chancel, sanctuary, and a fine tower of the quasi-fortified South Pembrokeshire type. The church lay in ruins for many years until a restoration of 1878–87 by the Rev. David Bowen, vicar between 1877 and 1926.

Above the large, late 12c S porch there used to be a room, or a parvise, and the steps which led to it can still be seen from inside the thickness of the wall. A fine, plain, Norman arch covers the doorway to the church, and was only rediscovered at the restoration.

The long narrow nave reflects its past as a priory church in its lofty spaciousness, and because of its length and height is probably a unique example of its type in the country. The N side is double-walled and is supported outside by three huge buttresses – the oldest part of the church. From traces of two small half-blocked windows on the N exterior of the nave it has been suggested that the masonry incorporates the S wall of the pre-Norman church.

The tombs on the N side are of the Meyricks of Bush, the Owens of Orielton, and the Corston family. The altar tomb of Sir Francis

Meyrick (d.1603), under the tower on the S side, has the figures of his seven sons and one daughter kneeling in perpetual prayer for their father's soul. The upper part of the tomb is in a style suggesting Italian Renaissance influences.

In 1887 the wall dividing the nave from the choir was removed and the present chancel arch was built. The chancel and sanctuary, formerly the Benedictine choir, are on an unusually large scale – 69ft/21m high – and are in the Decorated style. The great S window was erected to commemorate the visit, on 23 August 1902, of King Edward VIII, Queen Alexandra and Princess Victoria.

N of the chancel is a doorway that leads to a large chapel, which in all probability was the prior's private chapel. It is detached from the church and was in ruins, but was restored by Bowen in 1878. The windows were the gift of the Castlemartin Lodge of Freemasonry, and depict Old Testament figures and various symbols associated with freemasonry. One can see a large opening in the upper wall, which comes through the N wall into the chancel: through this the sick monks in the infirmary could see the High Altar and the Elevation of the Host at Mass.

Monkton (Quoits Mill) to Pwllcrochan 4.5ml/7.2km
The 'official' Coast Path begins again where the B4320 road turns inland to the village of Hundleton. A lane passes Quoits Mill at the head of a small pill, where a raised footpath has thoughtfully been provided when the road is flooded at spring tides.

Between Quoits Mill and Pwllcrochan the Coast Path passes through some pleasant countryside, but the route of the Path itself is somewhat unsatisfactory, and it is over-grown and muddy in several places. In all but perfect conditions – when it is dry underfoot and the undergrowth has not had time to assert itself – it will be better to take the lane from Quoits Mill to Hundleton, then the track called Goldborough Road to Wallaston Cross, and then follow the road past the entrance to the Pembroke Power Station to reach Pwllcrochan.

Pwllcrochan is a tiny place, with a couple of cottages, an old school, an old vicarage, and a weathered cruciform church. The church was rebuilt in 1342 with a small tower and spire, but its

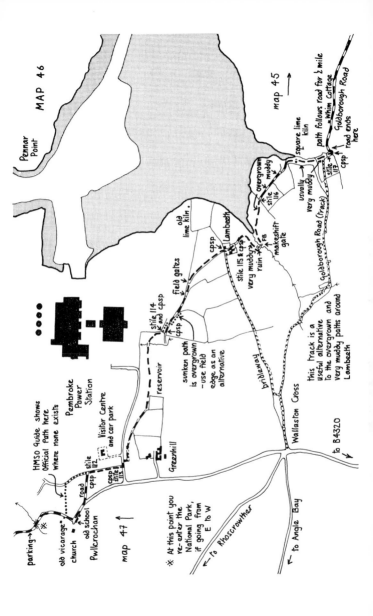

MAP 46

Pennar Point

map 45

path follows road for ½ mile
Whim Cottage
Goldborough Road
road ends here

square lime kiln
cpsp
stile 116

overgrown
stile muddy
116

usually
very muddy

old lime kiln

Lambeath

Goldborough Road (Track)

cpsp

stile 115 & cpsp
very muddy
ruin
Fes
makeshift gate

this Track is a
useful alternative
to the overgrown and
very muddy paths around
Lambeath

field gates

stile 114
and cpsp

cpsp

sunken path
is overgrown —
use field
edge as an
alternative

bridleway

Wallaston Cross

HMSO Guide shows
Official Path here
where none exists

Pembroke Power
Station

Visitor Centre
and car park

stile
112
cpsp
road
cpsp stile
113

reservoir

to B4320

old vicarage"
church
old school
Pwllcrochan

parking→

Greenhill

map 47

※ At this point you
re-enter the
National Park, if going from
E to W

to Rhoscrowther

to Angle Bay

furnishings are mid-19c: semi-box pews with doors, clear glass
throughout, and slate floors. It is closed and empty: some of its
artefacts have been removed to Rhoscrowther church. In the
churchyard there is a well of pure water, which runs into a stream
down to Pwllcrochan Flats, once renowned for its cockle beds.

The setting sounds idyllic, but the land around is now occupied by
the towers and tanks of the nearby Texaco refinery, while just
across the field is the massive bulk of the Pembroke Power Station
which pours warm water into the Haven, causing the cockles to stir
uneasily in their beds.

The building of the *Pembroke Power Station* was begun in 1964 as
part of the enlarged CEGB's programme of generating plant
construction, but it did not become fully operational until early
1972. Clearly the increasing importance of the Haven as an oil
refining centre encouraged the location of the plant there, some
60ml/96km from the nearest large electricity consumer, Swansea.
The station was opened in June 1973 by the Rt Hon. Edward Heath
MP, then Prime Minister. At the time of its completion it had cost
£110 million to build, and was the largest single item of capital
investment in Wales; it remains one of the largest oil-fired power
stations in Europe.

The power station has been built on largely reclaimed land which
formed part of the dry valley known as Pennar Gut, and most of the
buildings on the 480 acre/194ha site are well screened by the ridge of
Old Red Sandstone to the N, on the edge of the Haven. The
750ft/213m main chimney stack is somewhat difficult to hide, but
since the proportions are similar to those of the smaller oil refinery
stacks, its real height is not often appreciated.

Fuel is delivered to the station by pipeline from the neighbouring
Texaco and Gulf refineries. The station has a capacity of 2000
megawatts distributed between four 500-megawatt turbo-generators
and boiler units, each of which can generate more electricity than
Battersea Power Station ever could, with four auxiliary gas turbine
turbo-generators of 25 megawatts each as standby service.

Although the power station appears well landscaped from the
waters of the Haven, its full environmental effects have never been
measured. The CEGB says that 'The height of the chimney was

carefully chosen after exhaustive model and site testing to prevent annoyance in the neighbourhood and the efflux velocity ensures that the gases are sent into the higher levels of the atmosphere.'* Government regulations do not insist on the installation of 'scrubbers' to remove poisonous substances, and the simplest and cheapest method of disposal is to eject the waste gases at high velocity up to an altitude of 2000ft/610m in the hope that the wind will carry them away. The CEGB says that 'The need to avoid air pollution has long been foremost in the design requirements' and 'the effluent gases are constantly monitored and advanced control systems ensure that where there is a danger of harmful emission immediate remedial action is taken.'

The European Commission's demands in June 1988 for a reduction in the emissions from power stations have not been endorsed by the British government and the CEGB. There are no plans to have anti-pollution equipment fitted to Pembroke Power Station before the industry is privatized as planned in 1991.

All in all, the Milford Haven oil installations and power station are capable of ejecting perhaps 1000 tonnes of poison into the Pembrokeshire atmosphere each day. Current concern about the effects of 'acid rain' pollution may result in the full social and biological cost being reflected in the price of the product. The station's operating costs were at one time claimed to be lower than those of even the best coal-fired power stations, but with the tenfold increase in the cost of fuel in the first ten years that the station has been operating this claim to efficiency must be seriously doubted.

The CEGB says that 'two of the four main turbo-generator units should be capable of meeting the electrical power requirements of S Wales' and 'The present site comprises an area large enough for the erection of a second station should the need arise.' Because of the increase in the cost of heavy fuel oil, and the deterioration in the overall economic situation in the past few years, the load required from the station has been reduced, and it seems unlikely that such a need will arise in the foreseeable future.

* Quotations are taken from CEGB publications on Pembroke Power Station available to the public from the Visitor Centre, Pembroke Power Station, West Pennar, Pembroke.

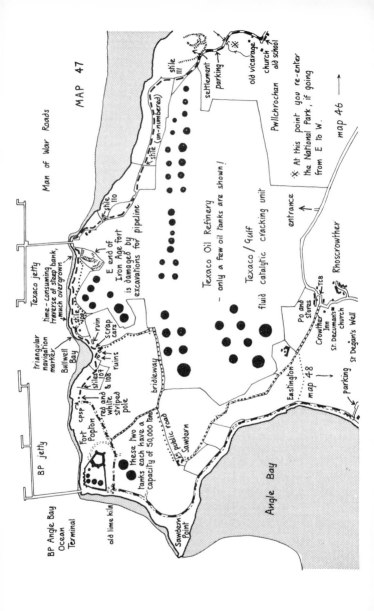

MAP 47

Man of War Roads

BP jetty

Texaco jetty

Triangular navigation marker

BP Angle Bay Ocean Terminal

old lime kiln

Sawdern Point

Sawdern

public road

These two tanks each have a capacity of 50,000 tons

red and white striped pole

Fort Popton CPSP

stiles 107 & 108

ruins

scrap cars

ruin

Bullwell Bay

lime-consuming traverse of steep bank, much overgrown

E end of Iron Age fort is damaged by excavations for pipeline

stile 109

stile 110

stile (un-numbered)

stile III

settlement

parking

old vicarage church old school

Pwllchrochan

map 46 →

※ At this point you re-enter the National Park, if going from E to W.

bridleway

Eastington

map 48 →

Texaco Oil Refinery - only a few oil tanks are shown!

Texaco/Gulf fluid catalytic cracking unit

entrance

Rhoscrowther

Po and stores

TCB

Crowther Inn

St Decuman's church

St Degan's Well

parking

Angle Bay

Hours of admission

The power station is open to the public for guided tours on
Tuesdays, Wednesdays and Thursdays between 1 June and 29
September (excluding Bank Holidays) at 1400 and 1500. Parties of
30–100 people can only be shown around by prior application to the
Station Manager. Refreshments are available in the Visitor Centre.

Pwllcrochan to Kilpaison 4ml/6.4km

The Coast Path regains the coast beyond Pwllcrochan and goes
around the Texaco refinery and the British Petroleum Angle Bay
Ocean Terminal on Popton Point, before following the shore of
Angle Bay and continuing past the village of Rhoscrowther. The
Path is good except for a short distance around Bullwell Bay –
between the Texaco and BP jetties – where it is hard to see and
follow in the undergrowth of the woods.

The *Texaco Oil refinery* is the only one on the S side of the Haven
and it came into operation on 27 October 1964 after being formally
opened by HM Queen Elizabeth, the Queen Mother. It was later
expanded to its present refining capacity of 180,000 barrels (6.3
million gallons/28.6 million litres) of crude oil a day (or 8.5 million
tonnes per annum), and in July 1975 it received the first North Sea
crude oil to be refined in Wales.

Texaco owns 925 acres/375ha of land; just over half of this area –
500 acres/210ha – is occupied by the refinery; the rest is mainly
green fields outside the refinery fence. The plant complex contains
some 111 oil tanks, the largest of which can each hold nearly
600,000 barrels/21 million gallons/95.4 million litres of crude oil.

The marine terminal is a T-shaped jetty extending 1400ft/426m
into the Haven, and it has five berths along its 3400ft/1036m long
trunkway. The largest berth is designed to handle tankers such as
the 270,000-ton *Texaco Caribbean*.

In 1977 Texaco and Gulf formed a consortium – called the
Pembroke Cracking Company – to build jointly a fluid catalytic
cracking unit, more popularly known as a '*cat cracker*'. This facility
converts heavy fuel oil into lighter, higher-value products such as
petrol, diesel oil and domestic heating oil, and improves the
manufacturing flexibility and product mix of the two refineries.

Each of the refineries was designed primarily to produce large quantities of fuel oil – more than is now required for the British market. The quantity of light products, especially of petrol, that could be made by this refining process was less than the two companies actually sold in the United Kingdom: they had to import petrol from foreign refineries to meet the shortfall in their share of the British market.

The cat cracker cost over £400 million to build, came on stream in 1982, and produces over 65,000 barrels/2.2 million gallons/10.2 million litres a day. Fuel oil yield is radically reduced, and the resulting ratio of products matches more closely the current market requirements. Texaco has announced a further major investment in plant to produce lead-free gasoline.

The British Petroleum Company's *Angle Bay Ocean Terminal* was brought into operation in August 1960 having cost about £7 million to build. It was officially opened by the Rt Hon. Richard Wood MP, Minister of Fuel and Power, on 20 April 1961.

The jetty of the terminal extends 1350ft/411m and the jetty head, 3820ft/1164m long, has three berthing heads capable of handling tankers up to 250,000dwt fully loaded. On 28 August 1965 the first 100,000dwt tanker was brought into the Haven when BP's *British Admiral* arrived on her maiden voyage with 104,000 tons of Middle East crude oil. In October 1973 one of the largest ships ever to enter the Haven, the 327,000dwt *Universe Kuwait*, discharged a part cargo of crude oil; while the first cargo of crude oil from BP's Forties Field in the North Sea was brought to the terminal by the *British Dragoon* in February 1976.

The administration centre of the BP tanker terminal was at *Fort Popton*, at the shore end of the jetty. This fort was built in 1859–64 and was ingeniously adapted and preserved by BP. The fort was contemporary with South Hook, Stack Rock and Hubberston. It had 31 guns, with eleven of these in casements with iron shields and it cost £90,227 to build. The defensible barracks form an irregular hexagon, and housed a garrison of 274 men. It is now new laboratories, research and a consultancy base for the Field Studies Council.

Adjoining Fort Popton to the S are two tanks, each having a

capacity of 50,000 tonnes. These tanks receive BP fuel oil from the terminal which is held here prior to delivery to the Pembroke Power Station.

From Fort Popton on Popton Point the Coast Path follows the urban-style private service road past Sawdern Point and around the eastern shore of Angle Bay, a kidney-shaped embayment some 2ml/3.2km wide. Halfway down this road a bridleway goes inland to Eastington Farm and the village of Rhoscrowther, whose substantial medieval church is well worth a visit.

Rhoscrowther is a small settlement of a church, rectory (now a guest house, the Crowther Inn), cottages, council houses and a farm on a hillside, overlooked by the tanks and towers of the Texaco refinery. Eastington is a small farmhouse with a square tower on its seaward side, having an embattled parapet and turret, and a fortified wall-walk.

The church is dedicated to St Decumanus, the Latin name of St Tegfan. Tegfan is reputed to have been born here and apparently sailed out of the Haven and up the Bristol Channel in a coracle, landing near Dunster in Somerset, where he settled as a hermit until a pagan Dane cut off his head in 706. Tegfan, however, surprised the Dane by walking away with his head tucked under his arm in the approved fashion, and he became a saint as a result.

The interesting church has a strong tower and a large N porch. It is irregular in plan and alignment, typical of South Pembrokeshire churches, and consists of nave and chancel, probably of 13c date, 14c transepts – the S one is the ground floor of the tower – and a S chancel chapel.

The church was 'restored' in 1910 and the inside walls and the diagonal passages which connect the N transept with the chancel and side chapel were whitewashed and heavily plastered. All windows were replaced in incongruous Bath stone, and the floor was laid with blue and cream tiles.

Beneath the church, in the shallow valley that runs into Angle Bay, is the site of St Degan's Well, a corruption of the saint's name. This well may have given the settlement its Welsh name, Rhoscrowther, meaning 'the moor with fresh water'.

Kilpaison to Angle East 2.2ml/3.5km

The low red sandstone cliffs which form the S shore of the Haven are eaten out by the wide, shallow, kidney-shaped bite of Angle Bay. The shallow stretch of water is visited by waders and duck, and it was from the Middle Ages until quite recently an important area for cockle-fishing. The bay dries a long way out at low water, leaving a muddy and sandy expanse.

At the end of the public road on the E side of Angle Bay there is a parking area, and pedestrians are permitted to pass through the BP security gate to gain access to a picnic area on the coast. The Coast Path is easy to follow along the northern edge of the BP Kilpaison Tank Farm, but once past this point it is best to walk on the shore, as no path exists on the land.

Tankers at BP's Ocean Terminal discharged crude oil through pipelines to *Kilpaison Tank Farm* and pumping station. This tank farm had a holding capacity of 500,000 tons: four of the tanks, each holding 75,000 tons, were among the largest in Europe, and were linked to BP's refinery at Llandarcy near Swansea by a 62ml/100km buried pipeline. Oil was pumped continuously at approximately 11,000 tonnes per hour to Llandarcy, and it took about 10 hours to make the journey. Operations ceased in 1985.

Until a few years ago the village of *Angle* used to be a very remote hamlet at the tip of the long peninsula, but today, partly as a result of improvements to the road from Pembroke to the power station and oil developments, and partly as a result of the Mirehouse Estate selling off some of its village properties, enabling outsiders and second-home owners to move in, the place is now well known to holiday-makers.

The village lies in a low valley which follows the axis of a downfold (syncline) in rocks of Carboniferous and Old Red Sandstone age. The soil and rocks are a rich red: the sandstone belt runs right across the Haven to Dale and under the sea to Skokholm. The village consists of a single delightful street with attractive cottages and is bounded by long and extraordinarily narrow fields which are enclosed strips of the Norman manorial field system.

The epitome of pre-railway Pembrokeshire, Angle is characterised by the rotting timbers of two schooners, a ruined quay

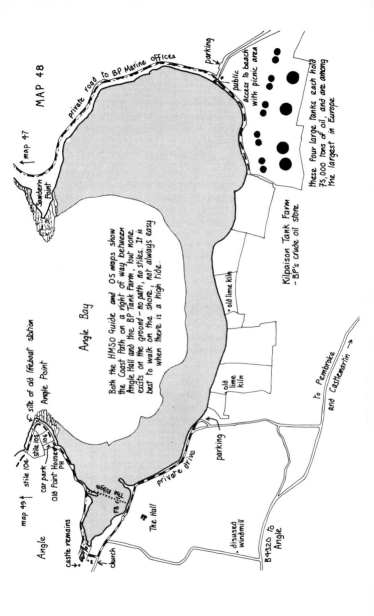

MAP 48

↑ MAP 47

Sawdern Point

private road to BP Marine offices

parking

public access to beach with picnic area

These four large tanks each hold 75,000 tons of oil, and are among the largest in Europe

Kilpaison Tank Farm – BP's crude oil store.

old lime kiln

Angle Bay

Both the HMSO Guide and OS maps show the Coast Path on a right of way between Angle Hall and the BP Tank Farm, but none exists on the ground – no path, no stiles. It is best to walk on the shore, not always easy when there is a high tide.

old lime kiln

to Pembroke and Castlemartin →

parking

private drive

disused windmill

B4320 to Angle

The Hall

FB

The Ridge

church

castle remains

Angle

map 49 ↑

stile 104

stile 105

106

car park

Old Point House PH

Angle Point

site of old lifeboat station

and harbour walls. Both bays – Angle Bay and West Angle Bay – have been used by fishermen for centuries. One of the wrecked schooners in the creek of Angle Bay, the *Progress*, was reputedly the fastest ship in her day on the cod run from Newfoundland; the other, further up the creek, was the two-masted ketch *Mary Jane*, the last ship to be built at Jacobs Pill in Pennar Gut in 1899. The main bay provides a sheltered anchorage, but moorings for yachtsmen may be difficult except at high water. The harbour entrance is obstructed by The Ridge, a spit of shingle running S from the northern shore, and may present difficulties for boats entering on a following tide. At low water The Ridge may be crossed on foot, saving 0.5ml/800m in that final dash for a pint in the pub on Angle Point.

The centrepiece of the charming village is the Globe Hotel, a three-storied building with a six-columned portico forming a colonnade across the pavement, its front topped by a battlement. Adjoining the Globe Hotel is the village Post Office and opposite this is a monument 'Erected by the tenantry of the Angle and Eastington Estates as a lasting tribute of respect for their late sincerely beloved and deeply lamented landlord, John Mirehouse. AD 1846.' Such were the effects of the ruling classes in those early Victorian times. Where are the monuments erected by the landlords praising the loyalty of their suffering workmen?

The nearby church of St Mary the Virgin was thoroughly restored in the 1850s, when it was given salmon-pink tiles on the chancel roof. Behind the church, in the churchyard, is a miniature detached fishermen's chapel, dedicated to St Anthony, and founded by Edward de Shirburn of Nangle in 1447. The chapel is raised above a crypt, and is reached by outside steps. The vaulted crypt is an ossuary chamber (depository of bones), while the chapel above contains a medieval effigy, narrow lancet windows, and modern stained glass in the E window showing Christ walking on the waters.

To the N of the church, and also reached by footpaths leading from the village street near the Globe Hotel, are the ruins of 'Angle Castle'. The 'castle' is a free-standing tower, with a moat on its

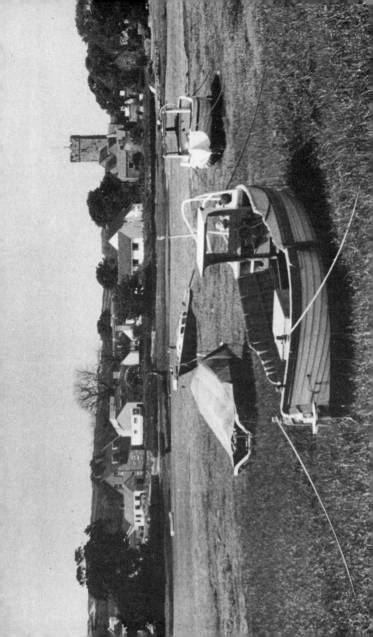

N and W sides, and its S side protected by the creek of the bay. The tower remains, roughly rectangular in plan, and having a rounded projection accommodating a corner stair. It was probably three storeys high, and entered at first-floor level across a drawbridge. Stone corbels projecting from the top of the tower could have supported a wooden walkway. Nothing is known of the castle's history. Nearby is a small, domed dovecote of uncertain date. Both castle and dovecote are on private land.

Angle Bay to West Angle Bay, via Chapel Bay 3ml/4.8km
Whatever you do, do not be tempted to make a short cut and follow the road between Angle Bay and West Angle Bay. The Coast Path around North Hill is a pleasant stroll, and as it is the highest point on the coast on the S side of the Haven it provides an unrivalled vantage point for the Haven and its shipping. The Path is good all the way, although you have to beware of the cliff-falls on the N side of West Angle Bay.

Due N of the village, on the cliff at Chapel Bay, are the remains of the battery of Chapel Bay Fort. This was built between 1868 and 1870 at a cost of £13,784 and accommodated a garrison of 65 men. It had a battery of six 9in/228mm rifled muzzle-loading guns, and it was remodelled in 1900 as an open battery for heavy guns, with magazines below. The fort is notable because of the scale of its revetted ditch, flanked by polygonal caponieres, looped for musketry. A MOD wireless station occupies land nearby.

Thorn Island is an offshore rock surmounted by a Victorian fort, one of the few forts still occupied and in good repair, and commanding a fine view of the entrance to the Haven. Thorn Island Battery was built in 1852–9 at a cost of £85,000 and held a garrison of 100 men. It had a casemented battery of nine guns, improved in 1860 to give fire all round. The building was turned into an hotel in the mid-1930s, and is accessible by motor launch from West Angle Bay.

West Angle Bay illustrates one of the many E–W trending faults of South Pembrokeshire which run out to the coast. The rocks on both sides of the sandy bay belong to the Lower Limestone Shales at the base of the Carboniferous Series; those on the N side of the bay dip to the S, and those on the S side dip into the bay, the axis of the syncline passing down the beach and into the sea. The bay has obviously been developed along the axis, the sea exploiting the comparatively soft alternations of shale and limestone: a similar pattern is evident at Lydstep Haven.

The bay is small and very pleasant, its sands flanked by low cliffs. It has many rock pools at low tide, when gently shelving gritty sand is revealed. There is good, free car parking, and immediate access to the beach, and there are public toilets, a beach café and a caravan site nearby, which tell of the beach's popularity.

Brick-making was once an important local industry, and limestone was also burnt for the farming community. An old lime-kiln is one the N side of the bay, and a brick-pit and brickworks are immediately behind the beach on the S side. The bricks were originally made by Staffordshire workmen, and the works had its own small tramway. The red brick buildings still stand near the beach café, but the brick-pit is now filled in. The bay was a landing place 3500 years ago for copper shipped from the Wicklow Mountains in Ireland.

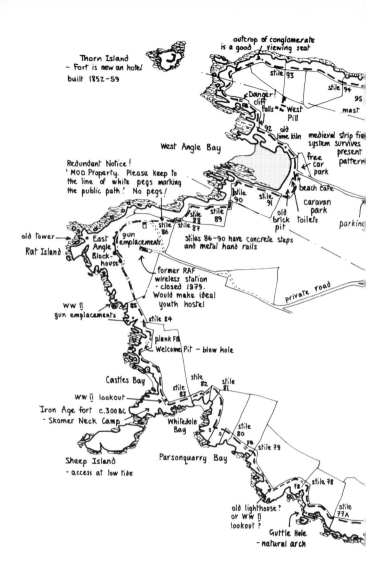

Thorn Island
– Fort is now an hotel
built 1852-59

outcrop of conglomerate
is a good viewing seat

stile 93

stile 94

95

mast

Danger!
cliff
falls

West
Pill

92

old
lime kiln

medieval strip field
system survives
present
pattern

West Angle Bay

free
car
park

Redundant Notice!
'MOD Property. Please keep to
the line of white pegs marking
the public path.' No pegs!

stile
90

stile
91

beach café

caravan
park

old
brick
pit

toilets

parking

stile
88

stile
89

old tower

Rat Island

East
Angle
Block-
house

gun
emplacements

stile
86

stile
87

stiles 86-90 have concrete steps
and metal hand rails

ww II
gun emplacements

85

former RAF
wireless station
– closed 1979.
Would make ideal
youth hostel

stile 84

plank FB

Welcome Pit – blow hole

Castles Bay

stile
83

stile
82

stile
81

ww II lookout

Iron Age fort c.300 BC
– Skomer Neck Camp

Whitedole
Bay

s

s

stile
80

FB

stile 79

Sheep Island
– access at low tide

Parsonquarry Bay

FB

stile 78

old lighthouse?
or WW II
lookout?

Guttle Hole
– natural arch

FB

stile
77A

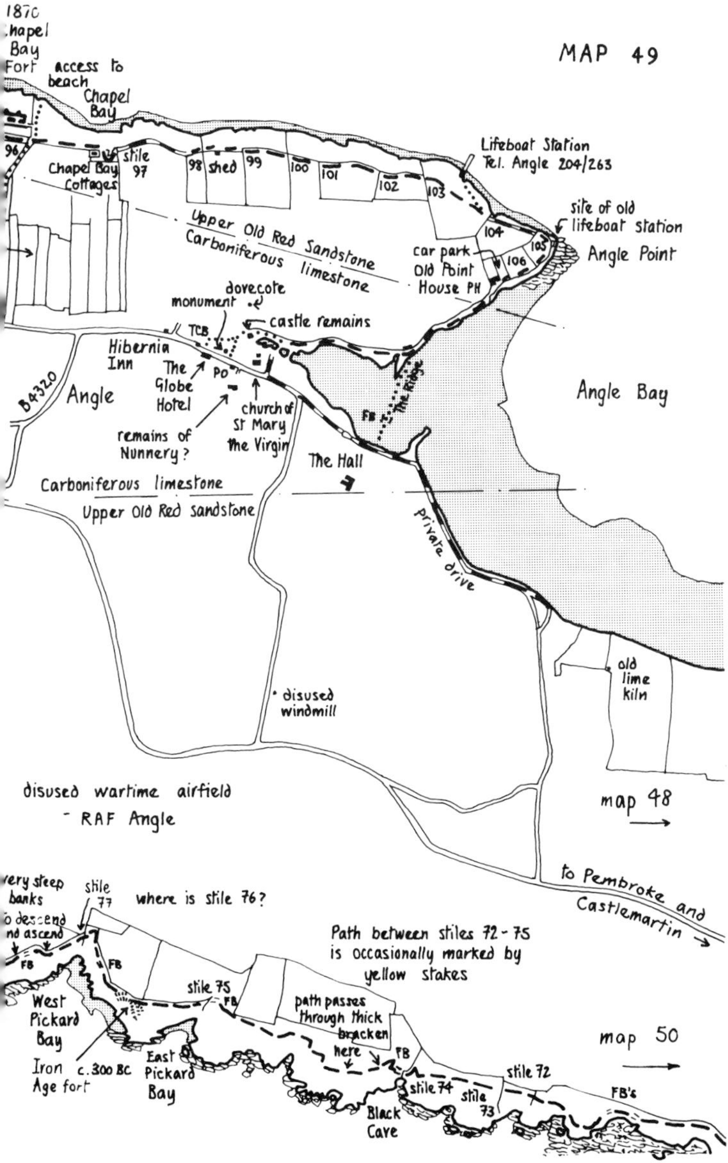

MAP 49

1870
Chapel
Bay
Fort

access to
beach
Chapel
Bay

96?

Chapel Bay
Cottages

stile
97

98 shed

99

100

101

102

103

Lifeboat Station
Tel. Angle 204/263

site of old
lifeboat station

104

car park
Old Point
House PH

105

106

Angle Point

Upper Old Red Sandstone
Carboniferous limestone

dovecote

monument

TCB

castle remains

Hibernia
Inn

The
Globe
Hotel

PO

B4320

Angle

remains of
Nunnery?

church of
St Mary
the Virgin

FB

The Ridge

Angle Bay

The Hall

Carboniferous limestone
Upper Old Red Sandstone

private drive

disused
windmill

old
lime
kiln

disused wartime airfield
- RAF Angle

map 48

very steep
banks

stile
77

where is stile 76?

to descend
and ascend

FB

FB

West
Pickard
Bay

stile 75

FB

Path between stiles 72 - 75
is occasionally marked by
yellow stakes

path passes
through thick
bracken
here

FB

map 50

Iron
Age fort

c.300 BC

East
Pickard
Bay

stile 74

Black
Cave

stile
73

stile 72

FB's

to Pembroke and
Castlemartin

Part five

South Pembrokeshire

24   Angle to St Govan's Head (Maps 49–55)   14.3ml/23km

From the tip of the Angle or Castlemartin Peninsula the Coast Path follows a magnificent coastline to St Govan's Head, the southernmost point of Pembrokeshire. The sandstone headlands of the Angle Peninsula give way to the broad sweep of the bay of Freshwater West, and then follows a superb stretch of limestone cliffs. Sadly these cannot be followed all the way because the Castlemartin Armoured Corps Tank Range intervenes, and a good part of the way has to be on the road.

West Angle Bay to Freshwater West   5.4ml/8.7km
This is a fine stretch of coast, with cliffs, bays, headlands and islands fronting the open Atlantic. It is scenically as exciting as, and possibly more satisfying than, the similar sandstone cliffs of the Dale Peninsula. This is not a stretch for young children, dogs, or the elderly, and, as the Path passes through thickets of gorse and blackthorn, is not for bare legs and sandals.

  After climbing up gradually from West Angle Bay you come to a disused RAF wireless station, which was built on the site of East Angle Blockhouse. The 19c fort was demolished, and only the open battery, dating from 1900, remains. Nearby is an old tower, the only surviving ruin of the post-Armada defences, built c1580. Rat Island – not really an island, but a promontory – has a fine colony of great black-backed gulls and choughs. Sheep Island, on the other hand, is an island, and it can be reached at low water. On its sloping top there are a large number of oblong hut-hollows and, in common with those of Gateholm Island, they are different from the more or less circular depressions that are characteristic of Iron Age huts. The site has not been excavated.

Sheep Island lies off a peninsula between Castles Bay and Whitedole Bay, and this headland carries an Iron Age fort called Skomer Neck Camp. It dates from about 300BC and has a defence of a single bank and a natural gully, cutting it off from the rest of the promontory. Within the fort built in 1914 a World War I lookout, which provides rudimentary shelter.

Between West and East Pickard Bays there is another single-banked Iron Age fort, also dating from about 300BC, with its causeway entrance on the E: its original stone walling is visible.

The coast soon changes from cliffs of Old Red Sandstone to the impressive sandy beach of *Freshwater West*. This is a splendid sweep of sands backed by wind-blown sand dunes, and is perhaps the most beautiful beach along the whole coast. The Atlantic rollers make a glorious display when the western wind gets behind them, and in a storm they are more than magnificent. The beach faces just S of W and receives waves bigger and more consistent than any other beach in Wales: all through the year, and at all stages of the tide, every swell that comes off the Atlantic hits the beach head-on, and oceanic rollers pound the shore unceasingly.

The whole beach is not considered to be very safe, as there are some bad rips – water draining back to the sea after a huge wave has broken and run up the beach – achieving speeds of several knots, generally showing about the middle of the beach; there are also patches of quicksands near the low-water mark at the northern end of the beach. The quicksands, currents and undertows make bathing, boating and paddling very dangerous – more drownings have occurred here than anywhere else around the coast – but it is nevertheless an excellent beach if you are an experienced surfer.

The superb and fragile dune system is a Site of Special Scientific Interest and is owned mainly by the NT. The official Coast Path follows the B4319 road to avoid the dunes, but if the tide is out you can walk along the high-water mark. Visitors in cars are requested to avoid the dunes and to walk to the beach only by the N and S access points. The dunes, known locally as burrows, sprawl far inland, rising as high as 200ft/60m toward the reclaimed and fertile valley near Castlemartin village. The extensive dunes of Linney, **Brownslade, Gupton, Broomhill and Kilpaison Burrows have**

MAP 50

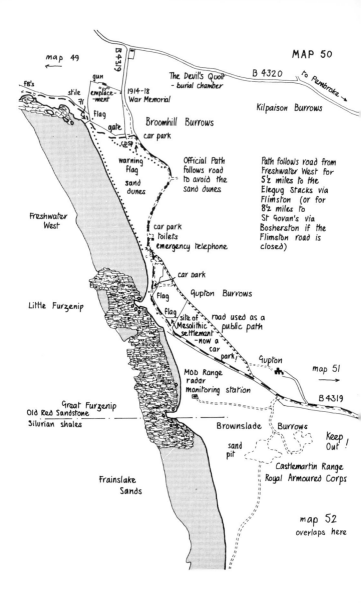

map 49 ←

B 4319

The Devil's Quoit
– burial chamber

B 4320   to Pembroke →

Kilpaison Burrows

FB's

stile
71

gun
emplace-
ment

flag

gate

1914–18
War Memorial

Broomhill Burrows

car park

CPS?

warning
flag

sand
dunes

Official Path
follows road
to avoid the
sand dunes

Path follows road from
Freshwater West for
5½ miles to the
Elegug Stacks via
Flimston (or for
8½ miles to
St Govan's via
Bosherston if the
Flimston road is
closed)

Freshwater
West

car park
toilets
emergency telephone

car park

flag

Gupton Burrows

flag

site of
Mesolithic
settlement

road used as a
public path

– now a
car
park!

Gupton

map 51 →

B 4319

Little Furzenip

MOD Range
radar
monitoring station

Great Furzenip
Old Red Sandstone
Silurian shales

Brownslade Burrows

Keep
Out!

sand
pit

Castlemartin Range
Royal Armoured Corps

Frainslake
Sands

map 52
overlaps here

covered several Mesolithic and Bronze Age sites, and have yielded quantities of Neolithic tools.

On the southern headland of Freshwater West at *Little Furzenip* stands the last of the seaweed collectors' huts – reed-thatched, A-shaped huts, once used to dry the edible seaweed before it was washed and finally boiled to produce laver bread. In the 1920s nearly twenty such huts were sited in this area: this one was restored by the PNPA.

The long, bubbly strands of seaweed *Porphyra umbilicalis*, red-brown and leathery, found on the rocks at low water, were gathered and boiled into a green mass, and called laver bread. It is a delicacy peculiarly Welsh, and was sold in Swansea, Cardiff and Llanelli. It is highly nutritious, full of vitamins, and was much in demand among colliers of S Wales, as it was said to supply a deficiency in their normal diet due to their working long hours underground, though why this practice did not catch on in other mining areas of Britain has never been explained. Laver bread is also said to be specially good against diabetes. Its full flavour can be appreciated only when it is cooked with bacon or gammon, though some say it is even better when rolled and cooked in oatmeal.

Across the road from the seaweed collectors' hut, at Little Furzenip Quarry, now a car park, was a Mesolithic site which when excavated recently revealed 7700 flints. Had they been brought here from the flint works on The Nab Head, overlooking St Bride's Bay?

Low tide at Little Furzenip reveals the remains of a post-glacial forest, almost 6000 years old. Fragmentary tree-trunks and branches matted with roots and the remains of plants, all in a pulpy condition, lie upon bluish clay and scattered rocks, at low-water mark of spring tides. The forest developed as the ice slowly disappeared. Sea level at that time was lower than it is now, and as the ice was finally melted there was a rise in sea level which caused the forest to be inundated and partially buried by sediment.

Access to the southern end of Freshwater Bay – called Frainslake Sands – is prohibited by the MOD. Watch-towers and red flags mark the Royal Armoured Corps Castlemartin Range, and the Coast Path has to go inland. A description of the continuation of the Coast Path follows on p. 315 but for completeness the continuation of the coastline is described in the next sub-section.

The Forbidden Coast

From Freshwater Bay round to Linney Head, past Stack Rocks – the Elegug Stacks – and on to St Govan's Head is one of the most deserted windswept areas of Pembrokeshire, uncompromising in winter but alight with wild flowers and ideal for a long walk in summer. Unfortunately a tank gunnery range – one of the most important NATO training areas in Western Europe – denies access to about 6ml/4.8km of the coast, and only when firing is not in progress is another 3ml/4.8km open. The coast from Freshwater Bay round Linney Head to Stack Rocks is permanently closed.

I have been fortunate in obtaining the permission of the military to walk round this magnificent but forbidden coast in the course of preparing this guide, and I have annotated the entire coastline of the range on Map 52 in preparation for the day when the Army goes away and we can walk round Linney Head once more.

The *Castlemartin Royal Armoured Corps Range* occupies 5884 acres/2381ha of some of the best agricultural land in Wales, and prevents access to a glorious stretch of limestone cliff coastline within the Pembrokeshire National Park. The area was renowned for its cereal production and was the home of the famous long-haired Castlemartin breed of Welsh Black cattle, a breed now merged into the Welsh Blacks. Fenton wrote, at the beginning of the last century, that this was 'a place worthy of the attention of every traveller, as a specimen of farming brought to a degree of perfection, unexampled in the country, and not to be outdone in any, and highly worthy of imitation.'

It is not worthy of imitation now. Its arable potential is virtually sterilised by military activity: the only farming is in winter, when about 5.6 per cent of the range area is grazed by cattle, and 90 per cent by sheep, mainly from the Prescelly Hills for over-wintering and fattening. The fertile limestone fields are despoiled in a misuse of valuable agricultural land (although, to give them their due, the Army spends considerable time and money clearing up at the end of the summer firing period to enable the range to be grazed in

The scene on Castlemartin Range

winter). Nevertheless, a vast area has been depopulated, its big old farmhouses and small country cottages have been demolished and left in ruins, shot to pieces or levelled to the ground. The fields have been turned into tank-courses, anti-tank bunkers have been thrown up, and the ground is littered with blown-up tanks, broken targets, bunkers and the debris of warfare.

Castlemartin Ranges form only one of a number of defensive sites which are such a notable feature of the Pembrokeshire coast; changes in the area's strategic importance and the technology of warfare are reflected in the many prehistoric earthworks, medieval castles, Victorian forts, airfields, tank ranges and 20c military installations. In the great majority of cases the fabric of these sites has outlived their original defensive purposes and those constructed before the present century are regarded as important assets in the historic legacy of the National Park. The MOD holds about 5 per cent of the land in the National Park and 24 per cent of Pembrokeshire's 'Heritage Coast', affecting about 11ml/17.7km of the Coast Path.

Military uses in a National Park are a classic illustration of competing national purposes, those of national defence and those of conservation and enjoyment of nationally important coast and countryside. Whilst we lament the continued use of the coastline for weapons training, here at Castlemartin, as well as at Manorbier and Penally, it must be recognised that the defence activities in the National Park were established before the Park was designated. One must feel gratitude that these stretches of coast were thus saved in the immediate post-war period from the pressure of caravans and holiday development – look at Freshwater East and Lydstep Haven, for example – when the area could all too easily have been inundated. The military presence also has an indirect but nonetheless valuable role in wildlife conservation, and the social and economic contribution of the armed forces is a traditional and important feature of the region.

In 1960 the Federal German Army Panzer Division (Bundeswehr) started coming with their Leopard tanks to the RAC firing ranges here under NATO agreements. About 3200 of them, and 1300 British troops, receive training on the range each year.

MAP 51

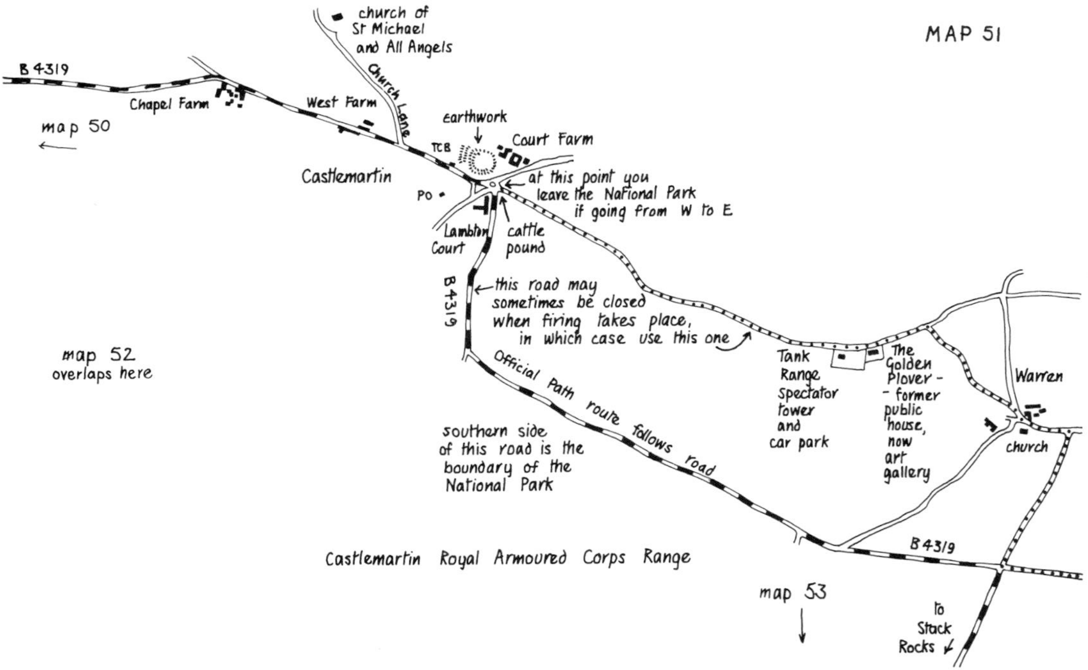

church of St Michael and All Angels

West Farm

Chapel Farm

B 4319

map 50

Church Lane

Castlemartin

earthwork

Court Farm

PO

PT8

Lambin Court

cattle pound

B 4319

at this point you leave the National Park if going from W to E

this road may sometimes be closed when firing takes place, in which case use this one

Official Path route follows road

southern side of this road is the boundary of the National Park

Castlemartin Royal Armoured Corps Range

map 52 overlaps here

Tank Range Spectator Tower and car park

The Golden Plover – former public house, now art gallery

Warren

church

B 4319

map 53

To Stack Rocks

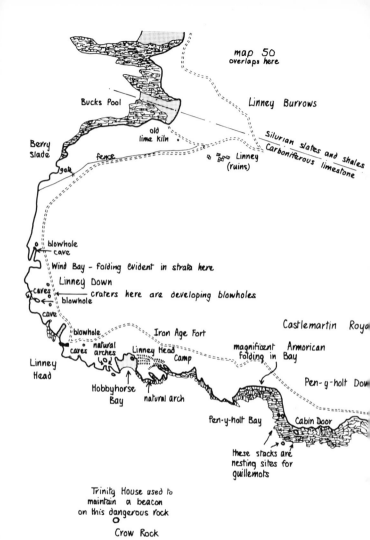

map 50
overlaps here

Linney Burrows

Bucks Pool

old
lime kiln

Silurian slates and shales
Carboniferous limestone

Berry
Slade

fence

gate

Linney
(ruins)

blowhole
cave

Wind Bay - folding evident in strata here

Linney Down

caves

craters here are developing blowholes

blowhole

cave

blowhole

Iron Age Fort

Castlemartin Roya

caves

natural
arches

Linney Head
Camp

magnificent
folding in

Armorican
Bay

Linney
Head

Hobbyhorse
Bay

natural arch

Pen-y-holt Dow

Pen-y-holt Bay

Cabin Door

these stacks are
nesting sites for
guillemots

Trinity House used to
maintain a beacon
on this dangerous rock

Crow Rock

MAP 52

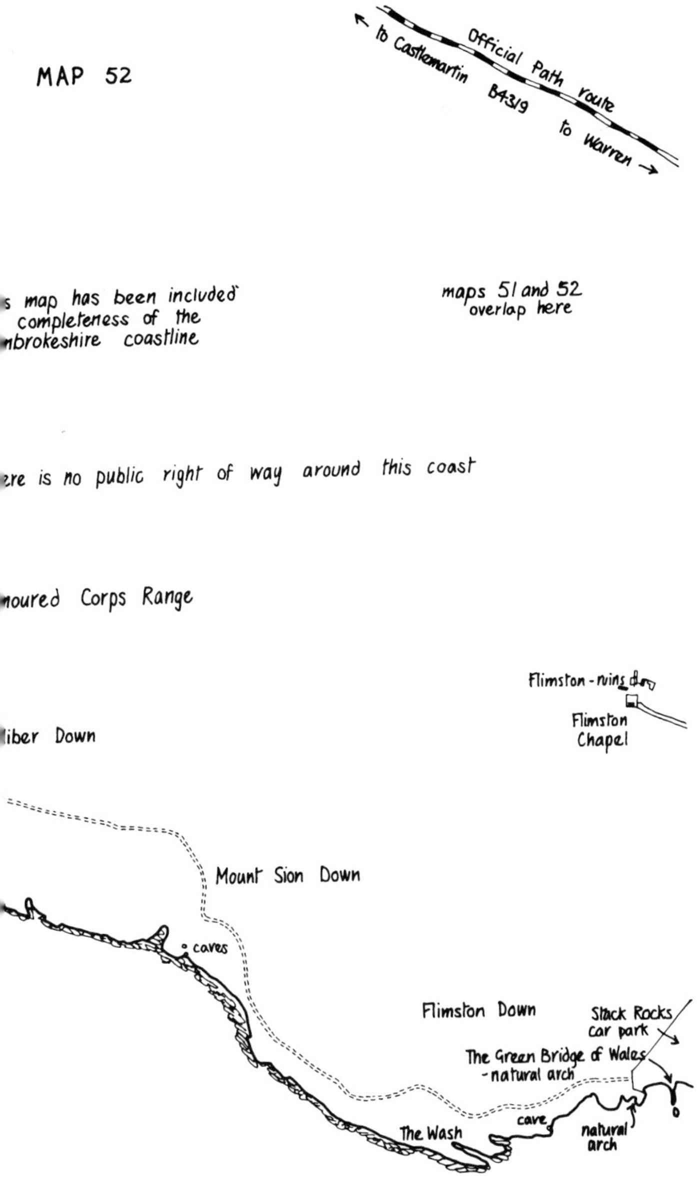

← to Castlemartin
Official Path route
B4319
to Warren →

...s map has been included
...completeness of the
...mbrokeshire coastline

maps 51 and 52
overlap here

...ere is no public right of way around this coast

...moured Corps Range

Flimston - ruins of
Flimston
Chapel

...liber Down

Mount Sion Down

. caves

Flimston Down

Stack Rocks
car park

The Green Bridge of Wales
- natural arch

The Wash   cave   natural
                                arch

The hostility to the Germans' presence, which was expressed more by English visitors than by local people, has long since gone. The presence of the camp is appreciated in the towns of Pembroke, Pembroke Dock and Haverfordwest, where the troops spend part of their free time, and money. Bilingual road signs are an unexpected result of the military presence: not, in Little England, in Welsh and English, but in German and English.

Information as to when the range is open is plainly displayed on notices on roads to Stack Rocks and St Govan's. The firing programme is published in the local press and posted at least ten days in advance in Bosherston Post Office (tel. Castlemartin 286). Information may also be obtained by telephoning Merrion Camp (tel. Castlemartin 321). In addition, red flags are flown around the perimeter when firing is in progress.

Firing normally takes place on the range between 15 May and early November, during weekdays, and usually between 0900 and 1630. Night firing is restricted to two nights a week, normally Tuesdays and Thursdays. Firing never takes place at weekends or on Bank Holidays.

The coast is permanently closed to the public between Freshwater Bay and Stack Rocks, but on days and at times when firing does not take place the splendours of the coast between Stack Rocks and Trevallen are available to walkers, and occasionally the section between St Govan's Chapel and Trevallen may remain open when the rest of the range is closed.

The stretch of coastline between Linney Head and St Govan's Head reveals some of the finest Carboniferous limestone cliff scenery in Britain. Magnificent cliffs 100–160ft/30–49m high are spectacularly developed with stacks, natural arches, blowholes and sea caves in abundance. The coast along here is subject to a 25ft/ 7.6m tidal range which causes violent currents under the high cliffs, and the scouring action by the sea creates fantastic shapes in the rocks.

There are several blowholes in various stages of development on Linney Head, which receives the full brunt of westerly and southwesterly gales, and the limestone is superbly displayed in horizontal strata. The coast between Linney Head and Mount Sion

Down shows a particularly clear example of Armorican folding, superbly epitomised in Pen-y-holt Bay, which is best seen from the W side. The sequence of folding from seaward is an arch through a steep anticline in Cabin Door, followed by a syncline through the beach and up to the cliff-top, which curls over into an anticline which leads down to northward into yet another complete syncline. This magnificent sequence of folding is found nowhere else on the coast: it's a pity it can't be seen by the public here.

The prohibited coastline ends at a range boundary fence close to the Green Bridge of Wales, a superb natural arch near to Stack Rocks, to which the public can gain occasional access, and where the Coast Path regains the coast.

Freshwater West to Stack Rocks 5.4ml/8.7km
From Freshwater West it is necessary to follow a road for a minimum of 5.4ml/8.7km, and possibly a maximum of 8.5ml/ 13.6km, depending on whether there is any firing on the Castlemartin Ranges. The shorter distance, to the Elegug Stacks (or Stack Rocks) via Flimston, is only possible when the range is open, but if the red flags are flying there is no access from Warren to the Stack Rocks, nor maybe from Bosherston to St Govan's Chapel, necessitating the longer route.

If you can get access to the Stack Rocks via Flimston you will be able to walk along the coast between the Stack Rocks and St Govan's Chapel, but it doesn't always follow that you will be able to walk in the reverse direction if you can gain access to St Govan's. Always enquire locally what the access restrictions are before you set off on this stage of your journey (see p. 314). If the red flags are not flying you can go through the desolate, treeless, farmless waste. When the red flags are flying gunfire is unceasing, and it disturbs the peace of most of the peninsula.

Castlemartin is a straggling, wind-swept village in the middle of an area noted for its early potatoes, or it was in the middle until it lost a lot of its potato-growing potential to the Army. The church of St Michael and All Angels hides down a side road on the NW side of the village. It is not architecturally important. In the centre of the village is a unique circular cattle pound, once used as a gun-site and an air-raid shelter, and now used as a roundabout at a road junction. It was built in 1870 and restored in July 1972.

At this junction the Coast Path follows the B4319 road to Merrion Camp, but this road may sometimes be closed when firing takes place, in which case you have to use a parallel road to Warren: there is no difference in the distance to be covered.

Warren is a small village consisting of a disused church, a couple of farms and a few cottages, but it boasts a one-way traffic system. The towers of three churches – Warren, St Twynell's and St Petrox – stand out conspicuously on the high open ridge which runs through the peninsula from Castlemartin. As with other towers in South Pembrokeshire they are tall and slender, battlemented and with a corbel table, and with a stair turret climbing higher than the main tower. These towers were useful as beacons and watch-towers as well as belfries, and they make a powerful contribution to this open landscape.

Merrion Camp is the headquarters of the RAC Castlemartin Range. Two famous tanks stand guard outside its main entrance: *Romulus*, a 65-ton Conqueror tank which was in service from 1958 to 1963, and *Remus*, a 33-ton Comet tank which saw service from 1944 to 1949.

There is access to the coast from Warren past Flimston to Stack Rocks when the range is open. If the road to Stack Rocks is closed so is that stretch of the coast between Stack Rocks and St Govan's Chapel, in which case you have to continue on the B4319 past Merrion Camp and on to Bosherston.

On the road to Stack Rocks you pass the isolated Flimston Chapel, standing beside a deserted farm in the middle of the tank range. This medieval vaulted chapel had become a barn until it was thoroughly restored in 1903 and again following World War II by the 'self-help' efforts of the troops stationed at Castlemartin at that time: it has therefore almost become a military memorial. Boulders carried by the glaciers are used as gravestones.

The coast and cliffs from the Stack Rocks towards St Govan's Head are within the Castlemartin Range (Range East). Public access is restricted to the approach roads to Stack Rocks (from Warren via Flimston) and St Govan's Chapel (via Bosherston), and the linking Coast Path, only when the range is not being used. Access when the range is in use is an offence under the range bye-laws.

Until only recently no climbing at all was permitted on the sea cliffs within the range, unless climbers had written permission from the range Commandant. Anyone caught roping down the cliffs or coming up them with a rope and without a permit was liable to be marched off to the guardhouse as a suspected spy landed from a submarine. Cliff climbing, however, is now permitted, subject only to the usual public access and other restrictions (see pages 37 and 314).

The first authorised climbs on the Stack Rocks took place in October 1970, and a brief account of these is given in *Sea Cliff Climbing in Britain* (see Bibliography).

Stack Rocks to St Govan's Head 3.5ml/5.6km

The road from Warren ends in a car park, and your arrival at the coast comes as a relief and as a complete surprise. The cliff-tops are level lawns of turf which end without warning, dropping vertically into the sea. The flat coastal platform is occasionally pock-marked with features of limestone erosion near the cliff edge, and the booming tide and shingle can be heard pounding the foot of the cliffs far below.

Sea birds are numerous: razorbills, guillemots, puffins, gulls and fulmars are the most common; raven, chough, peregrine falcon and jackdaw are land birds also nesting on these cliffs. The turf is rich in wild flowers, including the vernal squill and sea lavender. This short stretch of Path is one which the walker should savour to the full. It is a fine walk on flat open turf above splendid sheer cliffs, and the condition of the Path is everywhere excellent. The coastline along these limestone cliffs is superb, specially if a big sea is running.

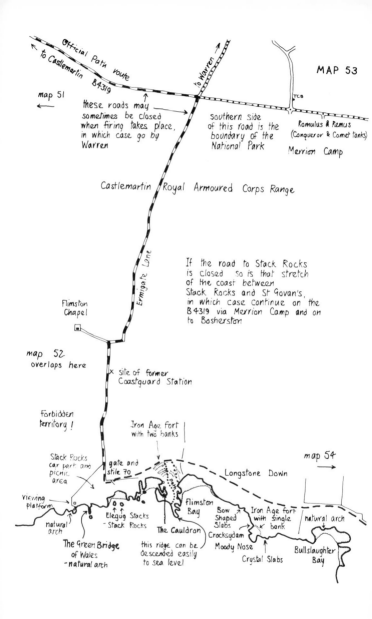

to Castlemartin B4319

Official Path route

to Warren

MAP 53

map 51

these roads may sometimes be closed when firing takes place, in which case go by Warren

southern side of this road is the boundary of the National Park

TCB

Romulus & Remus
(Conqueror & Comet tanks)

Merrion Camp

Castlemartin Royal Armoured Corps Range

Ermigate Lane

If the road to Stack Rocks is closed so is that stretch of the coast between Stack Rocks and St Govan's, in which case continue on the B4319 via Merrion Camp and on to Bosherston

Flimston Chapel

map 52 overlaps here

× site of former Coastguard Station

Forbidden Territory!

Iron Age fort with two banks

map 54

Stack Rocks car park and picnic area

gate and stile 70

Longstone Down

Viewing Platform

natural arch

Elegug Stacks - Stack Rocks

Flimston Bay

Bow Shaped Slabs

Iron Age fort with single bank

natural arch

The Green Bridge of Wales - natural arch

The Cauldron

this ridge can be descended easily to sea level

Crocksydam

Moody Nose

Crystal Slabs

Bullslaughter Bay

At the extreme westward point of the Stack Rocks car park there is a viewing platform beside the range boundary fence, and from here three fine natural arches may be seen in line. The best and most famous is the Green Bridge of Wales, formed by the coalescence of two caves from opposite sides of an old headland. The arch has a height of about 80ft/24m and at its narrowest point the apex is only about 4ft/1.2m wide.

The Stack Rocks, or Elegug Stacks, are two isolated and lofty towers of limestone, and represent the final development of the erosion cycle: at one time they were both natural arches like the Green Bridge, but their arches have collapsed and they are no longer connected to the mainland. They are a magnificent sight at any time but especially in spring and early summer when they are the haunt of innumerable nesting sea birds.

The Stack Rocks are the home of the largest sea-bird colony to be seen from the Path, and it is probably the most easily seen auk colony in Great Britain. Elegug – or guillemots – razorbills and other sea birds such as fulmars, shags and kittiwakes occupy the stacks only from between late April or early May until the end of July or early August, and are so thickly massed that it astonishes the observer that the individual bird can recognise its own mate, egg or chick, or find room to alight.

About 1000 pairs of guillemots occupy broad ledges and the tops of the stacks, and about 130 pairs of razorbills are scattered under overhangs and in cracks. Kittiwakes nest in colonies on the steep cliff-faces and fulmar petrels on wider ledges are sometimes in full view from the cliff-top. A few shags nest in larger holes in the cliff-face, and herring gulls occupy the very tops of the stacks.

The Elegug Tower is the larger of the two, a massive chunk of rock 150ft/45m high with overhanging walls, topped with a grassy crown of sea cabbage, sea beet and tree mallows. By contrast the Elegug Spire is needle-sharp and about 130ft/39.6m high.

A little way to the E of the Stack Rocks is the peninsula of Flimston, a name famous among geographers. Marine erosion is producing caves, blowholes, arches and stacks as a result of the weaknesses of faults and folds in the rocks. The peninsula is topped by an early Iron Age encampment, Flimston **Castle, which has a**

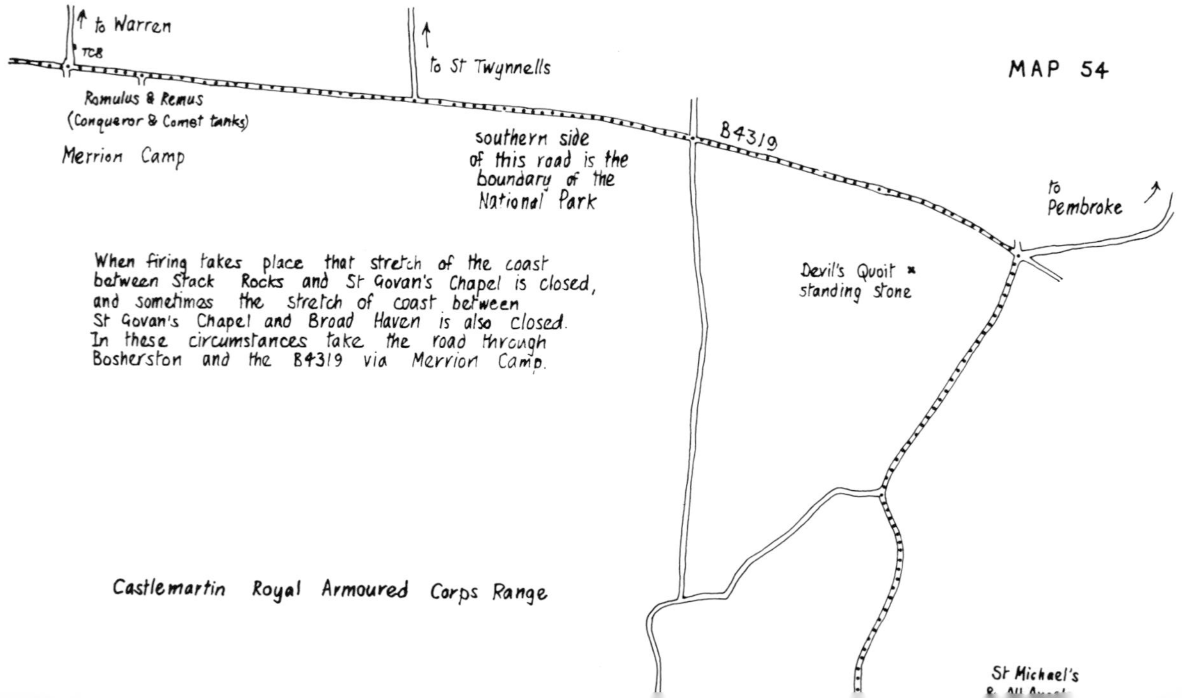

MAP 54

to Pembroke ↑

to Warren ↑

TCB

Romulus & Remus
(Conqueror & Comet tanks)

Merrion Camp

↑ to St Twynnells

B43/9

southern side
of this road is the
Boundary of the
National Park

Devil's Quoit ✕
standing stone

When firing takes place that stretch of the coast
between Stack Rocks and St Govan's Chapel is closed,
and sometimes the stretch of coast between
St Govan's Chapel and Broad Haven is also closed.
In these circumstances take the road through
Bosherston and the B4319 via Merrion Camp.

Castlemartin Royal Armoured Corps Range

St Michael's
& All Angels

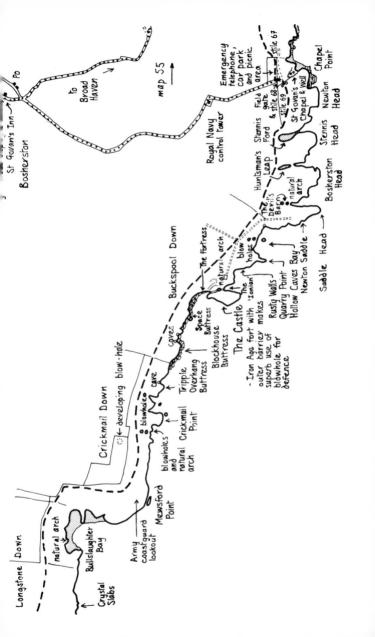

St Govan's Inn
Bosherston
Po

to Broad Haven

map 55 →

Emergency
telephone, car
park and picnic
area

stile 67

Royal Navy
control tower

Huntsman's Stennis
Leap Ford

Field gate
& stile 69

stile 68

St Govan's
Chapel & Well

Chapel
Point

Newton
Head

Stennis Head

Bosherston Head

natural arch

The Devil's
Barn

Saddle Head

Newton Saddle

Hollow Caves Bay

Quarry Point

Rusty Walls

The
blow
holes

The Castle
- Iron Age fort with
outer barrier makes
superb use of
blowhole for defence

'Ionian'

natural arch

The Fortress

Buckspool Down

Space
Buttress

Blockhouse Buttress

Tripple
Overhang
Buttress

Caves

Caves

cave

Crickmail Down

← developing blow-hole

blowhole

Crickmail Point

blowholes and
natural arch

Mewsford Point

Army coastguard
lookout

Bullslaughter Bay

natural arch

Longstone Down

Crystal Slabs

triple rampart and traces of hut-circles. The defensive works enclose the wild and beautiful Cauldron, and you soon find yourself looking down into a stupendous abyss, a vast blowhole 150ft/45m deep, into which the sea boils below at high tide. The hole is connected to the sea by arches through which sea birds fly to their nests inside the Cauldron itself. The best view of the Cauldron is from the narrow neck of land between it and the sea, but the cliffs should be approached with caution.

On the eastern side of the peninsula a path goes down to what is sometimes called the Danish or Viking Landing, a natural harbour in the rocks, accessible by boat in calm or offshore winds. It is said that here have landed in their primitive boats all the races which came by sea to colonise S Wales – the stone tomb-builders from Iberia, the Celts from mid-Europe, the first Christian saints from Ireland, the Vikings from Scandinavia, the Normans, and the Flemings, and, in the last century, the coastal traders in their schooners and ketches collecting limestone and Castlemartin corn.

A little further along the coast, at Crocksydam, are the worn but unmistakable banks of another promontory fort, with only one slight stone-faced rampart and ditch, best seen from the top of the outcrop inside the fort. It is somewhat earlier in date than the Flimston Castle fort, being occupied in the 2c.

As you walk on the Coast Path across Longstone Down you pass on the L the Sunken Forest, a small bush-like patch where a clump of ash trees grows in a shallow pit, the top of a collapsed blowhole, their tops neatly shaved off by the salt-laden wind. You go round Bullslaughter Bay to Mewsford Point, and as you look back you can see the large caverns and remarkable contorted strata in Bullslaughter Bay, and get a good view westwards of Stack Rocks and the Green Bridge of Wales.

The line of cliffs now turns more southeasterly, and as you go along the edge of Crickmail Down and Buckspool Down you pass several small blowholes. When the sea dashes into the caves below, under certain conditions, the air is driven out through the funnels and carries with it clouds of foam, and during westerly gales they spout like geysers. The Castle is an Iron Age fort on a peninsula with a defensive barrier which makes beautiful military use of a blowhole. A World War I troopship, the *Ionian*, ran aground in fog on the cliffs E of The Castle and her boilers may be seen at low tide.

You pass more blowholes on the way to Saddle Head and Bosherston Head, and then you come to a remarkable narrow fissure known as Huntsman's Leap, a fearsome gap through which the sea is visible 130ft/40m below, caused by the sea eroding a relatively small fault. It owes its name to the tradition that a huntsman, escaping from his creditors, leapt the chasm on horseback, and on returning to reflect on his feat, died from the shock. The chasm used to be called both Penny's Leap and Adam's Leap.

In a few minutes you pass the head of another ravine, Stennis Ford, and in a few minutes more you reach the car park and picnic area above St Govan's Chapel. A road leads inland for just over 1ml/*c*2km to the village of Bosherston, which we shall visit when we turn inland at Broad Haven to view the Bosherston Lily Ponds.

St Govan's Chapel is a diminutive building, wedged between two cliffs at the only point on the coast where there is an approach to the sea for several miles on either side. A path descends the cliff, a steep flight of polished limestone steps, and actually passes through the building to continue its descent to the rocky shore. There is a superstition that if you count the steps going down and then going up you never get the same total: I've counted 74.

The tiny chapel is a primitive, plain building with a ridged roof and bell-cote completely blocking the cleft. The interior measures 17.5ft/5.3m × 12.5ft/3.8m, and has a plain arched stone-vaulted roof, a typical feature of early medieval Pembrokeshire buildings. It was rebuilt *c*13c, but much of the walls, stone altar and nearby holy well are probably original. The floor of the chapel is of earth, washed down by storm water from the ravine above through the back door. There is a stone altar and to the R of it are a piscina and an aumbry. A remarkable feature is the doorway N of the altar, which leads to a smaller chamber or cell cut into the rock behind the chapel by enlarging a natural cavity. The chapel is dedicated to Gobhan, Abbot of the monastery of Dairinis in Wexford, Ireland, who died here in his cell in 586; it was erected by his followers.

Between the chapel and the sea is a well whose waters were

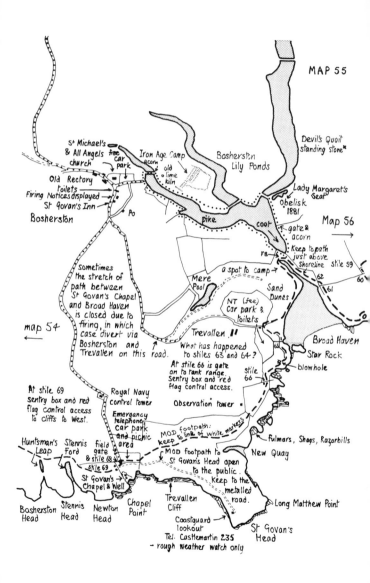

MAP 55

Devil's Quoit standing stone*

St Michael's & All Angels church · free car park · Iron Age Camp · acorn · old lime kiln · Bosherston Lily Ponds

Lady Margaret's Seat

Old Rectory · toilets · Firing Notices displayed · St Govan's Inn

Bosherston

Po

Obelisk 1881

Map 56

pike

coot

gate & acorn

F8

Keep to path just above shoreline · stile 59

Sometimes the stretch of path between St Govan's Chapel and Broad Haven is closed due to firing, in which case divert via Bosherston and Trevallen on this road.

map 54

a spot to camp

Mere Pool

62

61

60

Sand Dunes

NT (fee) Car park & toilets

Trevallen

What has happened to stiles 63 and 64?

At stile 66 is gate on to tank range. Sentry box and red flag control access.

Broad Haven

Star Rock

blowhole

stile 66

At stile 69 sentry box and red flag control access to cliffs to West.

Royal Navy control tower

Observation tower

Emergency telephone, car park and picnic area

MOD footpath: keep to line of white markers

fulmars, Shags, Razorbills

New Quay

Huntsman's Leap · Stennis Ford · field gate & stile 68 · stile 69

St Govan's Chapel & Well

MOD footpath to St Govan's Head open to the public.

keep to the metalled road

Long Matthew Point

Bosherston Head · Stennis Head · Newton Head · Chapel Point · Trevallen Cliff

Coastguard lookout Tel. Castlemartin 235 – rough weather watch only

St Govan's Head

supposed to have miraculous healing powers. Fenton described how 'crippled patients bathe their limbs, many of whom come from the remotest parts of the Principality to seek relief here and leave their crutches behind, a votive offering on the altar.' The well was frequented for cures as late as the mid-19c: it is now dry.

It is said that the empty bell-cote of the chapel held a silver bell which was stolen by pirates, but a tempest rose and sank their ship. Sea-nymphs rescued the bell and placed it beside the holy well, between the chapel and the sea, entombed in a rock that rings out on being struck.

St Govan's Chapel has recently been restored by the PNPA with the aid of a grant by the Ancient Monuments Branch of the Welsh Office and by the agreement of the MOD, on whose land the building stands. The restoration has won a Prince of Wales Award for its contribution to conservation in Wales.

The MOD permits access along a path from the car park to *St Govan's Head*, the most southerly point of Pembrokeshire. From the coastguard station on the lofty heights of this bold headland there are broad views over the Bristol Channel. In ideal conditions the view includes Worms Head on the tip of the Gower Peninsula, about 30ml/48km away; Lundy Island, 35ml/56km away; and parts of Somerset, Devon and Cornwall. St Govan's Head is a grand spot from which to watch the waves crashing on to the rocks during a southwesterly gale. Great blocks at the foot of the cliffs show that they are still retreating under attack from the sea.

25   St Govan's Head to Tenby (Maps 55–62)   19.5ml/31.5km

St Govan's Head to Broad Haven 1.5ml/2.4km
At times until only recently access to St Govan's Head was denied and you had to walk from St Govan's Chapel by road into Bosherston and then by another road to Trevallen in order to reach Broad Haven. However, the MOD has voluntarily released the path from St Govan's Chapel to Broad Haven and up to St Govan's

Head, although they reserve the right to close it when firing takes place. In practice you will usually find it open, and if you have been permitted to walk through the range from Stack Rocks to St Govan's Chapel you will generally find that you can continue to Broad Haven. Keep to the waymarked path, of course – unfortunately this denies us access to the old harbour of New Quay, an inlet sheltered from the southwesterlies by St Govan's Head.

The Coast Path reaches the NT's cliff-top car park at Trevallen. It may be thought a pity that the Trust should choose a prominent hill-top site for their car park: the old sand pit to the N would have been quite unobtrusive, but perhaps it might have resulted in disturbance to wild life in Mere Pool. Certainly damage to the dunes cannot have been the argument, as people have free access everywhere.

Broad Haven – or Broad Haven South as it is sometimes called, to distinguish it from the Broad Haven on St Bride's Bay – is a splendid expanse of golden sands, gently shelving, and flanked by sand dunes and low cliffs. It formed part of the Stackpole estate, acquired by the NT in 1976. Stackpole is a Norse name, from 'stac', a rock, and 'pollr', a small inlet. The 'stac' refers to the rock stacks in Broad Haven – Star Rock and Church Rock; the 'pollr' to what are now lily and fish ponds just inland.

The sand dunes that back the beach have been built up only since the end of the 18c after a retaining wall was built to form the ponds inland. The dunes are being extended seaward at the rate of about 1ft/304mm a year, as sand is swept inland by the wind.

The 'young' dunes nearest the sea can be damaged by walkers and should be avoided. These dunes are held together by marram grass, which thrives in conditions which most plants find inhospitable. The marram stretches back for about 45ft/13m and then gives way to a variety of other plants, among them the fast-spreading sea buckthorn, bright blue viper's bugloss and, in June and July, small pink-and-white restharrow, looking rather like a sweet pea. Various types of mosses and lichens grow on the older dunes.

This coast was uplifted from the sea in prehistoric times. On the E side of the bay, between the ponds and Saddle Point, a rough ledge, about 5ft/1.5m above the high-water mark, is evidence of this.

The *lily ponds* between Broad Haven and the village of Bosherston formed part of the enchanting landscape of the Stackpole Estate belonging to the Earl of Cawdor, a Scottish peer whose family have been connected with this part of Wales since the 17c. The pools are a system of inter-connecting fish ponds, extending finger-like over an area of some 80 acres/32ha, filling in a drowned river valley. They are cut off from the sea by a high bank of shingle and a natural bar of wind-blown sand, assisted by a retaining wall built by the Cawdors.

Leaving Broad Haven behind you, it is worthwhile taking a short walk around the lily ponds to visit Bosherston – a distance of about 2.5ml/4km (but not part of the Coast Path). It is an idyllic walk around the ponds, especially on tranquil evenings, across three delightful footbridges, and in spring and summer there are wild flowers everywhere. The sheltered pools, and the woods that overlook them, attract a wide variety of birds, including heron, kingfisher, moorhens, swans, coots, and mallard. The waters are renowned for their water lilies, at their best in June. The ponds form part of the Stackpole National Nature Reserve, owned by the NT and managed jointly by the NT and NCC.

Between the central and western fingers of the ponds there are the remains of a 5 acre/2ha Iron Age camp, known as Fishponds Camp. Ditches and ramparts have been added to the natural defences formed by steep slopes – the formidable defences include an inner (original) mound and ditch, and three outer lines of banks and ditches were added later. The camp is easily discernible on the ground, but the earthworks are overgrown by gorse and bramble and are generally inaccessible. Occupied during the earliest Iron Age (*c*400–300BC), its position between valleys which were once open to the sea would have been suitable as a landing place and base for newcomers seeking settlement sites. In its size, defences and siting Fishponds or Bosherston Camp resembles two other promontory forts – Great Castle Head and Deer Park, Marloes – which also command good landing places for people coming by sea.

Bosherston is a small village of a few cottages and farms and pub standing close to the parish church of St Michael and All Angels, a fine old Norman cruciform church of local type, built in 1250–70. It is interesting for a remarkable passage-hagioscope which projects externally in the angle between the S transept chapel and the chancel, and is lit by a window so that worshippers in the side chapel could see the altar. The Cawdors restored the church in 1855 and plastered the walls and ceiling, and they replaced the Norman windows with the present Gothic-style ones.

Broad Haven to Stackpole Head 2ml/3.2km
This is a fine unspoiled stretch of cliff coastline, with a good Path on delightful turf, and the grey limestone cliffs plunging sheer into the sea below. There is rock climbing at Saddle Bay and Gunn Cliff, while the cliffs of Mowingword and Stackpole Head offer some of the best climbing on limestone anywhere around this Pembrokeshire coast. Although the cliffs are only 100–150ft/30–45m high the massive horizontal strata and exposed positions give steep routes on high quality limestone.

Stackpole Head is a high, square-ended promontory hollowed by a natural arch that is spectacular when stormy seas burst through it. At low tide a wave-cut platform is revealed at the foot of the cliffs at Gunn Cliff, Mowingword and Stackpole Head, and this provides access to some of the cliff climbs.

Stackpole Head to Stackpole Quay 1.1ml/1.76km
This is a pleasant half-hour stroll, but the attractions of the cliffs, the blowholes, the birds, and the golden sands, will cause you to linger. The view from the Path between Stackpole Head and Barafundle Bay looks directly down on colonies of kittiwakes, guillemots and razorbills – some of the largest congregations of breeding sea birds on the mainland coast of Pembrokeshire. Gulls and fulmars also breed along the entire coast from Broad Haven South to Barafundle Bay, and choughs may be seen along the cliff-top.

Barafundle Bay is an unspoilt bay, accessible only by walkers along the Coast Path. The well-sheltered sands are backed by low dunes and flanked by cliffs, and are popular for picnics for those who have walked from their cars at Stackpole Quay only 10–15

MAP 56

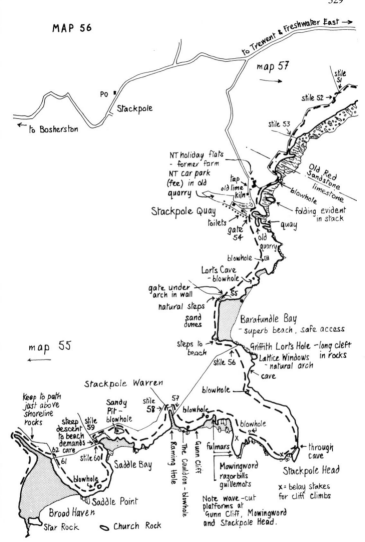

to Trewent & Freshwater East →

map 57

stile S1

stile S2

stile 53

Po Stackpole

← to Bosherston

Old Red
Sandstone

NT holiday flats
– former farm

NT car park
(fee) in old
quarry

tap
old lime
kiln

limestone

blowhole

Stackpole Quay

folding evident
in stack

toilets

gate
54

quay

old
quarry

blowhole

Lort's Cave
– blowhole

gate under
arch in wall

55

natural steps

Barafundle Bay
– superb beach, safe access

sand
dunes

map 55

steps to
beach

Griffith Lort's Hole – long cleft
in rocks

Lattice Windows
– natural arch

stile 56

cave

Stackpole Warren

stile
57

blowhole

keep to path
just above
shoreline
rocks

Sandy
Pit –
blowhole

stile
58

blowhole

blowhole

steep
descent
to beach
demands
care

stile
59

through
cave

62

61

stile 60

The Cauldron – blowhole

Gunn Cliff

fulmars

Raming Hole

Saddle Bay

Mowingword
razorbills
guillemots

Stackpole Head

blowhole

x = belay stakes
for cliff climbs

Saddle Point

Broad Haven

Note wave-cut
platforms at
Gunn Cliff, Mowingword
and Stackpole Head.

Star Rock

Church Rock

minutes away. This is a charming spot, said to be the smallest harbour in Britain. The harbour has a stone jetty from which limestone was once exported from a nearby quarry, which is now used as the NT's car park. The harbour is now no longer used commercially, but sailing craft may be moored there. High water is Milford time plus 10 minutes. There are rocks and cliffs around the quay, and the bay is shingly, with little sand at low water, so it is not a place for bathing. Fossils of shells and corals which thrived in the warm Carboniferous seas are well displayed in the rocks hereabouts.

The early history of *Stackpole* is vague, but in the 11c a castle was erected by a Norman lord, one Elidur de Stackpole, and in later centuries a mansion was built on its site. The last house, Stackpole Court, was a 50-bedroomed mansion built in 1735 on severely classical lines, extended in 1845, demolished in 1962–3.

In the Civil War Stackpole was held by Roger Lort, and 40 years later, in 1689, the estate came to the Campbell family of Cawdor, Scotland, as a result of a fairytale romance. Alexander Campbell, heir to Cawdor, and Gilbert Lort, Roger's son and heir to Stackpole, were undergraduate friends at Cambridge. On Alexander's way home to Scotland he would journey with his friend to Stackpole, spend a night or two there, and then sail around Pembrokeshire and up the W coast to Fort William and ride across the Great Glen to Cawdor. On one of these occasions storms prevented the young Campbell from sailing from Stackpole, and he had time to meet and fall in love with Elizabeth, Gilbert's sister. They were married in 1689, and when Elizabeth inherited Stackpole from her brother the estate passed into the Campbell family. Alexander and Elizabeth's great-grandson was ultimately created Baron Cawdor in 1796, and his son the first Earl Cawdor.

The Cawdor family, whose castle (and Macbeth's) is at Nairn, is one of the country's biggest landowners, with about 90,000 acres/ 36,423ha, of which 30,000 acres/12,141ha are in Wales. One story of how the family estates were increased relates how the first Earl Cawdor and John Vaughan, heir to Golden Grove, Carmarthenshire, set out on the Grand Tour of Europe together and, as was the fashion, each made a will in favour of the other, such being the dangers of travel at that time. Upon their safe return Vaughan destroyed his friend's will, but the Scot kept Vaughan's: when the heir to Golden Grove died unmarried, Cawdor produced the will and claimed the estate.

The fifth Earl Cawdor, John Duncan Vaughan Campbell, was interested in preservation. He was a trustee of the National Museum of Antiquities of Scotland and he became chairman of the Government's Historic Buildings Council for Scotland, set up in 1953 to provide money to preserve the best examples of Scottish heritage. It was said that he fell out with the government of the time ten years later because he couldn't get an Historic Buildings Act grant for the repair, upkeep and maintenance of Stackpole Court, so he demolished it. His son, the Viscount Emlyn, born in 1933 and qualified as a land agent, directed the sale of Stackpole's contents on 19 November 1962, and he had much of the family land holdings, including the Welsh property, transferred to him before his father died in 1970, thereby saving a considerable sum in death duty.

The property's transfer to the nation in July 1976 was through the Treasury as part of a death-duty deal on tax owed on assets of the late Earl. The NT thereby acquired some 1992.5 acres/806ha of the Stackpole estate, including the major sand dune systems at Freshwater West and some 8ml/12.8km of impressive coastline stretching from Stackpole Quay round to Broad Haven. This coastline was one of the most important acquisitions of Enterprise Neptune, the Trust's save-the-coastline campaign which was launched in 1965.

Stackpole Quay had no services, but when the Trust took over they brought in water from Stackpole village, connected electricity and installed a small sewage treatment plant. The old farm was converted into a complex of holiday cottages, a two-year task funded by the Manpower Services Commission, and they were opened in April 1979. The Trust are planning to repeat this success at the site of Stackpole Court, where the former brewery and dairy are to be converted into a tearoom, information centre and shop. The NT, which acquired in 1976 restrictive covenants over another 5285 acres/2138ha, bought out of the Enterprise Neptune account, sold the land in 1977 to the CEGB's pension fund.

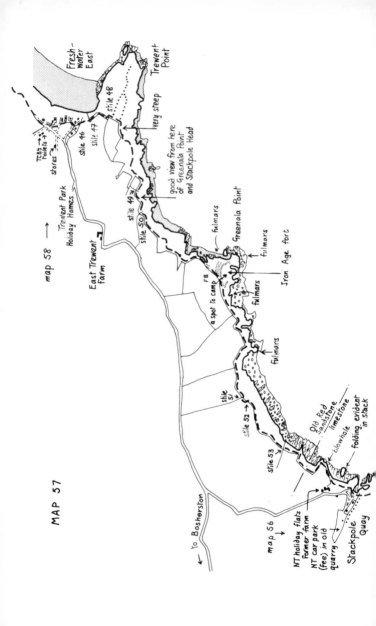

MAP 57

Stackpole Quay to Freshwater East 2.9ml/4.6km

The cliff scenery changes just N of Stackpole Quay to Old Red Sandstone, and the coastline becomes more undulating, with headlands at Greenala Point and Trewent Point. You can see the transition from the Carboniferous limestone quite clearly in a small bay just N of the old Stackpole Farm. The Old Red Sandstone extends as far as Old Castle Head, 5ml/8km across the bay at Manorbier, and then there is limestone again up to Tenby (except for the sand dunes in the Ritec estuary). The Path is good but steep and overgrown in parts.

Greenala Point is surmounted by a remarkably powerful and elaborate Iron Age earthwork. The small area enclosed seems quite out of proportion to the scale of the multiple defences, which consist of two banks and ditches on the N side. The entrance to the fort was on the W side, and the Coast Path passes through the ramparts at the W end.

Trewent Point has a fine view over Freshwater East and Swanlake Bay to the N, but the view S, looking back towards Greenala Point and Stackpole Head, is especially good, the colour and the formation of the underlying rock being very evident.

Freshwater East is an excellent, safe and favourite expanse of sand, good for bathing, sailing and boating. It is sheltered from westerly gales, but surfing takes place here mainly in the winter when the wind and swell come in from the SE.

The Old Red Sandstone rocks on the N side of the bay dip steeply northwards whilst those on the S side dip less steeply southwards. To stand in the centre of the bay is therefore to stand within the core of a large, unroofed anticline. The beach is gently shelving with a scattering of pebbles, running out a long way, and it is backed by low dunes, badly eroded as a result of uncontrolled access.

The bay is beautiful, but the hinterland is a chaotic shambles. The land has been subjected to intensive development following the decision to concentrate various forms of tourist accommodation here. Scores of bungalows, summer huts and houses have grown up all over the place, mostly unplanned. A former caravan park has been converted into a holiday home 'village' with lots of little boxes, but it is doubtful if this is an improvement, visually or in any other way. The visual squalor produced by shack development before the designation of the National Park was no doubt the reason that determined plans to develop the area into a small resort, but the place is depressing, and there is nothing much in the way of accommodation to cater for the casual visitor or the Coast Path walker passing through.

Freshwater East to Manorbier Bay 3.4ml/5.5km
This short stretch of the Coast Path will only take about 1½ hours to walk. It is not too strenuous and the Path is good, although sometimes a little overgrown in summer between Freshwater East and Swanlake Bay. It winds across the sand dunes at Freshwater East and then climbs up a low cliff at the transition of the Silurian shales of the bay with the Old Red Sandstone. Up here is a small Iron Age fort, but it is rapidly being destroyed by the erosion caused by human feet, so close is it to the popular beach. The skill in the siting of the fort is apparent only when standing on the top of the inner bank: the slopes are surprisingly steep, and there is a good view across the bay. Clearly children playing here can imagine that they are the king of the castle!

Swanlake Bay is a delightful sandy bay roughly midway between Freshwater East and Manorbier Bay, and unusually quiet when compared with the crowds that frequent the other two. The bay is somewhat isolated, it has no facilities, and there is no access to it by car, all important factors to consider when you are looking for a beach away from the crowds.

Swanlake Bay is flanked by two cliffs, East Moor Cliff being the more impressive, where exposed ribs of rock give an impression of embanked defences of a promontory fort. These geological irregularities provide some rock climbs and have created a deep zawn, which can be viewed, with care, from a position between the Path and the sea cliff.

The Path follows a long steep rock rib and provides an excellent view over Manorbier Bay. Rocks dominate the western and central bay at low water, but at the far end, facing SW, is a fine sandy beach with gently sloping sands, edged by cliffs on its E side. The Path touches the edge of a free roadside car park, and from here, or from

MAP 58

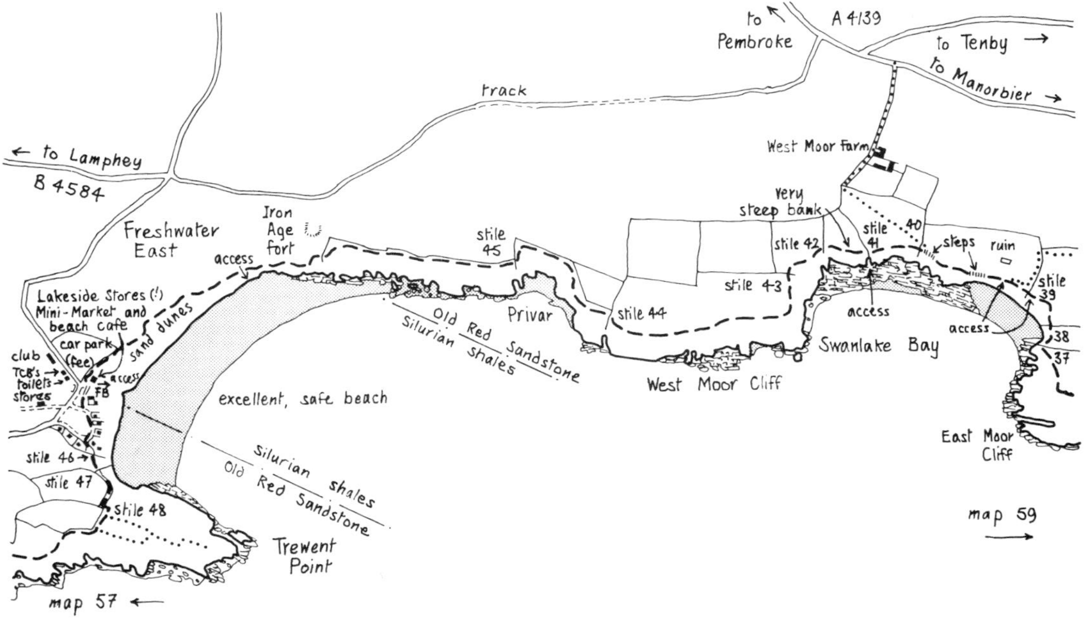

to Tenby →
to Manorbier →

A 4139

to Pembroke

to Lamphey

B 4584

Track

West Moor Farm

stile 39
stile 38
stile 37

stile 40
steps
ruin
access

stile 41
access

Swanlake Bay

East Moor Cliff

map 59 →

very steep bank

stile 42

stile 43

West Moor Cliff

stile 44

stile 45

Old Red Sandstone
Silurian Shales

Privar

Iron Age fort

Freshwater East

access

excellent, safe beach

Silurian shales
Old Red Sandstone

Trewent Point

Lakeside Stores (†)
Mini-Market and
beach cafe

car park

club
TICs
toilets
stores

access

P
PO

access

stile 46

stile 47

stile 48

map 57 →

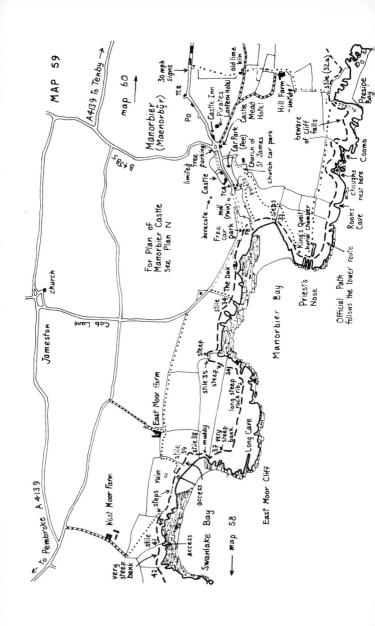

the centre of the bay, there is access inland to Manorbier.

The romantic Norman castle of *Manorbier* dominates the bay standing on the N slope of the valley that feeds into the bay, with a church set apart on the opposite slope. The name is said to be derived from the old Welsh Maenor Pyrr – the manor of Pyrrus, the first Abbot of Caldey in the 6c.

Manorbier is famous for being the birthplace of Gerald de Barri, grandson of the founder of the castle, who was born about 1146 and died in 1223. He became known as Giraldus Cambrensis and was famous mainly because of his unsuccessful struggle with Henry II to create a Welsh National Church by making St David's independent of Canterbury. He failed because he was probably seen as too capable and energetic, and too Welsh for the job. He was an eminent ecclesiastic, a powerful politician, distinguished intellectual, historian, chronicler and topographer, passionately Welsh, and widely respected. Today he is chiefly known for his detailed and descriptive accounts of life in Wales and Ireland. He wrote, in Latin, *Topography of Ireland*, and *The Description of Wales*, and his most famous work, *Itinerary through Wales*, which resulted from his tour through Wales in 1188 with Archbishop Baldwin on the recruiting campaign for the Third Crusade.

The temptation to quote the description of Manorbier by Giraldus is too great to resist: 'The castle . . . is excellently well defended by turrets and bulwarks, and is situated on the summit of a hill extending on the western side to the sea-port, having on the northern and southern sides a fine fish-pond under its walls, as conspicuous for its grand appearance as for the depth of its waters, and a beautiful orchard on the same side, inclosed on one part by a vineyard, and on the other by a wood, remarkable for the projection of its rocks and the height of its hazel trees. On the right hand of the promontory, between the castle and the church, near the site of a very large lake and mill, a rivulet of never-failing water flows through a valley, rendered sandy by the violence of the winds . . . The country is well supplied with corn, sea-fish, and imported wines; and what is preferable to every other advantage, from its vicinity to Ireland, is tempered by a salubrious air. Demetia [*as the Romans called Pembrokeshire, or Dyfed*], therefore, with its seven

cantrefs, is the most beautiful as well as the most powerful part of
Wales; Penfro, the finest province of Demetia; and the place I have
just described, the most beautiful part of Penfro. It is evident,
therefore, the Maenor Pirr is the pleasantest spot in Wales.'
Giraldus rounds off his soliloquy with an apology 'for having thus
extolled his native soul, his genial territory, with a profusion of
praise and admiration'.

King William II had entrusted the conquest of this part of Wales
to Earl Roger de Montgomery, and he in turn had granted the
stewardship of Pembroke Castle to Gerald de Windsor. The
lordship of Manorbier was held for Gerald by Odo de Barri, and it
was probably he who built the first *Manorbier Castle* some time
before his death in 1130. Odo was succeeded by his son William,
who greatly extended his influence by marrying Angharad de
Carew, the daughter of the aforementioned Gerald de Windsor,
and of the famous Nest, who had been Henry I's mistress, and
whose father, Rhys ap Tewdwr, was the ruling Prince of S Wales
until his death in 1093. Their fourth son was Gerald, or Giraldus
Cambrensis as he became known. Nearly all the present buildings
and fortifications were erected by the de Barris in the 12c and 13c.

The de Barris died out c1336 and by 1417 the castle had passed to
the Earl of Huntingdon. It was seized by the Crown in 1491 and
then granted out from time to time to a variety of individuals, until
it was sold by Elizabeth I to Thomas Bowen of nearby Trefloyne in
1601. In 1670 his grandson, another Thomas Bowen, married into
the distinguished Philipps family of Picton Castle: the castle has
descended through that family to the present day, the present
owner being Lady Dunsany.

The castle is still a private residence, though not occupied by the
owner, but it is open to the public daily, including Sundays, from
1100–1800, 19 May-30 September, and at Easter. There is an
admission charge.

Tour of the Castle

Manorbier is one of the very few Norman castles containing
comfortable living quarters for its inhabitants (although the present
residence is converted out of a great barn which was built in the

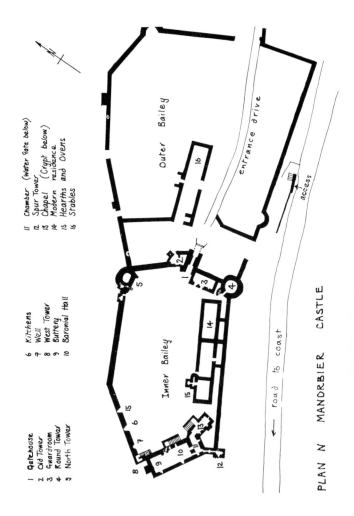

1 Gatehouse
2 Old Tower
3 Guardroom
4 Round Tower
5 North Tower

6 Kitchens
7 Well
8 West Tower
9 Buttery
10 Baronial Hall

11 Chamber (Water Gate below)
12 Spur Tower
13 Chapel (Crypt below)
14 Modern residence
15 Hearths and Ovens
16 Stables

Outer Bailey

Inner Bailey

entrance drive

access

← road to coast

PLAN N   MANORBIER   CASTLE

mid- or late 17c). Leyland described it in his *Itinerary* at the end of the Middle Ages as 'the most perfect model of an old Norman baron's residence, with all its appendages, church, mill, dove-house, ponds, park and grove, still to be seen and traced'.

The castle occupies the crest of a low spur which divides the valley below Manorbier village into two. The road from the beach to the village runs below the S wall of the castle, and steps lead up directly to the castle gatehouse. Alternatively, if approaching from the village, the main entrance follows a drive through the outer bailey. Little of the outer bailey remains, and the visitor from either entrance is confronted by the impressive mass of the defences of the inner bailey, where round towers are linked by a curtain wall, with two rectangular towers projecting to form the gateway.

Entrance into the castle through the gatehouse is over a wooden bridge where once there was a drawbridge, past two portcullises and doors, and into the inner ward. The upper floors of the gatehouse can only be reached by way of the stairs of the Round Tower (to the S) and then along a fighting gallery in the thickness of the curtain wall: at the far end a passage leads into the gatehouse's portcullis chamber, while a spiral stair leads up to the second floor which would have been the living quarters of the castle's constable. The spiral stair continues up to the roof and a lookout turret.

Immediately joining the gatehouse on the N side is the Old Tower; next comes the North Tower, a round-fronted three-storey tower. Its ground and first floors are reached by a stair in the thickness of the wall, but the second floor can only be reached from the wall-walk of the curtains.

At the far W end of the inner bailey is the Great Hall – the residential part of the castle, with its hall, chapel, and solar, forming an inverted 'Y' in plan. The hall and its buttery, forming the stem of the 'Y', date from the 12c, while the arms of the 'Y' forming the chapel and its vaulted basement, date from *c*1260. At the junction of the arms and stem of the 'Y' is a three-storied building containing two living rooms above a vaulted Watergate Passage, dating from the 13c. Both the hall and the chapel are raised above pointed barrel vaults and each is approached from the bailey by its own individual external staircase.

The S curtain is long and straight and terminates at the E end in the Round Tower, a completely cylindrical tower, four storeys high, and well preserved. Access to the first floor is from an outside stair in the courtyard, while upward access to the second and third floors and the roof is by a series of curving stairs, rising in the thickness of the inward segment of the wall, so as not to weaken the part of the tower exposed to the missiles of an enemy. The second floor gives access to the wall-walk, the northern one now being the fighting gallery leading to the gatehouse. The roof of the tower is a dome-shaped vault, copied from the great keep at Pembroke.

Below the castle on the N side runs a stream through a large flat area of marshy land, marking the site of the mill-pond, which was stocked with fish. Beside the track leading to the present-day village sewage works are the ruins of the mill, and beyond is the well preserved round tower of the Columbarium, or dove-house.

Although the castle, the church, the mill and the dove-house form a satisfying little manorial group, Manorbier is no longer 'the most perfect model' that Leyland saw. However, the PNPA hopes to restore the mill, the dovecote and two lime-kilns near the castle, as well as to undertake management of the marsh, control scrub, and plant trees. They have already improved the footpaths and the badly eroded sand dune system. The fact that some 48 acres/19.5ha of land around the bay and cliffs belong to the NT should assist the planners in carrying out their objective.

On the opposite side of the valley to the castle is *Manorbier church* dedicated to St James the Great, Apostle and Martyr, an extremely interesting building. It was originally Norman, and the oldest part of the nave, *c*1150, pre-dates most of the castle; the chancel was rebuilt, and the transepts and N aisle were built about 100 years later, at the same time as the oldest parts of the castle.

The church has a very irregular and curious appearance as a result of successive additions: the tower was built *c*1270, and the S aisle built and N transept extended in the 14c. The very thick walls of the original Norman nave had odd-sized and primitive-looking arches cut through them, and aisles added on either side; the tower is oddly placed, and the chancel is out of line with the nave. The result is a clumsy medley of arches and pillars, which was not improved by heavier and still clumsier plastering in the 1867 restoration. Steps lead down into the church through a vaulted porch (note the medieval painting, and a large squint which enables the altar to be seen) and you get the impression of entering a cavern.

Originally the Early English N transept was short: and of it only the gable, with a sort of clerestory window, remains. At a later date this was lengthened to form a Chantry Chapel, possibly for John de Barri, who died in 1324. The lower, or lengthened, transept has, instead of a plain vault, a vault consisting of five ribs of coarse rubble set near together, more like the arches of a bridge than a church roof.

It is said that the orientation of the chancel allowed the early sun on St James's Day (25 July) to shine through the E window. Before the restoration of 1867–70 the chancel had Perpendicular windows, but then these were changed for the present three-light window.

The effigy in the chancel, removed from the N transept, shows a knight wearing mail ring armour with a mixture of plate, goaded spurs and sleeveless surcoat. There is a small plate on the front of the crossed legs. The identity of the knight is uncertain, but the shield bears the arms of the de Barri family. The date of the effigy is 1325 or earlier – it may be of John de Barri himself: similar examples are to be seen at Stackpole and Carew.

The tower has an unusual position in the angle between the chancel and N transept. It was formerly apart, but has been incorporated into the growing building. It was built c1270, in the time of William de Valence (1250–96), at about the same time as the original short N transept, and clearly before this transept was lengthened, for part of the tower was cut away to receive the transept wall: this can easily be seen from outside the church. The tower is a good example of the corbelled Pembrokeshire vaulted tower of the type without spiral stairs. The only way into it was by a tiny doorway high up above the lectern. Access to this door was originally by a ladder kept on a stone crook high up on the face of the chancel wall, and drawn in during an emergency. The stone crook is still there. The 14c oak loft leading into the tower is one of the few remaining examples of medieval church woodwork in Pembrokeshire. The tower has very few lights, and none on the S side. Its base is only 15.5ft/4.57m square, which suggests that it was not originally intended to be as high as it is now.

Manorbier Church has an early connection with Monkton Priory, the Benedictine house near Pembroke, and the earliest recorded rector of Manorbier was Richard, Prior of Monkton, in 1251. The land, tithes and advowsons were given by John de Barri in 1301 to the Priory of Pembroke, and this may account for the monastic grange or priory, now in ruins, above the church on the S side.

Manorbier Bay to Lydstep Haven 3.9ml/6.2km
The condition of the Path is good, but it has to make a diversion around part of the Royal Armoured Corps' Manorbier Camp.

Access to the coast around Old Castle Head to Skrinkle Haven and Skomar was prohibited until 1983, then the situation changed as the cliff land between Skrinkle Haven and Skomar was acquired by the PNPA from the MOD. As a result a new path has been created between Presipe Bay and Skomar, but the military still occupy Old Castle Head.

From the car park below Manorbier Castle a path leads down to the beach to rejoin the Coast Path. Alternatively another path from the church car park traverses above the valley to join the Coast Path at King's Quoit, a Stone Age burial chamber on the S side of Manorbier Bay right beside the Coast Path. It originally rested on three short supporting stones, but one has fallen and lies underneath. The capstone has an overall length of 16.75ft/5.1m, a breadth of 8.5ft/2.59m, and is 1.5ft/0.45m–2ft/0.61m thick.

The coast and 48 acres/19.4ha of land here were bought out of Enterprise Neptune funds by the NT in 1965 from Christ's College, Cambridge. The Coast Path turns the headland at Priest's Nose, taking the lower of two paths, and heads towards the small sandy Presipe Bay.

Between Presipe Bay and Lydstep the fine cliffs around Old Castle Head and Skrinkle Haven were until 1983 enclosed by the largely disused artillery range of Manorbier Camp. In World War I airships from this camp operated photographic reconnaissance sorties over the sea in the search for enemy submarines in conjunction with the hydrophone station on Carn Llidi, near St David's.

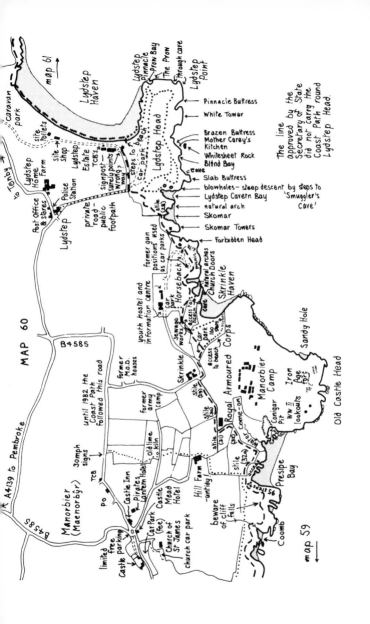

MAP 60

map 61

Caravan park

Lydstep Haven

site toilets

site shop

Lydstep Point

through cave

The Prow

Prow Bay

Lydstep Pinnacle

Pinnacle Buttress

White Tower

Brazen Buttress
Mother Carey's Kitchen
Whitesheet Rock
Blind Bay
cave
Slab Buttress
blowholes — steep descent by steps to 'Smuggler's Cave'
Lydstep Cavern Bay
natural arch
Skomar
Skomar Towers
Forbidden Head

The line approved by the Secretary of State did not carry the Coast Path round Lydstep Head.

to Tenby

Lydstep Home Farm

Lydstep Estate

signpost — surely points wrong way?

steps to beach

Lydstep Head car park

car park

stile (23)

stile

former gun positions used (as car parks)

Post Office & Stores

Lydstep

Police Station

private road — public footpath

Horseback

natural arches Church Doors

Skrinkle Haven

Sandy Hole

youth hostel and information centre

car park

Car park

access road

Sewage works

access 160 steps road to beach

B4585

until 1982 the Coast Path followed this road

former M.O.D. houses

former army camp

old lime kiln

Skrinkle

stile (29)

stile (30)

Royal Armoured Corps

come on

Manorbier Camp

Iron Age Fort

Caniger Pit

WW II lookouts

Old Castle Head

A4139 to Pembroke

30mph signs

TCB

Castle Inn

Pirates' Lantern Hotel

PO

Castle Mead Hotel

stile (32a)

stile

Hill Farm — unfaig

beware of cliff falls

Presipe Bay

Coomb

map 59

Manorbier (Maenorbŷr)

Limited free Castle parking

Car Park (fee)

Church of St James

Church car park

The anti-aircraft gunnery school of the Royal Artillery closed a few years ago, having been in use since 1939. Plans to reduce the area of the camp in the 1970s were frustrated by cuts in defence spending which delayed the introduction of new weapons needing smaller training areas. With the advent in the early 1980s of compact ground-to-air missile systems with shorter training needs, and an increase in defence spending, the MOD was at last able to release most of its range.

Old Castle Head and its Iron Age promontory fort still cannot be visited, but we can look across to it. The broad headland is separated from the mainland and higher ground by a hollow, something like a glacial overflow channel, which extends to the sea at both ends, that on the E running down to the beach of Sandy Hole. The camp takes advantage of this natural formation: it is small, in an exposed position, and has no water, but when it was described in 1871 there were 'evident traces of rows of hut-circles, numerous and perfect'.

Many examples of vertical bedding can be seen along the coast between Freshwater East and Lydstep Point, but the most striking are at Skrinkle Haven. Two large buttresses of limestone project like walls into the sea, and divide the Haven into three beautiful coves. The coves were created by faults which were readily exploited by the sea, and some of the thinly bedded limestone of the projecting ribs has been torn out to form caves and natural arches.

Skrinkle Haven is famous geologically as being on the fault line of the Devonian Old Red Sandstone and the Carboniferous limestone. On the W, towards Old Castle Head, the cliffs are red; on the E, towards Skomar and Lydstep, they are grey. A substantial flight of about 160 steps, built by the Army, descends the cliff to the Haven, a safe bathing beach, and in December 1983 the PNPA constructed a new access (with 134 steps) to the cove to the E, between Church Doors and Horseback.

In 1983 the PNPA purchased from the MOD for £51,000 about 45 acres/18ha of cliff-top and redundant military buildings and has set about creating car parks and picnic areas on the former concrete gun positions overlooking Skrinkle Haven and Skomar. Some of the acquired buildings have been earmarked for an outdoor pursuits centre and a PNPA information and education centre. One building has been acquired by the YHA for conversion into a youth hostel: it opened on 30 July 1988.

At the eastern limit of the PNPA's land are the superb limestone cliffs of Skomar Towers and the inaccessible bay of Skomar. On the top of the cliffs is the Iron Age Skomar Camp, an earthwork defended on three sides by perpendicular cliffs and on the landward side by a massive rampart and ditch. The single bank has suffered from erosion over the centuries but is seen at its best on the W side where it rises from the inside to a height of 10ft/3m then falls 30ft/9.1m to a ditch 9ft/2.7m wide. The entrance to the enclosure was at the NE angle.

Lydstep Point is a magnificent limestone promontory, its 54 acres/ 21.8ha being the property of the NT with free access. The headland was acquired with a grant by the Pilgrim Trust in 1936. Unfortunately the means of approach to the headland from the village is not too clear for first-time visitors. Car-borne visitors are expected to park on the main road A4139 near Lydstep Post Office – but parking spaces do not exist – and walk down the private road just W of the Post Office. As an alternative, motorists may enter the Lydstep Bay Caravan Park at an entrance on the Tenby side of Lydstep village, paying for the privilege, and park close to the beach of Lydstep Haven, but this approach is available only in summer when the caravan park is open. NT members may drive down this way, free on production of their membership card, and park free of charge in the headland car park. Walkers on the Coast Path have none of these problems.

For some reason the route of the official Coast Path as approved by the Secretary of State does not run around Lydstep Head. Presumably because this was already NT land before the Coast Path was designated, there was *de facto* access, and a right of way was not necessary. There is a well defined path around the headland from the car park, and also a nature trail laid out by the DWT, but there is no real convenient link from this path to the Coast Path except at the car park: there is a path dropping down from the plateau to Lydstep Pinnacle and then on the rocks below the northern cliffs to the Haven, but it is a bit of a scramble and you risk getting your feet wet at high tide.

Lydstep Head is a major climbing area in Pembrokeshire with an impressive and ever-growing number of routes on its superb limestone cliffs. Most visitors will be content to see the Lydstep Caverns at the W end of the headland: with the exception of the Smuggler's Cave they can only be visited at low tide.

The well-developed E-W folds which traverse South Pembrokeshire, and which were formed during the Hercynian Earth Movements, commonly have inclined, sometimes vertical, flanks. Along the S cliffs of Lydstep around Mother Carey's Kitchen and Whitesheet Rock the limestone layers rise vertically, and erosion has exploited the less resistant layers. Below the cliffs is a remnant of a wave-cut platform, excavated on steeply dipping limestone strata when the sea stood at a higher level in relation to the land, probably during an inter-glacial phase of the Pleistocene sequence of glaciations.

Lydstep Point is an excellent viewpoint in clear conditions for St Margaret's Island and Caldey Island, Worms Head on the Gower Peninsula, Lundy Island, about 35ml/56km to the S in the middle of the Bristol Channel, and on occasions the distant coastline and hills of Somerset and Devon.

Below the old disused quarry on the N side of the Point is the 'step' on which schooners lay as they were loaded with limestone for export to Bideford, Cardigan and other ports around the Bristol Channel and the Irish Sea.

Lydstep Haven is an exceptional bay, a beautiful crescent of shelving sand below a shingle bank in a wooded setting, more impressive than Freshwater East. The Haven is the core of a syncline similar to West Angle Bay, with the rocks rising upwards on both S and N sides. On the S side of the bay the limestone beds composing Lydstep Head, and which represent the southern limb of the downfold, are arranged vertically, whereas on the N side the limestone cliffs around Proud Giltar dip steeply towards the S. The opposite arrangement of rocks is evident at Freshwater East. The bay has been cut into the softer shales by the advancing sea, while the limbs of the bay remain in the more resistant cliffs and headland.

The Haven was formerly secluded, but it is now part of the Lydstep Beach Estate holiday village, with a caravan park, beach shop and licensed premises. The estate charges an admission fee for cars, inclusive of parking, but access on foot is free.

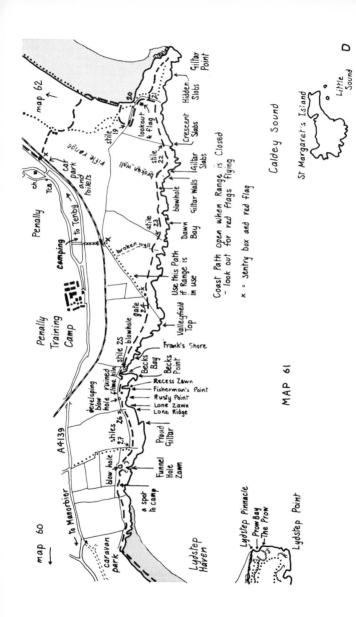

MAP 61

map 62 →

map 60 →

to Manorbier

A4139

to Tenby

Penally

Penally Training Camp

Camping

caravan park

car park and toilets

ch.

Tea

Rifle Range

stile 19

stile 20

21

lookout & flag

Gillar Point

Hidden Slabs

Crescent Slabs

Gillar Slabs

stile 22

broken wall

blowhole

Dawn Bay

stile 23

Gillar Walls

broken wall

Use this Path if Range is in use

gate 24

Valleyfield Top

blowhole

stile 25

blowhole

Frank's Shore

Becks Bay

Becks Point

Recess Zawn

ruined lime kiln

developing blow hole

Fisherman's Point

Rusty Point

Lone Zawn

Lone Ridge

stiles 27 26

Proud Giltar

blow hole

28

Funnel Hole Zawn

a spot to camp

Lydstep Haven

Coast Path open when Range is Closed
- look out for red Flags Flying

x = Sentry box and red flag

Caldey Sound

St Margaret's Island

Little Sound

Lydstep Pinnacle

Prow Bay
The Prow

Lydstep Point

D

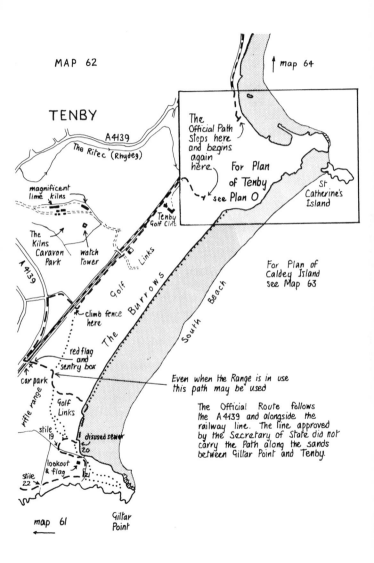

MAP 62

TENBY

A4139

The Ritec (Rhydeg)

↑ map 64

The Official Path stops here and begins again here.

For Plan of Tenby see Plan O

St Catherine's Island

magnificent lime kilns

The Kilns Caravan Park

watch tower

Tenby Golf Club

A4139

Golf Links

The Burrows

climb fence here

South Beach

red flag and sentry box

For Plan of Caldey Island see Map 63

car park

rifle range

Golf Links

stile 19

disused sewer

20

Even when the Range is in use this path may be used

The Official Route follows the A4139 and alongside the railway line. The line approved by the Secretary of State did not carry the Path along the sands between Giltar Point and Tenby.

stile 22

lookout & flag

21

map 61 ←

Giltar Point

Lydstep Haven to Giltar Point 2.5ml/4km
The Coast Path follows a line above high water across the Haven, in
front of the caravans, and you will notice that at the northern end of
the beach there is more wind-blown sand than at the southern end,
where the bay is more sheltered by Lydstep Head. The Path climbs
up to the level of the cliffs, 120ft/36.5m above the sea, and follows
them as far as Giltar Point. Collectively these cliffs are called the
Giltar Cliffs and they provide a good introduction to the limestone
climbing of South Pembrokeshire. Because of their general low
height, good rock, lack of verticality, and ease of approach, it is a
good area both for climbers not familiar with limestone and for bad
weather. Most of the climbs are concentrated on Proud Giltar,
Beck's Bay and Giltar Slabs.

Part of the Path round Giltar Point is sometimes closed when the
Penally rifle range is in use – red flags are flown when it is – and you
have to go inland and follow the main road A4139 through Penally.
Penally is a picturesque village on the eastern end of the Ridgeway,
a ridge of Old Red Sandstone running E–W which carried a
prehistoric trackway from the sea across to Pembroke. The village
overlooks a broad area of sand dunes (The Burrows) and the sea.
The cliffs that were formed before the sand dunes were created can
clearly be seen as you drive along the main road: the village was
once on the edge of the sea.

Giltar Point to Tenby 2.25ml/3.6km
As the Coast Path swings round over Giltar Point you are faced with
the magnificent sweep of Tenby's South Beach, backed by high
sand dunes, with the town perched on the cliffs in the distance. The
South Beach is a 2ml/3.2km stretch of gently shelving sand with a
scattering of shingle, but instead of following the shore line the
official Coast Path turns inland slightly to run behind the sand dunes
and alongside the railway line. The Path also crosses and runs
alongside the golf links of Tenby Golf Club, a championship
eighteen-hole course, the oldest in Wales.

Between Penally and Tenby is the valley of the River Ritec

The Tudor Merchant's House, Tenby

(Rhydeg) which flows from St Florence past Gumfreston to the coast. This was once an estuary and at high tide ships went far inland. Land reclamation started in 1811 by the construction of an embankment, and when the railway came in 1865 the line was laid along this, and the Ritec was diverted. The embankment acted as a dam which accelerated the accumulation of sand which is carried towards Tenby on a southerly wind. The sandhills have increased and smothered the river, which now runs in an underground drain. In heavy rain this cannot accommodate the swollen waters, and the low land is deeply flooded.

This low land is the Tenby Marsh, noted for its wealth of wild flowers, including yellow flag, willow herb, the fascinating hanging blossoms of touch-me-not, and a rare daffodil – the Tenby Daffodil (*Narcissus obvallaris*). It appears to be native only to the Tenby area, usually grows to a height of 8–10in/203–250mm, and is uniformly a golden yellow colour, upward-looking, with a trumpet rather longer than the petals. There is much local distress if it is not in flower on St David's Day (1 March).

On the southern side of Tenby Marsh is the Kiln Park Caravan Site, its name derived from the magnificent lime-kilns built there to meet the demands of Tenby. John Nash is supposed to have had a hand in designing them. They are in two blocks; one has 12 main archways, pointed, and the other six, round. They are stone-built, in good condition, and quite impressive. They were last used in about 1890.

The official Coast Path breaks off where the sand dunes meet the cliffs on which the town is built, at a point where the road to the golf club and a huge beach café development meets the Esplanade. The Coast Path begins again at the junction of The Croft with the High Street, just S of the Information Centre. There is a minimum distance of 0.5ml/800m between these two points, and I have described a route between them in the next chapter, as a Tenby town trail. The continuation of the Path is described in Chapter 28, since Chapter 27 is devoted to Caldey Island.

26   **Tenby** (Dinbych-y-Pyscod) (Plan O)

Tenby is an attractive and popular seaside resort, finely placed on a limestone promontory with beautiful beaches on each side. On a fine summer's day with the sea rolling in on South Beach the view of the Victorian hotels on the Esplanade rising above the cliffs, with the castle on its promontory at the far end of the beach, together with the bastion on St Catherine's Island, can give one an impression of a resort on the Bay of Naples. The town faces E across Carmarthen Bay and has lovely views. It has a picturesque old harbour surrounded by attractive houses; it has an ancient castle and town walls; and it is an old town and sea port. Its Welsh name means 'The small fort of the fishes'.

Tenby may have existed in Roman times, but the first known record is a mention as a Danish fishing station. During the 14c Tenby was a principal herring port, and in 1328 the first breakwater was built, with a grant from Edward III, to provide protection, and was the first such breakwater to be built in Wales.

Henry, Earl of Richmond (afterwards Henry VII) and the Earl of Pembroke took refuge here after the Battle of Tewkesbury in 1471, and escaped hence to Brittany. Henry was assisted by Thomas White, mayor and merchant, who on the return of Henry VII to power was given a lease of all the Crown lands about Tenby. He lies under one of the many monuments in St Mary's Church (qv).

Tenby became a walled town in the 13c. The walls were strengthened in 1457 and again under the threat of the Armada in 1588. The town had a rough time in the Civil War: it was garrisoned for the King, but surrendered to the Parliamentarians in 1644 after a siege of three days; it was retaken in 1648 after defecting during the Second Civil War. It was twice bombarded from the sea.

The town extended beyond its walls with the coming of the railway in 1853. The railway caused a gradual decline of the coastal trade, but at the same time the town's potential as a fashionable holiday resort began to be realised, with visitors from Bristol and elsewhere flocking in. A certain Sir William Paxton, a flamboyant **magnate of Llanarthney, Carmarthenshire,** in the 1790s, took Tenby in hand in 1806 and began its conversion from a decaying medieval port into one of the most charming and elegant watering-places of Wales.

Paxton employed the architect S P Cockerell to design the public baths, 1810–11, now called Laston House, in Castle Square. A Greek inscription cut into the stone above the entrance doorway is an appropriate quotation from Euripides (c480–406BC): 'The sea washes away all the ills of mankind.' The quotation has been adopted as the town's motto. (Cockerell had recently designed Paxton's house in Carmarthenshire – Middleton Hall – and was responsible for the folly there known as Paxton's Tower in memory of Lord Nelson. Paxton had made a princely fortune in India and had set himself up as a banker in London.)

Tenby owes a lot to Paxton's energy and imagination. Elegant houses were built on the cliff-tops under his leadership. Paxton was responsible for improvements to the streets and, most important of all, to the water supply. He died, much lamented, in 1824.

Bay-windowed hotels rose along the cliffs above the North Beach and the South Beach between 1866 and 1939, but since World War II the Tenby holiday trade has changed in response to the increasing popularity of the private motor car, caravan accommodation, and self-catering holidays. The growth of the town has continued unabated: ill-conceived post-war planning led to the despoliation of much of the area around Tenby, Saundersfoot and Begelly.

Tenby is a bright, clean-looking town. The buildings are mostly in stone, and many are colour-washed stucco. The tall terraces of lodging houses have a pleasant Regency and early Victorian atmosphere and, together with the patches of colour overlooking the beaches and the harbour, give the place quite a foreign appearance. As a seaside resort (out of the high season) Tenby cannot fail to please even those who detest the average British watering-place.

A Tenby town trail

There is no official Coast Path through Tenby, but the town has many attractions and Coast Path walkers would do well to savour them before spending the last day walking the Coast Path to its conclusion. Readers are advised to follow my Town Trail with the aid of Plan O, overleaf.

At the break-off point of the official Coast Path, walk along the Esplanade above the South Cliff, passing the house where the artist Augustus John was born in 1878. At the eastern end of the Esplanade the road comes to a stop in front of the town wall, and you have to turn inland.

Tenby's town walls may have been first built by William de Valence, Earl of Pembroke, who was half-brother to Henry III and who died in 1296, but there is reason to believe that they were not erected until later: the earliest known historical reference to them relates to a grant made to the town in 1328 by Edward III of certain dues for seven years to help the inhabitants to enclose their town and build a quay.

The curtain wall has four gates and towers. It is about 20ft/6m high, has a wall-walk and battlements, strengthened externally by bastions, of which all except one are cylindrical. The broad walk along St Florence Parade and South Parade shaded by elms may have been a shallow moat. The walls were strengthened in 1457 by Jasper, Earl of Pembroke, and again in 1588, a reflection of Tenby's Elizabethan importance: a small tablet inscribed 'AD1588 ER30' relates to the strengthening of the wall in the thirtieth year of Queen Elizabeth I's reign – the year of the Spanish Armada.

All the town gates except one were demolished in the 18c: the Royal Lion Hotel stands on the site of the North Gate. It suffered damage from a Parliamentarian bombardment in 1644, and was removed in 1797.

The surviving section of the town wall begins at the junction of the Esplanade and St Florence Parade at the South Cliff, where a small square watch-tower still stands on the cliff terminating the southern end of the wall. Near to it is a round tower, the interior of which is now part of the kitchen of the Imperial Hotel, and next N is the tall Belmont Archway with an entry into the old town by a street called Paragon. Next N is a splendid square tower flanked on the N side by a corbelled-out opening which is the remains of an old latrine which overhung the moat, and further N is a round tower with small windows.

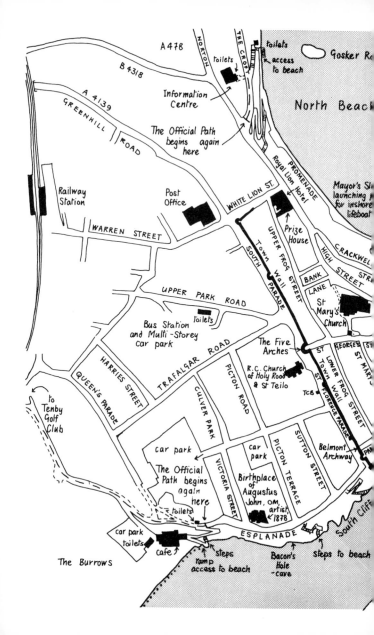

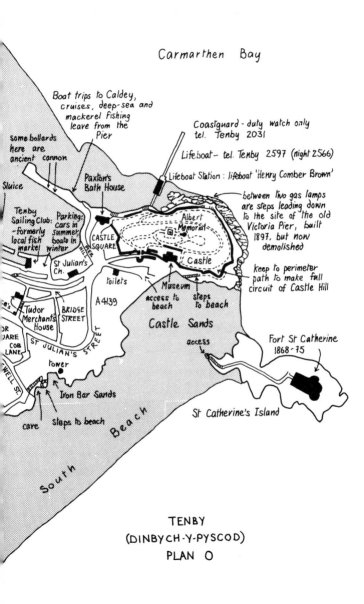

Carmarthen Bay

Boat trips to Caldey, cruises, deep-sea and mackerel fishing leave from the Pier

Coastguard – duty watch only tel. Tenby 2031

Lifeboat – tel. Tenby 2597 (night 2566)

Lifeboat Station: lifeboat 'Henry Comber Brown'

Some bollards here are ancient cannon

Paxton's Bath House

Sluice

between two gas lamps are steps leading down to the site of the old Victoria Pier, built 1897, but now demolished

Tenby Sailing Club: – formerly local fish market

Parking: cars in summer, boats in winter

Albert Memorial

CASTLE SQUARE

St Julian's Ch.

Castle

keep to perimeter path to make full circuit of Castle Hill

toilets

Museum

A4139

access to beach

steps to beach

Castle Sands

Tudor Merchants' House

BRIDGE STREET

ST JULIAN'S STREET

access

Fort St Catherine 1868-75

COB LANE

QUARE

WELL ST.

tower

Iron Bar Sands

cave

steps to beach

South Beach

St Catherine's Island

TENBY
(DINBYCH-Y-PYSCOD)
PLAN O

The sole remaining gate, near the middle of the wall, is a massive open-roofed tower with a vaulted gallery. Locally known as the Five Arches, this remarkable semi-circular barbican originally had one arch. The original entrance is on the N side, with a portcullis slot in the arch, and with the favourite medieval trap for attackers, consisting of a right-angled turn. The other three openings are modern: the fifth is the archway in the wall itself. Once the town walls were no longer necessary for defence a battle for their preservation continued throughout the 19c. The gatehouse is a traffic bottleneck, and the arches are constantly under threat as traffic increases, but neither residents nor visitors would do without them.

We enter the old walled town by passing through the Five Arches and into St George's Street, going straight ahead, passing the junction of Upper and Lower Frog Streets on our way to the southern approach to the parish church. Inside the walls is a fascinating maze of narrow streets and crooked lanes, a medieval layout, although there are few signs left of any medieval buildings. The medieval Town Hall stands beside the original entrance archway to the churchyard, as the main approach to the church was from St George's Street, and we shall turn off here to pay a visit to the parish church.

St Mary's Church is the largest in Pembrokeshire (with the exception of St David's Cathedral) and is one of the finest medieval survivals of the town. The oldest surviving parts date from the 13c but when Tenby was a prosperous trading port in the 15c the church was more than doubled in size in a series of additions over a period of 100 years, proudly reflecting the town's prosperity. The Victorian popularity of the resort led to extensive changes in the 1850s to accord with the mid-Victorian ideas of 'correct' style, but managing to retain the W of England influences.

The building is of the Early English and Perpendicular styles, the latter predominating. The church is 145ft/44m long, 80ft/24.3m broad, and has seating for 1500. The tower is 83ft/25.2m high and is topped by a stone octagonal spire 69ft/21m high, forming a landmark for mariners.

If we come to the church by the S porch we enter the S aisle, an unusually wide aisle created in the 15c alterations by incorporating the aisle and side chapels of the original church. To the N is the nave, part of the original 13c church but much altered in the 15c when first the arches on the N side were inserted in what had been the outside wall of the older church, then later an entirely new row of arches was erected on the S side, and finally the walls were heightened for a new 'wagon' roof and the former chancel arch was removed. The arches to the N aisle are unusual in having no capitals to separate the arched head from the column, while those on the S have capitals decorated in stylised foliage of W Country pattern. The panelled nave roof has 89 carved bosses including five figures.

The chancel was built in the 13c with the tower as part of its S side, and it was enlarged c1470 by adding on the E the broad steps and raised sanctuary. Dr John Smith, rector of the church from 1461–75, erected the chancel roof when he became Bishop of Llandaff: eight bosses over the N side of the sanctuary inscribed in Latin record the fact. Of the 80 bosses in the chancel roof 75 are original, and they are carved with a variety of foliage designs, grotesque faces, mitred heads, mythical beasts, fishes, and even a mermaid holding a mirror and comb. The arch-braces of the roof rest on corbels carved as robed figures, each holding a shield, 32 in all, decorated with the initials of all the known rectors of the parish.

The tower has a chapel on its first floor, reached by a stone newel stair in its SW corner. To the E of the tower is St Thomas's Chapel, added in the mid-15c. The corresponding chapel on the N side of the chancel is St Nicholas's Chapel, added c1475–80. As might be expected in a prosperous medieval town there were several wealthy merchants, and there are a number of good tombs in the church commemorating them. The two chapels display some of the best.

In St Thomas's Chapel are two very fine carved alabaster altar-tombs with recumbent effigies in freestone to the White family: Thomas White (on the E) and his son John, both prosperous merchants and mayors of Tenby. It was this Thomas White (d.1482) who aided the escape of the Earl of Richmond to France after Tewkesbury. His son John died c1507. Both are dressed in the long garments of their day, the head resting on a peacock and the feet on a hart. The Latin inscription records their respective wives – each married twice – and the alabaster panels below show their families: on the L John's tomb shows, in four panels, one of his wives and a daughter kneeling before a saint, then another wife and daughter kneeling before another saint, then John himself kneeling at a desk with his three sons behind him, and finally a coffin with infants who died at birth; Thomas's shows first his second wife and a daughter kneeling before a saint, then his first wife and a daughter doing the same, then Thomas himself with his six sons, and finally a coffin with three infants who died at birth.

On the E wall of the chapel is the kneeling figure of William Risam, another wealthy merchant and mayor, who died in 1633. On the S wall a modern plaque commemorates Robert Recorde, who was born in Tenby in 1510. Recorde was a pioneer in mathematics, and in algebra in particular. He invented the equals, minus and plus signs, and was the first man to work out square roots.

In St Nicholas's Chapel is the largest monument in the church, an elaborate and colourful tomb to Margaret Mercer, the first wife of Thomas ap Rees of Scotsborough, a former mansion near Tenby. There are life-sized figures of them both. Mrs Rees died in childbirth on 1 May 1610, aged 30. She had been married twelve years and bore ten children. Her seven surviving children – four boys and three girls – are shown in miniature at the tomb base.

On our way out of the church by the N door we pass more effigies and monuments. In the far NW corner of the N aisle, to the R of the W window, is a tablet to: Peggy Davies, 'Bathing Woman 42 years to the Ladies who visited Tenby,' and who died of apoplexy in the water at the age of 82. As we leave the church we pass on the L side of the N door a ghastly *memento mori* – a shrouded skeleton of a priest, dating from about 1500.

We emerge from St Mary's Church on to the broad High Street and turn R into Tudor Square, then at the TCBs turn L down the steps of narrow Quay Hill towards the harbour. Here are the best surviving medieval buildings in Tenby – the Tudor Merchant's House and Plantagenet House.

The Tudor Merchant's House gives some idea how the more prosperous Tenby citizen lived in the late 15c. It is an example of a merchant's house with a fine 'Flemish' chimney, remains of fresco

wall paintings and largely original Tudor interior. It has a gabled
front and a corbelled chimney-breast. The building was presented
by Tenby Corporation to the NT in 1937 and is now a NT
information centre with a museum housing a collection of Tudor
relics. The building is open from Easter until the end of September
at the following times: Mondays-Fridays 1000–1300 and 1430–1800,
and Sundays 1400–1800. It is closed on Saturdays.

Adjoining the Tudor Merchant's House is Plantagenet House,
also having a 'Flemish' chimney but dating from the early 15c. It too
is owned by the NT, but it is open to members only by appointment.

These two houses face down Bridge Street, and we go down here
towards the harbour. On the L is Norris's House, home of Charles
Norris (1779–1858), artist and author of *Etchings of Tenby*, 1812.
He lived here *c*1805–21. Facing the bottom of Bridge Street, at the
end of St Julian's Street, is St Julian's Terrace, the best terrace of
late Georgian houses in W Wales.

The streets turn into Castle Square and from here there is access
not only to the castle and the harbour but also to Castle Sands and
St Catherine's Island. Castle Sands are easily reached from the town
on foot, but car parking is a different matter. A short walk down a
ramp or steps leads to gently shelving sands, which are really a
northwards extension of South Beach. There are the usual beach
amenities.

St Catherine's Island is accessible on foot at low water across
Castle Sands. The island is dominated by Fort St Catherine, an
outlier of the Milford Haven defensive scheme. It was built in
1868–75 at a cost of £16,260 for a garrison of 60 men and an
armament of 11 guns in casements. It has been partly dismantled.

Castle Hill is a projecting promontory which divides the splendid
sandy beaches of Tenby into two. On its summit are the scanty
remains of a castle, and its grounds are laid out as a public park; it is
freely accessible.

The present castle was built in the late 13c by William de
Valence, and probably many years later the D-shaped barbican and
a small watch-tower were added. Much of the castle's strength,
however, came from its site and from the wall already encircling the
town: any attack was expected from the land, not the sea. In the

Civil War of 1642 the town and castle were garrisoned and besieged by both sides in turn, and they twice suffered bombardment from the sea. In 1643 Parliamentary ships exchanged fire with the Royalist batteries on Castle Hill; some of the cannon survive there and also serve as bollards on the harbour. The castle fell to the Parliamentarians in 1644. Tenby was also involved in the revolt in 1648 when so many Parliamentarians joined the Royalist cause and began the Second Civil War. In May 1648 Cromwell came to Tenby as it was being besieged by his own troops. He took the castle and it yielded twenty pieces of ordnance and other booty.

The scanty remains of the castle include a gatehouse to which a barbican was added – note the grooves for the portcullis – a double tower, fragments of walls, and parts of domestic buildings, one of which was adapted as a school and now houses the *Tenby Museum*. This has excellent collections on display relating to Pembrokeshire, and particularly to Tenby. They cover geology, archaeology, natural history and medieval history. They include the Smith Collection of implements and animal bones taken from limestone caves on Caldey Island and Hoyle's Mouth, and the Lyons Collection of sea shells. There are also some weapons taken from the French invaders at Goodwick in 1797, and some of the books Recorde wrote.

Museum admission hours: 1 June-30 September, weekdays only 1000–1800; 1 October-31March, weekdays only 1000–1300 and 1400–1600 but closed on Friday afternoons; 1 April–31 May, weekdays only 1000–1300 and 1400–1800 but closed Friday afternoons.

Elsewhere on Castle Hill is the house which was once a coastguard station, and an old stone watch-tower where beacons were once lit to signal danger. The summit of Castle Hill is surmounted by a conspicuous marble statue, the Welsh National Monument to Queen Victoria's Consort, Prince Albert (b. 26 August 1819, d. 14 December 1861). The memorial was erected on the third anniversary of Albert's death, although it was not unveiled until 2 August 1865, by HRH Prince Arthur.

There are several ancient cannon mounted on the hill, consisting of early 17c Culverins (weighing about 4000lb/1816kg and capable of firing a 15lb/6.8kg shot about 2000ft/610m) and later 17c Sakers (weighing 2500lb/1135kg and capable of firing a 5.5lb/2.5kg shot about 1500ft/457m). The cannon have been remounted by the School of Artillery, Manorbier.

Castle Hill shelters the small harbour, which is protected by a long stone pier, and provides good shelter for many small boats, sailing craft, motor cruisers and a few trawlers. Most of the inshore fishing boats are used in the summer for short trips by holiday-makers in search of mackerel, tope and shark. A dozen or so passenger vessels run a shuttle service to Caldey Island in the summer; there are cruises along the coast, to Saundersfoot, and around the bay; and there are also boats for hire.

The Harbour Beach is small, busy with boats, and sheltered from the wind, and there is immediate access to gently shelving sand, running out to the North Beach and Gosker Rock. There are the usual beach amenities. High water is Milford time minus 12 minutes.

Down by the harbour is St Julian's Seamen's Church, a little chapel where fishermen's services were held. St Julian the Hospitaller is the patron saint of boatmen. This building was converted into a public bath house in 1781 by John Jones, Bachelor of Physic at Haverfordwest, but in 1878 it was converted into a chapel to replace the old St Julian's Chapel on the old pier. Until the reign of Charles II this old pier was the only one of which there is any record in S Wales.

From the harbour we can continue past the sailing club and The Sluice to the traffic-free Promenade, which runs along the back of the North Beach and comes out at the mid-point of the bay opposite the great sandstone rock called Gosker. At its end steps climb up to join The Croft, where the Coast Path to Saundersfoot begins. Alternatively, we can leave the harbour and go along Crackwell Street, where some gaily painted late Georgian and early Victorian terrace houses look out over the bay. Crackwell Street joins High Street and The Norton: No. 3 High Street, next but one to the Royal Lion Hotel, is a stone mid-Victorian building with three small balconies, now called North Bay House, but known locally as the **Prize House**. Designed by a Bath architect, it won a prize in a

MAP 63

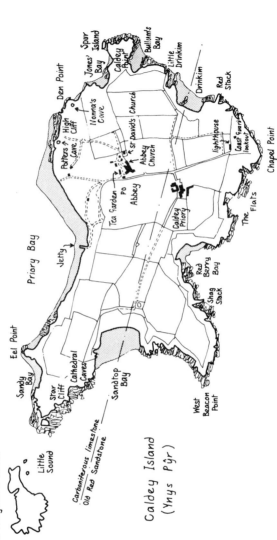

St. Margaret's Island

Little Sound

Caldey Island
(Ynys Pŷr)

Carboniferous limestone
Old Red Sandstone

Sandy Bay

Eel Point

Star Cliff

Cathedral Caves

Sandtop Bay

Priory Bay

Jetty

West Beacon Point

Shag Stack

Red Berry Bay

Caldey Priory

Tea Garden

Po

Abbey

Abbey Church

St. David's Church

Potters Lane

High Cliff

Nonna's Cave

Den Point

Jones' Bay

Spur Island

Caldey Point

Bullum's Bay

Little Drinkim

Drinkim

Red Stack

lighthouse

Coast guard lookout

The Flats

Chapel Point

competition connected with the Great Exhibition of 1851. It was
assembled in Tenby from marked stones shipped from Bath.

The official Coast Path begins again at the junction of The Croft
with High Street and The Norton and we shall start the final stage of
our journey from here after we have paid a visit to Caldey Island.

27   **Caldey Island** (Ynys Pyr) (Map 63)

Caldey Island lies about 2ml/3.2km S of Tenby but only about
0.5ml/800m off the coast of Giltar Point. It has had a history of
religious settlement from the earliest times until the present day.
The first record of a monastic community on the island is during the
6c when a man called Pyro or Piro retired here as a hermit, and the
island became known as Ynys Pyr – the Island of St Pyr. Pyro had
probably come from a community of St Illtyd's foundation at
Llantwit Major in Glamorgan (although some authorities maintain
that Caldey was the earlier foundation), and he was drowned in 521.
Archbishop Dubricius, the reputed first Bishop of Llandaff
(Cardiff), who happened to be in retreat on the island at the time of
Pyr's death, appointed St Samson, a pupil of St Illtyd, to succeed
Pyr as abbot. Samson later sailed to Brittany to become the first
Bishop of Dol, where he died in 565.

In 1113 the island was given by Henry I to Robert, son of Martin
de Turribus, the Norman conqueror of North Pembrokeshire and
first Lord of Cemaes. Robert gave it to his mother Geva, and she
transferred it in turn to the Benedictines from the Abbey of Tiron
who had already founded a monastery at St Dogmael's near
Cardigan. Caldey remained a cell of the Congregation of Tiron for
over 400 years, the Benedictine monks holding peaceful possession
until the Dissolution of the monasteries in 1534 by Henry VIII.

The island was granted to the Bradshaw family of Presteigne in
Radnorshire who held it from 1536 to 1612, then it passed through
the hands of changing owners until 1897 when it was bought by the
Rev. W Done Bushell, chaplain of Harrow school, **who restored the**

Priory Church and St David's Church, and repaired other ruined buildings.

In 1906 Bushell sold the island to a young man, Benjamin Fearnley Carlyle. In 1896 Carlyle had founded a brotherhood of Reformed Anglican Benedictines, and in 1903 he had become Abbot Aelred of Painsthorpe Abbey in Yorkshire. Aelred and his community built most of the present monastery and the abbey church in 1910–12. Aelred 'Poped' in 1913 and his community lost most of its financial support when it was received into the Roman Catholic Church. Aelred resigned in 1921, leaving his affairs in a mess and going to N America. The Benedictines had to sell the island to remove their burden, which they did in 1926, and in 1928 they were established at Prinknash Abbey in Gloucestershire.

The island was bought by the Order of Reformed Cistercians and a group of monks came in 1929 from the Abbey of Chimay in Belgium. About 800 years earlier the Cistercians had established monasteries at Tintern Abbey in Monmouthshire and at Rievaulx Abbey and Fountains Abbey in Yorkshire, but today their only other house in Britain is at Mount St Bernard's Abbey in Leicestershire. The present community live, as far as possible, by the work of their own hands: apart from the summer cash-flow from the tourists the monks earn their living by working a mixed stock and arable farm on the island's 556 acres/225ha, and by exporting, since 1953, the now-famous herbs and scents made from the island's lavender, gorse and other flowers.

A Tour of the Island
Visitors to Caldey land at Priory Bay, where they have unrestricted bathing and picnicking. Beyond that they are restricted to the defined lanes and footpaths leading to the village, around the monastery, to the three churches, and to the lighthouse (although there is no visiting permitted into the lighthouse). The monastery is open to male visitors only: ladies have to be content with visiting the churches.

From the landing stage follow the road for a short way and then take a path up steps towards the village green, where a group of buildings house the weaving, perfume and chocolate-making rooms. Turn L at the Post Office and gift shop, and you have an impressive view of the monastery ahead: the building was constructed of limestone quarried on the island and designed in a Romanesque Rhenish style, clad in white stucco, with steep-pitched red Roman tile roofs, lofty turrets and slender pinnacles.

At the E end of the monastery buildings is the Abbey Church of Our Lady and St Samson, where the monks have their services. It was restored in 1951 in the Cistercian tradition of austerity. Further to the E is the village church of St David's, which serves the islanders. It is a small and simple building, closely resembling the early Celtic churches of the 8c and 9c.

The third church on the island is St Illtyd's, standing high up on the hill in the centre of the island. The church was probably built up gradually by the Benedictines from St Dogmael's, and the nave, porch and tower were added on to the chancel in the 14c–15c. The chancel has thick walls and a barrel-vaulted ceiling, and a floor paved with beach cobbles. Attached to the church is the cloister garth of the twelve-celled priory, having a cobbled courtyard with an arched doorway leading to the gatehouse and dovecote.

S of St Illtyd's a field track leads to the lighthouse on the highest part of the island. The lighthouse was erected by Trinity House in 1829, and on either side of the circular tower and connected to it are the two keepers' dwellings. The lighthouse is now fully automatic: the gas-burning light is regulated by natural daylight variations. The tower is 52ft/16m high, and the light, some 213ft/65m above the sea, is visible over a range of 14 nautical miles. The signal is a white and red group flashing three times every 20 seconds. There is no fog signal. The lighthouse cannot be visited.

From this vantage point, 188ft/57m above the sea, the whole layout of the island can be seen, together with the southern coastline of Pembrokeshire, the town of Tenby directly to the N and St Govan's Head in the far W. To the E, 12ml/20km across the sea, you may see the Gower Peninsula and Worms Head, while 27ml/43km to the S Lundy Island can be seen: to its E you can make out, in good weather, the mainland of Devon, about 37ml/60km away.

This is all we are allowed to see on Caldey. Most of the island is farmed by the monks and there is no public access, not even to the cliffs and beaches (other than Priory Bay where the boat lands). We must return to the village and jetty, keeping to the main routes. This short tour of the island is about 2ml/3.2km and takes about 1–1½ hours, plus the boat crossing.

Caldey is often included in the excursions that can be made from Tenby and thousands of tourists visit the island in the summer months. A regular service of motorboats operates from Tenby harbour to the island, normally from about the third week in May (Whitsuntide) until the third week in September, every day except Saturdays and Sundays, weather permitting. The fleet of vessels is known as 'The Pool', and tickets for them can be obtained on the harbour side. The first boat to the island departs from Tenby at about 0945, and the last boat at about 1530: the last boat returns at about 1800. The crossing takes about 20 minutes, and at the height of the season boats depart every few minutes, but even so there are often queues.

At all other seasons, save in very rough weather, a place can usually be obtained in the abbey boat which calls at Tenby for mail and supplies.

Facilities on the island include a shop, Post Office, café and toilets. Dogs are allowed if on a lead. Conducted tours around the monastery, for male visitors only, at 1100, 1500 and 1630 in summer.

Boat trips around Caldey and St Margaret's Island – but not visiting the islands – are also run from Tenby harbour. A 75-minute cruise operates from Easter to the end of September, and boats depart at intervals from 1030 onwards, with frequent departures at the height of the season. The *Enterprise* (96 seats) and *St Keyne* (94 seats) are twice as large as the vessels in 'The Pool' and have licensed bars, snack bars and toilets on board. Make sure that you are boarding the correct vessel, as places of embarkation vary according to the state of winds and tides.

St Margaret's Island

Lying to the W of Caldey, and once originally connected to it, is the 20 acre/8ha island of St Margaret's. The size of the island was gradually reduced by the quarrying of its limestone. In 1841 there were 22 inhabitants farming and quarrying, but these activities have now ceased. Ruins of the old quarrymen's cottages can still be seen.

The island is the property of the Picton Castle estate and is leased by them to the DWT as a nature reserve. There is a fine cormorant colony, the largest in England and Wales, with over 300 breeding pairs of birds, and razorbills, guillemots, shags and kittiwake also flourish. Rats have driven out the burrow-nesting Manx Shearwaters and puffins, although a few pairs of puffins regularly nest in the inaccessible crevices of the cliffs.

There is no landing permitted on the island except by special permit from the DWT. If on Caldey Island, do not be tempted to cross the rocky natural causeway across Little Sound which is revealed at low tide. A shore visit is not necessary, as the island and its birds can be better viewed by boat on round trips from Tenby.

28   Tenby to Amroth (Maps 64–66)   7ml/11.2km

The final stage of the Coast Path commences at the junction of The Croft with High Street and The Norton. In good conditions this stretch can be walked in 3½ hours, enabling one to make the return journey to Tenby for transport home by road or rail. Alternatively a morning could be spent on Caldey Island, and this last walk undertaken in the afternoon. In general the Path beyond Tenby is suitable for all walkers except the elderly, who would be advised to go no further than Waterwynch, after which the Path becomes surprisingly strenuous here and there on its way to Saundersfoot.

Tenby to Saundersfoot 3.75ml/6km

The shores between Tenby and Saundersfoot are the most sheltered in Pembrokeshire. They are dominated by woods of scrub oak and sycamore along the fringe, with plantations of Sitka spruce and larch behind and amongst them. The wooded cliffs are broken by a series of secluded coves: First Bay and Second Bay are accessible only at low tide from Tenby's North Beach, and at low water you can get round Bowman's Point to Waterwynch Bay, but if you follow the shore you have to be very careful not to get cut off by the incoming tides.

At the termination of The Croft, by a gate, the Coast Path continues along Waterwynch Lane, a pleasant shady bridleway. It passes Allen's View, a viewpoint 275ft/83m above the sea. There is access to Waterwynch Bay by a lane running down from the A478, but there is no car park. From the Coast Path steps lead down to a beach of gently shelving sand and shingle in a pretty little cove backed by low cliffs with caves. If you go N or S from the centre of this bay take care not to get cut off by incoming tides.

Just E of Trevayne (which is reached by road from the A478 at Twy Cross), at a junction of paths, there is a signpost which says 'Saundersfoot 1.25ml' and 'Tenby 1.5ml'. In fact Tenby is 2.5ml from this point by the Coast Path, which does not run out to Monkstone Point but cuts across the headland. A path runs down steep ground and a number of steps to reach the superb gently shelving sands of Monkstone Beach, while an even steeper path runs down off the tip of Monkstone Point. This headland, which separates Tenby Roads from Saundersfoot Bay, is a good viewpoint: it is possible to see the Black Mountains and The Vans 40ml/64km away, and Llanelli 23ml/37km away. The Gower Peninsula is only 20ml/32km away; and in the same direction across Carmarthen Bay is the Helwick Light Vessel, visible at night 15ml/24km away. To the S is Lundy Island, 33ml/53km, with Exmoor 52ml/83km behind.

N of Monkstone Point a fine, safe, stretch of sand runs for nearly 1.5ml/2.5km to Saundersfoot harbour. It is possible to gain access to this beach at low water at Monkstone Point or from Trevayne Wood and to walk to Saundersfoot (and beyond) when the tide is out. The beach is scattered with shingle and at the foot of the cliffs are splendid rock pools, and a walk along the shore gives excellent views of the exposure of the Lower Coal Measures strata. These rocks are equivalent in age to the anthracite-bearing rocks of the S Wales Coalfield. They are severely shattered and folded, and beds of sandstone and shale may frequently be seen standing on edge or at steep angles, having been produced by the Hercynian Earth Movements some 250 million years ago, which had compressed and

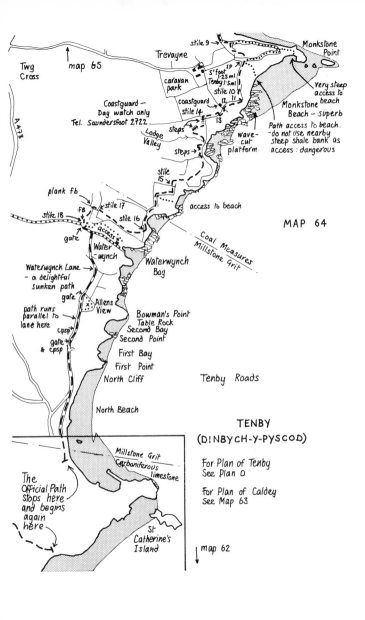

Twg
Cross

map 65

A 478

Trevayne

stile 9

Monkstone
Point

caravan
park

S'foot sp
Tenby 1·5ml
stile 10

Very steep
access to
beach

Coastguard –
Day watch only
Tel. Saundersfoot 2722.

coastguard
stile 14

12   11

13

Monkstone
Beach – superb

Lodge
Valley

steps

wave-
cut
platform

Path access to beach.
do not use nearby
steep shale bank as
access : dangerous

steps

stile
15

plank fb

stile 17

FB

access to beach

stile 18

FB

stile 16

MAP 64

gate

Water
wynch

access

Coal Measures
Millstone Grit

Waterwynch Lane
– a delightful
sunken path

gate

Waterwynch
Bay

Allens
View

path runs
parallel to
lane here

x

cpsp

Bowman's Point
Table Rock
Second Bay
Second Point

gate &
cpsp

First Bay

First Point

North Cliff

Tenby Roads

North Beach

TENBY
(D!NBYCH-Y-PYSCOD)

Millstone Grit
Carboniferous
limestone

For Plan of Tenby
See Plan O

For Plan of Caldey
See Map 63

The
Official Path
stops here
and begins
again
here

St
Catherine's
Island

↓ map 62

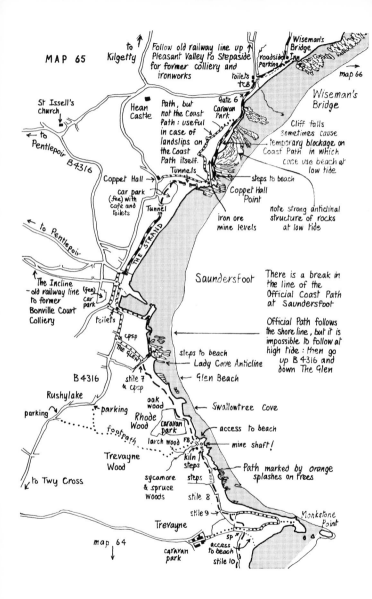

MAP 65

to Kilgetty

Follow old railway line up Pleasant Valley to Stepaside for former colliery and ironworks

Wiseman's Bridge

roadside parking

toilets TC8

map 66

Wiseman's Bridge

St Issell's church

to Pentlepoir B4316

Hean Castle

Path, but not the Coast Path: useful in case of landslips on the Coast Path itself.

Gate 6
Caravan Park

Cliff falls sometimes cause temporary blockage on Coast Path in which case use beach at low tide

Coppet Hall

car park (fee) with café and toilets

Tunnels

Tunnel

to Pentlepoir

steps to beach

Coppet Hall Point

iron ore mine levels

note strong anticlinal structure of rocks at low tide

THE STRAND

Saundersfoot

The Incline – old railway line to former Bonville Court Colliery

(fee) car park

toilets

cpsp

THE GLEN

There is a break in the line of the Official Coast Path at Saundersfoot

Official Path follows the shore line, but it is impossible to follow at high tide: then go up B4316 and down The Glen

steps to beach

Lady Cove Anticline

Glen Beach

stile 7 & cpsp

B4316

Rushylake

parking

parking

oak wood

Rhode Wood

caravan park

larch wood

FB

Swallowtree Cove

access to beach

mine shaft!

footpath

Trevayne Wood

kiln steps

steps

Path marked by orange splashes on trees

to Twy Cross

sycamore & spruce woods

steps

stile 8

stile 9

Monkstone Point

Trevayne

sp

access to beach

map 64

caravan park

stile 10

uplifted the Carboniferous and older rocks of S Wales into an E-W mountain range. Just S of an access to the beach near Saundersfoot harbour is the Lady Cave anticline, a famous geological monument. The steeply-crested anticlinal structure is clearly exposed here because the less resistant beds of shales have been exploited by the processes of marine erosion, and a small cave developed. The more resistant layers of sandstone left behind form the limbs of the fold, and remnants are preserved in strike-ridges on the foreshore.

The official Coast Path follows the shoreline N of the Lady Cave as far as Saundersfoot harbour, where it stops. This route is impossible to follow at high tide, and you have to go inland. There is a gap of about 0.25ml/400m in the Coast Path in the centre of Saundersfoot, and we shall break off to see what the town offers.

Once a busy coaling port, *Saundersfoot* is now an excellent and popular small seaside resort, some 3ml/4.8km by road N of Tenby. The village owes its development to the local coalfield. In 1829 a company was formed to construct a harbour for the export of high-quality anthracite coal mined in the hinterland, and the coal was transported to the harbour by narrow-gauge railway which operated until the last colliery closed in 1939. The harbour was built so that the locally mined anthracite, iron ore and locally manufactured firebricks and iron castings could be loaded into wooden schooners, ketches and barges, much of it being exported to Bristol, Ireland and France.

The holiday trade has now superseded the industrial past, of which little evidence remains. The harbour is in a fine state of repair and still provides shelter for many sailing boats and cruisers, although it is now almost silted up with mud and sand, and at low tide is unapproachable by sea. It is perhaps the best appointed sailing centre in Pembrokeshire. High tide is Milford time minus 13 minutes.

From the town there is immediate access, or a short walk and some steps, down to gently shelving sand. The golden sands offer safe bathing and are among the most popular along the whole Pembrokeshire coastline. The town has several car parks, and a large one on the harbour, all crowded in summer, and if you can find a parking space very little walking is needed. All the usual resort amenities are available down by the harbour.

The parish church of St Issell's is situated 0.75ml/1.2km inland in a pleasant wooded valley on the B4316 road to Pentlepoir. The building is of Norman foundation, with Early English arches in nave and chancel, and is dedicated to the Welsh saint Usullt. The typical and distinctive Pembrokeshire tower is probably 14c. Restoration in 1864 has given the interior the usual Victorian flavour.

The most important colliery district in Pembrokeshire was that around Saundersfoot and Kilgetty. In the early 18c coal was worked largely on the surface, and transported by horse and cart to the beaches of Saundersfoot and Wiseman's Bridge, where it was loaded on to sailing vessels at low tide. There were sometimes 30 vessels or more being loaded on Coppet Hall beach.

Everything was changed after 1829 with the building of Saundersfoot harbour and the various narrow-gauge mineral railway lines from nearby collieries. Now coal could be exported more easily, and in the middle of the century the industry prospered. By 1864 over 30,000 tons of coal were being exported from Saundersfoot harbour, and production reached a peak in the 1880s, with over 100,000 tons produced in some years.

Pembrokeshire coal-mining was always rather inefficient, and there is not the same wealth of coal seams here as in the major S Wales coalfields. As the best seams were worked out and as high transport and drainage costs began to affect the collieries, they were closed one after another. By 1900 Bonville's Court, W of Saundersfoot, was the only large colliery left open in the area. It survived until 1930. With the closure of the last colliery in 1939, the long industrial history of the Saundersfoot area came to an end. There are said to be over 200 million tons of coal still underground.

The coal deposits were largely worked by the Vickerman family, who controlled many of the industrial enterprises in the area. They also rebuilt Hean Castle in 1876. The local spelling 'Hean' is an erroneous form of the word 'Hen', the Welsh for 'old', and is pronounced 'hayne'. Nothing much is known about its origins. The well-wooded site is still privately owned, and the castle is now the home of Mr Lewis, son of Lord Merthyr, the former owner.

Saundersfoot to Wiseman's Bridge 1.2ml/1.9km

The Coast Path begins again immediately N of the centre of the village, and follows the line of the former railway line, here called The Strand. It passes through a tunnel and across the car park serving Coppet Hall beach. This is really an extension of Saundersfoot's beach, and is usually crowded in summer.

Stepaside Colliery once had a tram line to bring anthracite down to Saundersfoot harbour. It passed through tunnels in the cliff, and the Coast Path follows its route between Saundersfoot and Wiseman's Bridge without the need to take the alternative cliff path through the wooded grounds of Hean Castle, although this route would be useful if (and when) the Coast Path is blocked by land-slips from the cliffs above. (A fall that had blocked the Path for a number of years was finally blasted away in 1983 – an offer by Territorial Army Royal Engineers to clear away the debris, at no cost, had to be declined by the PNPA because of objections on behalf of commercial demolition interests, and a private operator subsequently received at £17,000 contract for the work.) From this stretch of Path two horizontal mine shafts (adits) are seen running into the cliff-face.

Wiseman's Bridge is a hamlet built on a hillside near the mouth of a stream. The road runs along the top of a storm bank of large pebbles, and there is immediate access to gently shelving sand. There is roadside car parking, café, pub and toilets, and the place is crowded in summer. The beach played a vital and secret part in the build-up to the invasion of Europe by Allied forces in 1944. A full-scale rehearsal for the D-Day landings took place here in 1943 and Eisenhower, Churchill and Montgomery met here to view the exercises.

During the 19c ironstone from local cliffs was used in the production of iron at Stepaside Ironworks, and a firebrick works was also established here. The ironworks and three collieries were served by the Saundersfoot Railway which headed inland from Wiseman's Bridge up Pleasant Valley, and you can make a detour to see them.

The *Stepaside Ironworks*, in Pleasant Valley below the small village of Stepaside, is about 1ml/1.6km inland from Wiseman's

Bridge. It was opened in 1849 by the Pembrokeshire Iron and Coal Company and used locally mined anthracite (from the Grove Colliery on the hillside above the ironworks) and iron ore taken from the cliffs between Wiseman's Bridge and Coppet Hall. The remains of the colliery can still be seen, together with part of the railway track which connected it to the works; the iron-ore tunnels into the sea cliffs can be seen adjacent to the track of the old mineral railway, which is now the Coast Path.

By 1864 the Stepaside Ironworks was producing over 4000 tons of pig iron annually, some 3000 tons being exported from Saundersfoot harbour and the remainder being sold and used locally. There were also substantial exports of iron ore, particularly during periods when the furnaces were not 'in blast'. In the national depression of 1873 production declined, and smelting operations were forced to cease in 1877. Although the Stepaside Ironworks buildings are in a ruinous state, ivy-covered and surrounded by caravans, we can still see something of its architecture. The old casting-shed is the most impressive building, and nearby are old workshops now becoming very dilapidated. At the foot of the hillside are the remains of two blast furnaces. At the time of its greatest success, in the 1860s, the works also had an enormous blowing engine and a line of lime-kilns. Out on the valley floor there are traces of an old canal and of the mineral railway lines used for importing raw materials and for exporting pig iron. The original main tramway consisted of 'fish-belly' rails laid on stone sleeper-blocks. A branch of the line passed through its own separate arch beneath the present road bridge carrying the A477, and was reputedly built by Thomas Telford.

The second ironworks was close to Wiseman's Bridge. It opened in 1850 and was worked until about 1924 or 1926, specialising in castings and a wide variety of other metal goods for colliery plant, ships and agricultural machinery. The traces of the foundry are now difficult to find.

Wiseman's Bridge to Amroth 2.05ml/3.3km
The coast continues as a sequence of shingle and sands below crumbling cliffs. Although you can walk along the sands all the way

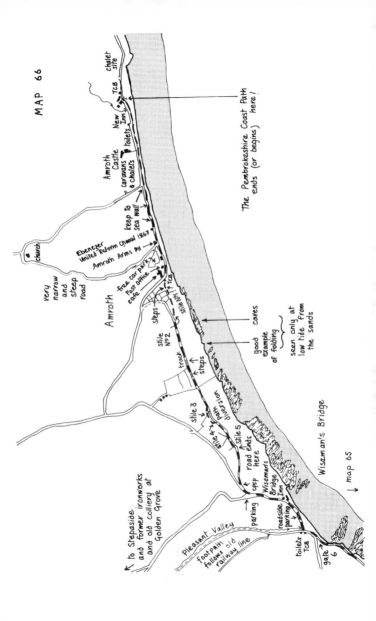

MAP 66

The Pembrokeshire Coast Path ends (or begins) here!

chalet site

TCB

New Inn

toilets

Amroth Castle caravans & chalets

keep to sea wall

church

very narrow and steep road

Ebenezer United Reform Chapel 1867

Amroth Arms PH

Amroth

free car park
Post Office
café office

stile No.1 Tea

steps

stile No.2

caves

good example of folding

seen only at low tide from the sands

track

steps

stile 3

diversion

stile 4

stiles

road ends here

opp.

Wiseman's Bridge

Wiseman's Bridge Inn

roadside parking

parking

Pleasant Valley footpath follows old railway line

to Stepaside and former ironworks and old colliery at Golden Grove

Wiseman's Bridge

map 65

toilets
TCB

gate

6

at low tide the Coast Path follows a track above the cliff between Wiseman's Bridge and Amroth, and there are splendid views over Carmarthen Bay. As you drop down to Amroth village and climb over Stile No. 1 you recall that you have passed or climbed over some 479 (or more!) stiles on this Coast Path.

Amroth is a small former miners' village tending to straggle along the coast road. The few houses face their enemy the sea across a long bank of pebbles, beyond which lies a fine, wide, sandy beach at low tide. The village fights a constant battle with stormy seas: when the tide comes in during winter storms it has the habit of washing the road and an odd house or two into the sea. Long lines of groynes try to prevent the sea encroaching on the land.

At very low tide – when exceptional tidal conditions lower the sand level – tree trunks and stumps of trees of a submerged forest dating from c5000BC are occasionally exposed. Fossilised hazel nuts picked here may be seen in Tenby Museum. Bones of long-extinct animals and flakes of primitive flint tools have also been yielded from the sands.

As a seaside resort the village is growing in popularity: new holiday bungalows, caravan and chalet sites abound. Even Amroth Castle has been converted into holiday flats and a caravan park is sited behind the long wall on the sea-front of its grounds. The Castle is a late 18c house with a castellated façade on the site of a vanished medieval castle, and is one of the many places in these parts that were proud to welcome Lord Nelson during his S Wales tour of 1802.

At the mouth of a pebbly stream Pembrokeshire ends, and with it the Coast Path. It comes somewhat as an anti-climax: the sands continue into Carmarthenshire to Marros Sands and the famous Pendine Sands, but the way to Dylan Thomas's Laugharne and the estuary of the Afon Taf and Afon Tywi is barred by a MOD Proof and Experimental Station. This is all forbidden territory, so we had better stop at Amroth.

The Lady Cave anticline near Saundersfoot

References and bibliography

J H Barrett, *The Pembrokeshire Coast Path* (HMSO, 1974)

J H Barrett and C M Yonge, *Collins Pocket Guide to the Sea Shore* (Collins, 1958)

E G Bowen, *Saints, Seaways and Settlements* (University of Wales Press, Cardiff, 1977)

E G Bowen (editor), *Wales – A Physical, Historical and Regional Geography* (Methuen, 1957)

J Cleare and R Collomb, *Sea Cliff Climbing in Britain* (Constable, 1973)

William Condry, *Exploring Wales* (Faber & Faber, 1970)

T H Warren Davies, *Plants of Pembrokeshire* (DWT, 1970)

G A Gibson-Hill (revised and updated by B Campbell, R Campbell and R Prytherch), *A Guide to the Birds of the Coast* (Constable, 1976)

Ted Goddard, *Pembrokeshire Shipwrecks* (Hughes, Swansea, 1983)

R J W Hammond (editor), *Red Guide: Complete Wales* (Ward Lock Black, 1981)

L G Higgins and N D Ridley, *Field Guide to the Butterflies of Britain and Europe* (Collins, 1970)

P Howell and E Beazley, *Companion Guide to South Wales* (Collins, 1977)

Roscoe Howells, *Across the Sounds to the Pembrokeshire Islands* (J D Lewis & Sons, 1972)

Roscoe Howells, *The Sounds Between* (J D Lewis & Sons, 1968)

Brian John, *Pembrokeshire – British Topographical Series* (David & Charles, 1976)

Ronald M Lockley, *Pembrokeshire – Regional Book Series* (Robert Hale, 1957, 1965, 1969)

Ronald M Lockley, *The Island* (Story of Skokholm) (André Deutsch, 1969; Penguin, 1980)

Dilwyn Miles, *Portrait of Pembrokeshire* (Robert Hale, 1984)

Jon de Montjoye and Mike Harber, *Pembroke* (*Sea Cliff Climbs Guide*) (Climbers' Club, 1985)

Colin Mortlock, *Rock Climbing in Pembrokeshire* (H G Waters, Tenby, 1974)

National Park Committee, *Pembrokeshire Coast National Park Plan 1977–82* (Dyfed County Council, 1977)

Sir Frederick Rees, *The Story of Milford* (Milford Haven) (Cardiff, 1954)

Vyvyan Rees, *South West Wales – Pembrokeshire and Carmarthen* (Shell Guide, Faber & Faber, 1963)

Alan Reid, *The Castles of Wales* (Letts Guide/George Philip, 1973)

Stuart Rossiter (editor), *Blue Guide to Wales* (Benn, 1969)

D Saunders, *A Guide to the Birds of Wales* (Constable, 1974)

Patrick Stark, *Walking the Pembrokeshire Coast Path* (H G Waters, Tenby, 1972)

Prof. Steers, *The Coastline of England and Wales* (Cambridge University Press, 1946)

Wynford Vaughan Thomas and Alun Llewllyn, *Shell Guide to Wales* (Michael Joseph, 1969)

Carl Thompson, *Surfing in Great Britain* (Constable, 1972)

Sidney Toy, *The Castles of Great Britain* (Heinemann, 1963)

Herbert Williams, *Pembrokeshire Coast National Park Guide* (Webb & Bower/Michael Joseph, 1987)

Index

Bold figures indicate main references in the text.